Russia's Road to the Cold War

Russia's Road to the Cold War

Diplomacy, Warfare, and the Politics of Communism, 1941-1945

Vojtech Mastny

Columbia University Press / New York / 1979

Vojtech Mastny is associate professor of history at the University of Illinois at Urbana–Champaign.

Library of Congress Cataloging in Publication Data

Mastny, Vojtech, 1936–
  Russia's road to the cold war.

Includes bibliographical references and index.
  1. Russia—Foreign relations—1917–1945.
2. World War, 1939–1945.   I. Title.
DK273.M4   327.47   78-13433
ISBN 0-231-04360-0

Columbia University Press
New York and Guildford, Surrey

Copyright © 1979 Columbia University Press
All rights reserved
Printed in the United States of America

For Kitty and the children, Katja, John, and Lisa

contents

preface

By its nature, contemporary history imposes upon a scholar a more personal commitment than do other periods of the past. Rather than determining the topic of his inquiry solely because of its intrinsic merit, he can hardly pretend that he was not influenced in his choice by direct exposure to his subject matter. This book grew out of my preoccupation with the German policies, collaboration, and resistance during World War II—the theme of my earlier study on the Czechs under Nazi rule. The deeper one delves into the complexities of that era, the more one is led to perceive it as the true watershed between the past and our own times; in countless ways, we still live with the problems the war created or failed to solve. Among these, the East–West conflict remains pre-eminent, and the memory of living in eastern Europe through the climactic years of the Cold War added to the fascination of exploring its origins as part of history. Finally, the confusion that muddled the understanding of the subject in this country, especially at American universities, during the 1960s reinforced my conviction that here was a topic eminently worth investigating.

Several institutions and individuals contributed to making possible an endeavor which, because of the many controversial ramifications of its subject, proved more protracted than originally anticipated. In 1969 and 1970, the Columbia University Council for Research in the Social Sciences provided summer grants, and two years later the Alexander von Humboldt Foundation gave me a fellowship; together they enabled me to initiate the necessary research in the United States and Europe. All this time, Columbia's Institute on East Central Europe offered both stimulating working conditions and funds to keep the project going.

Midway in the process, when an author can greatly benefit from exposing his preliminary findings to critical judgment by a distinguished sample of his future readers, the Lehrman Institute furnished this very experience. I acknowledge with profound gratitude the research fellowship I held in 1974–1975 at that incomparable New York institution, which combines its dedication to high standards of intellectual inquiry with a keen concern for the crucial issues of public policy. During its brief existence, the Institute has already proved an outstanding testimonial not only to the vision and energy of its founder but also to the enduring influence of the great surrounding metropolis that fertilizes it with its own vitality.

The members of the study group on the "Aims and Motives of Soviet Policies in 1944–45," which I conducted at the Lehrman Institute, helped me to clarify my thoughts and focus my reasoning before proceeding to the final stage. Besides the ever-helpful Nicholas X. Rizopoulos, the Executive Director of the Institute, they included especially Cyril Black, Thomson Bradley, John C. Campbell, James Chace, Herbert Dinerstein, Warren F. Kimball, Henry Krisch, Walter LaFeber, Ivo J. Lederer, Hans Morgenthau, Forrest C. Pogue, Joseph Rothschild, Benjamin Rowland, Harrison Salisbury, Gaddis Smith, Stanley W. Stillman, Robert C. Tucker, and Daniel Yergin.

Toward the end of my work, the University of Illinois's Research Board and its Russian and East European Center generously supplied further financial aid while the Harry S. Truman Library Institute awarded me a travel grant. Finally, the School of Advanced International Studies of the Johns Hopkins University in Washington provided me with a congenial environment when I was putting the last touches on a manuscript already prepared for publication.

Besides the staff of the archives and libraries enumerated in the Note on Sources, several of my research assistants and graduate students, who aided me at different times, deserve special appreciation. At Columbia University, these were Vladimir Socor, Andre Kaldi, and George Deak. At the University of Illinois, I was assisted by Edward Tabler and, above all, Tom Dyman, whose skill, efficiency, and dedication were crucial to help bring the manuscript and the footnotes to the final shape.

At Columbia University Press, Bernard Gronert expertly saw the book through all the stages of the publication process. Maria B. Caliandro proved very much the ideal editor that every author wishes to work with.

While ever ready to share her critical opinion as an experienced researcher and writer, my wife maintained both a detachment from the subject of my study and an attachment to its author which proved an unfailing inspiration. To her and to our children, who, for having to endure all the tribulations of my prolonged involvement with Stalin, have surely earned the distinction of ranking among his many innocent victims, the book is dedicated.

Washington, D.C.
January 1978

introduction

F or a third of a century, the East–West rivalry has provided a
reassuringly familiar and conveniently simple yardstick for
sizing up and reducing the complexities of international relations.
That yardstick may no longer serve so well in a world setting
where the relative (though not absolute) stature of the two superpowers, the United States and the Soviet Union, is diminishing.
Besides, their relationship itself has become more problematic, as
evident from the inconclusive debate about the true meaning of
détente. Does the evolving new relationship herald an eventual
withering away of their competition? Or does détente mean "continuation of tension by other means,"[1] if not a prelude to their
final catastrophic confrontation?

Any attempt to sort out the promise and the peril in the new
situation would be flawed if not informed by an understanding of
the reasons that led to the original clash of interests. To wit, we
ought to know why and how the American–Soviet rivalry assumed
the extreme form of a total conflict short of armed struggle that is
conveyed by the notion of the Cold War. The question is not exactly novel, given the countless books and articles that have been
devoted to it. But since so many of them have been shots in the
Cold War rather than distinterested explanations, the answer remains elusive—as the continued public interest in the his-
toriographical controversy about the Cold War's origins abun-
dantly shows.

During the 1960s, the controversy took on a new dimension because of the "revisionist" school that emerged in the West from the frustrations of the Vietnam war. Projecting their cherished images of the present into the past, the adherents of that school proved ever ready to affix on the United States the main responsibility for the ills of the world. In interpreting the origins of the Cold War accordingly, they managed to shatter many of the old certainties but not to replace them with new ones. The debate they provoked sometimes resembled a trial in an American courtroom, where the adversaries excel in advancing not only every reasonable but also every conceivable argument to buttress or demolish a case. It is a procedure that does not always result in a triumph of truth and justice; instead, it often leads to dismissal of the case for lack of satisfactory evidence.

Similarly, in their zeal to try and condemn the United States in the court of history, the revisionists tended to obfuscate the role of the other defendants; they especially tended to exonerate the Soviet Union by default. At their best, they asked the right questions; they seldom found or even sought the right answers. Relentlessly dissecting and censuring the American policies, they were conspicuously less adept at progressing beyond mere assumptions about the Soviet ones. Usually these experts and dilettantes in the field of United States foreign relations could not read Russian, much less the more exotic eastern European languages. In neglecting the Soviet side of the story, they could always rationalize that the pertinent sources remained out of reach.

In his critique of the revisionist school, the late Herbert Feis once lamented that "without the Soviet documents and memoirs all accounts of the Cold War must be lopsided."[2] This is a truism rather than the truth. Admittedly, the Russian sources are a mere trickle compared with the torrent of American, British, and German documentation. But this regrettable state of affairs does not make the students of Soviet policies substantially worse off than historians of the more remote past who also have to form their judgment from fragmentary evidence. And yet that judgment does not necessarily suffer as a result. In fact, on recent events as well, some of the best books have been written before the archives opened their doors and some of the worst have been the product of extensive abuse of archival material.

In contemporary history, little of substance can remain concealed for long because alternative sources abound to substitute for those we may wish to have but do not. Indeed, in surveying the Russian road to the Cold War, the true challenge is not so much in having to make do without the inaccessible ones as in coming to grips with those actually at hand. So much new evidence has been coming to light, from the recently opened Western archives and from eastern Europe itself, that its mass and variety alone make another look at the old problems imperative. While not aspiring to a definitive account—an elusive goal anyway—we can certainly do better than we have done so far in establishing "such truth as is publicly available to us."[3]

An air of déjà vu lingers about writings on Russia and the advent of the Cold War as their authors have scrutinized the same familiar pieces of evidence over and over again. Worse still, that limited base has sometimes served to prop up mutually incompatible interpretations, adding to the confusion about Soviet motives. All too often, these have been depicted as either transparently simple or hopelessly inscrutable. The new evidence calls for a more nuanced treatment, starting with a rigorous examination of all the pertinent information we have. Instead, it has become fashionable to pontificate, persuasively but beside the point, about the inevitability of the whole East–West confrontation.

Surely there is more to scholarship than merely registering that what happened was bound to happen. Forces beyond men's control do have a strong influence on the course of history, and statesmen in particular labor under irresistible pressures constraining their freedom of action in multiple ways. But we are concerned about the developments within men's control as well. How do nations and their leaders use or misuse the chances they have? After all, to perceive and exercise choices is the essence of statecraft. Likewise, it is the essence of the historian's craft to understand the choices in terms of their time and interpret them for the benefit of his own.

What, then, were the Russian choices that failed to prevent the Cold War? Reminiscing about the crucial period of World War II from the perspective of thirty years later, Nikita S. Khrushchev deplored the inadequacy of all Soviet writing about this heroic and tragic era. He expressed a longing for another Tolstoy to recreate the past reality by the power of artistic imagination and for historians to complete the task by drawing on all the evidence that has been preserved.[4] Khrushchev's erstwhile protégé Alexander Solzhenitsyn has since discharged the first part of the assignment with distinction. But for Soviet historians who (similar to their revisionist counterparts in the West) would have both the documents and the urge to challenge the accepted version of events, the time is yet to come. The failure of so prominent a dissident as Roy Medvedev to even perceive the real issues of the Cold War origins in his magnum opus on Stalinism is indicative of the void.[5]

A Western scholar seeking to grasp those issues thus acts as something of a surrogate for putative Soviet revisionist historians. To draw a balance sheet of Stalin's stewardship of Russia's foreign policy, he inevitably has to come to grips first with the dictator's extraordinary personality. Quite apart from the moral aspects involved, any interpretation of Soviet policies at that time implies assumptions about the manner in which that personality influenced events.[6] The question is not only whether decisions followed from a fundamentally rational or substantially irrational assessment. In a broader sense, we also have to determine to what extent Soviet policies were simply Stalin's policies.

From what we know today about the inner workings of the Nazi dictatorship, we should not be overly impressed by any ruler's pretensions of total control. Behind the formidable façade of Stalinism there loomed inefficiency, opportunism, and drift. Yet never did the totalitarian ideal of a fully regimented body politic come closer to perfection in Russia than under Stalin. This is not to say that whatever happened necessarily conformed to his intentions, merely that any discrepancies need to be explained rather than taken for granted.[7]

The totalitarian thrust of the Soviet system at once facilitates and complicates the historian's task. It simplifies the subject matter but makes explanations more difficult. In particular, the necessity to account for seemingly disparate manifestations of policies often requires putting together widely scattered pieces of evidence. How, then, could the inquiry be sensibly narrowed down and focused without distortion?

The point at issue is Moscow's presumed "grand strategy" in 1941–1945, that is, the selection and pursuit of its long-term objectives during and immediately after the war against Germany. What was the vision of the postwar world that inspired Soviet actions at that time? What were the Russian aims in east central Europe especially, the area where both world wars and also the Cold War originated? How were those aims related to the historic Russian interests there? And how did the results measure up to the expectations?

A few standard assumptions have been common to Western authors of both the traditional and the revisionist variety: Stalin's determination to regain the territorial acquisitions he had achieved during his pact with Hitler, his quest for a division of Europe into spheres of influence, his desire to establish dependent regimes in neighboring countries. Yet such readings of Stalin's aspirations, though not necessarily wrong, may be misleading. While plausible with the benefit of hindsight, they do not always conform to the contemporary evidence without important qualifications. In any case, they mark the beginning rather than the end of serious research.

In all fairness to the deficiencies of Soviet power and the unpredictability of events in wartime, Stalin's goals should be considered as evolving rather than as a design firmly fixed and single-mindedly pursued. How did he, the faithful disciple of

Lenin, proceed in implementing the master's formula postulating minimum and maximum aims? It would seem that the striving for the optimum presupposed at all times an effort to match the feasible with the desirable and a continuous reassessment of both from the dictator's particular perspective. How did short-term situations influence long-term policies? And how did these depend on opportunities provided by others, friends and enemies alike?

To be convincing, the answers ought to heed the intricate interrelationship among Moscow's military strategy, its diplomacy, and its management of international communism. During the war, military force ruled supreme. But how willing was Stalin to rely on it in promoting his political ambitions? How did calculations of cost influence his aims at different times? Is it true, as is usually presumed, that he always subordinated his military moves to political considerations?

As an art of compensating for the deficiency of power, diplomacy loomed large in the Russian conduct of the war. Although diplomats ranked rather low in the Soviet hierarchy, Stalin himself acquired a high reputation for his expertise in their trade. Did he really deserve it? If a comparison between the expectations and the results is the true measure of accomplishment, did he have reasons to be dissatisfied with his record? How well did he serve his nation's interests as he and others perceived them?

Moscow's manipulation of foreign followers who were receptive to its guidance on grounds of ideological affinity was an integral, even if not always the decisive, feature of its international behavior. Certainly this is potentially the most revealing but also the most confusing feature of that behavior. Whatever Moscow wanted the Communists to do reflected its long-term interests the most directly, yet the esoteric language habitually used in their mutual communications inhibits understanding of the real issues involved. How can the actual objectives be reliably distinguished from lip service to the messianic tenets of the doctrine that is the minimal attribute of any Communist aspiring to good standing? Where is the line to be drawn between operational and tactical goals, between the truth and its deliberate distortion? Moreover, not only outsiders but also the Communists themselves and even their Soviet mentors could get fooled.

Misperception and miscalculation are the salient themes linking the study of the Cold War with the problems of today's public policy. Although much has changed since Stalin's days, much has also remained the same, and the point is to grasp the extent and consequences of the change. Again, anxiety about Soviet intentions is the topic of the day. But if that topic is no less urgent than thirty years ago, neither is it any less liable to misinterpretation. Like generals, historians and politicians tend to learn the wrong lessons from the last war they fought, and the lessons of the Cold War are by no means self-evident. To help discover them, this book has been written.

Russia's Road to the Cold War

chapter one

Traditions and Antecedents

The Russian Tradition

In the affairs of nations, the influence of character on policies is as crucial as it is elusive. Different nations, much like different individuals, often do not act the same way in similar situations, yet the reasons for their particular behavior are not easy to grasp. Ever since the theory of the nation as a living organism first appeared at the end of the eighteenth century, recourse to the "national soul" has provided facile explanations. Quite apart from its marked susceptibility to abuse, that notion belongs to the realm of faith, thus precluding further discussion; by explaining everything, it explains nothing. So, too, the celebrated "Russian soul" should be regarded as an inspiration for poets at best and a subterfuge for impostors at worst.

Whether or not there are innate and immutable characteristics that distinguish nations from one another—and we are unlikely ever to know for sure—they can safely be disregarded in favor of characteristics acquired over definite periods of time in specific environments. Informed social philosophers in general and those concerned with Russia in particular have gravitated overwhelmingly toward geopolitical explanations.[1] They have sensibly stressed the formative impact of the external circumstances of life on political culture, that sum total of attitudes that give each nation's politics its particular flavor. Accordingly, such attitudes are permanent only insofar as the external circumstances remain unchanged, and change is as much the stuff of history as continuity is.

Consciousness of the past, whether as a legacy to be fulfilled

1

or a burden to be overcome, has been a more prominent ingredient of politics in eastern Europe than in the West, where the peoples' historical experiences have tended to be less traumatic. In the case of the Russians especially, their remarkable homogeneity as a people bordering on ethnically heterogeneous areas has further heightened that collective consciousness. And the Marxist ideology of the Soviet leaders, with its emphasis on historical inevitability, has added specifically the postulate of conformity with long-term historical trends as an indispensable requirement of any sound policy.

Political culture, elusive as it is, does not determine with any finality the kind of decisions that nations and their leaders make. But the collective experience does shape both their perception of the available choices and the manner in which the decisions are reached. It has been a truism that the memory of recurrent foreign invasions of their geographically vulnerable country has haunted the Russians throughout their history. Yet as a magic formula to explain the guiding motives of successive generations of their statesmen, this "defensive complex" can be a misleading oversimplification unless internal factors are sufficiently taken into account.

Over the centuries, the Russian rulers' preoccupation with maintaining their power in a huge and unwieldy empire has institutionalized repression to a degree unparalleled elsewhere in Europe. It is also true, however, that nowhere else has anarchy (whether expressed in the people's spontaneous aversion to discipline or in the Byzantine in-fighting among the elite) been so integral a part of the political scene as in Russia. A painful awareness of the country's backwardness, itself both the cause and the consequence of the repressive society, has generated a basically tragic and pessimistic view of man's condition in it, as well as of the nation's place in the world. But that view has by no means fostered resignation; on the contrary, it has bred an extraordinary urge to prove Russia's vitality in international competition. Few other nations can provide more persuasive arguments in favor of

2

the *Primat der Innenpolitik*, the determination of foreign policy by domestic issues.

Ever since the country opened itself to the outside world in the eighteenth century, bright and brash foreigners have been fascinated by what they perceived as quintessential attributes of "eternal Russia." Their efforts to identify those attributes have produced an impressive consensus, ranging from reactionaries, like the caustic Marquis de Custine,[2] to such superprogressives as Karl Marx and Friedrich Engels. These two notorious Russophobes were particularly irritated by the discrepancy between Russia's assertiveness abroad and its fundamental internal weakness. Suspecting a brazen bluff, Marx maintained with characteristic arrogance that "the idea of Russian diplomatic supremacy owes its efficacy to the imbecility and timidity of the Western nations, and . . . the belief in Russia's superior military power is hardly less a delusion."[3] Such sweeping judgments, though not lacking merit, underrate the extent to which the Russians have overcome or at least mitigated their deficiencies by diplomatic ingenuity, often enhanced by skillful deployment of military power.

It has been a great paradox of the Russian conduct of foreign affairs that the policy-makers, although caught up in internal problems, have been singularly uninhibited in their operations by formal constraints. In a classic essay written in 1890, Engels criticized bitingly the small, exclusive, and self-perpetuating caste to which the czars entrusted their foreign relations. He held up for reproof the arrogance and amorality of these arbitrary guardians of Russia's destiny (many of whom, ironically, were not Russian by origin) and singled out habitual mendacity as one of their salient traits. So timeless was his critique that forty years later Stalin, that Russianized Georgian who had stepped into their shoes, saw fit to ban the treatise from circulation, for he greatly admired what his mentor had despised.[4]

Unencumbered by public opinion, which scarcely existed, those in charge of Russia's foreign policies have customarily enjoyed the extraordinary advantage of being able to harness the

3

country's considerable resources in pursuit of whatever they decided were its national interests. This power and discretion have no doubt simplified their job and sometimes enhanced the effectiveness of their policies as well. Yet the system has also had its pitfalls, which no amount of purely professional competence could entirely surmount. In particular, exclusiveness has bred a narrow and distorted view of international realities, while the excessive concentration of power has repeatedly led to the wrong choice of priorities.[5] Consequently, the practical accomplishments have not been nearly so impressive as one might expect. In fact, the record of Russia's foreign pursuits includes numerous failures resulting from striking miscalculations—perhaps the reason why cautious opportunism, rather than reckless adventurism, has tended to be the hallmark of its practitioners.

Even so, the obsession with security, poorly conceived and elastically defined, has been a dangerous source of instability. The rulers' quest for expansion of Russia's power has often required exertions that aggravated the internal problems they hoped to mitigate. Also, their ventures have frequently precipitated abroad the very confrontations that they most needed to avoid. The Russian tradition has been one of perpetual contradiction, as if to prove the applicability of the Marxist dialectics that the Soviet leaders embraced as their guide for action. As materialists, they have never thought much of the "Russian soul," their own nationalist leanings notwithstanding. But they have all the more eagerly heeded their predecessors' accomplishments and failures as antecedents from which many useful lessons could be learned.

Once Peter the Great had vigorously begun Russia's drive to the west, he and his successors first concentrated their efforts on the lands along the Baltic coast. But repeated conflicts with the declining Ottoman Empire subsequently diverted their energies more to the Balkans. There the prize was control of the Black Sea straits, which they coveted as a solution to Russia's perennial problem of access to the open sea. Most of the time they sought support, or at least connivance, of the leading central European

4

powers, Austria and Prussia. As a result, partitions, territorial compensations, and spheres of influence became staple fare of international politics in east central Europe—the amorphous area extending between Russia and Germany from the Baltic to the Aegean Sea. Although in the short run these devices sometimes proved useful expedients to reduce tensions, they all too often became counterproductive in the long run.

Before the age of nationalism and mass politics, there was nothing unusual or disreputable about these typical transactions of the "old diplomacy." Yet at least one of them—the Russian-sponsored dismemberment of Poland at the end of the eighteenth century—shocked even contemporaries. This was the first time that a sovereign state was obliterated cold-bloodedly in peacetime rather than as a result of military defeat. By taking the bulk of the partitioned territory, the Russians rounded out their possession of the Baltic lands known today as Estonia, Latvia, and Lithuania, to which they soon added Finland as well. In ruling their new subjects, the czar's administrators combined repression with conciliation but were understandably more at ease with the methods they knew best from their homeland. As a result, they never managed to inspire genuine loyalty (not to speak of affection) in the hearts of peoples who, rightly or wrongly, considered themselves culturally superior to the Russians.

After Napoleon's fall, the sudden ideological twist of the czar's policies further differentiated Russia from other contemporary powers. In 1815, the year his victorious troops camped in the streets of Paris, Alexander I cast himself as the chief defender of the shattered old order against the rising tides of liberalism and nationalism. He tried to win his fellow monarchs to the sweeping yet disconcertingly vague project of the Holy Alliance, in effect a precept for Russian intervention on a continental scale. Although the scheme never got off the ground, mainly because of British resistance, later developments emphasized the cleavage between the perennially repressive Russia and the increasingly liberal West. However, for nearly half a century a desire to preserve the

5

status quo nurtured the czarist regime's rapprochement with Prussia and Austria.

Owing to similarities in political culture, Russia had more in common with Prussia than with Austria. Much as the Russian autocracy differed from the Prussian-German *Rechtsstaat*, they both exalted the state's power to circumscribe the freedoms of citizens, thus setting themselves apart from the liberal tradition. These affinities did not rule out conflict but would time and again inspire attempts at collusion, accentuating the ambivalent love–hate sentiments that Germans and Russians frequently harbored toward one another.[6]

No similar affinities existed between the oppressively cumbersome Russian empire and the benignly inefficient Austrian one, but the threats they both faced from numerous restive nationalities within their boundaries drew them together. In 1849, Czar Nicholas I demonstrated his feeling of solidarity by sending an army to help his Austrian confrere suppress insurgency in Hungary—a painful episode that left the Magyars with a lasting grudge against the Russians. That solidarity soon fell victim, however, to tensions radiating from the disintegration of the Ottoman Empire, which was accelerated by the nationalist revolts of the Balkan peoples.

Invoking a right supposedly granted by the Turks in the controversial treaty of Kuchuk Kainardji in 1774, the czars posed as the protectors of Christians in the Ottoman Empire. Quite apart from this dubious interpretation of the actual contents of the treaty,[7] the pretense hardly concealed the more profane goal of carving out of the Sultan's domain vassal states that would owe their liberation to Russia or would for other reasons look to St. Petersburg for protection. In this effort, the czarist regime was not beyond abetting the forces of nationalism, provided that these were susceptible to Russian guidance.[8]

On the whole, Russian interests in different parts of southeast Europe were shaped by geopolitical considerations, while the local peoples' readiness to follow Russian leadership reflected closely the ethnic divisions.[9] As early as the eighteenth century, the remote Slavic principality of Montenegro dramatized its defiance of the Turks by symbolically proclaiming political and religious allegiance to the czar.[10] However, two other subsequently independent Slavic states, Serbia and Bulgaria, became the strongholds of Russian influence in the area, the frequent vacillations of their shaky governments notwithstanding. Conversely, non-Slavic Greece and Romania, though benefiting from Russian aid during the early stages of their liberation struggles, eventually sought and found their protectors elsewhere.

The czarist regime's involvement in the "eastern question" led to the Crimean War and a defeat that badly shook the domestic foundations of the autocracy. Yet the Russian diplomats at the 1856 Paris peace conference succeeded in mitigating the adverse international consequences of that defeat, showing that they were at their best when distress stimulated their ingenuity.[11] By contrast, they tended to be at their worst whenever tempting opportunities encouraged their greed—as when, twenty years later, they tried to impose the notorious Treaty of San Stefano on a prostrated Turkey. That attempt to create a "Greater Bulgaria" as a Russian bastion only led the other powers to close ranks and administer a humiliating rebuff to St. Petersburg.[12]

Although the Balkans served as the main arena of czarist imperialism, Poland never ceased to be its principal trouble spot. Throughout the nineteenth century, the most visible result of clumsy Russification efforts was a further exacerbation of the Poles' deeply ingrained Russophobia. Because of its narrow-minded nationalism, the czarist regime repeatedly let pass opportunities to tackle the Polish problem seriously.[13] And the Poles, while differing among themselves about whether the Russians or the Germans were the greater scourge, clung all the more stubbornly to their national identity, yearning for the opportunity to regain their independence. This was not the only reason, however, why they were the most subversive foreign element in the czar's lands.

7

Unlike the majority of their compatriots, the most radical Polish Socialists were prepared to replace the goal of national independence with the presumably higher one of a classless society to be achieved together with their Russian comrades. They figured prominently among the Russian revolutionaries who directly threatened the czar's throne. Yet this particular linkage also led many other Poles to associate revolutionary socialism with subservience to the hereditary enemy, a view heralding a further complication of the already untractable relationship between the two peoples.[14]

No such dilemmas vexed the Czechs and Slovaks who, having had little physical contact with the Russians throughout their history, developed an exalted image of the Slavic Big Brother. That image not only served as a psychological prop in their hard struggle for self-assertion against their German and Magyar masters; it also assumed a political meaning in the writings of Czech and Slovak literati who distinguished themselves as prophets of Slavic unification under Russian leadership. Thus the 1856 treatise by Slovak nationalist L'udevít Štúr, *The Slavs and the World of the Future*,[15] became a classic of Pan-Slavism.

This new ideology, better suited to the spirit of the times than the obsolescent doctrine of monarchic solidarity, found ardent promoters in Russia as well. Yet the architects of Russian foreign policy, though favorable enough to the theory, proved singularly hesitant about its practical implementation.[16] They especially shunned extending unequivocal support to Austria-Hungary's disaffected Slavic subjects lest such a policy backfire in the czar's own multinational empire. Accordingly, in 1871 when Czech politicians waved the banner of Pan-Slavism in soliciting the czar's backing in their quarrel with Vienna, he turned a deaf ear. At least in the Czech case Foreign Minister Alexander M. Gorchakov was right when he virtuously commented, *"nous ne nous mêlons pas des affaires d'autrui."*[17]

As long as German Chancellor Otto von Bismarck dominated European politics, he deftly managed to keep Russia away from central Europe. Having first won the czar's gratitude by offering him help against his rebellious Polish subjects in 1863, the "honest broker" proceeded to facilitate Russian advance elsewhere while at the same time trying to impose definite limits upon it. He was instrumental in having the London Conference of 1871 abrogate clauses restricting Russian naval activities in the Black Sea. He crowned his efforts, but also reached the limits of his ingenuity, with his controversial Reinsurance Treaty of 1887. The two governments pledged to agree in advance on any territorial changes in the Balkans and promised each other neutrality in case of war with a third power—from Bismarck's point of view a pledge dangerously verging on incompatibility with his Austrian alliance.[18]

The eclipse of ideological motivation in St. Petersburg's foreign policies did not necessarily encourage restraint. In the succession of international crises that eventually plunged Europe into World War I, the czarist regime played an increasingly aggressive role. This is not to say that it became the chief menace to world order; that dubious distinction belonged to Germany, which after Bismarck's dismissal embarked on its drive for global power. In a situation where action and reaction could not always be easily sorted out, Russian policies were conspicuous more for aggravating existing problems than for creating new ones.

After Bismarck's successors had allowed the Reinsurance Treaty to lapse, the Russians brought their tentative rapprochement with France to a full-fledged military alliance in 1894. This unprecedented liaison of Europe's most oppressive regime with one of the most liberal was a landmark in the development on the continent of two hostile blocs, each of which was held together by interlocking mutual-defense commitments. In particular, the alliance with a new and distant friend expanded dramatically the scope of Russia's potential involvement. This prospect, rather than fostering sobriety, excited the imagination of Russia's leaders when Germany finally provoked war in 1914.

Although woefully unprepared to fight, St. Petersburg

9

grasped eagerly at what it perceived as the golden opportunity to forestall permanently "German and Austrian attempts to challenge Russia's prestige as a Great Power,"[19] an objective both sweeping and vague. In a pointed allusion to Pan-Slavism, the czar proclaimed at the onset of the struggle that "according to her historical traditions, Russia united by faith and blood with the Slav peoples, has never regarded their fate with indifference."[20] Yet at no time during the war did Russian notions of the desirable postwar order actually mature into a coherent policy.

There was, to be sure, no shortage of exceedingly specific proposals suggesting the official thinking. In September 1914, in a confidential memorandum Foreign Minister Sergei D. Sazonov singled out the separation of East Prussia as a necessary prerequisite for the destruction of German power.[21] He envisaged an east central Europe divided into small, nominally independent Russian client states. Among these, Poland was to be enlarged at Germany's expense by eastern Poznania and Silesia.[22] Two years later, other Foreign Office memoranda foresaw the dismantling of Austria-Hungary and the creation of a vassal Czech kingdom.[23] As late as 1918, the czar's self-appointed caretaker Admiral Alexander V. Kolchak contemplated a mighty Pan-Slav "federation" that would include not only genuine Slavs but also such honorary ones as the Magyars, Romanians, and Greeks.[24]

While the dreams flourished in inverse ratio with Russia's military fortunes, the czar's diplomats sought promissory notes from their allies. In 1915, as a reward for Russian assistance to the Entente, Britain and France endorsed the Russian claim for control of the Black Sea straits. Two years later, the Russians elicited a French promise of *désintéressement* in Poland which entitled the czar to settle that nation's future to his own liking.[25] But this was the farthest his regime ever went in preparing a postwar settlement.

In both their extent and their implementation, the Russian war aims lagged conspicuously behind the vast and elaborate ambitions of imperial Germany. In a different sense, they were more

10

part of what Engels subsumed under "eternal Russia." They not only had grown out of a long and consistent tradition, but also were to prove durable in the future. Rich in experience and tempered by a keen awareness of its limitations, Russian imperialism was less malevolent and destructive than the upstart German variety; it was more deeply rooted and pervasive in the long run.

In 1917, nevertheless, this imperialism went thoroughly bankrupt. Although the czarist regime collapsed primarily for domestic reasons, its ignominious end discredited both the goals and the style of its foreign policy, which was held responsible for the nation's military catastrophe. The czar's Bolshevik successors solemnly renounced "Great Russian chauvinism" and all its works, vowing instead to start with a clean slate. The break with tradition could not have seemed more complete.

The Bolshevik Experience

Despite their pretensions, the Bolsheviks started with a slate that was highly tainted by their Marxist preconceptions. In conformity with their doctrine, Russia's new rulers initially tended to spurn all foreign policy as an inherently evil and ultimately dispensable by-product of the rotten capitalist system. On the premise that states were instruments of class domination, they also considered the relations among them to be temporary, pending the worldwide establishment of a classless Communist society. In anticipation of that happy event, the first People's Commissar for Foreign Affairs, Leon Trotsky, reportedly expected to "issue a few revolutionary proclamations to the peoples of the world, and then shut up shop."[26] But the shop remained open and busier than ever.

The new outlook led to both an expansion of the scope of foreign policy and a shift in its geographical thrust. Bound by their sense of duty to promote revolutions wherever the conditions seemed promising, the Bolsheviks became involved in colo-

11

nial countries where the European powers' control had faltered as a result of the war. In Europe, they turned hopeful eyes toward Austria-Hungary and Germany, whose impending defeat held the greatest promise of instant upheaval. There were also other reasons, however, why central Europe now replaced the Balkans as the focal area of Russian interest.[27]

Even before they seized power, the Bolsheviks had been tantalized by Austria-Hungary's nationality problem. Duly appreciating its explosive potential, they had reserved some of their most acrimonious verbiage for the "Austro-Marxists"—men like Karl Renner and Otto Bauer—who had been looking for a nonrevoluntary cure for the empire's fatal disease. In 1913, Lenin as the head of the Bolshevik party had commissioned Stalin (at that time still a minor figure in it) to refute that distasteful idea in a pamphlet, *Marxism and the Nationality Question*, which established the future Soviet dictator's claim to expertise on that topic.[28] The outbreak of World War I had actually found Lenin living in Austrian territory in Galicia, although afterward he had moved his center of operations to Switzerland.[29]

The Bolsheviks had been even more preoccupied with Germany, the nation that had given mankind their mentors, Marx and Engels. According to their theory, Germany, with its highly developed capitalist society and its large, well-organized, and politically conscious working class, had seemed the most ripe for revolution. Consequently, when the news about the upheaval in Russia and the ensuing overthrow of the czar first reached Lenin in Switzerland, he was caught unprepared. Although he and his associates subsequently exploited the unexpected opportunity very well indeed, they still believed that the dictatorship of the proletariat must prevail in advanced Germany before their own rule in backward Russia could be safe.[30]

That thesis acquired urgent importance when the Soviet leaders, eager to liquidate the lost war they had inherited, received the armistice terms from the German generals at Brest-Litovsk. In vain did they drag their feet, counting on the glorious

German proletariat to save them from these rapacious militarists. The peace, signed in March 1918, forced Russia to relinquish all the lands the czars had amassed in Europe during the previous two hundred years, and much more. Although the disastrous treaty was soon nullified (ironically, by the fiercely anti-Soviet Entente statesmen who dictated their terms to defeated Germany at Versailles) Germany continued to loom in Moscow's calculations.

Having lost many of the former czarist possessions—among them, Poland, Finland, and the Baltic provinces had become independent and Bessarabia had been annexed by Romania—the Bolsheviks pinned their hopes on world revolution all the more strongly, and they saw the road to it as leading through Germany. That country was the foremost concern of the Communist International (Comintern) they established in Moscow in March 1919 to serve as the general staff of the revolution.[31] The Communist Spartacist uprising in Berlin that year proved a dismal failure, but in 1921 and 1923 the organization again encouraged its German sympathizers to revolt—with no greater success.[32] In the meantime, more promising opportunities had arisen elsewhere in central Europe.

In 1919, the revolution that failed to come off in Germany succeeded temporarily in Hungary, which, according to the Marxist book, should have been no more ready for it than Russia. Nonetheless, Lenin welcomed the emergence of the Communist government of Béla Kun, saying that "the Hungarian Revolution perhaps plays a larger role in history than the Russian Revolution."[33] This was the heady time when yet another Soviet regime emerged in Bavaria while Austria, infiltrated by Kun's agents, seemed on the verge of following suit.[34] By the end of the year, these ventures—to which Moscow had been unable to contribute more than verbal encouragement and modest financial aid—had all collapsed.

The new republic of Czechoslovakia had equally unexpectedly earned a prominent place on the Bolshevik blacklist. Even

13

before the state's official proclamation, Czech and Slovak "legionnaires" (former Austrian deserters and prisoners of war) had been busy fighting the Reds in the Russian civil war. They wished nothing more than to get home, but they had been drawn into the conflict partly by the Entente's design, partly by the Bolsheviks' own clumsiness. In July 1918, their approach to the city of Yekaterinburg had prompted the local Soviet chiefs to massacre there the deposed czar and his family.[35] Later that year, Lenin dispatched a special emissary to foment revolution in the Czech lands. His mission proved no more successful than the ephemeral "Soviet republic" that Béla Kun's troops had fostered in eastern Slovakia.[36] Nevertheless, the traditionally straightforward Czech–Russian relations had suddenly become rather complicated.

It was against the background of these multiple frustrations that in 1920 Lenin made his fateful decision to spread revolution abroad by force of arms. Having repelled a Polish invasion of the Ukraine, the Soviet leadership (misinformed by the ultraradical Polish Communists about the true disposition of the Polish proletariat) pursued the invaders into their homeland. The Bolsheviks not only envisaged installing a kindred regime in Poland but, as the Red Army approached Warsaw, they also indulged in visions of a triumphant march farther west.[37] In their exuberance they refused to consider peace on the basis of the "Curzon line," the approximate ethnic frontier suggested by the British Foreign Secretary. Nor did the reported attempt by Czechoslovak Foreign Minister Edvard Beneš to placate them with an offer of his country's easternmost province, the Carpathian Ukraine, bring any immediate effect.[38] But both episodes were to have important implications in the more distant future. For the moment, the most significant result of the Polish campaign was its utter failure. Having rallied against the hereditary enemy, the Poles forced the Russians back, and the 1921 peace of Riga established the Polish–Russian frontier quite far east of the Curzon line.

Despite the ebbing of the revolutionary tide, as late as 1923

Moscow backed an abortive Communist bid for power in Bulgaria.[39] But it was central Europe, not the Balkans, that remained the focus of Russian attention, the disproportionate number of Bulgarian employees in the Comintern apparatus notwithstanding. The Bolsheviks never forgot their humiliation in Poland, and among them Stalin (who was said to have contributed greatly to the debacle by his incompetence and insubordination during the campaign)[40] harbored a particular grudge. Relations with Czechoslovakia also remained strained, as the country became a major haven for anti-Soviet Russian refugees.

As for Germany, the inflated revolutionary reputation of its workers plummeted in Moscow. Later on, Stalin often recounted the apocryphal story of how their delegation once missed an important Socialist meeting simply because its members could not get their tickets punched at a railroad station.[41] But the virtues of the German capitalists seemed to compensate for the deficiencies of the German proletariat—as suggested by the fruits of the Russian-instigated rapprochement between the two nations, both ostracized by the respectable international community. Their 1922 Treaty of Rapallo was the first postwar triumph of Soviet diplomacy, which has been invoked ever since then as an antecedent to justify German–Soviet collaboration at the expense of the West.

Even so, the results of Rapallo accentuated Russia's weakness rather than contributing decisively to its strength. The extent of German–Western estrangement fell notably short of Soviet expectations. Gustav Stresemann, who guided Berlin's policies for the rest of the 1920s, had no illusions about the liaison: "to enter into a marriage with Communist Russia would mean to lay oneself in bed with the murderer of one's own nation."[42] The rapprochement did lead to secret collaboration between the Red Army and the *Reichswehr,* as the Russians granted the German army training and testing facilities on their territory in return for technical assistance.[43] But in the long term, the main beneficiary

15

proved to be German militarism—and that is the main reason, besides the moral opprobrium, why Moscow never officially acknowledged this embarrassing episode.

The unsavory relationship highlighted the Bolsheviks' loss of innocence since their advent to power, a transformation eased by their notion that in dealing with class enemies honor was irrelevant. Yet their reversion to the execrated practices of czarist diplomacy did not imply abandonment of their original goals. No soul-searching is known to have taken place in the Kremlin after the failure of the postwar experiments with revolutionary foreign policy; rather, the managers of international Communism shifted the blame onto their followers abroad.[44] The new slogan of "Socialism in One Country" assigned top priority to consolidation of the Soviet state. But this task presupposed fostering of divisions among its capitalist enemies while merely postponing the final reckoning. Side by side with conventional Russian diplomacy, subversive operations of the Comintern therefore continued apace.

The duality provided the Soviet leadership with an extraordinary flexibility, as well as with means to differentiate in the pursuit of long-term and short-term goals. The Comintern's fifth congress in 1924, for example, endorsed the right of complete political separation for all "oppressed minorities" in Poland, Czechoslovakia, Romania, Yugoslavia, and Greece. In particular, its resolution called for incorporation of the Carpathian Ukraine, eastern Galicia, Bessarabia, and Bukovina into the Soviet Ukraine, thus giving a hint of Moscow's long-term hopes.[45] Nevertheless, five years later, Foreign Commissar Maxim Litvinov concluded friendship treaties with some of the very states that the Comintern had declared to be its targets. Here the purpose was to lure into the Russian fold the eastern European countries that anti-Soviet Western statesmen had hoped would serve as a *cordon sanitaire* against the further spread of Communism. The aim of the deceptively reassuring nonaggression pledge of the "Litvinov Protocol" was to reduce their reliance on the West and to convince them that any mutual combinations were superfluous.

During the late 1920s the role of the Communist parties as tools of Soviet foreign policy further increased as a result of their "Bolshevization," the wholesale expulsion of nonconformist elements from their ranks. Yet this accomplishment, particularly successful in the German party, led to intellectual sterility that Moscow could ill afford at a time when the rise of Fascism and the advent of the Great Depression called rather for far-sighted and imaginative leadership.[46] The apparent success turned into a disaster by assuring docile acceptance of the Soviet misassessment of Fascism as gravedigger of a capitalist system that was now seemingly on its last legs.

In its eagerness to hasten the funeral, Moscow went so far as to abet tactical alliances between the Communists and the Nazis, as during the 1931 electoral campaign against Prussia's Social Democratic government or during the Berlin transit strike the next year.[47] Nor did the Comintern show an understanding of what Hitler's appointment as Chancellor really meant when it congratulated itself that "the establishment of an open Fascist dictatorship destroys all illusions of the masses and liberates the masses from the influence of the Social Democracy."[48] Playing down the event as a mere incident on the road to capitalism's impending demise, Moscow directed the German Communists to assault Nazism head on by launching an overt rather than an underground campaign—advice which made them easy targets for the Gestapo.

Thus Germany, having again served as the main testing ground of the Soviet leaders' world strategy (to prove the validity of the theory that Fascism was the terminal disease of capitalism), fooled them a second time. So great was their incredulity that they only reluctantly drew the appropriate conclusions. Neither the ordeal of the German comrades nor the Nazi harassment of Soviet officials in Germany prompted a decisive response. Indeed, four months after Hitler's seizure of power Moscow demonstrated its readiness to conduct business as usual by renewing its

1926 commercial treaty with Berlin.[49] Only the January 1934 nonaggression pact between Germany and Poland, which raised the specter of their collusion, set in motion an agonizing reappraisal.

Moscow's failure was, of course, a failure of its Marxist ideology, and the role of that ideology in Soviet foreign policy would never again be the same. Nor, for that matter, did Stalin, who by then had prevailed in the power struggle within the Bolshevik establishment, possess much of the ideological fervor that had driven Lenin and Trotsky. Although he, too, viewed international politics through the prism of Marxism, his categories, unrefined by any intimate knowledge of a foreign milieu, were mainly the product of the grim domestic struggle for power in which he had bested his competitors by superior cunning and a lack of scruples. Stalin had great admiration for diplomacy, particularly the British, but regarded it as little more than the art of deception: "A diplomat's words must have no relation to action—otherwise what kind of diplomacy is it? Words are one thing, actions another. . . . Sincere diplomacy is no more possible than dry water or iron wood."[50]

Only many years later did Soviet historians offer rare glimpses of how the most consequential reorientation of the Bolshevik foreign policy since the 1917 revolution was accomplished. It was actually spearheaded by western European Communist parties, and Stalin only reluctantly followed suit. But unlike the pretense that had been used to cover up the earlier miscalculation with world revolution, this time the soul-searching was real and its results were tangible.[51] In 1934 the Soviet Union joined the League of Nations, which it had previously denounced as an agency of imperialism. The next year it allied itself with France, the chief instigator of the *cordon sanitaire*. It embraced enthusiastically the idea of collective security, of which Litvinov became the chief prophet.

Significantly, the ideological corollary of the turnabout came second. Here Litvinov's role was played by Georgi M. Dimitrov, the Bulgarian Communist who had achieved fame by his agile self-defense in the Nazi court that had charged him with complicity in the 1933 Reichstag fire. Dimitrov presided over the Comintern's seventh (and last) congress in 1935, which launched the new "popular front" strategy of collaboration among all left-wing enemies of Fascism, including the Social Democrats—the "Social Fascists" of yesterday. The forces of international Communism were thus harnessed to help bring to power governments willing to act to stem the Fascist tide.

All too often, latter-day critics of the Western policies have taken at face value Moscow's professions of devotion to the cause of collective security. In reality, Russian self-interest was only too palpable in a campaign designed to mobilize international action to stop Hitler but at the same time to shift onto others the main risks of that uncertain enterprise. While Soviet fear of war was clear enough, Soviet readiness to avert it by other than merely diplomatic means was not. Even Litvinov, despite his quest for alliance with the West, did not hide his contempt for "allies" that his Marxist convictions taught him were moribund in the long run. Stalin could find more congenial traits in the Nazi Führer, a fellow dictator and self-proclaimed revolutionary whose ethics and methods were akin to his own, than in the democratic statesmen whose motives eluded him. Even in the heyday of collective security, Moscow therefore kept the door open to possible accommodation with Berlin and in fact undertook several probes toward rapprochement. [52]

To explain the apparent inconsistencies of the Soviet behavior, it has been suggested that in matters of foreign policy Stalin may not have achieved full control over his party rivals until as late as 1938. [53] It is more likely that, although he was in a position to exercise such control, at first he deliberately abstained from a domineering role. In any case, as a perceptive observer in the League of Nations noted, Litvinov enjoyed there "at least as free a hand as was generally given to the Foreign Ministers of the democratic powers." [54] It would have been very sensible for Stalin

19

to keep a low profile in matters about which he knew so little. Besides, he acted as if he were convinced that the key to success abroad lay in success at home, thus reducing foreign affairs to a secondary Soviet concern during most of the 1930s.[55]

In Stalin's case, however, this otherwise sound notion had bizarre consequences. The traumatic upheaval of the great purge, which he masterminded in 1935–1938, nearly demolished the machinery of his foreign policy. It all but wiped out the Soviet diplomatic service, with the notable exception of Litvinov, as well as the elite of international Communism, especially those who had proved their faith in the "fatherland of Socialism" by taking refuge there from the persecution they faced in their home countries. The victims included Béla Kun (the leader of the most successful Communist revolution outside Russia, which Stalin had characteristically denounced as not authentic), not to mention the Polish Communist party, dissolved en bloc on Comintern orders.[56] In addition the Red Army's officer corps was decimated. The motives behind the ghastly spectacle continue to defy rational explanations.

Conceivably, Stalin was preparing for the worst by trying to eliminate ahead of time anyone within reach who might challenge him in the dreaded event of a German attack.[57] Yet by doing so he was actually courting the worst by shattering the society's moral resilience, on which its ability to withstand the ordeal ultimately hinged. He further played into the hands of those Westerners who justifiably doubted the desirability of Russia as an ally, on both moral and military grounds. If, alternately, the dictator was already aiming at an understanding with his German counterpart and accordingly was getting rid of those who might stand in his way,[58] the procedure was not suited to impress the Nazis with Soviet strength—the only way, if any, to achieve a durable accommodation with them. As much a mistake as a crime, the bloody extravaganza betrayed the irrational streak in Stalin's personality, his celebrated realism notwithstanding.[59]

The Soviet weakness was evident as the crisis mounted in

central Europe, where Austria and Czechoslovakia had become Hitler's main targets. Having previously questioned Austria's very qualifications for nationhood, Moscow now began to vigorously champion its independence, even directing the local Communists to support the authoritarian regime that had outlawed them.[60] When the Nazis marched into Austria in March 1938, the Soviet government reacted with indignation. Litvinov went on record with the impressive statement that "it may be too late tomorrow, but today the time . . . is not yet gone if all the States and the Great Powers in particular take a firm and unambiguous stand."[61] But his proposal to convene an international conference for that purpose was his last serious endeavor in collective security. During the subsequent crisis over Czechoslovakia, when not only diplomatic but also military action was at stake, the Soviet Union took an ambiguous stand.

Czechoslovakia had become the pivot of Russia's central European policy in 1935 when Foreign Minister Beneš went to Moscow and signed a mutual defense treaty subsidiary to his country's alliance with France. Simultaneously the Czechoslovak Communists had become advocates of national defense, a metamorphosis that enabled them to make their party the largest legal one in Europe after the French and, of course, the Soviet. As the threat of a German invasion loomed more ominously over Czechoslovakia, the Russians had every reason to stand by it as the last bulwark against the further spread of Hitler's power. Yet their professions of readiness to do so even if France defaulted are open to doubt.[62]

At no time during the September 1938 crisis did the Soviet government attempt to clarify how it would deal with Poland's and Romania's refusal to grant the Red Army the necessary rights of passage. Nor did German and other foreign diplomats in Moscow ever seriously expect it to move. Stalin himself later privately confessed that "personally he had never believed the Czechs meant to fight."[63] And indeed, Beneš, by then the President of Czechoslovakia, did not await Moscow's reply to his last-minute inquiry before deciding to yield to the blackmail exercised by his Western friends and Nazi enemies at the Munich conference. Czechoslovakia surrendered its borderlands to Germany without a fight, in return for a promise of survival of what was left.

Moscow's readiness to help was never really tested, thus enabling the Soviet Union to later pose as the Czechs' only friend in distress. At the time, however, the Russians were very much the losers; they appeared to be next on Hitler's agenda. In the wake of Munich, Berlin encouraged proponents of a "Greater Ukraine," which inevitably would be carved out of Soviet territory. This disturbing prospect brought about an unusual Russian rapprochement with Poland, another nation threatened by the Ukrainian irredenta. Suddenly the Carpathian Ukraine, still part of Czechoslovakia but the nucleus of the entity contemplated by Germany, achieved on the diplomatic scene a prominence scarcely warranted by its intrinsic value. An economic liability for anyone who possessed it, the wretched piece of land was also coveted by Poland and Hungary.[64] Above all, for Stalin it came to symbolize the vulnerability of his multiethnic empire to foreign intrigue.

In London, the exiled President Beneš reached the prescient conclusion that Hitler "would help us get Russia for a neighbor"; in fact, he believed "it ought to be our goal to have the Russians in Uzhgorod," the province's capital.[65] For the time being, to be sure, the Russians were on the run before a Germany that seemed to be inexorably moving east. And at Munich the Western powers had given the impression of having written off east central Europe as a German backyard. Never had Stalin's chances of either obtaining their backing against Hitler or else achieving an accommodation with him appeared slimmer. Running out of options, the Soviet dictator faced the dismal prospect of having to cope alone with his sworn enemy.

From the perspective of late 1938, the past experience of Soviet ventures on the international stage offered little to cheer their proponents. In twenty years of strenuous efforts, the successive Bolshevik chiefs had managed neither to spread their system in Europe nor to safeguard their own country's security. Their ideological preconceptions were mostly to blame. Their doctrine had driven them to entertain goals far beyond those the czars had dreamed of, thus generating recurrent frustrations. And this doctrine, while imbuing the Soviet policies with an extraordinary vigor and sense of purpose, had also made them more susceptible to failure because of Marxism's inherent flaws. In this respect, however, the Bolsheviks' capitalist adversaries were hardly better off. Not knowing what was good for themselves either, they could sometimes unintentionally rescue Moscow from an impasse. This is precisely what happened in 1939.

Stalin and Hitler: The Formative Relationship

Hitler set events in motion at the beginning of 1939. After he had shelved his Ukrainian designs, his next target was the Poles, who had recently sinned in his eyes by their tentative rapprochement with Moscow. In an effort to outflank them and soften them up, in mid-March he invaded what was left of Czechoslovakia, annexed its Czech parts as a "Protectorate," and turned Slovakia into a satellite state. This flagrant violation of the Munich pact prompted the British "diplomatic revolution": the repudiation of appeasement and a commitment to the defense of countries in eastern Europe, especially Poland.[66] To be sure, London's declared intention to defend that country's integrity was not convincing enough to deter Hitler, but it enraged him quite sufficiently to begin preparations for the outright military subjugation of Poland. Moreover, since Soviet neutrality was indispensable for this enterprise, the British turnabout enabled Stalin to play off Germany and the West for the highest bid.

Ironically, then, much as the Western appeasement may have tempted Stalin to come to terms with Hitler if he could, only its reversal created the possibility. Accordingly, the various Soviet moves following the Polish guarantee served less to deter than to entice the Germans. On April 17, the Russians replied quickly but evasively to a British proposal for a joint guarantee for Poland and intimated to Berlin their desire for rapprochement.[67] On May 3, Stalin finally opened the way for actual negotiations with Germany by dismissing Litvinov, who epitomized the opposite policy and, as a Jew, was anathema to the Nazis.[68]

Litvinov's successor, Vyacheslav M. Molotov, used to be disparaged as "the best filing clerk in Russia."[69] Indeed, he was cheerless, inflexible, and unimaginative—but also alert, precise, and hard-driving. Even his opponents were to be impressed by these qualities although their prevalent reaction would be exasperation with a man who sometimes seemed more like a machine.[70] For Stalin, Molotov was a perfect choice. Having no greater ambition than to serve his master faithfully, he was eminently qualified to become the chief executor of the Stalinist diplomacy now rapidly coming of age.

Although the Germans had been the first to propose a nonaggression agreement, Stalin was the true architect of the pact of August 23, 1939. As a long-time American observer of Soviet politics, Louis Fischer, succinctly put it,

If Stalin had wanted an agreement with the West he would have negotiated openly with Hitler. That would have put pressure on the West to give Russia a better bargain. Instead, Stalin negotiated openly with the West. That put pressure on Hitler to give Russia a better bargain.[71]

The Soviet dictator both controlled the timing and fixed the terms. So much was the pact his personal work that no other members of the Politburo besides Molotov learned about the deal until after it had been made.[72] The feat set the tone of all Stalin's subsequent diplomacy. But its author came to value the master stroke too highly.

Initially, the Soviet Union had by far the better part of the

24

bargain. Hitler had calculated that the central public provision of the pact—mutual neutrality in case of war with a third power—would compel Britain and France to tolerate his invasion of Poland. But they declared war on him all the same. Admittedly, he had at least secured Moscow's neutrality, but that achievement was more apparent than real since its military intervention on behalf of Poland had been most unlikely from the beginning. Nor did the Russian-inspired secret protocol, supplementing the public nonaggression pledge and providing for a division of east central Europe into spheres of influence, offer any advantages to the Nazis. Indeed, by extending the Soviet domain farther west, it hampered rather than facilitated the resumption of Hitler's drive to the east, which remained his foremost long-term ambition despite his momentary entanglement in the west.

In contrast, Stalin's gains were real, or so they seemed at the time. Without a shot, by a sober bargain with his chief ideological adversary, he achieved more than Lenin and Trotsky had with all their revolutionary brainstorming. In particular, the demise of Poland and the Soviet annexation of its territory even beyond the Curzon line reversed the humiliating verdict of 1920. Moscow further obtained German recognition of its predominant interest in other parts of the former czarist empire: Finland, Latvia, Estonia, and Bessarabia. Most important, the destructive war among the capitalists, which the pact had helped to unleash, deflected Hitler's aggressive impulse from the Soviet Union. Of course, this desirable situation might not last and the rapacious Führer might still turn east later on; even so, the newly acquired lands provided a priceless strategic shield. But the Nazi leader's very benevolence in conceding that shield suggested that he might well have postponed indefinitely his dream about living space in Russia, much as Stalin had done with his own dream about the victory of Communism in the world.

This comforting estimate seemed further corroborated by Berlin's ready assent, after Poland's defeat, to a second secret agreement the Russians proposed—a document so shameful that officially they have never even admitted its existence.[73] It added Lithuania to the Soviet sphere of influence and committed the partners in plunder to suppress any "Polish agitation," a euphemism soon translated into mass executions and deportations, the former preferred by Hitler, the latter by Stalin.[74] In appreciation of the Nazis' accommodating attitude, Moscow now dropped its original assessment of the war as a contest between two equally despicable groups of imperialists and clearly began to favor the German ones.

The Soviet Union tried to promote reciprocity on Hitler's part by ostentatiously displaying its respect for what he regarded as his own. When anti-German demonstrations broke out in Prague in October, the Comintern directed the underground Czech Communists to use "all their strength to paralyze the chauvinistic elements."[75] In November a declaration assaulting Social Democracy and Western (but not German) imperialists was issued jointly in Moscow by exiled representatives of the German, Austrian, and Czech Communist parties; this move was a sign that Russia accepted the Nazi-enforced merger of the three countries.[76] Soon afterward, the government made an even more telling gesture recognizing Hitler's new order in central Europe: it closed the Czechoslovak Legation in Moscow and invited instead an envoy of the pro-German regime in Slovakia.

To be sure, Stalin did not want Hitler to win the war. As explained clearly in the confidential messages the Comintern sent at that time to the leaders of the American Communist party, he was instead using the means at his disposal to encourage a stalemate that would benefit the Soviet Union at the expense of the exhausted belligerents.[77] Because Stalin, like most of his contemporaries, overestimated the military prowess of Germany's enemies (he judged the French army to be "worthy of consideration"),[78] he evidently thought it clever to give comfort to the ostensibly weaker side by distributing favors to it in carefully measured doses.

At the same time, the Soviet leader used the favorable circumstances to bolster his position vis-à-vis Germany in case the calculation did not work out as anticipated. He unceremoniously imposed treaties on the three Baltic republics, providing for Red Army bases on their territories. But if he hoped to impress Berlin by Russia's might, he achieved the opposite after Finland refused his demands for similar concessions and he foolishly resorted to war.

According to later testimony by Nikita S. Khrushchev (the most important Soviet source concerning the motives behind Stalin's policies in these eventful years), the dictator intended to annex Finland with the help of the puppet government of Otto Kuusinen which he attempted to install in the border town of Vyborg. Yet the actual Soviet treatment of that government, particularly Moscow's conclusion with it of treaties similar to those with the Baltic states, suggests instead that Stalin considered the status of these states a satisfactory model for Finland as well, at least for the time being.[79] He also assigned to the prospective Kuusinen regime much of Soviet Karelia in exchange for smaller territorial concessions of strategic value. In any case, however, the whole operation miscarried, as successful Finnish resistance led to a protracted and costly war. Then rumors spread, hinting at Western plans to help the Finns and simultaneously strike at Germany by striking at its Soviet ally—an alarming prospect which, by creating an acute need for German good will, made a shambles of Stalin's policy of limited favors.[80]

In his frantic effort to secure that good will, the Russian ruler, according to Khrushchev's running commentary, "now literally groveled before Hitler."[81] In early 1940 the Soviet Union stepped up dramatically its shipments of strategic raw materials to Germany.[82] It also handed over to the Gestapo several hundred German Communist refugees, a gesture that gave a special meaning to the Comintern's exhortations to "unmask" enemies of German–Soviet understanding.[83] There was a curious symbiosis between the Communist "undergrounds" and the Nazis, particularly in some western European countries where the Germans

27

temporarily even allowed the Communists to publish and hold local offices. [84]

The most atrocious, as well as the most puzzling, Soviet misdeed in the spring of 1940 was the massacre of several thousand interned Polish army officers at Katyn. So crude a mass murder was not typical of Stalin's style of disposing of his opponents, an aspect suggesting that it may have been committed by overzealous subordinates who misinterpreted his wishes. Nor are the motives for the crime clear, although its coincidence with Nazi grumblings that Polish officers were being harbored by the Russians for ulterior purposes offers a clue. [85] But if Stalin's thugs killed the men in order to ingratiate him with Hitler, as he was trying hard to do at that time, they failed to inform Berlin about the job well done. So for the time being the crime remained concealed, only to become an intense embarrassment when later discovered by the Germans in entirely different circumstances.

Conceivably, Stalin did not think it expedient to convey the Katyn news to Berlin because his need to court Germany had already diminished. Having overwhelmed the Finns by sheer numbers, he was soon able to dictate peace terms to them. Considering his original intention to absorb the country, these terms proved remarkably lenient. Finland had to give up a good tenth of its territory, particularly Karelia and the Baltic naval base of Hangö. But the rest survived as an independent state, thus testifying that the Russian dictator was far from indifferent to the cost of conquest. Stalin was not Hitler; he was ready to moderate his goals if he met determined resistance, whereas his Nazi counterpart, provoked by it, often did the opposite.

In June 1940, Khrushchev further tells us, "Stalin's nerves cracked when he learned about the fall of France." [86] If they did, the damage was not lasting, for the Soviet Union soon responded with a vigor hard to find in those days outside of Britain. In moral terms, there was of course a world of difference between the British struggle to preserve the freedom of this embattled island and Stalin's drive to unscrupulously extend his tyranny into neighbor-

28

ing countries; still, the desire to check Hitler's advance was common to both. In essence, Stalin sought to offset the growth of the German domain in the west by expanding his own in the east.

In June and July, Moscow used military blackmail and supported pseudorevolutionary movements in order to annex Estonia, Latvia, and Lithuania. It also tried to grab from Romania both Bessarabia, which had been mentioned in its spheres-of-influence agreement with Germany, and Bukovina, which had not; the latter, in fact, had never belonged to the Russian empire. After Berlin protested, Stalin exempted southern Bukovina from the package but, threatening Romania with an ultimatum, speedily occupied the rest. In a further effort to hurt Hitler's principal oil supplier, Russia incited Hungarian designs against Romania. It prodded the Hungarians to follow its example by reclaiming Transylvania, which the Romanians had seized after World War I.[87]

It was against the background of these momentous developments that the new British government of Winston Churchill undertook a bid for rapprochement with Moscow. The British documentation does not permit definite conclusions about how far Ambassador Sir Stafford Cripps exceeded his instructions by offering Stalin specific inducements. However, his conduct during their July 1 interview allowed the Soviet leader to act as if Britain had offered to recognize Russian hegemony in the Balkans. The dictator showed a prudent disinclination to get bogged down in an area where "an army of pacification" might be required.[88] He did indicate interest in British mediation to revise the 1936 Montreux Convention, which restricted Soviet military traffic through the Black Sea straits. But he showed a singular lack of faith in Britain's ability to deliver what it proffered, for he promptly leaked the whole conversation to the German ambassador.

Stalin's friendly gesture did not entirely mollify Hitler's indignation at the Soviet advances in southeast Europe. Later in July the Führer issued his first secret order anticipating a final settlement of accounts with Russia by war.[89] In the meantime, he regained the initiative in the Balkans by sponsoring the Vienna

Award, which transferred northern Tranyslvania to Hungary, thus earning Budapest's gratitude. Soon afterward, the Romanians also lost southern Dobruja to Bulgaria. This only increased Romanian dependence on German protection against further depredations, and in October German troops were stationed in the country.[90]

The Russo-German tug of war continued; Moscow made an abortive attempt to gain joint control of the Danube delta with Romania, and dispatched Arkadii A. Sobolev (a rising star in Molotov's foreign service) on a special mission to Bulgaria. Sobolev offered a Soviet guarantee of its integrity and indicated that his government would view favorably a Bulgarian bid for Greek Thrace and most of European Turkey. Although the offer, duly publicized by the local Communists, impressed the Russophile populace favorably, its net effect on the Sofia government was to draw it closer to Berlin.[91]

In a pattern that later became characteristic of his diplomacy, Stalin explored additional vulnerable spots to help redress the deteriorating balance of power. He again put pressure on the Finns, eyeing their northern district of Petsamo (which was rich in nickel ore) and dropping broad hints about the country's possible transformation into a Soviet republic.[92] In allusion to its defunct revolutionary heritage, the Comintern assisted Russian diplomacy by developing the pseudoradical theory that the imperialist war would ultimately result in the creation of such republics throughout Europe. Assiduously cultivated by Communists in Slovakia, the theory carried particular poignancy in this country with a small but compact Ukrainian minority.[93]

Reflecting a Soviet reassessment of the relative standing of the belligerents, the Comintern-inspired propaganda in the second half of 1940 no longer gave comfort to the German imperialists, tending instead in the opposite direction.[94] For their part, the Nazis discarded whatever inhibitions they had had about clamping down on Communists as hard as they could. They badly mauled Moscow's clandestine contacts in the countries under

German control, particularly Austria and the Czech Protectorate.[95] The outcome dramatized the continuing decline of international Communism as a useful tool of Soviet foreign policy; accordingly, in his pursuits abroad Stalin showed a growing readiness to rely exclusively on conventional devices of power politics.

Molotov's historic visit to Berlin in November 1940 was a case in point. At that time, the behavior of his Nazi hosts still suggested that Hitler's intention to attack might be reversible. Bent on subjugating Russia without resort to force, the Führer proposed to Molotov that the Soviet Union join the Tripartite Pact, which linked Germany, Italy, and Japan with Berlin's eastern European satellites. As a reward, the Nazi chiefs tried to dazzle him with the prospect of Russian advance in the Black Sea area and in central Asia toward India.[96]

Evading a reply pending consultation with his boss, Molotov countered with an astounding list of other desiderata, focused pointedly on Europe. These envisaged effective subordination of Finland and incorporation of southern Bukovina, both of which had previously eluded the Soviet net. Molotov further demanded that Bulgaria be recognized as part of a Russian security zone, to which Sweden also supposedly belonged. He declared his government's long-term interest in Hungary, Yugoslavia, Greece, and even the portion of Poland currently occupied by the Germans. Finally, he expressed the Soviet desire for military bases in the Dardanelles and, for good measure, a Russian–Danish condominium over the Baltic straits.[97]

Never before had Soviet leaders put forward so unashamedly an imperialistic program; its different ingredients were to crop up again on various later occasions. Of course, in November 1940 the discrepancy between Stalin's appetite and the means available to satisfy it was such that he could hardly have expected to get all that his aide was asking for. Rather, in his growing uneasiness about German intentions, he wished to ascertain how much the

Nazis were prepared to pay for his friendship. After all, this tactic had worked well by yielding reassuring results during the German–Polish war the year before.

However, the circumstances were different now, and so were the results. While Molotov's resistance to German blandishments infuriated Hitler, the extravagant Soviet greed impressed him as a sign of weakness—which indeed it was. Moscow's inglorious acceptance ten days later of the invitation to join the Tripartite Pact did not help matters, accompanied as it was by further demands, particularly for recognition of the Soviet right to expand through Iran toward the Persian Gulf.[98] No sooner had the Foreign Commissar left Berlin empty-handed than Hitler began to prepare for an invasion of Russia the next spring. Although his ideology and thirst for conquest, besides misperceived military exigency, had long predisposed him toward this decision, the Soviet arrogance assured it.[99]

In the shrinking area where the Russians could still aspire to compete for influence, the fate of Hungary assumed a significance somewhat reminiscent of Czechoslovakia's fate before Munich. The Budapest government still seemed to be resisting complete subservience to Berlin. Never had Soviet–Hungarian relations been better than in late 1940 and early 1941 when the Russians, in a gesture of appreciation, returned to Budapest some of the flags the czar's soldiers had captured from Magyar insurgents in 1849. The regime of Admiral Nicholas Horthy reciprocated by releasing to Moscow the imprisoned Communist party chief, Matyás Rákosi. That trade-off later inspired the quip about the splendid bargain the Hungarians made, for in four years they would have Rákosi back as their boss while keeping the flags, too.[100]

It is only fair to stress that, in those days of German ascendancy, Stalin could not have anticipated this outcome any more than he appreciated all the future benefits of his evolving special relationship with Czechoslovakia. Since the summer of 1940, intelligence had been passing from the Czech underground to the Russian Consulate in Prague. Meanwhile in London the Czechoslovak government-in-exile, presided over by Beneš, had established cordial relations with Soviet Ambassador Ivan M. Maiskii, at that time still widely ostracized because of his country's German connection.[101] In southeast Europe, Czechoslovak secret agents entered into a liaison with their Russian counterparts. And in April 1941, the Beneš government's dispatching of a military mission to Moscow heralded a further rapprochement.[102]

In the spring of 1941, Yugoslavia unexpectedly became the catalyst of events; in March an upsurge of patriotism brought to power a new government that was more disposed to resist German pressure. The Soviet Union quickly seized the opportunity to conclude a friendship treaty with Belgrade that provided for diplomatic assistance against a threat by a third power.[103] No sooner did the threat materialize as a Nazi invasion of Yugoslavia than Moscow hastily reneged on its pledge. Much like the British after Hitler's attack on Poland, Stalin was brutally reminded of his impotence; his response, however, was different. Ironically the lesson he learned was "hands off"—at the very time when the Yugoslav Communists were about to launch the most powerful pro-Soviet resistance movement in all of Europe!

The ten weeks that followed the collapse of Yugoslavia marked the all-time nadir of Soviet diplomacy.[104] As the Nazis triumphantly completed their conquest of the Balkans, Moscow in a frantic effort to appease them broke off relations not only with the exiled governments of Yugoslavia and Greece but, in an orgy of self-degradation, with those of Norway and Belgium as well. There is even evidence of a Russian feeler toward recognition of the pro-Nazi Ustashi regime in Croatia.[105] On April 13, Stalin made an unprecedented public appearance on the occasion of the German ambassador's departure; he pathetically embraced the envoy, insisting that their two countries must remain friends.[106]

The subsequent story of how, despite many warnings, Stalin was caught unwares by the Nazi attack has often been recounted as a case study of both his personal gullibility and the pitfalls of a system that discourages dissent. The true story is rather one of successful German dissimulation, calculated to generate the impression that the troop concentrations along the borders merely provided the proper setting for an ultimatum that would demand Moscow's unequivocal subordination to Berlin's leadership. The scheme fooled not only Stalin but also nearly all contemporary statesmen and intelligence services.[107] Thus neither his personality nor the system he created was primarily to blame for the disastrous misjudgment; they did account, however, for the extremes of appeasement that made it worse.

As reports of the imminent invasion piled up in the Kremlin, Stalin increasingly suspected a British ploy to embroil him in a war with Germany; the astonishing Tass communiqué of June 14, denying such reports as slanderous, bespoke his dread and the utter bankruptcy of his policy.[108] Meanwhile in Berlin Soviet diplomats were reportedly instructed to find out the terms of the imaginary ultimatum. There are indications that, in his panic to stave off fate, Stalin was at last prepared to offer concessions so drastic that they would have reduced his country to the status of Germany's junior partner—the status Hitler had seemed to desire at the time of Molotov's visit.[109]

Whatever the doubtful rationale of these desperate moves, and Khrushchev may have been right in implying that toward the end Stalin simply lost his nerve,[110] they showed how genuinely devoted the Soviet dictator was to the pact with his Nazi counterpart. So enthralled had he become by the mutually beneficial relationship that he could not imagine how Hitler might possibly see any advantage in wantonly destroying it. Even later, he appeared less indignant at his former partner's depravity (an irrelevant consideration) than contemptuous of the Führer's stupidity.[111] According to Stalin's daughter, her father never ceased to regret the demise of the liaison: "With the Germans," she recalls him saying nostalgically, "we would have been invincible."[112]

The crucial years of the Stalin–Hitler pact left a durable imprint on both the content and the style of Soviet foreign policy. It was in collusion and competition with his congenial Nazi rival that Stalin had formulated the main objectives of that policy in Europe and had developed the means for their attainment as well. Those objectives had not proved very different from the traditional goals of Russian imperialism. Nor had the principal means—the pursuit of a balance of power, with a special predilection for the time-honored device of spheres of influence—been unknown in the arsenal of the "old diplomacy." Nonetheless, in pursuing his goals Stalin had added and perfected a blend of opportunism and savagery that was peculiarly his own. He did not regard it as his fault that the mixture had failed to protect him from Hitler; therefore neither his aims nor his methods were likely to alter in the future—provided, that is, that he could survive the catastrophe he had been so instrumental in bringing on the heads of his people.

chapter two

The Minimum Aims
June 1941–February 1943

The Improbable Allies

Stalin's later detractors have described graphically his erratic behavior in the wake of the Nazi invasion on June 22, 1941. According to Maiskii, "he locked himself in his study and would not see anybody," lamenting, as Khrushchev has testified, that "all Lenin created we have lost forever."[1] Whether these self-serving assertions are accurate or (more likely) exaggerated, Stalin did act as if he were "depressed, nervous, and of uneven disposition"[2] for at least two weeks. He not only failed to take immediate, firm command of the nation's defense but also was not publicly heard from until July 3, when he finally recovered sufficiently to deliver his famous radio oration. Addressing his audience uncharacteristically as "brothers and sisters," he spoke haltingly and in a plaintive tone.[3]

Stalin's initial mood of uncertainty would seem altogether justified by a preoccupation with potential threats from within. It would have been natural for his associates to censure him for the catastrophic results of the policy to which he had so deeply committed himself. And indeed, that policy was indirectly criticized by Litvinov, now back from his enforced retirement. In an address broadcast on July 8, over the foreign rather than the domestic service of the Moscow radio, he ridiculed the belief that any "agreements or treaties . . . signed by Hitler could be trusted."[4] As for the rank and file of the citizenry, a great many were, as officially admitted, "given to panic and even oriented toward the enemy"[5]—so many in fact that the Soviet Union eventually supplied Hitler with more collaborators than any other country he occupied.

Stalin soon found himself surrounded, however, by devoted servants and harmless sycophants rather than angry critics; even Litvinov's gibe may have been unintentional. And the sullen populace, subdued by the years of terror, in no way took advantage of the tyrant's distress; in this respect at least, the purges seemed to be paying off. Not without a touch of amazement would Stalin later pay tribute to the Russians' docility by comparing them with other peoples who "would have said to the Government: 'You have failed to justify our expectations. Go away. We shall install another government.' "[6] Hitler deserved credit, too, because his atrocities provided compelling evidence that his rule was even worse than Stalin's.

Many complexities of the crucial aftermath of the Nazi attack will probably not become known for a long time. Even the trickle of revelations publicized under Khrushchev was soon dammed by his successors. The June breakdown not only reflected on Stalin personally but also exposed basic weaknesses of the whole Soviet system at the moment of its greatest peril. Its margin of survival may have been paper thin.

The military outcome of the Russian–German confrontation hung in the balance for months to come. With commendable candor, Stalin himself later acknowledged that if the Soviet territory had not been so deep the Red Army would have succumbed,[7] as had the French army amid similar chaos and incompetence in 1940. But long before the military verdict, Stalin had already won the war politically and morally, for better or for worse. Both the members of the ruling clique and the people at large had given him absolution. With his rule vindicated, he was under little compulsion to reform it substantially. Despite temporary concessions for wartime expediency, he continued to treat his subjects as callously as before. Soviet soldiers would soon discover that they had to face not only the enemy in front but also sinister detachments behind them, handpicked to deal brutally with any real or fancied "traitors and cowards."[8]

A favorable international response to Russia's plight was not a foregone conclusion. The West could well have followed Stalin's recent example and have kept aloof if not, indeed, lent one or the other of its avowed enemies just enough support to assure that both would perish. That idea was entertained by various people, among them Harry S. Truman (then still an obscure junior senator from Missouri). On the day after the Nazi invasion he said: "If we see that Germany is winning we ought to help Russia and if Russia is winning we ought to help Germany and that way let them kill as many as possible, although I don't want to see Hitler victorious in any circumstances."[9]

Opinions were one thing and policies quite another. On the day of the Nazi invasion, Churchill took the critical step by extending his unsolicited and unrestricted offer to assist "Russia and the Russian people" with all means at Britain's disposal. The old crusader against Bolshevism stated publicly that "the past, with its crimes, its follies, and its tragedies, flashes away"; privately he confessed that "if Hitler invaded Hell . . . [I] would make at least a favorable reference to the Devil in the House of Commons."[10] A few days later, the United States also offered the Soviet Union all possible help, even though it did not officially become a belligerent until December.[11]

Thus the "Grand Alliance," unlike the pact with Hitler, was not Stalin's creation. It seemed so improbable that the Soviet leader could hardly have avoided wondering about the capitalists' true motives. Ironically, their very generosity to someone as thoroughly compromised as he was, and under such circumstances, was apt to enhance rather than allay his suspicions. Significantly, the person whom Stalin sent to negotiate the aid agreements in London and Washington was General F. I. Golikov—the chief of the intelligence department of the Red Army General Staff.[12]

39

Whatever perfidious motives he may have thought had inspired the Western assistance, Stalin had every reason to welcome the aid with open arms. It was against the background of this windfall of unexpected, undeserved, and altogether unbelievable gains that his war aims began to evolve. As early as June 27, Molotov proposed to Sir Stafford Cripps "a political agreement to define the basis of cooperation." [13] The British ambassador replied that "it was better to wait till we had learnt to trust each other," a pertinent remark in view of the Soviet insistence that a clause barring separate peace be inserted prominently into the preliminary military agreement between the two countries. [14] This terse document was signed on July 12, by which time Moscow had also made clear that it continued to claim all the lands it had acquired during the collusion with Hitler.

The West was unlikely to contest claims to the territories taken from Germany's associates Finland and Romania, especially not after London at Soviet behest declared war on these two countries. Nor was the Russian intention to keep the Baltic states (none of which ever established a government-in-exile) likely to meet effective opposition despite the United States' refusal, until the present day, to formally endorse their subjugation and its continued recognition of their phantom diplomatic representatives. But Stalin's claim to eastern Poland portended trouble from the start.

Despite the Soviet Union's new status as an Allied nation, the exiled Polish government in London remained notably reserved toward a nation it regarded as a predator of Polish lands. And the Russians failed conspicuously to offer incentives and assurances to dispel the mistrust of their intentions so amply justified by their past record. It was therefore left to the British to press the two enemies into reluctantly establishing diplomatic ties on July 30. [15] As part of the deal, Moscow agreed to the formula that "the Soviet–German treaties of 1939 as to territorial changes in Poland . . . [have] lost their validity." [16] Yet only five days later, an authoritative *Pravda* article invalidated this concession by insisting that the prewar Polish frontiers were not "immutable," defending the changes the Soviet Union had enforced in 1939, and maintaining that the question remained open for a final settlement in the future.[17]

Aware of the popular feelings in the lands it coveted, Moscow harbored no enthusiasm for the Atlantic Charter—that lofty declaration of Allied war aims that Churchill and Roosevelt issued on August 14, reaffirming all peoples' right to self-determination.[18] Maiskii conveyed to British Foreign Secretary Anthony Eden his government's unhappiness at not having been consulted in advance on the wording of so important a document.[19] At the inter-Allied conference in London on September 24, the Soviet Union did endorse it but with a significant reservation. Maiskii stated that the application of the Charter had to be adapted to "the circumstances, needs and historic peculiarities of particular countries," a formulation casting doubt on his simultaneous profession of Soviet respect for "the sovereign rights of peoples" and for every nation's "independence and territorial integrity."[20]

Stalin's overwhelming reluctance to part with any of his questionable acquisitions, despite the complications this was sure to cause with his much-needed allies, is not easily explicable. In his July 18 message to Churchill, he argued how much harder it would have been for the Red Army to face the invaders on the old frontier than on the one of June 1941.[21] This was a specious argument, however; he had shown his lack of faith in the military value of those territories by neglecting to build up their defenses,[22] a negligence which had made the Germans more willing to risk attacking them. Stalin desired the land less for strictly military than for psychological reasons; the possession, though not providing real security, at least enhanced the feeling of it. And his craving for security was limitless.

On December 16, Stalin tackled the question of war aims during a conversation with Eden, who had come to Moscow to promote closer ties. Stressing pointedly that "if our aims were different, then there would be no alliance," the Soviet leader revealed desiderata strikingly similar to those Molotov had raised in Berlin the year before.[23] Besides recognition of the June 1941 frontier, he demanded military bases in Finland and Romania; in return, he invited Britain to help itself to the same in Norway, Denmark, Belgium, the Netherlands, and possibly France. He wanted to sign immediately a secret political understanding that would spell out the future European settlement.

As he had done with Hitler in 1939, Stalin was again proposing a partition of Europe into spheres of influence, except that this time he did not draw a clear line between them. In the middle, he recommended that some of Hitler's victims be rewarded at the expense of Germany and its accomplices. Czechoslovakia was to be restored within its pre-Munich boundaries, with the addition of unspecified portions of Hungary. Yugoslavia was to be reestablished and enlarged with both Hungarian and Italian territory. Further at the expense of Italy, Albania would again become independent and Turkey would receive the Dodecanese Islands. The Turks might also get a piece of Bulgaria, the country that only a year earlier Moscow had lured with an offer of Turkish territory.

This reshuffling of frontiers would not necessarily have drawn the beneficiaries closer to one or the other of the great powers, although Turkey might have been expected to become accommodating toward Russian demands for control of the Black Sea straits. Other proposed changes, however, were plainly calculated to promote dependence on the Soviet Union. Thus Romania was to be compensated by Hungary for its loss of Bessarabia and northern Bukovina, a Vienna Award in reverse that would compel Bucharest to look for protection to Moscow. And Poland was to get East Prussia (except for the area north of the Nemen river which Stalin thought could be added to Soviet Lithuania) along with other parts of Germany, possibly up to the Oder.[24]

Blending radicalism with respectability, Stalin's suggestions about Germany were tailored to appeal to the supposed preferences of Hitler's capitalist enemies. He spoke in favor of an independent Austria, as established by the 1919 Paris peace settlement. He further mentioned possible separation of the Rhineland (the pet project of French chauvinists) and quasi-autonomy for Bavaria, reminiscent of its position during the Bismarckian Reich. He advocated the restoration of the Sudetenland to Czechoslovakia, a return to the uneasy prewar situation.

These operations, if implemented literally, would have left Germany drastically smaller if not dismembered; none of them, however, was to be a Soviet responsibility. According to subsequent hints by Russian diplomats, the British were to be the ones who would police that troublesome country, and indeed the whole of western Europe.[25] Since the Bolshevik revolution, Moscow had already burned its fingers badly three times in Germany—when it had misjudged the country's revolutionary potential in the early 1920s, when it had misunderstood the vitality of Nazism in the early 1930s, and of course most recently when it had mishandled the pact with Hitler. For Stalin, the obvious lesson was to let others take the lead in coping with a people so dangerously unpredictable as the Germans, lest too definite a policy on his part again result in a bitter disappointment.

Friends and foes alike have often credited Stalin with an uncanny prescience and sense of purpose. After all, did not the Europe that emerged from the war conform quite closely to the vision he had expounded to Eden in 1941? Yet that vision was no blueprint for achieving unalterable aims. Rather, the Soviet ruler was exhibiting the same "incurable taste for future precision to offset . . . present confusions"[26] that had characterized his czarist predecessors during World War I. Admittedly, he had his preferences, but precisely because his chances of realizing most of them on his own seemed remote, he tried to pin down his indispensable allies to as many specifics as possible, and that required flexibility and improvisation.

Soviet diplomacy displayed these traits in abundance after the talks with Eden had ended inconclusively. During the subsequent negotiations for a formal alliance, Moscow reluctantly retreated from Stalin's original demand for a comprehensive political agreement. On May 5, 1942, Maiskii proposed a secret, or even public, understanding that would at least authorize his government to exact any military privileges it desired from Finland and Romania, while the British would affirm their right to do likewise with the Low Countries.[27] Although London showed no inclination to subject its traditional friends to such heavy-handed treatment, the Russians were not easily dissuaded. They submitted an amended proposal that did not name Belgium or the Netherlands but suggested that the British might still wish to proclaim their special interest "in the Straits of Dover and the southern part of the North Sea."[28] This pathetic search for a crutch that would enable Stalin to salvage even part of his grandiose scheme showed how severely his military predicament limited his diplomatic leverage in those days.

So bad was this predicament that initially many Western officials suspected Stalin might attempt to come to terms with Hitler again. United States Assistant Secretary of State Adolf A. Berle, Jr., considered such an attempt quite possible as early as July 1941; the British Embassy in Moscow anticipated a Soviet bid for peace two months later.[29] Although during the winter the Red Army's position improved, in the spring of 1942 the British fears were even greater, mainly as a result of dire predictions by the Ambassador to Washington, Lord Halifax.[30] But such fears were groundless so long as the Red Army's plight remained desperate. In Stalin's view, any overtures to Berlin would have heightened the danger of a dreaded Western reversal of alliances; they would also have given additional comfort to the enemy at a time when Russia could least afford it. In any case, the Nazis proved by their behavior that as long as they retained the upper hand the only terms he could expect from them were complete submission.

Nevertheless, on March 7, 1942, in a letter to Roosevelt Churchill insisted that because of the urgent need for Soviet help in the Allied war effort, "the principles of the Atlantic Charter ought not to be construed so as to deny Russia the frontiers which she occupied when Germany attacked her."[31] Eden, fresh from his Moscow experience, had been trying to impress this view upon the British government during an agonizing debate in which he played Stalin's advocate. He startled Alexander Cadogan, the Permanent Under Secretary in the Foreign Office, by his disposition "to throw to the winds all principles."[32] In the end, the British decided to endorse all of the Soviet territorial claims except those against Poland. They hoped that by sanctioning most of the claims now they would be better able to discourage Stalin from seeking more later on.[33]

The Americans, for their part, disapproved. Haunted by the memory of President Woodrow Wilson's sorry experience with secret treaties in World War I, they opposed any advance territorial arrangements that might later prove embarrassing. With both logic and foresight, Secretary of State Cordell Hull suspected

[that] the Soviet Government has tremendous ambitions with regard to Europe and that at some time or other the U.S. and Great Britain will be forced to state that they cannot agree, at least in advance, to all of its demands. It would seem that it is preferable to take a firm attitude now, rather than to retreat and to be compelled to take a firm attitude later when our position had been weakened by the abandonment of the general principles.[34]

Actually, there was much to be said for both the British and the American approaches, provided that the one chosen had been applied jointly and consistently by the two governments. But this did not happen in 1942 or, for that matter, during the rest of the war—a deficiency that only tended to confuse the Russians and encourage them to act unilaterally.[35]

Alert to the differences between its two partners, Moscow ignored Roosevelt's plea to exclude any territorial provisions from the proposed pact with Britain; at the same time, it prodded London to resist American pressure.[36] This the British could not afford to do, nor did they really want to. It is not clear whether Hull warned them as bluntly as he later asserted in his memoirs, that Washington would publicly dissociate itself from the agreement if it included territorial clauses; there is no other evidence of the alleged warning.[37] According to the British records, Eden on his own initiative proposed to Molotov (who had come to London at the end of May for the final stage of the talks) a straight military alliance without any such clauses. Surprisingly, the Foreign Commissar accepted the formula quite readily, although not before checking with United States Ambassador John C. Winant, to assure himself that it enjoyed American approval.[38] The alliance was signed on May 26.

Molotov's concession, which gratified the British and the Americans after so many months of frustrating bickering, brought into focus the evolving Allied controversy about the "Second Front." (The term, of Russian origin, had come to signify in Moscow's parlance an Anglo-American invasion of France across the English Channel; it carried the insulting connotation that the Soviet Union alone was really fighting.) In fact, Stalin had only consented to dispatch Molotov to London after he had received an encouraging message on this subject from Roosevelt. In that message, the President had mentioned he had "in mind a very important military proposal involving the utilization of our armed forces in a manner to relieve your critical Western Front."[39] To Stalin, this could hardly have meant anything other than the ardently desired Second Front, and it had prompted him to add Washington to Molotov's itinerary. In the Soviet mind, though not necessarily yet in reality, America was rapidly replacing Britain as the decisive factor of war and peace.

There was an intricate connection between the Second Front and Soviet aims in eastern Europe. Molotov reached Washington expecting a major military reward for his London concession, a reward all the more imperative to offset the painful setback the Red Army had recently suffered as a result of its abortive offensive at Kharkov. But when he first met with Roosevelt on May 30, the President did not volunteer any promise. Pressed by Molotov about the Second Front, he asked General George C. Marshall, the Army Chief of Staff also present in the room, whether it was fair to say that the United States was preparing the operation. Given an affirmative answer, Roosevelt went a step further and "authorized Mr. Molotov to inform Mr. Stalin that we expect the formation of a second front this year."[40]

Since the United States was planning a landing in North Africa later that year, the statement was not technically incorrect but it was nevertheless rash and misleading; as the President ought to have known, the prospective campaign did not meet the Soviet criteria for a Second Front. Roosevelt made a further blunder by discarding the State Department's carefully worded draft of the public communiqué and accepting instead one prepared by Molotov. Thus the world was informed that "in the course of the conversations full understanding was reached with regard to the urgent tasks of creating a second front in Europe in 1942."[41]

An understanding had indeed been reached, but about the very opposite! For Roosevelt was well aware that he could not deliver the Second Front in Europe that year and Molotov, having witnessed the Americans' behavior, could not have left with any illusions about this. Even in the unlikely case that he did, the residual illusions were effectively destroyed a week later by Churchill. The Prime Minister, appalled at the President's casual handling of a serious business, took special care to impress upon Molotov that the operation was entirely contingent on favorable conditions, which were unlikely to exist in 1942.[42] However, what Roosevelt had privately said and publicly confirmed enabled the Russians to pose as if they believed that they had been tricked. Frustrated by their inability to exact the commitment they wanted, they found both solace and political capital in maintaining the pretense.[43] And there was at least a chance that the President might try to lessen his embarrassment by speeding up matters.

For all his ideological obeisance to the impersonal Marxist categories, Stalin assigned an inordinate significance to the role of personality in politics. This incident gave him an opportunity to ponder the different qualities of his two peers. In one of his revealing conversations with Milovan Djilas, the Yugoslav Communist chief, he expressed his utter mistrust of and contempt for both Western statesmen:

> Churchill is the kind who, if you don't watch him, will slip a kopeck out of your pocket! By God, a kopeck out of your pocket! And Roosevelt? Roosevelt is not like that. He dips in his hand only for bigger coins. But Churchill? Churchill—even for a kopeck.[44]

There was, to be sure, a good deal of self-conscious pose in these ruminations; still, the smearing distinction betrayed a keen, though distorted, perception of some real differences between these leaders.

Of the two, Roosevelt was more difficult to fathom. The creator of the New Deal did not fit easily into the Soviet stereotype of a capitalist statesman unflinchingly pursuing the narrow interests of his class; his approach could be seen alternatively as devious and as inconsistent. He left no doubt about wielding enormous power but otherwise gave few clues to what direction, if any, he intended to use it in. In this respect, his ebullient but fuzzy language was of little help. There was something positively alarming about a person who "didn't much care what interpretations other people put on it . . . as long as he could put his own interpretation on the language."[45]

Roosevelt had treated the Russians shabbily in the matter of the Second Front. However, he also gave Molotov reason to believe that he was less formidable an opponent of Soviet power than would appear from his vetoing of British recognition of Soviet territorial claims. He confided to Molotov his preference for a world to be run by "four policemen" and, while he failed to elaborate about the size or location of the Russian precinct, the design clearly implied Moscow's strong presence in Europe.[46] On balance, although the President's erratic style of diplomacy was annoying, it did not necessarily augur ill for Soviet interests and, with luck, might even redound to their advantage.

In contrast, Churchill was no enigma. To the Bolsheviks he had been the quintessential capitalist statesman ever since he had advocated military intervention to overthrow them after they had seized power. When Stalin first met him, during the Moscow visit that Churchill undertook in August 1942 to soothe the Russian ire about the Second Front, the two seemed to understand each other perfectly. After Churchill had genially touched on his anti-Communist past, Stalin answered in kind that "we like a down-right enemy better than a pretending friend."[47] From the Soviet perspective, the British leader appeared perhaps more dangerous but also more easily manageable than the American one.

Meanwhile, for Stalin the Second Front remained the crucial test of his improbable allies' adherence to the common cause. He was a most unlikely person to ever believe the truth that the operation was repeatedly postponed for purely military rather than political reasons.[48] He had grounds, though the wrong ones, for questioning the motives of his partners, and therefore he demanded constant reassurance that their aid was not being husbanded to promote a stalemate. Nothing within their power at that time could allay his anxiety. "The paucity of your offers," he once gratuitously reproached American officials, "shows that you want the Soviet Union defeated."[49] And the rebuff that Stalin had suffered in his quest for recognition of his country's June 1941 frontier did not help matters. But then, what his allies were reluctant to grant, the disruption of Europe by his enemies promised to yield.

Reversing the *Cordon Sanitaire*

By sowing discord throughout Europe, the Nazis played into Stalin's hands. However, their particular division of peoples into victims and accomplices did not always coincide with his preferences. Thus in east central Europe the war pitted the Poles, Czechs, Serbs, Albanians, and Greeks against the Finns, Slovaks, Hungarians, Croats, Romanians, and Bulgarians; it left the ambiguous status of the three Baltic nations, as well as of Austria, open to interpretation. Any Soviet aspirations to transform the execrated *cordon sanitaire* into a comfortable shield of genuinely, or at least effectively, friendly states had to take into account this complex situation. The ensuing policies were therefore bound to be considerably more tortuous than the ostensibly straightforward design Stalin had unfolded before Eden in December 1941 might seem to indicate. In an important sense, his insistence on definite territorial annexations suggested perceived limitations regarding Russia's ability to control a wider area by more subtle means. His preoccupation with the Soviet Union's immediate western neighbors contrasted with his initial lack of concern for other countries.

Among the neighbors, Estonia, Latvia, and Lithuania were the only ones whose independence Stalin appeared firmly resolved to extinguish. In the wake of Hitler's invasion, their peoples had demonstrated their true feelings by spontaneously revolting against Russian rule, before being subjugated by the Germans.[50] For its part, Moscow never faltered in maintaining that the three countries remained integral parts of its national territory. After all, they were small enough to be absorbed, they had belonged to the Russian empire before, and the Soviet Union had always regarded them as vitally important for its defense because of their strategic location.

Stalin proved more lenient in his designs against Germany's most active accomplices, Finland and Romania, which had declared war on him to regain their territories that he had seized in 1940. In both countries, he aimed to establish military facilities and the concomitant political control, but he differentiated between them in regard to territorial issues. In August 1941, he began his wartime correspondence with Roosevelt by a message which, in soliciting American mediation of the conflict with Finland, hinted at the possibility of "certain territorial concessions",[51] he never indicated a willingness to do likewise with Romania.

Stalin's grudging respect for the Finns and contempt for the
Romanians seem to have accounted in part for the difference. But
there were also two legal points—something that the dictator, for
all his willfulness, was seldom prepared to disregard entirely.
First, the Soviet government had never acknowledged the validity of Romania's possession of Bessarabia. Second, in making war
on Russia, Finland had prudently abstained from joining with the
Germans formally in an alliance. Indeed, the Russians had been
the ones who had first launched massive air attacks against Finland, possibly because they had assumed the Finns and the Germans were acting in concert.[52]

Soviet diplomats made their British counterparts believe that
their government was aiming at a similar arrangement with military bases in Bulgaria, although Bulgaria was at war only with the
Western powers and not with Russia.[53] The country, renowned
for its Russophile traditions, offered throughout the war the extraordinary sight of hosting the only Soviet legation in Hitler's
Europe. But in 1941, this situation seemed unlikely to last, although it is difficult to determine who was principally responsible
for the strain in Bulgarian–Soviet relations at that time. In the
summer of 1941, the Bulgarians attributed mysterious air raids on
their territory to Soviet planes. Accusing Sofia of bellicose intentions, the Russians pleaded innocence;[54] in the absence of reliable evidence, German provocation is as likely as Russian.

The circumstances of Hungary's entering the war against
Russia were as curious as those of Bulgaria's avoiding it. The day
after the German invasion, Molotov summoned the Hungarian
Minister in Moscow, József Kristóffy, to assure him of the Soviet
desire for continued friendship with Budapest.[55] Five days later,
Hungary declared war all the same following another tantalizing
incident supposedly involving Soviet aircraft—the bombing of the
city of Kassa, or Košice, which the Hungarians had recaptured
from Czechoslovakia in 1939. Again, the Russians denied any responsibility, professing indignation at Budapest's treachery.

The best available opinion, based on a judicious examination
of circumstantial evidence, is that those planes were indeed flown

by Russian pilots, who believed mistakenly that they were bombing a city in Slovakia.[56] That country had already joined Hitler's crusade against Bolshevism a few days before—without any provocation or other compelling reasons. The explanation of the incident seems plausible in view of not only the momentary confusion that seized the Soviet High Command at that time but also the subsequent Russian tendency to set Hungary apart from Hitler's other accomplices. In a public address on February 23, 1942, Stalin conspicuously exempted it from his enumeration of the nations that had gratuitously assaulted the Soviet state.[57]

In another public statement, on November 6, 1941, Stalin made an equally meaningful allusion to Austria. By juxtaposing its *Anschluss* in 1938 and the Nazis' later conquests, he seemed to implicitly legitimize its incorporation into Germany. Johann Koplenig, a leading Austrian Communist exile, later testified that his nation's right to independence had indeed been a matter of discussion in Moscow in those days.[58] On the one hand, the Russians found it expedient to maintain a separate Austrian broadcasting service among the many they had established following Hitler's invasion in order to beam propaganda into his dependencies. On the other hand, Dmitrii Z. Manuiliskii, the chief Russian liaison man in the Comintern, paid his Austrian comrades the dubious compliment that their compatriots were only "a charming variety of Germans."[59]

Nor was Moscow's attitude toward Hitler's genuine victims free of disconcerting ambiguities. In trying to revive contacts that had lapsed during Stalin's exercise in appeasement, soon after its enforced termination the Russians formally recognized the foreign-based liberation movements representing most German-occupied countries. The notable exceptions were France and Denmark (the former until August 1943, the latter until as late as July 1944), ostensibly because they had "opened the gates to the enemy," but in reality for more tangible reasons as well.[60] There was something to be said for trying to make an outcast of France, the only continental nation potentially strong enough to compete

52

with Russia for influence after Germany's demise. The pretense depicting Denmark as Hitler's accomplice also had its special purpose, considering the desire to share control of the Baltic straits that Moscow had expressed in November 1940.

Apart from the territorial issues concerning them directly, the Russians proved notably reluctant to commit themselves on the changes that Stalin had advocated in his conversation with Eden. They evaded Czechoslovakia's demand for recognition of its pre-Munich frontiers. Indeed, Maiskii shocked Beneš by indicating his doubts about the benefits the Czechs could possibly derive from the possession of the German-inhabited Sudetenland.[61] A separate Sudeten German service of the Moscow radio conveyed the disturbing notion that the area was more a special part of Germany than of Czechoslovakia.[62]

On July 4, 1941, the Soviet Union proposed to the Czechoslovak, Polish, and Yugoslav governments-in-exile that they form their "national committees" and military forces on its territory.[63] The offer aroused apprehension and retrospectively has usually been viewed as a ploy to set up rival puppet regimes. This was hardly Moscow's intention at that time; if it had been, the proposal would not have been addressed to the governments supposedly to be replaced, nor would Maiskii have consulted with the British beforehand as he did.[64] For the time being, the Russians were instead trying clumsily to emulate the support the czarist regime had extended to fellow Slavs under similar circumstances during World War I. Only the Czechs availed themselves of the opportunity by organizing an army formation as the first foreign military unit to be established on Soviet soil, and the initial results were quite reassuring. Until the summer of 1942, the Russians let the Beneš government select its officer corps without any interference.[65]

The Poles preferred to evacuate to the West the many potential recruits available in Soviet territory once Stalin had begun releasing them from his prisons and labor camps. This sensitive topic was one of several that Polish Premier Władysław Sikorski tackled with Stalin during his Kremlin visit on December 4, 1941. The German armies were then converging on Moscow, and enemy guns firing in the suburbs were audible during the meeting. In this eerie setting, the Soviet leader went the farthest ever in suggesting a compromise about the frontiers. According to Sikorski's account, Stalin specifically hinted at leaving the Poles Lvov (ethnically a predominantly Polish city) along with the overwhelmingly Ukrainian surrounding area:

Stalin proposed to me a conversation of this nature. He told me of Soviet good will in this direction, and of the assistance which Russia was ready to give us in our disputes with the Ukrainians in the matter of the Polish city of Lwów. He told me of the need to bargain with Russia. [66]

Stalin also supposedly mentioned that all of East Prussia and other German territories east of the Oder should become Polish. [67]

No bargaining ensued, however, because the Premier felt that his hands were tied. And indeed, given the feelings of his countrymen, entering into a discussion which might cast doubt on the nation's integrity would have been tantamount to his political suicide. He tried to impress the seriousness of the matter upon Stalin, reportedly commenting that "the world would burst with laughter" [68] at the Poles' parting voluntarily with their prewar territory. Sikorski was later criticized for having missed a precious "opportunity for Russian–Polish friendship," [69] since Stalin never again repeated his offer. In mid-December, when the Soviet leader met with Eden, he no longer mentioned anything about Lvov and also proposed that a part of East Prussia should go to Soviet Lithuania rather than to Poland. In the interval, the Red Army had repelled the immediate German threat to Moscow—a sequence of events demonstrating a critical correlation between Stalin's military outlook and his political aspirations.

The opportunity may not have really existed, for even though Stalin seemed willing to compromise so long as his military emergency lasted, the frontier question was a symptom rather than a cause of the deeper Russian–Polish hostility. It was further enmeshed with the question of the nation's future political system. The Poles feared that the Soviet territorial demands were the first step toward the eventual establishment in Warsaw of a pro-Soviet Communist regime, as the Bolsheviks had attempted in 1920, and that any concession on the frontier issue would only encourage Moscow to proceed with its presumed scheme.[70] In theory, Stalin had a whole range of alternatives in his quest for a friendly Poland, from outright incorporation to some form of compulsory nonalignment. The West's well-known concern for the country's independence, and plain common sense, were conducive to his seeking the least painful solution. But even if he hoped for such a solution, was he qualified to achieve it? A prisoner of his misdeeds, he may not have realized how intractable the Polish question really was.

Whatever Stalin's preferred settlement of that question—and he is not likely to have made up his mind immediately—the Polish government was unwilling to take chances. It sought strength by combining forces with other small nations of east central Europe. Ever since World War I, the Poles had been the foremost proponents of such combinations, which were generally mistrusted, however, as vehicles of their own exaggerated great-power ambitions. Now the idea struck a more responsive chord among peoples whom Hitler had taught the lesson of disunity; their common predicament seemed to give them a fair chance for association as equals. In November 1940, Poland and Czechoslovakia set an example by concluding a preliminary agreement about postwar confederation.[71]

Britain warmly supported the project. It suited perfectly Churchill's vision of a future Europe where a strong France would be resurrected in the west while several confederations would emerge in the east: one in the Balkans, another consisting of Hungary, Austria, and portions of a dismembered Germany, a third uniting Poland and Czechoslovakia. Since Churchill also

55

feared that "it would be a measureless disaster if Russian barbarism overlaid the culture and independence of the ancient States of Europe,"[72] the scheme has often been regarded as being aimed primarily at averting the disaster; contemporary British documents, however, justified regional integration solely as a defense against future resurgence of German imperialism.

Stalin could hardly have avoided thinking differently. Even so, he did not initially rule out eastern Europe's supranational integration. In August 1941, Maiskii told the Yugoslav Minister to Britain that a Balkan union might be a good solution to the Yugoslav–Bulgarian problems.[73] He also conveyed to Beneš his government's approval of the Polish–Czechoslovak project, provided this would result in a loose confederation rather than any close federation.[74] Stalin himself told Eden on December 16 that in principle he had nothing against confederations.[75] However, as soon as the victory at Moscow had given Stalin his first taste of success, this benevolent attitude changed, especially since the unification efforts were beginning to gain momentum.

In January 1942, Poland and Czechoslovakia reaffirmed their intention to unite, and a similar declaration was issued by Yugoslavia and Greece. Both statements raised the prospect of still larger groupings.[76] Sikorski approached the Dutch, Belgians, and Norwegians with a comprehensive proposal for a bloc of small nations.[77] His move prompted the unkind remark by Alexander E. Bogomolov (the Soviet envoy to the exiled governments resident in London) that someday the Poles might have to choose between "Russia and Luxembourg."[78] Commentaries by Radio Moscow seconded the censure.[79]

During the subsequent negotiations for the British–Soviet pact, London tried to pin the Russians down to a clause committing them to encourage the regional integration efforts.[80] In March, Sikorski traveled to the United States to campaign for additional support. But Washington felt less strongly about confederations than about frontiers. Roosevelt decided that the Polish Premier "should be definitely discouraged on his proposition.

This is no time to talk about the post-war position of small nations and it would cause serious trouble with Russia."[81] Without the American backing, Molotov easily managed to have the troublesome item deleted from the final version of the pact, which he signed in London on May 26.

On the same day, Molotov also gave to Yugoslav Foreign Minister Momčilo Ninčić a positive reply to Yugoslavia's earlier proposal to revive the friendship treaty between the two countries; it had been in abeyance since the Soviet Union had failed to live up to its spirit the previous spring. There was a difference, however, between the Yugoslav and the Russian concepts. The royal government would have been content with restoration of the original relationship, limited to diplomatic cooperation. Molotov wanted a full-fledged mutual assistance pact, complete with a guarantee of territorial integrity and a provision about close collaboration after the war. This meant that Yugoslavia would rely on Moscow rather than any Balkan union for its security. Though not entirely opposed to the idea, the King's government sought reassurance about Russian good faith. In particular, it tried to solicit Soviet help to uphold its authority, which was challenged by the Communist partisans active in the occupied country.[82]

British intervention frustrated the pact project. When Molotov passed through London again on his way home from Washington, on June 9 Eden broached the whole subject of relations with small countries.[83] Eden expressed concern that these might be encouraged to rush for the favors of the great powers. He urged that the major and minor Allies abstain from any bilateral treaties that might prejudice their postwar relations. In his preoccupation with more pressing issues, notably the Second Front, Molotov shelved the Yugoslav project, and Eden gained the impression that there was a meeting of minds. These were the circumstances of the "gentlemen's agreement" that supposedly obligated both Moscow and London to desist from any special arrangements with smaller countries or at least to consult with each other before seeking any.

57

The Soviet Union, prudently refusing to be drawn into internal Balkan squabbles, continued doing business with the legitimate Yugoslav government. To the indignation of the Yugoslav Communists, in August 1942 the two governments elevated their legations to embassies.[84] Moscow pursued the same cautious policy in the two neighboring countries where Communist guerrillas were active, Greece and Albania. It maintained correct diplomatic relations with the Greek government-in-exile in Cairo. And it joined Britain and the United States in issuing, on December 18, a declaration in favor of restoring an independent Albania.[85]

In conformity with the Soviet departure from the czarist tradition, Moscow's interest thus focused on the northern rather than the southern tier of east central Europe, as Molotov further demonstrated on the night after he had ostensibly agreed with Eden not to seek any deals with the minor Allies. At the Soviet Embassy, he had an important conversation with Beneš, who was pressing for Russian recognition of Czechoslovakia's pre-Munich boundaries. Seizing an opportunity for a *quid pro quo*, the Foreign Commissar kept raising the subject of the Czechoslovak–Polish confederation. At last a deal was struck: Molotov promised the recognition, and Beneš declared that "if your relations with Poland are not friendly there would be no confederation."[86] The special relationship that the Czech leader had sought, even before the Soviet entry into the Allied camp, was beginning to bear fruit.

The Czechoslovak President deserved his reputation as "one of the most astute and devious politicians of Europe."[87] He was also one of the most frustrated, after the Munich experience had taught him about both the limits of Western friendship and his own impotence. Haunted by what he viewed as the perennial German menace, he came to regard future Russian predominance in east central Europe as not only inevitable but desirable. He never lost his preference for Western values, but he was prepared to compromise them for security. Unlike the Poles, he did not harbor overly strong feelings about sovereignty; rather, he hoped to gain for his nation the status of Moscow's favorite protégé. This did not necessarily contradict his pet notion of Czechoslovakia serving as a bridge between West and East, for he envisaged the future Western influences as mainly economic while the Eastern ones would be political and military.[88]

No other established eastern European leader was to play a more important role in the wartime Soviet designs than this unconventional bourgeois statesman. Although the Russians were not likely to ever trust him entirely, neither did they, as Dimitrov pointedly stressed in a confidential Comintern directive, ignore the fact that "Beneš's political position is after all quite different" from that of his Polish or Yugoslav counterparts.[89] Certainly the Russians had little reason to discourage his government's growing tendency to offer itself as their tool. In the spring of 1942, some Western diplomats in the Soviet Union assessed their Czechoslovak colleagues as "Soviet agents." The American Embassy reported that "evidence was accumulating to the effect that the Czechoslovak Legation is spending a good deal of its time in serving the interests of the Soviet government."[90]

Under these circumstances the result of Moscow's diplomatic offensive against the Polish confederation project was a foregone conclusion. The Russians chose the favorable moment of an impasse in the Czechoslovak–Polish talks about the future of Teschen, the disputed territory that Poland had snatched from the Czechs after Munich. On July 16, Bogomolov sent a blunt warning to Beneš that the Soviet government disapproved of the prospective confederation.[91] Undeterred, the Poles wanted to go ahead anyway but the Czechs lost enthusiasm,[92] and the less advanced plans of the other countries also remained stalled.

The eclipse of the movement that the British were known to regard with special favor coincided with mounting Allied tensions over the Second Front. Two days after Bogomolov's veto, Stalin sent to Churchill his most intemperate complaint thus far, stopping just short of an outright accusation of treachery.[93] This precipitated the Prime Minister's August visit to Moscow, during which the subject of confederations was not even mentioned. The Soviet Union had won a decisive round.

As hope faded for eastern European integration plans, Stalin found an unlikely ally in his quest for the Second Front: the Polish Premier. Sikorski was prominent among those who tried to expedite the invasion to assure an Allied presence in central Europe before the Russians could get there. In a memorandum he submitted to Roosevelt later that year, he argued vigorously (though speciously) that if the landings were extended to Germany proper they could actually terminate the war, thus preventing Soviet hegemony over the continent.[94] This desire to speed up, rather than to delay, the Second Front was indeed one political consideration that entered into the debates among Western officials.[95] But Sikorski was no more successful than Stalin in swaying the cautious military planners who controlled the timetable of the crucial operation.

Pondering on the Soviet policy of promoting divisions among smaller nations, even Beneš was moved to confide to his associates that he did "not like very much what the Russians are doing to us now; they are already showing their cards."[96] Toward the end of 1942, other eastern European exiles wondered even more anxiously what indeed was in those cards. But diplomacy alone was unlikely to tell; the guidance that foreign Communist parties had, or had not, been receiving from the Moscow headquarters provided an additional clue.

A Role for the Communists

Hitler's June 22 invasion of Russia had rescued from oblivion that forlorn group of Communist exiles who had survived the tribulations of Stalin's hospitality. On the day of the attack, their doyen, Dimitrov, reported to the Kremlin to consult about the Comintern's new tasks.[97] It is not clear whether he was summoned there or acted on his own initiative, perhaps the more likely explanation in view of the chaos prevailing in high Soviet councils. In any case, the results of Dimitrov's call became immediately visible; the Comintern issued urgent directives to foreign Communists to join in their peoples' patriotic struggle against the Nazi oppressors, thus assisting the endangered Fatherland of Socialism. The text of the message received that day by the party leadership in Yugoslavia testifies vividly to the Comintern's turnabout.[98]

Yet on closer scrutiny the turnabout was not unequivocal. For several days, Stalin's wishful illusion that the German blow might prove a misunderstanding influenced Moscow's attitudes. The illusion is evident in the plaintive, self-pitying tone that pervaded Molotov's June 22 address to the nation—the first official Soviet reaction to the attack.[99] As late as June 24, a declaration issued by the émigré leadership of the German Communist party still mumbled about an "indestructible alliance" between the German and Russian peoples, invoking Bismarck as its forerunner.[100] And two days later, party secretary Walter Ulbricht wrote an overly devious manifesto, intended for German soldiers, in which he contrasted their regrettable invasion of the Soviet Union with their presumably less reprehensible war against the Western "plutocrats."[101] By this time, however, the situation had become sufficiently clear that the draft was filed without further action. It was perhaps in allusion to these awkward ideas that Stalin, in a July 10 conversation with Ambassador Cripps, made a curious remark about the émigrés' pro-German talk that must be stopped.[102]

In less extreme forms, the awkwardness persisted as the Moscow-based "German People's Radio" resurrected the old formulas glorifying the German proletariat. Again Hitler was being misrepresented as an agent and benefactor of Big Capital. The October 1941 manifesto of 158 captured German soldiers, prepared by Ulbricht and his associates, abounded in crude class-struggle phraseology reminiscent of an earlier decade.[103] So did a proclamation of the party central committee later that month.[104] On the front, Red Army loudspeakers tried to lure potential deserters by addressing them as fellow proletarians, with predictable results.[105] As in the early 1930s, the policy implied a belief that Germany was on the verge of an internal explosion.

The prevalence of such fallacies suggests a significant degree of émigré influence in shaping the Soviet psychological warfare at that time.[106] Catapulted by their Russian protectors into positions of unaccustomed responsibility, the exiles tended to project their hopes and prejudices, magnified by their long absence from the homeland, into the present. Both from Germany and from other parts of Hitler's Europe, reliable news was exceedingly scarce. Ernst Fischer (the chief commentator of the Austrian service of the Moscow radio) later recalled having felt, in front of the microphone, as if he were speaking "into a void";[107] similarly, the program directors of the "Kossuth Radio" had to conjecture "what the Hungarian working class and forward-looking intellectuals *might think.*"[108] Such a state of affairs again showed how woefully unprepared Moscow was for the war that came.

The new concept of the "national front," to be implemented throughout Europe except for Germany, was hastily improvised. Despite its superficial resemblance to the prewar "popular front" formula, there was the significant difference that now the Communists were to join hands with all, rather than just left-wing, enemies of Fascism.[109] Yet the strategy did not go well with the anticapitalist harangues still emanating from Moscow, and initially little effort was made to smother the inconsistencies. The Comintern did prepare a comprehensive program for at least one country, Romania, testifying to the high priority Stalin assigned to Romanian affairs. Issued on September 6, 1941, ostensibly by the Romanian party's central committee, the document dwelt on immediate, practical goals: overthrow of Marshal Ion Antonescu's pro-German dictatorship, cessation of hostilities against the Soviet

Union and declaration of war on Germany, "liberation" of Transylvania from Hungary. [110]

To promote the new line, Communist parties had to be implanted in areas where none had hitherto existed. These happened to be the country for which Stalin cared least, Albania, and the one which concerned him most, Poland. In November 1941, emissaries of the Yugoslav Communists were given the job of establishing the party in Albania as their subsidiary. [111] In Poland, the Russians themselves took charge. In December they parachuted in a task force of their own, selected from among the few Polish Communists who were still available to them after Stalin had liquidated the party four years earlier. The group formally reconstituted the party in Poland at the beginning of January 1942. [112] Neither of the new creations, however, became formally part of the Comintern—a sign even then that the days of the ex-revolutionary International may have been numbered.

The Comintern's pronouncements after June 1941, lacking even the ersatz vision of a Soviet Europe invented during the last year of Stalin's ill-fated alliance with Hitler, were singularly devoid of long-term perspectives. [113] When some Comintern followers (notably the Yugoslavs) showed an inclination to take that notion seriously, they were called to order. In the spring of 1942, the Yugoslav Communists received a warning to abstain from anything that might convey the impression of aiming at "the sovietization of Yugoslavia." [114] And in November 1942, Moscow ruled explicitly that "the question of the regime in Yugoslavia, as you understand it, will come up for settlement after the German–Italian coalition has been smashed and the country freed from the invaders." [115]

Similarly, the platform the Comintern supplied shortly afterward to the exiled Czechoslovak party leaders stressed that the political system, as well as international status, of their country was "to be determined after its liberation." [116] Obviously these formulations concerned tactics rather than strategy. Yet in the absence of clearly expressed long-term goals, other than the ultimate victory of socialism, they inevitably carried strategic implications as well, especially since they were confidential directives to the faithful rather than propaganda statements for public consumption. They showed Stalin's reluctance to commit himself in a fluid situation that was beyond his control. In this respect, his attitude was quite similar to that of Roosevelt, who also preferred to postpone controversial decisions affecting the future of small nations.

Moscow's reluctance to enlighten its foreign disciples about the ultimate purpose of their struggle reflected faithfully the tentative nature of Stalin's designs for the postwar order. Nevertheless, it would be unfair to say that the Comintern had degenerated into an instrument of opportunism pure and simple. Ernst Fischer, who combined first-hand experience with an incisive mind, passed a well-reasoned judgment on the organization's contradictory qualities under Dimitrov's stewardship. He described it as

an amalgam of genuine analysis and peremptory voluntarism, of critical intelligence and bureaucratic red tape, of interparty consultation and Soviet-determined objectives, a "General Staff of world revolution" in an epoch of defensive action in which it was becoming increasingly difficult to uphold the postulate of a "World" Communist Party—but a general staff none the less, whose business it was to coordinate revolutionary resistance to Fascism.[117]

How effective was the Comintern in performing this new task? During the first months of the German–Soviet war, its exhortations tended to emphasize propaganda and sabotage rather than guerrilla warfare. Stalin was never genuinely enthusiastic about guerrilla resistance, with its reliance on both mass spontaneity and individual initiative.[118] When the Yugoslav Communists first notified Moscow about the popular insurrection that had been spreading under their auspices in Serbia, Russian eyebrows were raised about this supposedly irresponsible venture doomed to failure.[119] Even after the partisans had triumphantly proved this estimate wrong, they still waited in vain for Soviet aid other than the Comintern's patronizing messages.[120]

The Russians preferred the infiltration of agents to conduct sabotage and gather intelligence. Recruited by the Comintern mainly from among the émigrés, the first of these agents left the Soviet Union shortly after the June invasion. In 1941 most of them went to, of all places, nonbelligerent Bulgaria. By air and by submarine, a total of 58 Soviet personnel landed there clandestinely within the span of two months.[121] The choice may have resulted from an irrepressible desire of the Comintern's numerous Bulgarian employees to prove their own and their nation's worth. More likely, this traditionally pro-Russian country had simply been chosen in the hopeful belief that it would be the easiest to penetrate.

If this was the belief, events quickly disproved it. All the infiltrators were captured in a matter of days or weeks at most, perhaps the main reason for the strain in Bulgarian–Soviet relations at that time. The story of the agents dispatched to Czechoslovakia and Hungary was similar.[122] Their fate was less a tribute to the competence of the local police than an indictment of the dilettantism of their Russian mentors. Having discovered the contrast between their high expectations and the dispiriting reality, many of the agents turned themselves and their comrades in. "Lamentably poor" preparation was an equally visible defect of the Russian intelligence personnel whom the British were assisting to penetrate into Germany in the fall of 1941.[123]

Although it was not obvious to contemporaries, the astonishing Soviet underestimation of enemy strength, at a time when the Red Army was experiencing almost uninterrupted setbacks, is as conspicuous as it is puzzling. Oddly enough, the fact that Russia survived, despite those setbacks, may have been more responsible for the misapprehension than mere ignorance and imprudence. Stalin seems to have reasoned that since the Soviet

65

Union proved stronger than nearly everybody (including himself) had thought possible, therefore Germany must be much weaker than its formidable appearance suggested. He spoke and acted as if he believed Hitler's regime was so rotten that it needed merely a little push to collapse. On November 7, 1941, when the Nazis were at the gates of Moscow, the otherwise cautious Russian leader went on record with the prediction that in "another few months, another half year . . . , Hitlerite Germany must burst under the pressure of her crimes."[124]

A month later, the Red Army's first successful counterattack in the battle of Moscow so elated Stalin that his generals believed he now genuinely expected them to be able to push the invaders out of the country in one quick sweep.[125] So excessive an optimism after so deep a pessimism half a year earlier betrayed a curious susceptibility to extreme moods in the essentially insecure dictatorship. It contrasted sharply with the grim sobriety and calm dignity that had been the response of the self-assured British democracy at its time of trial in 1940.

Stalin's exultation lasted only until the Soviet offensive ran out of steam in early 1942, but his delusion about Nazism's fundamental feebleness died hard. In his February 23 Order of the Day, he declared that "Hitlers come and go, but the German people and the German State remain."[126] With the benefit of hindsight, these much-quoted words have often been misinterpreted, either as a sign of willingness for accommodation with Germany or else as a forecast of its transformation into a Communist state. At the time, they conveyed hardly more than a hope that the prospect of a protracted struggle might at last teach the German people where the interests of their state lay and prompt them to stop their Führer's war.

Far from fulfilling that hope, the Germans soon resumed their march eastward with full vigor. In May, when they turned the Red Army's attempted offensive at Kharkov into a rout, the Soviet predicament was in important ways even worse than at Moscow the previous December; the Germans had penetrated deeper and the weather favored rather than hampered them. Under such circumstances, the question Molotov asked Churchill, what the British would do if the eastern front failed to hold, was not merely rhetorical.[127] At this critical time, the Russians also took another look at the whole issue of how much the faithful behind enemy lines could do to relieve the intolerable pressure.

The answer was resistance *à outrance*. Only now did the Comintern launch through both overt and clandestine channels a systematic campaign designed to ignite guerrilla wars and eventually national uprisings throughout Hitler's Europe. On May 30, the Soviet party's central committee created a "Central Staff of the Partisan Movement" as a coordinating body.[128] According to the Comintern journal, *Kommunisticheskii Internatsional,* "the shattering of the Fascists' European rear" would not only weaken German military potential but also "hasten the opening of the Second Front."[129]

The special targets of the campaign were Czechoslovakia and France, whose industries had been contributing a great deal to the Nazi war machine. Taken to task for Czechoslovakia's unsatisfactory resistance record, its exiled Communist leaders issued a fiery appeal urging their compatriots to open a "Second Front" right there in their homeland.[130] The French, too, were told by Moscow that passive resistance and sabotage would no longer suffice; a national uprising was the demand of the day.[131] Again, several teams of Comintern agents were dispatched into Hitler's Europe, this time particularly the Reich proper, to carry the message. Meanwhile Soviet news media reported prominently an upsurge of resistance in Poland, Norway, and Austria.[132] But the model they now began to acclaim as most worthy of emulation was the partisan movement in Yugoslavia—the movement the Comintern had previously censured as adventuristic.

Even so, Moscow did not endorse readily the cause of the Communist partisans under Josip Broz Tito against the rival royalist guerrillas led by Draža Mihajlović. For months, the Communists had been supplying Moscow with shocking details about collusion between Mihajlović's "chetniks" and the enemy, but the Russians had abstained from casting any shadow on this acclaimed hero of the Yugoslav government in London, with which they had been negotiating a friendship treaty. Only after that projected treaty had fallen victim to British intervention did they begin to publicize the incriminating evidence in July 1942, thus allowing their relations with the king to deteriorate.[133]

Moscow was not easily convinced that the damning accusations were true; they looked like malicious smears to enhance the Communists' own image, and sometimes they were.[134] Stalin himself was experienced in slander and cynical about Communist ability to earn respect by winning genuine popular support. Therefore, despite the public Soviet denunciations of Mihajlović, Soviet diplomats repeatedly intimated to the king's representatives that Moscow was willing to send a liaison mission to the chetnik headquarters and to supply Mihajlović with arms—the arms the Russians had been withholding from the partisans, pleading logistic difficulties.[135] Although the Soviet media lavishly praised the partisans, they abstained conspicuously from mentioning their leader, Tito, by name.

Early in 1943, the Comintern prepared a "Proclamation to the Peoples of Occupied Europe," which it wanted to have the partisans issue in their own name to prod other peoples, particularly the sluggish Czechs and French, to follow their example.[136] Yet at the last moment, Moscow withdrew the project, which would have amounted to a major gesture of recognition toward its Yugoslav disciples. Stalin evidently found it hard to believe that Tito, not Mihajlović, was both the more effective resistance leader and the man of the future; after all, the chetnik chief enjoyed so much better publicity and Western backing as well. Ironically Churchill, who took reports about Mihajlović's faults more seriously, was by that time preparing to shift British support to Tito. The Prime Minister judged the two rivals by the same standards of expediency as did Stalin; only his conclusions differed.

Elsewhere, resistance *à outrance* proved largely ineffective if not disastrous. Throughout Europe, the Communist undergrounds suffered their greatest setbacks when Moscow needed them most. In the spring of 1942, police raids all but obliterated the undergrounds in Hungary[137] and Bulgaria; in Bulgaria, a Soviet spy ring with connections in Czechoslovakia was broken up in the process.[138] In June, the Gestapo liquidated the Czech party's clandestine central committee in Prague;[139] four months later the "Red Orchestra," the famed intelligence network of German leftists working for Moscow from sheer revolutionary idealism, met the same fate.[140] Finally, the rudimentary party organization built by Comintern emissaries in Austria fell victim to the police in early 1943 and was not restored for the rest of the war.[141]

Some of these calamities antedated the campaign for all-out resistance, but in other instances the campaign itself had precipitated the disaster. The capture of inexperienced Comintern operatives sometimes helped the police to track down the more seasoned members of the underground serving as their contacts.[142] In addition, Moscow's incessant calls for action regardless of cost were bound to result in the greatest casualties among those most responsive to its guidance. Yet the Soviet Union was prepared to sacrifice these elite foreign cadres for momentary military advantage.

To broaden the impact of its exhortations, in the second half of 1942 the Comintern moved in a more pragmatic and less ideological direction. Its pronouncements about Germany were purged of their anachronistic revolutionary vocabulary; ruefully, Ulbricht and his associates accepted the distressing truth that most of their countrymen believed in Hitler's victory and feared chaos in case of a defeat. To reassure conservative sensibilities, Soviet broadcasts to Austria went as far as advising villagers to form resistance groups by uniting around their parish priests.[143] Also, the second comprehensive program Moscow elaborated for a specific country, the July 17 manifesto of the Bulgarian "Fatherland Front," was a more moderate document than its Romanian predecessor. It omitted social and economic items and demanded merely a break with Germany and friendship with the Soviet Union, not insisting on Bulgaria's active belligerence on the anti-German side.[144]

The Fatherland Front that ostensibly issued the manifesto was a fiction at the time its program was proclaimed over the Moscow radio; the real organization was not founded in Bulgaria until fourteen months later.[145] Similarly, Soviet broadcasts are the sole testimony to the existence of the Austrian "Freedom Front" that in October 1942 supposedly issued a manifesto calling for the "expulsion of the Nazi Prussians" and demanding "Austria for the Austrians."[146] It was a peculiar Russian stratagem to create imaginary resistance movements in the apparent hope of bringing to life real ones that would conform to the requisite model. As an Italian Communist author later admitted, in those days "a report about 'the appearance of partisan detachments' was in reality a directive to 'form partisan detachments.' "[147]

The most elaborate fabrication was the German "Peace Front" which, again according to Moscow radio, convened a clandestine conference somewhere in the Rhineland on December 6, 1942.[148] Its detailed record allegedly smuggled out and subsequently published in the Soviet Union as a pamphlet, listed speakers representing such diverse anti-Nazi elements as former unionists, businessmen, Social Democrats, "Christians," even disillusioned SA men, besides discreetly self-effacing Communists.[149] They all spoke in favor of the national front as preached by Moscow. Not until 1969 did an East German Politburo member finally admit the Comintern provenance of this document, which had long passed as genuine.[150]

For all the Soviet preoccupation with tactics and instant results, Moscow's theoreticians gradually refined the national front concept to assist their long-term aspirations as well. Although calling for broad unity and cooperation on the basis of anti-Fascism, they subtly differentiated between a coalition on the national level and a grass-roots resistance movement down below.[151] In the former the power relationships were to be spelled out in a formal compact that the Communists would conclude with representatives of other political groupings, while in the latter any party distinctions would be submerged in the local resistance committees. The Comintern urged its followers to take the lead in creating these committees, variously described as "fighting," "revolutionary," or later more innocuously as "national" and "national democratic."[152]

From October 1942 onward, the Czechoslovak Communists in Moscow pressed the Beneš government to sanction in advance the formation of "national committees" in their country.[153] Intended to eventually supplant the regular administration, which was supposedly compromised by collaboration with the enemy, these bore a striking resemblance to the 1917 Russian soviets whose decisive contribution in ushering the Bolsheviks to power was common knowledge. This is not to say that in 1942 Stalin contemplated the same scenario in Czechoslovakia or anywhere else. But neither was he indifferent to the head start that such institutions, created amidst chaos with scant regard for constitutional formalities, might offer to a dedicated Communist minority determined to magnify its influence out of proportion to its numbers.

Although military exigencies reduced the role of Stalin's potential "fifth columns" almost to dispensable tools of instant resistance, he did not entirely neglect the future. He sought to maintain in all countries a core of loyal followers, to be at hand to help implement whatever policies he would eventually decide to pursue. Accordingly, as Communists in occupied Europe sacrificed their lives by the thousands, substitutes were being trained deep in Russia, particularly in the Comintern facilities near Ufa in the Urals.[154] Recruited mainly from among the émigrés, these new cadres were supplemented by prisoners of war responsive to indoctrination.[155] Ready to step in when needed, they were Stalin's main investment in the future at a time when expediency ruled supreme.

During the first year and a half of the war with Hitler, neither a fixed design nor an entirely shapeless opportunism had

71

inspired Soviet policies. Faithful to the Leninist formula, Stalin's behavior was suggestive of his thinking in terms of minimum and maximum goals. To be sure, only the minimum ones were really pertinent under his extreme military duress: the restoration of the pre–June 1941 frontier, the prevention of any close groupings among Russia's western neighbors, the survival of useful Communist establishments abroad. Indeed, Stalin temporarily showed an inclination to compromise even about these vital matters, as indicated by his hints at concessions about the frontier, his initial grudging acceptance of the confederation projects, and his willingness to decimate his most devoted foreign disciples in dubious resistance ventures. Only gradually did he draw the line below which he would not go. Anything above the minimum goals, however, remained in the realm of vague desire rather than practical policy until, at Stalingrad, the changing fortunes of war during the winter of 1942–1943 began to open altogether new perspectives.

chapter three

Hazy Perspectives
February–October 1943

A Separate Peace?

Stalingrad opened new perspectives but also new complications.[1] The outcome of the great battle, which ended in February 1943, deprived Hitler of a chance to win the war; this only increased the uncertainty of who else might dominate Europe afterward. To the Russians, the triumph assured military survival but not complete victory. Indeed, in the opinion of E. A. Boltin, a leading Soviet authority on war history, Stalingrad merely resulted in a balance of forces between the two belligerents.[2] The cost of total victory must have still appeared staggering to Moscow; what is more, it could not be estimated with any accuracy so long as the Second Front remained suspended. Certainly past combat experience gave every reason to believe that the victory would be arduous, and the Soviet Union had already suffered appalling losses.

Now, if ever, the time was ripe for Stalin to weigh the assets of an imperfect peace against the liabilities of an elusive victory. The situation offered both the opportunity and the inducement to trade military gains for a political compromise. As an article in the January 1943 issue of the Moscow *Bolshevik* pointedly elaborated,

Separation of politics and strategy, and the neglect of the requirements of politics for "purely strategic" reasons, are fraught with dangerous consequences. . . . Politics and war influence each other but they are not factors of the same order; primacy always belongs to politics.[3]

In particular, Stalin could now try to obtain German confirmation of his territorial aims, which his Western allies had been conspicuously unwilling to give. For the first time since the war began, a negotiated peace leading to a Soviet–German condominium of Europe was no longer unthinkable. Any such arrangement would, of course, mean a complete turnabout, but that was something both Stalin and Hitler could perform if they wished. Their independence from domestic restraints was only one of many affinities between the two dictators, who hated but respected each other. Moreover, the Russian, though not the German, had a record of discounting the incompatibility of their interests.

Stalingrad inaugurated the most intriguing period in wartime Soviet diplomacy. As early as November 6, 1942, Stalin had hinted tantalizingly in a public speech that "it is not our aim to destroy all organized military force in Germany, for every literate person will understand that this is not only impossible . . . but . . . also inexpedient from the point of view of the victor."[4] This comment was in line with his remarks the previous February, but now the Red Army's ascendance gave his words a special edge. His statement was a scarcely veiled offer of friendship to the German military, among whom so many prominent Russophiles had been found in the past and with whom Moscow had experienced a thoroughly satisfactory liaison in the 1920s. The military were also the best qualified to perceive that Hitler's war was lost and seek their country's salvation in another Rapallo.

On December 12, shortly after the German army at Stalingrad had been encircled, in Stockholm a Soviet intermediary named Edgar Clauss reportedly told Peter Kleist (an aide of Nazi Foreign Minister Joachim von Ribbentrop) that Moscow was ready to sign an armistice in eight days if Berlin responded favorably.[5] Although Kleist's account of this episode has not been verified, subsequent Soviet actions give it weight. Whether aiming at accommodation with Hitler or with a military leadership that might replace him, they indicated a readiness to explore the separate peace option for whatever it was worth.

The Stalingrad victory enhanced Soviet prestige but not Allied solidarity, which was almost immediately tested by the Russians. Their unfriendly acts included harassment of British personnel accompanying arms convoys to Soviet Arctic ports.[6] The Soviet press also proved notably reticent about acknowledging the extent of American lend-lease deliveries, an attitude that prompted criticism by United States Ambassador William H. Standley and, in turn, Moscow's further displeasure.[7] Most important, both privately and publicly Stalin indicated doubts about the value of the coalition as a vehicle for his interests.

Stalin's "Order of the Day" for the Red Army's anniversary on February 23, 1943, did not even mention the Western Allies.[8] It presented the war as an exclusively Russian–German affair which, by implication, could be settled between the two belligerents. Three weeks later, in reply to Churchill's letter saying that the cross-Channel invasion had been postponed, Stalin warned "of the great danger with which further delay in opening a second front in France is fraught."[9] Although he had expressed dissatisfaction on this score before, this time other Soviet moves accentuated the gravity of the warning.

Shortly before Stalin dispatched his message to Churchill, the Red Army had begun curtailing its offensive operations.[10] The unprecedented calm on the battlefields was justifiable by exhaustion after the recent great exertions and by unfavorable weather conditions. It also coincided, however, with the sympathetic publicity Moscow gave to numerous manifestations of a "peace movement" that was allegedly taking hold in Germany but that was in reality a Russian invention.[11] At the same time, the Soviet Union shunned association with the demand for unconditional surrender which Roosevelt and Churchill had enunciated during their conference at Casablanca two months earlier. All these actions served to impress on the Germans the great differences between the Russian and Western attitudes toward them.

So disconcerting was this behavior that the British government instructed its Moscow ambassador, Sir Archibald Clark Kerr, to investigate what the Soviet intentions toward Germany really were. He quizzed both Molotov and Stalin, but the "reply was not in very friendly terms."[12] It seemed as if the Soviet leaders, aware of their new options, did not wish to prejudice their own course of action. This was the case not only with the German question but, more importantly, with the Polish question.

No sooner had Stalingrad bolstered their self-confidence than the Russians acted to aggravate the Polish question. On January 16, 1943, they served notice that all persons who in 1939 inhabited the parts of Poland the Soviet Union had seized would henceforth be considered Soviet citizens.[13] A *Pravda* article by Deputy Foreign Commissar Alexander Korneichuk strongly reaffirmed Moscow's territorial claims.[14] When the London Poles demurred, a Tass statement in March accused them of hostile designs against the Ukraine and Belorussia; in addition, the formation on Soviet territory of a Union of Polish Patriots raised the possibility of a rival government under Russian aegis.[15] By giving new publicity to the frontier that he had once fixed with Hitler, Stalin evoked the days of their collusion at the Poles' expense.

So great was the Nazis' arrogance and obstinacy that they ignored these enticing developments; indeed, they chose this moment to inflict a most painful blow on Stalin. Having unearthed the graves of the Polish officers who had been murdered at Katyn in the days of Russian–German friendship, on April 12 they announced the gruesome discovery to the world, dwelling on the overwhelming evidence of Soviet responsibility for the crime. Although Hitler's Propaganda Minister, Josef Goebbels, was reportedly inclined toward a possible understanding with the Russians,[16] he could not resist the splendid opportunity to embarrass them. So successful was he that Katyn still remains an unmentionable topic in the Soviet Union and its dependencies.[17]

The genuine dismay and studied indignation that Moscow displayed when confronted with the incriminating evidence are hardly surprising; more suggestive are the conspicuous limits and the particular direction of its anger. In an initial impulse to gloss over the German indiscretion, it offered the lame explanation that the Nazis might have mistaken archaeological excavations for graves.[18] Only when the Germans insisted on their version did the Soviet Union begin to charge them openly with an attempt to blame others for their own atrocity. Even so, the Russians soon diverted attention from the question of responsibility in a way that could hardly fail to please the Nazis. They brazenly accused the London Poles of collusion with Hitler after the Poles had unwisely, though not unreasonably, suggested taking advantage of the German offer to let an impartial international investigation determine the truth on the spot.[19] Brushing aside Churchill's and Roosevelt's urgent pleas to desist, the Russians proceeded to sever diplomatic relations with the Polish government-in-exile.[20]

Having thus made the Poles its whipping boys, Moscow avoided placing additional obstacles in the way of possible rapprochement with Berlin. There are indications of secret attempts at such a rapprochement despite the public insults the two capitals continued to exchange. In mid-April, the French Communists were rumored to have received a Comintern alert to be prepared for Soviet–German armistice talks.[21] According to Swedish informants of the American Office of Strategic Services, preliminary talks took place soon afterward at Russian initiative in Stockholm, involving diplomats from both sides.[22] The Germans were presumably ready to consider peace in return for a satellite Ukraine and economic concessions in other parts of the Soviet Union, but the Russians would accept no less than the frontier of 1941.[23] A deadlock over this issue would seem a plausible explanation of why, according to the same source, the Soviet side broke off the contact at the beginning of May.

On May 1, Stalin first publicly tackled the subject of a separate peace. In his May Day address, he attributed such machinations to the Nazis judging their adversaries by their own standards of treachery.[24] He insisted that only Germany's unconditional surrender could end the war, but he avoided relating this general phrase to the specific formula adopted at Casablanca. He sounded as if he had almost given up persuading the Germans that a compromise was not only in his but very much in their interest. He could also have meant his statement as an incentive for talks on terms more acceptable to him. In any case, his evolving triangular relationship with his Nazi enemies and Western allies now enabled him to alternate in showing a friendly face to one side and then the other.

The exercise was facilitated by the unseemly speed with which London and Washington ruled out *a priori* any suggestion of Soviet complicity in the Katyn massacre.[25] Their attitude, despite their better judgment of the evidence, proved their eagerness to maintain at least the appearance of Allied solidarity. And it was the appearance, rather than the substance, that Moscow proceeded to cultivate during the next few weeks of "record warmth *vis-à-vis* Britain and America."[26] The Russians celebrated the anniversaries of the 1942 alliance agreements with the two nations, extolling the recent Anglo-American victories in North Africa—a battlefield they had previously denigrated as insignificant.[27] Their commentators, seconding Stalin's call for Germany's surrender, ridiculed the idea of a separate peace.[28]

Yet no practical Soviet steps toward closer collaboration ensued. Stalin remained aloof to Roosevelt's urgent pleas for a summit meeting to clarify mutual war and peace aims.[29] It is difficult to judge to what extent Stalin's standard excuse that he needed to keep a close eye on the front was a pretense rather than a symptom of a genuine nervousness about German intentions, which was very noticeable in Moscow at that time.[30] The inexplicable delay of the enemy's anticipated and dreaded summer offensive could mean that Berlin might be ready to negotiate after all. However, as long as there was no positive evidence of such readiness, Stalin had to assume that the offensive would eventually come, in which case he might need all the help he could get. There was more than gentle prodding in the way the Soviet press systematically encouraged the belief that the recent Allied victory in North Africa had at last made the Second Front imminent.[31]

On June 4, at this time of high-pitched Russian hopes and anxieties, Churchill's and Roosevelt's notification about yet another delay in the crucial operation reached Moscow. Stalin's distress at hearing the news is easy to imagine. He not only gave vent to it privately in his replies to the Western leaders, but also recalled his reputedly pro-Western ambassadors to London and Washington, Maiskii and Litvinov, thus publicly accentuating the rift within the alliance.[32] On June 22, the official Sovinformburo news agency hinted obliquely that "without a second front, victory over Germany is impossible."[33] After the brief period of amity for the West, overtures to Berlin again came under consideration.

The June issue of the new journal *Voina i rabochii klass*, which henceforth served as a special outlet for authoritative policy pronouncements for foreign consumption, elaborated upon the distinction between "war aims" and "peace aims." It maintained that only the former, namely, military victory, were definite, whereas the latter remained flexible because "only the aggressor can declare his aims clearly."[34] The article went farther than any other wartime Soviet statement in suggesting leniency to the enemy. It took issue with various Western projects for punishment of the German people, expressing misgivings about subjecting them to reparations or even to military occupation. Moreover, by raising doubts about not only Polish but also Czech claims for territories that were currently part of the Reich, it hinted that the Germans might be allowed to keep some of their conquests, particularly the Sudetenland.

On June 16, the Swedish newspaper *Nya Dagligt Allehanda* created a sensation by printing a special edition with a report that high Soviet and German officials had been secretly negotiating near Stockholm.[35] Although promptly denied in official communiqués issued almost simultaneously in both Moscow and Berlin,[36] the allegation is given credibility by information available in American and British intelligence files, and also in Kleist's memoirs.[37] After the war, when an American magazine article revived the subject, the Russians considered it important enough to warrant a rebuttal in *Izvestia* by their former ambassador to Sweden, Alexandra M. Kollontai.[38] Significantly, rather than focusing on the merit of the case, the rebuttal centered on the mistaken identity of one of the alleged Soviet participants. All things considered, Moscow probably had extended feelers although the premature leak most likely prevented actual contacts. In any case, if a chance for a separate peace was lost that spring, the reason was Nazi unresponsiveness rather than any lack of trying on the Soviet side.[39]

At the beginning of July, the Germans finally launched a big offensive at Kursk, shattering whatever hopes Moscow had been entertaining about their disposition to compromise. Moreover, the campaign, foredoomed because the Russians had learned about enemy operational plans through their intelligence network in Switzerland, soon turned into a Russian victory even more decisive than Stalingrad.[40] This first summertime triumph of Soviet arms opened the prospect of their continuous and irreversible (though still far from easy) advance to the west. The military triumph provided the setting for a political initiative as well.

On July 12, while the battle was still in progress but its outcome was certain, the Russians stunned friend and foe alike by giving their blessing to the creation of the "National Committee for a Free Germany."[41] The conspicuous feature of the organization was not so much the predictable presence of Communist luminaries as the participation of individuals of impeccable nationalist and conservative reputation, recruited from among the prisoners of war. The Committee launched appeals to the German army, urging it to end the war by getting rid of Hitler and withdrawing to the present frontier of the Reich—a suggestion implying that this relatively modest concession would make possible a mutually acceptable peace. In fact, General Melnikov, who served as the Soviet liaison to the Committee, privately assured General Walther von Seydlitz, the most prominent of the cooperating prisoners, that Moscow was ready to support the restoration of Germany's 1937 frontiers, although he refused to confirm his assurance in writing.[42]

Retrospectively, both admirers and detractors have been inclined to view the Committee as the harbinger of the Communist East German state, as it materialized six years later.[43] Yet although Ulbricht was the key figure in both ventures, the Free Germany movement was rather a pragmatic Soviet response to the circumstances prevailing in mid-1943 (one East German author who dared to advance this sensible interpretation in 1962 was officially rebuked for his heresy).[44] After Kursk, the Russians had to ponder not only the high cost of ultimate victory but also the increasing probability that Hitler might be overthrown from within. As Rudolf Herrnstadt (the ideological watchdog of the Committee) said in 1944, the organization was desirable to help secure Soviet influence "in case of a successful German opposition movement. . . . We had to be prepared for such a possibility."[45]

The likelihood of such a movement increased as Kursk spread doubts about the wisdom of continued fighting even among the highest-ranking Nazis. Many of them could see what the future held, and a few tried on their own to learn what the Russian peace terms might be. In August, Ribbentrop again dispatched Kleist and another of his assistants, Rudolf Likus, to gather information in Stockholm.[46] The next month, Goebbels told Hitler that "we must come to an arrangement with one side or the other." The Führer replied that in that case "he would prefer negotiations with Stalin," although he did not "believe they would be successful."[47]

The mere prospect sent shivers through the small group of Germans who were planning to save their country by a coup d'état against Hitler. One of them, Ulrich von Hassell, noted in his diary that "if Hitler comes to terms with Stalin, the resultant disaster cannot be imagined."[48] Another, former ambassador to Russia Friedrich von der Schulenburg, thought of undertaking a secret mission to Moscow to prevent it.[49] Although the conspirators favored the West over the East, at least some of them (including especially Claus Schenk von Stauffenberg, the would-be assassin of Hitler) may have preferred seeking accommodation with the Soviet Union, either because they hoped to find it more responsive or because they regarded Communism as the wave of the future.[50]

Did the Russians know about the plot and attune their policies accordingly? Sándor Radó, who at that time headed the Soviet espionage network in Switzerland, has written in his memoirs that on April 20, 1943, he relayed to Moscow the message that "a group of generals, who already in January wanted to dispose of Hitler, are now determined to liquidate not only Hitler but also his supporting circles."[51] There may have been a connection between this message and preparations for the Free Germany Committee, which were set in motion on May 27.[52] Moreover, the credibility of the information was surely enhanced in Soviet eyes when the same Swiss channel accurately reported on enemy operational plans at Kursk—reports that proved so helpful to the Red Army in winning the battle.[53]

The overthrow of Mussolini in Italy on July 25 provided a worthy example for Germany, and Soviet moves following the event indicate a conviction that a revolt against Hitler might be imminent. Since the Italian coup had been carried out by members of the ruling class and not by the people, Moscow had all the more reason to cultivate Germany's elite rather than any imaginary "peace front." It therefore prepared to supplement the Free Germany Committee, on which Ulbricht and his team were perhaps too conspicuous, with the more respectable and exclusive "League of German Officers." The growing numbers of prominent war prisoners whom Germany's impending military catastrophe had persuaded to cooperate facilitated the venture.[54]

According to Wolfgang Leonhard, who as a young German Communist worked in the Committee's headquarters at that time, the Russians made an overture to Hitler before actually going ahead with the new project. He reports that at the beginning of September the planned inauguration of the League was suddenly postponed indefinitely and an armistice appeal, addressed to the Nazi leaders currently in power rather than to their potential challengers, was about to be issued instead. It was supposedly withdrawn in the last moment, whereupon the League's official proclamation followed on September 11.[55] Meanwhile in Stockholm, according to Kleist, another Soviet feeler through the familiar Clauss had been extended but not accepted.[56]

Despite the intriguing coincidence, the two stories invite caution. The sensational armistice appeal that was supposedly discarded is strikingly similar to the completely routine one actually broadcast by the Free Germany radio on September 1.[57] Nor does the reported feeler by Clauss necessarily prove Soviet initiative. What may have happened is that the intermediary, a braggart of dubious reputation, misled both the Germans and the Russians about each other's readiness to negotiate. If so, the episode shows at most that Moscow, while no longer actively seeking contacts with Berlin, was still willing to respond to initiatives by others. But even that willingness was quickly disappearing, and the experience with Clauss may have been the last straw. On September 13, Molotov snubbed Japanese Ambassador Naotake Sato with the meaningful remark that "under different circumstances the Soviet government would have considered it its duty to accept the Japanese offer of mediation."[58]

The longer that hopes for a negotiating partner in Germany remained unfulfilled, the greater was Stalin's need to seek an understanding about postwar settlement with the Western powers. The rules of the diplomatic triangle now required the Soviet leader to improve his relations with them, and he soon began to instill more life into the alliance, not only in words but in deeds. On September 8, he agreed to a conference of foreign ministers in October and to a meeting of the chiefs of state a month later.[59] He also notified Washington and London about the recent Japanese mediation attempt, thus giving proof that he was now more interested in promoting their trust than in keeping open any secret channels to the enemy.[60] Finally, a Russian diplomat in Stockholm revealed to an American colleague that "German agents and intermediaries" had approached Soviet personnel there and had been rebuffed,[61] a disclosure at variance with Ambassador Kollontai's September 22 statement in the London *Daily Express* that "there have never been any . . . feelers put by the Germans to my Legation."[62]

Ironically, only after the chances for a German–Russian rapprochement had already passed did a separate peace scare seize the West. Toward the end of the summer of 1943, proliferating rumors created an atmosphere "alarmingly reminiscent of that which preceded the Molotov–Ribbentrop pact of August, 1939."[63] Although Moscow was sometimes suspected of planting them, they emanated from so many unrelated sources that they could not have been disseminated from one center.[64] And Stalin would hardly have wished to risk a mystification that might backfire by tempting the Western capitalists and their German confreres to turn the tables on him. In any case, the Soviet government coped with the rumors in a fashion calculated to discourage rather than encourage further speculation.[65]

All the same, many Western officials were worried. In London, some were "battling with a paper on the possibility of a German–Russian *rapprochement*."[66] In Washington, others debated "The Proper Course of Action for the United Nations in the Event Russia and Germany Effect a Compromise Peace."[67] And in the October issue of the *American Magazine*, Roosevelt's right-hand man Harry Hopkins admitted the disturbing possibility publicly. He proceeded to reassure the American people: "Russia, the keystone of the war, is still fighting grimly. If we lose her, I do not believe for a moment that we will lose the war, but I would change my prediction about the time of victory."[68]

In the final analysis, the earlier peace probes, though without effect on their intended recipients, paid Stalin fringe benefits in two important ways. First, unable to achieve a negotiated peace at a time when this would have brought him only minor gains, he had no choice but to stay in the war and fight for a total victory that would eventually bring him greater gains than any conceivable deal with Germany would have brought. Second, the rumors about real or suspected probes enhanced the Western disposition to tolerate such gains. Significantly, Harry Hopkins, though fearing that a weakened Russia might seek peace because of the high price of victory, also concluded that Russia's "postwar position in Europe will be a dominant one"; accordingly, "every effort must be made to obtain her friendship."[69] Securing that friendship seemed all the more imperative because of the nagging suspicion that Moscow might be tempted to use its dominant position for a Communist crusade.

The Specter of Communism

Once the Red Army had embarked on its great trek westward from Stalingrad, the specter of Communism that Marx had seen haunting Europe a century before reappeared vividly before many eyes. To be sure, World War II generated significantly less revolutionary momentum than World War I. Hitler was able to keep a tighter rein over the peoples he ruled. Moreover, the struggle those peoples waged against his tyranny was a worthy, inspiring, and promising cause, not conducive to frustrations such as those that had been responsible for the radical tendencies of the previous generation. The powerful Red Army was now at hand, however, to compensate from without for whatever revolutionary potential might be in short supply within. The Soviet Union had never renounced its ideological commitment to promoting the cause of Communism abroad, and every new success of Russian arms stirred the imagination of its adherents and sympathizers. Their enthusiasm made it difficult for Moscow to sidetrack indefinitely the ultimate realization of their dreams, as the Comintern had been trying to do so far.

Stalin's wartime relationship with his revolutionary cohorts has been particularly susceptible to retrospective distortion. The experience of the Cold War has fostered an image of the Communist undergrounds ticking to his command with a clocklike precision resembling the responsiveness of the postwar "fraternal" parties in his eastern European satellites. Even critics have been prepared to regard this as an inevitable result of the Communists' proverbial dedication, discipline, and conspiratorial prowess—a heroic myth understandably dear to pro-Soviet propagandists as well. For the latter it has been axiomatic to presume full "concordance of the anti-fascist struggle for freedom, peace, and democracy with the wartime aims of the Soviet Union," as the ponderous title of one particularly crude essay would have it.[70]

The subsequent loosening of Russia's grip over international Communism has bred different, though hardly less misleading, projections of the present into the past. In some countries of eastern Europe, nationalist party historians have countered the Soviet propensity to take credit for the wartime achievements of Communist resistance movements.[71] Instead, they have glorified the indigenous roots of those movements as the main source of their alleged mass appeal. And Western "revisionist" authors, with their own axes to grind, have added their apotheosis of the vague but valiant European "Left" ultimately betrayed and crushed by an unholy alliance of Anglo-American and Soviet imperialists.[72] These assorted myths have almost obliterated the true dimensions of the accord and discord between Moscow and those who looked to it for inspiration.

The situation that had begun taking shape by 1943 was more complicated than the appearances suggest, as well as different from country to country. In particular, the geographic distribution of Communist strength was very uneven, and from the Soviet point of view was downright embarrassing. The appeal of the Communist creed showed almost an inverse ratio to proximity to the one country where its tenets had supposedly been put into practice. It was much greater in such faraway places as France or

Italy[73] than in the adjacent lands that were Stalin's principal concern but whose peoples had been taught by history to beware of the Russian neighbor. Thus, while the French Communists managed to build their "National Front" into a powerful and respected segment of the nation's resistance movement, their comrades in Poland had to struggle for life.

Soviet emissaries started building the Polish party organization from scratch at the beginning of 1942; half a year later they reported to Moscow a membership of 4,000, and in early 1943 double that figure.[74] Although the growth may seem impressive, the totals were not, particularly in a nation where belonging to some resistance organization or another was almost essential for a self-respecting citizen and where the various pro-London groups boasted hundreds of thousands of active supporters. Decimated by Stalin's henchmen and hunted down by Hitler's, the Communists were still despised by their compatriots as agents of "enemy number two."[75] They were widely suspected of provoking reprisals against their political competitors if not betraying them to the Germans outright.[76] If it was hard to be a Pole and face two enemies, it was even harder to be a Polish Communist and face three.

The underground Communist establishment was not significantly stronger among the pro-Russian Czechs or Bulgarians. In Czechoslovakia, its size reflected the modest dimensions of the resistance as a whole. In Bulgaria, according to official sources prone to overestimation, in 1941 the party numbered 10,000 members—actually two-thirds less than a decade earlier.[77] There had been declines in Romania and Hungary as well; in the former country down to a few hundred, in the latter to a pitiful seventy or eighty faithful by 1943.[78] In east central Europe, the only genuine mass Communist movements emerged, ironically, in Yugoslavia, Greece, and Albania, the areas most remote from the Soviet Union.

Membership figures may be deceptive indicators of real influence, especially since the Communists were under instructions to infiltrate other resistance groups. But in this respect, too, the results of their drive to gain acceptance left much to be desired, as the national front coalitions desired by Moscow remained the exception rather than the rule. One that did come into being was Hungary's ephemeral "Independence Front," which attracted attention by sponsoring a campaign against German interference at the end of 1941.[79] By contrast, the "National Revolutionary Committee" described (in Communist sources only) as the supreme organ of the entire Czech underground was almost certainly a product of wishful thinking.[80] Neither did the four men, two of them Communists, who in late 1942 posed as a similar committee in Slovakia represent any identifiable following.[81]

In Yugoslavia, Greece, and Albania the conditions were different but, from the Soviet point of view, not encouraging. Their "liberation fronts," formed in opposition to other resistance groupings rather than in any effort to enlist their cooperation, were not the kind of coalitions Moscow desired. "Are there really no other Yugoslav patriots—apart from Communists and Communist sympathizers," a Comintern message pointedly asked Tito in March 1942, "with whom you could join in a common struggle against the invaders?"[82]

Indeed, the Communist guerrillas in the Balkans sometimes seemed to be fighting their domestic rivals more vehemently than their foreign enemies. This was the impression British observers received in Greece.[83] Even the upright Yugoslav partisans had a stain on their record. In March 1943, their emissaries met with German army representatives in Zagreb to discuss a truce, so that Tito would be free to turn with full force against Mihajlović. The negotiations failed because of opposition in higher Nazi quarters, and the evidence remained buried in German archives for another thirty years; even then, its disclosure by an American scholar touched a raw nerve in Belgrade. Otherwise, only Milovan Djilas (one of the emissaries) confirmed the incident with his customary candor in his memoirs.[84]

At the heart of Stalin's problems was the disruption of Comintern lines of communication caused by the war and aggravated by the reverses the Communist undergrounds suffered in 1942, reverses for which his policy of all-out resistance was partly to blame. For most of the time, therefore, covert two-way contacts remained sporadic, depriving the local party chiefs and their Soviet mentors of the benefit of instant mutual consultation. The local chiefs had to rely for guidance mostly on Moscow's public broadcasts, while the Russians were left to worry constantly about heresies and deviations.

The indefatigable Yugoslav partisans maintained the best communications, first by courier and then from February 1942 regularly by secret radio.[85] Yet time and again they outflanked Moscow by their radical experiments. These included expropriation of "class enemies" and proclamations of "Soviet regimes," attempted in 1942 in Montenegro and Hercegovina.[86] The next year, Tito drew the Comintern's criticism for having his lieutenant, Svetozar Vukmanović-Tempo, promote the project of a "Balkan Staff" to direct all Communist guerrillas in the peninsula in preparation for its later political unification under Yugoslav auspices—an idea congenial perhaps to Lenin but certainly not to Stalin.[87] The trouble was not that Communists anywhere would deliberately defy the Soviet Union, at least for the time being; the Yugoslav ones especially wished to be considered Stalin's most faithful disciples. However, because of insufficient leverage, Moscow now had to use persuasion where previously it could have simply issued commands.

Poland was another case in point. When the Soviet organizers first reached there at the end of 1941, they found a rudimentary Communist underground already in place. Coming as envoys of a regime that had only yesterday competed with Hitler in stamping out everything Polish, they were not received enthusiastically.[88] Before being able to assert their authority, they had to delete from the new party's first platform any references to Soviet recognition of the London government-in-exile.[89] Not only were they not fully trusted by the indigenous radicals, but they also did

89

not trust one another: in December 1942, Marceli Nowotko, the head of the original Moscow team, was assassinated by another member of that team on suspicion of treason.[90] The Polish party, though Stalin's own creation, remained his problem child.

Viewed from Moscow, the darkest part of the continent was central Europe. Symptomatic of its inaccessibility is the fact that the 1940 slogan of "Soviet Slovakia" continued to be disseminated by local party militants until 1942, simply because the Comintern lacked the means to enlighten them properly about the new course.[91] In July of that year, a new central committee (already the fourth since the war began) came into being in Slovakia entirely on its own. By early 1943, its counterpart in the Czech Protectorate was formed under similar circumstances.[92] No such bodies claiming national authority ever existed in Germany or Austria although active regional organizations did emerge in Germany. They functioned especially in Berlin, Leipzig, and Thuringia.[93]

Just how much the Russians were able (or willing) to keep in touch with Communists in Germany, especially after the Red Orchestra had been liquidated in the summer of 1942, is doubtful. For East German authors, it has been obligatory to maintain that the country's entire party underground was always effectively steered from Moscow, a belief shared by many Western authors.[94] Yet no hard evidence has been produced; on the contrary, Ulbricht's close associate Otto Winzer has admitted that confidants of the émigré leadership were not able to deliver directives to the underground after March 1943.[95] Even that statement is misleading, for by that time the emissaries themselves had been cut off from their Moscow headquarters. Indeed, the available evidence adds up to a picture of deep isolation.

In the spring of 1943, the head of the Berlin group, Anton Saefkow, attempted to establish contact with Comintern agents operating from Stockholm. He used as an intermediary Arvid Lundgren, an employee of the Swedish Legation in Germany. Since Lundgren was a Social Democrat, however, and thus by definition suspect, nothing of substance is likely to have passed through this channel. Lundgren later described the highlights of his liaison with Saefkow as being excursions to the outskirts of Berlin where together they enjoyed the thrill of singing the "Internationale."[96]

The only recorded Soviet attempt to infiltrate agents into Germany during 1943 does not indicate much interest in the Communist underground at a time when separate peace with its enemies was most topical. In April a group of émigrés headed by Vinzent Porombka was parachuted into East Prussia, from where they subsequently moved into Silesia—neither being an area of significant Communist activity. Probably alone among all the Comintern's German emissaries, Porombka survived the war, but apparently at the cost of having accomplished little else. According to his own later account, he never made contact with any of the major party organizations; he also relayed little information to Moscow, because his radio transmitter broke down soon after he arrived.[97]

Some of Germany's forlorn Communist militants excelled in "sectarian" deviations. Elated by the Red Army's advances after Stalingrad, in 1943 they distributed leaflets anticipating a "genuine Socialist order" in close alliance with the Soviet Union; they saw the greatest peril in their country's possible subjugation by the "Anglo-American imperialists" who would bring a "slavery ten times worse than Versailles."[98] But again, rather than challenging Moscow, they tried to anticipate its wishes and act accordingly. The members of the Leipzig group, for example, kept redrafting their program until they were satisfied that it harmonized with the goals they deduced from listening to the Soviet radio.[99] Nonetheless, the Gestapo's liquidation of the last remnants of Germany's organized Communist underground in the summer of 1944 simplified the situation for the Russians.[100]

To ascertain whether such an underground existed in Czechoslovakia, and if so to assure its subordination, in early 1943 the Comintern dispatched two special missions to the country reputed to be the maverick of European resistance. The first mis-

91

sion, intended for the Czech lands and led by Rudolf Vetiška, reached its destination in April; its counterpart for Slovakia, headed by Karol Šmidke, arrived in July.[101] The emissaries were armed with the confidential resolution about "the political line and future tasks" adopted by the émigré party leadership shortly before their departure. Unlike their Polish counterparts a year earlier, they were welcomed warmly by their comrades in the homeland. But the program they had brought along, with its emphasis on instant resistance rather than inspiring long-term goals, aroused misgivings and was endorsed only after heated arguments.[102]

The further fate of the Czech mission highlighted the familiar deficiencies of the Comintern's clandestine operations. Its members had been equipped with packages of American dollars but with no local currency, and their identification papers were easily recognizable as forgeries; also they were not familiar with local names that had been changed since the beginning of the war.[103] It was probably thanks to the Gestapo that they managed to find their contacts at all, for by then the Czech party had been thoroughly infiltrated by informers. Even a member of its three-man directorate, an alumnus of the Moscow school for foreign cadres, had become one; there was a police confidant in the Slovak central committee as well.[104] The emissaries therefore were shadowed almost from the moment they set foot in the Protectorate, and the Communist underground operated under German surveillance until late 1944. By that time, the Nazis even organized "clandestine" conferences at which Gestapo agents masquerading as Soviet instructors distributed assignments to the unsuspecting participants.[105]

Although the Czech situation was probably the worst anywhere, the incidence of treason within Europe's Communist resistance, as revealed reluctantly in party sources, is striking. By way of comparison, among the 1784 agents the British infiltrated into France alone (a figure probably higher than the number Moscow dispatched into all countries), not one is known to have betrayed his cause.[106] It is not entirely impossible that at times Stalin's long reach may have been handing potential or real dissidents to the police; such a scheme is actually on record from Hungary in the 1930s.[107] More likely, however, the basic cause of the Communists' failings was ironically the same "Bolshevik discipline" that in other instances inspired them to heroic feats. Their exalted vigilance, ruthlessness, and readiness to sacrifice— the hallmarks of that discipline—were ever prone to degenerate into moral turpitude conducive to its undoing.

Soon after the assassination of Nowotko, his successor Paweł Finder, another of the Polish party's imported leaders, undertook a highly controversial bid for accommodation with the local representatives of the government-in-exile, the so-called "Delegation." In a manifesto, published in January 1943 in the underground press, the party secretary challenged the Delegation to consent to the creation of a "united resistance front."[108] London authorized its confidants to explore the proposal and next month its low-ranking representatives met in Warsaw with a high-powered Communist team. During the ensuing talks, the Communists urged the formation of a broad national coalition that would appoint a clandestine provisional government in Poland itself; the one in exile would continue functioning, but only as the nation's representative abroad.[109]

The scheme (originally devised by Nowotko) may have been initiated by the Polish party leaders independently, perhaps mainly to prove their worthiness to Moscow. But the implementation was almost certainly coordinated with the Russians. It coincided with the Soviet moves against the London Poles at the beginning of 1943, notably the reaffirmation of Soviet territorial claims and establishment of the Union of Polish Patriots. While the Warsaw talks were getting under way, Stalin also summoned Colonel Zygmunt Berling, who had long been advocating the formation of a separate Polish army under Soviet auspices and independent of London, although Stalin for the time being withheld permission for the project.[110]

If the Russians, in their typically overbearing fashion, hoped to impress upon the Poles the desirability of accepting the Communists as legitimate members of the nation's political underground, the effort was a dismal failure. The spokesmen for the Delegation, though willing enough to listen, had insisted that the Communists first pledge unconditional allegiance to London, disavow any connection with the Comintern, and endorse the inviolability of Poland's eastern frontiers—all this to be spelled out in a formal statement in the party press. Since the Communists were equally inflexible, the talks collapsed after only three meetings.

Conceivably, the Communists had wished this outcome anyway, in order to prove to the Russians both their readiness for accommodation with London and the impossibility of reaching it. Yet Moscow still seemed unconvinced: In mid-March, Dimitrov commented critically about the new party platform that Finder had drafted shortly after the abortive talks; according to Dimitrov, the goal remained a "democratic," not a "socialist," Poland.[111] Thus it is unlikely that the outcome of the talks significantly hardened the Soviet policy; it was rather the accident of the Katyn discoveries that did.

Precisely because the Katyn crime had been an imperfect one, Stalin tended to overreact to its intensely embarrassing publicity. His severance of diplomatic relations with the London Poles was one example; the drastic reorganization of the international Communist movement that he initiated soon afterward may have been another. Within three weeks after Katyn, the machinery was set into motion to liquidate the Communist International. At the beginning of May, the Yugoslav party received a confidential message that "on May 2 a proposal was sent to the Sections for the disbanding of the Comintern as the leading centre of the international workers' movement."[112] And on May 22 its dissolution was announced officially.

Whether because the organization had become obsolete or because it presumably continued to exist in another guise, the significance of this step has customarily been minimized.[113] According to Adam Ulam, a leading American scholar of Stalin's political behavior, "the main motives in the decision to dissolve the Comintern seem transparent and can be ranged under the heading *deception*."[114] With due respect for Stalin's aptitude at deception, however, his alleged desire to placate his capitalist allies could hardly have provided a sufficient motive for the dissolution, nor does this presumed motive shed any light on its timing. Since the Comintern's previous existence had proved no insuperable obstacle to his cooperation with the West, the move would seem superfluous; besides, his dependence on that cooperation was currently diminishing rather than increasing. Nor did the end of the organization mark the beginning of any new Soviet effort to strengthen the alliance; the opposite happened during the next three months of probes about a separate peace.

In any case, those most impressed by the dissolution were not the capitalists but rather the Communist true believers, some of whom later testified to their bewilderment at hearing the news.[115] The trainees in the Comintern school at Ufa were taken by surprise. In Hungary, the Communist leaders panicked to the point of precipitously disbanding their miniature party, which therefore had to be reconstituted later.[116] In confidentially explaining the rationale of the Comintern's demise, Moscow went out of its way to convince its faithful that the liquidation was genuine rather than merely pretended for propaganda purposes. It condemned in advance any "factionalism" by those who might think otherwise.[117]

A close reading of the Comintern's official obituary leaves little doubt that the intended audience was its followers rather than its adversaries. Justifying its abolition in their terms, the document dwelt especially on three themes: the widening cleavage between the nations allied with Germany and their opponents, the urgency of a mass war of liberation against the Axis, and the "growth and maturity of the communist parties," which had presumably rendered their direction from one center unnecessary.[118] These assertions are not to be taken literally, but they do offer clues about Moscow's principal concerns and aspirations.

Actually the war not only exacerbated national rivalries but also generated an unprecedented desire to eventually overcome those rivalries by closer association above national lines. The stress on obstacles to reconciliation conveyed Stalin's hope to exploit nationalism rather than to foster any form of internationalism. The ritualistic call for liberation wars, too, suggested more an effort to whip up nationalist passions than a wish to see any truly popular movement triumph in its own right anywhere in Europe. Nor did the compliment about the Communist parties' maturity signify Stalin's readiness to tolerate their independence. It did mean that because their situation varied so much from country to country a different institutional framework was needed to manipulate them.

Stalin's experience with the Comintern as the general staff of resistance had been discouraging. Despite prodigious exertions, few of the Communist resistance movements had challenged the enemy as effectively as he desired. Even fewer had succeeded in overcoming the mistrust of potential allies and gaining acceptance. They all had proved difficult to control because of the breakdown in communications. Indeed, it was often impossible to judge whether they might have actually turned into enemy tools.

The Soviet dictator discarded his established machinery for managing international Communism at a time when his prestige, as well as the movement's unity, was greater than ever. But as Jesús Hernández, the Comintern's disillusioned Spanish protagonist, has appropriately observed,

Stalin's vision extended far. He realized that his imperialist ambitions might create misgivings among the national parties. He did not want to be forced to justify his policy to the foreign Communists. He eliminated in advance any possibility of an uncontrolled reaction by an international body no matter how tame.[119]

96

From now on, Moscow would therefore deal with each of the "fraternal" parties directly and separately on a bilateral basis. [120]

The abolition of the Comintern was suggestive of Stalin's groping for the optimal use of his potential "fifth columns." He was no Lenin or Trotsky to pursue revolution for its own sake. Neither was he prepared, however, to forego whatever assistance his foreign disciples could offer to advance Soviet power and influence. To the question of how far Communism ought to be promoted, he had no categorical answer; it depended on circumstances, particularly on the attitude of his powerful coalition partners. In 1943, that attitude took a new turn as the Russian military ascendancy revived the issue of Europe's possible division into spheres of influence.

Toward Spheres of Influence

Since their rebuff in the spring of 1942, the Russians had abstained from actively pursuing the idea of spheres of influence. [121] Although on June 1, 1942 Stalin had assured Roosevelt that he liked very much the President's concept of "world policemen," [122] the unresolved issue of the Second Front had taken precedence over any further discussions about the postwar settlement. Nor had the prospect of a separate peace after Stalingrad provided the Russians with the right kind of incentive. Only on March 10, 1943, did Ambassador Maiskii return to the subject of war aims, made topical by Eden's imminent departure for Washington where these were to be on the agenda of his talks with American officials.

Maiskii asked to call on the Foreign Secretary, and during the conversation he recapitulated Stalin's familiar minimum aims, adding a few particulars reflecting the recent deterioration of Russian–Polish relations. Although he mentioned in general terms that Germany ought to be broken up, he only referred specifically to the award of East Prussia, not the area east of the Oder, to Poland. Regarding Poland's eastern frontier, he divulged for the first time that "something in the nature of the Curzon line" would be acceptable to his government.[123] That line, advanced by the British at the time the Bolsheviks seemed to be winning the 1920 war, roughly coincided not only with the ethnic divisions but also with the border that Stalin and Hitler had drawn in 1939.[124]

The ambassador also reiterated that the Baltic states were an integral part of the Soviet Union and that Romania and Finland should be linked with Moscow by special treaties providing for Russian bases on their territory. He further explained that his government might tolerate a Balkan federation without Romania and a Scandinavian one without Finland, for these would presumably be "vegetarian" and harmless. In reply to Eden's question about the Czechoslovak–Polish confederation, he expressed misgivings about any regional groupings other than merely economic ones. But the main purpose of Maiskii's call was to persuade Eden not to enter "into any definite commitments for any detailed postwar settlement" in Washington, a wish the British statesman promised to grant.

Maiskii's request conformed with Moscow's reticence regarding long-term commitments. The Soviet government delayed its reply to a British inquiry (which the Foreign Office happened to dispatch on the same day) about the principles to be used in handling possible peace approaches by Germany's satellites.[125] Such aloofness contrasted vividly with Stalin's efforts a year earlier to coax the British into a formal agreement that would spell out the respective rights and responsibilities in relation to different enemy countries. The Russian leader now evidently preferred to wait, exploring other scenarios for peace; in the meantime, a climate more receptive to his earlier proposals had been developing in the West.

In the United States, "through a curious kind of illogic the

Russians' vigorously successful resistance to Hitler purified them ideologically in the eyes of Americans." [126] Although conservative repugnance to any expansion of Communism was still more typical for the Americans than for the British, so was the liberal idealization of the Soviet regime because of its allegedly growing resemblance to a true democracy. In any case, 1943 marked an all-time peak of American good will toward Russia as measured by public opinion polls. [127] In Britain, the trend was less permeated by ideological preconceptions but equally pervasive. It reflected the great popular appeal of the view, promoted assiduously by such prestigious intellectuals as the historian Edward H. Carr, that only the Soviet Union could redress the balance of power Germany had upset to Britain's woe. [128] Thus on both sides of the Atlantic a growing opinion held that the Russians deserved what they wanted in eastern Europe, not so much because of their ability to take it as because of their presumed other virtues.

By coincidence, on March 10 when Maiskii met with Eden the London *Times* took a position in favor of a British–Soviet condominium of Europe much along the lines Stalin had suggested in December 1941. [129] This important editorial maintained that Britain's frontier was on the Rhine, Russia's on the Oder. Although similar ideas had been publicized before, this was the first time that they seemed to bear the stamp of official approval, for the *Times* was generally regarded as a mouthpiece of the government. The statement prompted some outcry in the West but only praise from the Soviet media, which gave it extensive coverage. [130] It made little difference that Eden informally denied that the suggestion in any way expressed the government's policy. [131] Nor did Churchill's eloquent but ambiguous speech in favor of European unity dispel the lingering suspicion that the opposite might be true. The Prime Minister pleaded for "the largest common measure of the integrated life of Europe" but cautioned that this must be compatible with "the high permanent interests of Britain, the United States, and Russia." [132]

For the Soviet Union, it was again the Katyn scandal that

shortly afterward helped to bring those interests into focus. At the height of the crisis, the Russians gave the first public hint that they favored Poland's extension to the river the *Times* had described as their western frontier. Expressed in an article published in Moscow on April 16 over the signature of Alfred Lampe (the chief ideologist of the Polish Communist exiles), the suggestion was a transparent attempt to soothe the Poles' profound indignation at the massacre they all but universally attributed to Stalin.[133]

The implied Soviet endorsement of Lampe's demand for the Oder as Poland's "strategic frontier" had far-reaching implications. Even before, much of the British press had been advocating compensation to the Poles in the west for the losses they were likely to suffer in the east.[134] Churchill himself conveyed his favorable opinion of the idea to Polish Foreign Minister Edward Raczyński the day before the Lampe article appeared.[135] But although the Poles entertained extensive designs on German territory, they refused to consider these as a compensation of any sort. In his December 1942 memorandum for Roosevelt, Sikorski described the Oder as Poland's natural security line; to Eden, he expressed a desire for East Prussia as well.[136] Most of his compatriots, regardless of political persuasion, favored such aggrandizements on presumed historical grounds or simply as a fair reward for their exceptional suffering and resistance record.[137] They did not appreciate, as Stalin did, how much the acquisition of the land might force them to rely on his backing against its former German owners. For once, his selfish interests were in harmony with a widely popular cause.

Katyn also provided the setting for the reply Moscow finally gave to several questions that Beneš had posed to Ambassador Bogomolov more than a month earlier. They concerned a friendship treaty that the Czechoslovak President had been contemplating with the Russians, the eligibility of Poland to join such a treaty later as a third party, and Soviet willingness to endorse his plan to expel his country's German minority after the war. On

April 23, Bogomolov answered the first question encouragingly, the second discouragingly, and the third evasively.[138] This timely reply sufficed to assure Czechoslovakia's quiescence when, the next day, the Soviet Union announced its diplomatic break with the Poles. In fact, the Czechs went so far as issuing on their own initiative an explicit statement certifying that the projected confederation with Poland was no longer topical.[139]

At this tense moment of the war, when the Russian–Polish row coincided with the Russian–Western estrangement induced by the prospects for a separate peace, Beneš undertook to mediate in his own way between the principals of the anti-Hitler alliance. He indicated that intention to Bogomolov before leaving for an official visit to the United States at the beginning of May, and the Soviet diplomat did not discourage him.[140] Once in America, the Czechoslovak President capitalized on his considerable prestige as a leader of a small nation who might be expected to fear Russian power yet did not. A widely respected expert on Soviet affairs, he stressed his confidence in the benign nature of that power in his numerous public speeches and private conversations with prominent Americans.

Beneš attributed the Bolsheviks' past hostility mainly to a lack of Western understanding for the ideals of their revolution. In conformity with Soviet preferences, he stressed the desirability of sovereign national states rather than of any supranational combinations. Yet he dwelt on safeguards for their sovereignty considerably less than on what he described as the beneficial effects of the Soviet Union's prospective primacy in eastern Europe. He defended the Russians' "influence in central and Western Europe which is rightly due to them as a great world power."[141] Commenting sympathetically about his remarks, the *New York Herald Tribune* of May 29 observed that the example of Czechoslovakia proved that "it is possible, even for a small country, to pursue a policy of friendship vis-à-vis Russia without sacrificing her political ideals, national interests or independence . . . the larger states can do the same."[142]

The subtle impact of Beneš's American visit on the wartime East–West relationship was significant. Although no American record of his two long interviews at the White House has been preserved (a not untypical example of the casual conduct of foreign affairs during World War II), his own account leaves little doubt that his reassuring estimates of Soviet intentions helped to reinforce congenial views held by Roosevelt.[143] Soon after the talks, ex-Ambassador Joseph Davies, whose main qualification was his uncritical admiration for anything Soviet, left for Moscow as a special presidential emissary, carrying Roosevelt's astounding invitation to Stalin for a tête-à-tête behind Churchill's back.[144] Davies's mission, during which he treated a startled Kremlin audience to a preview of the new Hollywood movie based on his memoirs, unabashedly whitewashing the atrocities of the great purge, marked the high point of the American courtship of Stalin's Russia.[145]

Stalin nevertheless seemed unimpressed. Davies's antics may well have backfired by arousing the dictator's suspicions about the motives behind so crude an approach. He snubbed the invitation, and on June 1 Maiskii confided to R. A. Butler (the British Conservative party's expert on postwar planning) the opinion that the United States was entering an imperialist phase; consequently, the Russians and the British should stick together.[146] But while the success of Beneš's mediation effort may thus have been too great for the Russians to believe, they still had every reason to be satisfied with his performance. They gave his speeches in the United States favorable publicity and after his return to London offered him a tangible sign of appreciation. On June 6, Bogomolov conveyed to him Soviet approval of the plan to expel the Sudeten German minority.[147] Although this was a mere verbal statement, the later evidence of Moscow's secret preparations gives it substance. In particular, at that time the Russians commissioned several Communist leaders from eastern Europe—Czechoslovakia's Rudolf Slánský, Hungary's János

Kádár, and Romania's Emil Bodnăraş—to study the specifics of possible population transfers in their respective countries.[148]

The most obvious repercussions of Beneš's trip concerned the British policy. No sooner did he return to London than his announced intention to go to Moscow provoked a critical British reaction. Eden particularly resented not having been consulted about Beneš's plan to sign a major treaty there.[149] He feared that such an ostentatious demonstration of Czech–Soviet amity would worsen the already deplorable state of Polish–Soviet relations and that the precedent might encourage Moscow's quest for client states. The British tried to impress upon the Czechs that they had no need to go so far as to formalize their friendship with Russia by an act that might rather give "everyone the impression that they were completely under the Soviet hat."[150]

Eden summoned Maiskii to remind him of the May 1942 "gentlemen's agreement" with Molotov which barred both Britain and the Soviet Union from concluding bilateral treaties with the minor Allies.[151] The Russians, taking advantage of the lack of an authoritative record of what exactly had transpired at that time, began to expound a different version. According to them, Molotov had only tentatively accepted Eden's original suggestion, whereupon a month later the Soviet government had sought further clarification by requesting a formal British proposal. Although the British had no recollection of any such request, Moscow blandly took the line that since no proposal had been submitted the supposed agreement amounted to a mere preliminary exchange of opinion without formal binding.[152]

Soon after Eden raised objections to the treaty with Czechoslovakia, the Russians apparently changed their opinion about its urgency: previously Beneš had been pressing them; now the roles became reversed. On July 5, the Czechoslovak ambassador to Moscow, Zdeněk Fierlinger (who was always more inclined to defend the Soviet viewpoint to his own government than vice versa) reported ominously that the Russians "do not say that they would not sign the treaty later but do not know when and under what circumstances it could be signed if not now."[153] The next month, Bogomolov flatly told the Czech officials in London that they had better hurry.[154] As Beneš's *chef de cabinet*, Jaromír Smutný, aptly observed, the Soviet Union had "found the Czechoslovak offer of the treaty opportune to drive home its own interpretation of the 1942 agreement."[155] Caught between his British and his Russian friends, Beneš tried to temporize.

Meanwhile Hungarian peace feelers to London moved the Russians to finally act on the three-month-old British inquiry about how to deal with Germany's satellites.[156] The Soviet reply, which Maiskii delivered to Eden on June 7, posited four principles that were to be incorporated into any armistice agreement: unconditional surrender, restoration of all conquests, obligation to pay reparations, and punishment of war criminals. In return, the victors would pledge to respect the territorial integrity and national independence of the vanquished. Described by the ambassador as "very important,"[157] the document seemed quite categorical; in practice, however, the subsequent Soviet implementation of it was governed by expediency rather than principles. In order to retain flexibility, Moscow was prepared to bend especially on the principle of territorial restoration, as its treatment of the Transylvanian question demonstrated.

The memorandum Maiskii handed to the British stated vaguely that the Soviet government did not consider "fully justified" the 1940 Vienna Award of northern Transylvania to Hungary. Two months later, however, Russian confidants hinted to the Hungarian Consul in Geneva, Ferenc Honti, that the area might actually remain within his country as an autonomous entity.[158] This was the time when Moscow was exploring the possibility of sponsoring a Hungarian counterpart of the Free Germany Committee; accordingly, the proposed Transylvanian arrangement could serve as an inducement to captured Hungarian officers to join the venture. Since, however, these officers proved more loyal to Horthy than their German comrades were to Hitler, the scheme never got off the ground. By October, the Russians therefore seem to have shifted their position in the dispute in favor of Romania. That month, General Melnikov, who was in charge of the various prisoner-of-war committees, informed the Romanian committee that "Transylvania will be Romanian."[159] Even so, Stalin would not commit himself either way for a long time, evidently preferring to prolongate both claimants' uncertainty about his true intentions.

On the whole, the principles outlined in Maiskii's June 7 memorandum served to enhance the small nations' dependence on Moscow. The obligation to pay reparations was not only intended to help postwar Soviet reconstruction but also to cripple the defeated countries economically and therefore politically. Likewise, the punishment of war criminals could be construed broadly enough to force the elimination from public life of any person the Russians deemed objectionable. Under such circumstances, of course, the promised guarantees of independence and integrity could hardly provide effective protection against Soviet interference. Rather, their purpose was to bar the various countries from joining the regional associations Stalin detested; the memorandum added Austria and Hungary to the list of those to be prohibited from forming them. To publicly reinforce the point, Moscow simultaneously resumed its propaganda campaign depicting such associations as an evil scheme of Polish reactionaries.[160]

It was the Western Allies rather than the Soviet Union, however, that took the lead in inaugurating the liberation of foreign countries from the Axis rule. On July 10, 1943, while the Red Army was still fighting deep inside its home territory, the Anglo-American forces landed in Sicily, from where they proceeded to the Italian mainland. Aware of the significance of the event as a precedent, the British government had already submitted to Washington and Moscow a comprehensive proposal concerning the administration of liberated Europe. Dated July 1, the document foresaw the establishment of a tripartite American–British–Soviet commission to supervise the execution of any armistice agreements.[161]

According to the British proposal, the local military commanders would have full responsibility for administering all the occupied areas, but a "United Nations Commission for Europe" would "direct and coordinate the activities of the several Armistice Commissions, the Allied Commanders-in-Chief, and any United Nations civilian authorities that may be established." Although both the major and the minor Allies were to sit on the commission, the will of the great powers would be safeguarded by a tripartite steering committee whose decisions would require unanimity. In effect, each of the victorious powers would control temporarily the parts of Europe it had occupied, while international bodies would help to mitigate any potentially divisive effects of the arrangement.

As with the previous British inquiry about the armistice conditions for Germany's satellites, Moscow did not react to the proposal until prodded by an enemy initiative, this time the overthrow of Mussolini and the prospect of Italy's impending surrender. On August 19, Churchill and Roosevelt notified Stalin that the new government of Marshal Pietro Badoglio had offered to capitulate and that instructions had been issued to General Dwight D. Eisenhower, the Allied Supreme Commander, to present it with surrender terms.[162] Three days later, the Soviet leader retorted with his own proposal for the creation of "a military-political commission of representatives of the three countries . . . for consideration of problems related to negotiations with various Governments falling away from Germany."[163]

In a later addendum Stalin said further that this single body should exercise authority "not only in relation to Italy but also correspondingly in relation to other countries."[164] In all of them, the Russians wanted the commission to wield executive power, which the British preferred to reserve to the commanders on the spot. The Soviet scheme, unlike the British one, also envisaged an exclusive great-power agency in which the minor Allies would have no voice. Its authority was to extend to all occupied countries regardless of whether these qualified as defeated or as liberated.[165]

The differences between the two approaches were subtle but significant. Whereas the British aimed at regulating the relations among the great powers, as well as between the great and the small ones, the Russians jockeyed for positions that would give them maximum leverage at the crucial moment of Europe's liberation. Hence they wished to take as much power as possible away from the local commanders and give it to the commission on which they would have a strong voice. Through the commission, empowered to regulate such vital matters as restoration of local government, they would then be able to influence the domestic politics of different countries—an effort in which they could count on aid from loyal Communist parties.

But why was Stalin advocating an arrangement which reciprocally entailed the risk of opening to Western influences the foreign countries that would eventually be liberated by the Red Army? It is hard to avoid the impression that in 1943 he simply did not consider his conquest of any such countries a foregone conclusion; accordingly, he devised the Military Political Commission to help project Soviet influence abroad by political means, irrespective of how far Soviet military power might reach at the end of the war. His diminished interest in a spheres-of-influence arrangement tends to support this interpretation.

On August 31, during a farewell call before his return to Moscow, Maiskii explained to Eden that "there were two possible ways of trying to organize Europe after the war." Either Russia and the Western powers "could agree each to have a sphere of interest," although "he did not himself think this was a good plan." Or they could "admit the right of the other to an interest in all parts of Europe," which he thought preferable.[166] The Soviet diplomat was no paragon of truthfulness, but he need not be suspected of having stated his government's priorities in reverse

107

order. It is not true that "the Kremlin . . . thought *only* of spheres of interest."[167] At a time when Russian military power was growing steadily but the extent of its eventual geographical advance remained an open question, it would not have been expedient for Stalin to seek a definite understanding about the future limits of Soviet influence, which would have only tied his hands.

The Soviet leader may not have realized how far his Western peers had already acquiesced in advance to his putative aspirations. Francis Cardinal Spellman of New York later recalled having been privately told by Roosevelt on September 3, 1943 that "the European people will simply have to endure the Russian domination in the hope that—in ten or twenty years—the European influence would bring the Russians to become less barbarian." In the President's opinion, Germany and Austria would become Communist, perhaps even without Soviet military intervention, and Austria, Hungary and Croatia would "fall under a sort of Russian protectorate."[168] Roosevelt indicated to the cardinal that he would try to obtain Stalin's pledge not to expand beyond a certain line but did not expect he would succeed.

Despite the overtone of pessimism and resignation conveyed by Spellman's account, the ever optimistic Roosevelt actually saw the future in bright colors. He glossed over the contradiction between the Soviet aims as he apparently perceived them and the principles of the Atlantic Charter to which he was committed; what is worse, he neglected to bring the dilemma to the attention of the American people.[169] He seems to have believed that in the end it would simply fade away amidst the profusion of good will to be generated by Nazism's ultimate defeat. The resulting ambiguity in American policies had fateful consequences.

Churchill's attitude was not so fundamentally different from Roosevelt's as the Prime Minister's reputed perspicacity and distaste for Communism may suggest. His advocacy (by then already faltering) of the unification of eastern European states can be retrospectively regarded as a scheme for the containment of Russia.

Yet a memorandum for internal guidance of top British government officials, which Eden issued on July 1, 1943, stressed unequivocally that the country to be contained was Germany.[170] Nor was Churchill's favorite plan to launch the main attack on Europe from the south instead of the west intended to inhibit Soviet penetration;[171] rather, considerations of military effectiveness inspired that controversial plan. It was both the strength and the weakness of Churchill's realism to tackle only one problem at a time, and that problem was Hitler.[172]

The differences between the two Western leaders concerning the prospect of Russia's dominant position in east central Europe boiled down to the fact that Churchill was more aware of the dilemma which Roosevelt preferred to ignore. The British did not have a coherent long-term policy any more than the Americans did. As Eden stated in his July 1 memorandum, "it may be, of course, that after the war is over, the fear of Russian aggression may be uppermost, but we cannot plan on that assumption now."[173] Accordingly, the basic directive he took from Churchill for the forthcoming foreign ministers' conference in Moscow was ambivalent:

We affirm the principles of the Atlantic Charter, noting that Russia's accession thereto is based upon the frontiers of the 22nd June 1941. We also take note of the historic frontiers of Russia before the two wars of aggression waged by Germany in 1914 and 1939.[174]

This could mean acceptance of Soviet domination of Poland and possibly of Russia's other western neighbors as well. At the very least, as Eden jotted down, when the time came Britain would raise no objections to the restoration of the frontier Stalin wanted.[175]

Thus the Western powers, though genuinely opposed to spheres of influence, showed a growing disposition to sanction in advance Soviet supremacy in a large, but as yet undefined, portion of Europe. Stalin himself was no longer pursuing that old-fashioned formula, striving instead to spread his influence wherever the conditions might seem favorable. Even so, an informal spheres-of-influence arrangement remained for him a second best but still eminently desirable solution. It promised that Russia's exclusive role in eastern Europe would be taken for granted while the rest of the continent could be regarded as open for competition. This was the new meaning the formula had acquired by 1943.

Of the new perspectives that the Red Army's ascendancy had opened to Stalin in 1943, a separate peace leading to a Soviet–German condominium over Europe had been of interest to him only during the brief span of time between Stalingrad and Kursk. The alternative possibility of using that ascendancy to advance the cause of Communism also did not appeal to the cautious dictator. Thus a gradual and "orderly" growth of Soviet strength from an eastern European base—perhaps with the help of his Communist followers in different countries but not at the cost of a confrontation with his powerful Western allies—emerged as the most desirable goal. The ever more accommodating Western attitude toward a possible division of the continent into spheres of influence abetted Stalin's quest for power and influence. Yet what exactly was worth striving for, in the wide range between his minimum aims and the enticing prospect of Russia's possible hegemony over a prostrate Europe, still remained undecided. The many unanswered questions were to be clarified at the great Allied conferences scheduled in Moscow and in Teheran later that year.

chapter four

The Crucial Conferences
October – December 1943

The Foreign Ministers at Moscow

As the foreign ministers were preparing for their deliberations, the pressures of war weighed on the three Allied powers heavily but unevenly.[1] For all their military feats, the Russians approached the impending conferences from a position of
weakness rather than strength. Their war-weariness, evident in
the behavior of the man in the street, shocked the newly appointed United States Ambassador, W. Averell Harriman, soon
after his arrival in Moscow in October 1943.[2] For some time Soviet authorities had been showing concern about the eventual re-
covery of their devastated country. In typically esoteric fashion,
an officially inspired debate about the proper interpretation of
Marx's theory of value tackled the formidable problem of mobiliz-
ing resources for postwar reconstruction.[3] More directly, the
prestigious economist Evgenii Varga made public for the first
time Soviet claims to extensive reparations from Germany, which
were to include contingents of forced labor.[4] In short, the Russians had won impressive victories but seemed to loathe the prospect of having to win many more. On the agenda of the forthcoming conference they placed only one item, suggestive of their
main priority: how to hasten the end of the war, by launching the
Second Front and by other means.[5]

In contrast, the Western powers, serene in their material superiority, regarded with equanimity what they perceived as an in-
exorable drive toward ultimate victory. Their expectations from
the conference were therefore of an altogether different order.
They wanted to discuss various political questions concerning the

111

relations among the members of the coalition and the preconditions of a postwar settlement. The British had prepared a long list of practical items, such as peace feelers from the Axis countries, administration of the liberated territories, spheres of influence, and the creation of a joint commission to deal with European problems.[6] The Americans introduced topics that were somewhat less practical but also politically important, especially a four-power declaration that envisaged the establishment of an international organization for the preservation of peace, and a proposal for the postwar treatment of Germany.[7]

So great was the discrepancy between the Western and the Soviet agendas that foreign correspondents in Moscow expected the conference to fail.[8] It seemed as if the Russians, having assigned so much prominence to the controversial subject of the Second Front, might actually desire a failure to dramatize their dissatisfaction with the slow progress of the operation they regarded as the crucial test of the alliance. The course of the conference soon showed differently. Molotov proved amenable to discussing political questions, although he let his Western partners take the initiative. In practice, all substantive negotiations were conducted between him and Eden. Cordell Hull, as Clark Kerr observed, "looked and moved like a magnificent old eagle" and was "swept . . . with all deference into acquiescence in the decisions that had been taken" by his two colleagues.[9] It was the last important international gathering at which the British, rather than the Americans, spoke for the West in dealing with the Soviet Union.[10]

The military topics raised in the Soviet agenda were discussed first. The Russians renewed their appeal for the Second Front and were satisfied to hear that May 1944 remained the target date for the invasion of France. As another measure to shorten the war, they advocated putting pressure on Sweden to let Allied aircraft operate from its territory. That proposition was not without political meaning, as suggested by the remark of a Soviet diplomat in Stockholm that the prevention of a Scandinavian

112

union was one of his main tasks.[11] But Molotov's most persistent demand was for Turkey's entry into the anti-Axis coalition.[12] Since the obvious area where the Turks could help was the Balkans, the demand could only have meant that at this time the Soviet Union did not seek to monopolize the liberation of that part of Europe. Stalin's priority, like Roosevelt's and Churchill's, was to defeat the enemy quickly by whatever means he considered the most effective.

Thus far the Russians had avoided taking sides in the great Anglo-American controversy about whether the main thrust into Europe should come from the west or the south. The southern option, which Churchill advocated for its presumed military merits, was vehemently opposed by the United States, likewise on purely military grounds. As for Stalin, back in 1941 he had implored the British to open a second front "somewhere in the Balkans *or* in France."[13] Since then, he had been emphasizing that he regarded the landing in France as more imperative but had not been saying that either operation excluded the other.

In the course of the conference, a message arrived from General Harold Alexander in Italy, warning that Allied setbacks there might delay the cross-Channel invasion.[14] On October 28, Eden apprehensively broke the awkward news to Stalin but found his reaction surprisingly mild. The Soviet leader even complimented the Allied military efforts, stressing that without them the recent Russian victories would have been impossible. He actually suggested that the operations on the peninsula might be expanded to supplement the eventual attack through France.[15]

Significantly, at that time American officials regarded the Soviet position as a threat to their concept of reserving all available resources for the cross-Channel invasion.[16] And the Russian viewpoint was in an important sense closer to the British one. Although Stalin, unlike Churchill, considered the invasion of France primary and the Mediterranean theater only secondary, they both thought that a major Western offensive from the south was feasible and desirable. Its likely result—Anglo-American mili-

113

tary control of not only Italy but possibly most of southeastern and central Europe as well—was the price Stalin seemed willing to pay for ending the war quickly. Inevitably, then, his political aspirations in that area could only be tentative.

Prior to the conference, the Russians had received an urgent request from Tito that they press the participants to bestow international recognition on his National Liberation Committee and repudiate the Yugoslav government in London.[17] Moscow ignored the plea. At the October 23 meeting, when Eden announced that Britain was shifting support from the chetniks to the partisans, Molotov at first did not respond; then he indicated that the Russians might still send a mission to Mihajlović.[18] He avoided any further discussion about the Balkans and merely submitted, at British request, a factual report about the situation in Bulgaria.[19] Like Churchill, now the main benefactor of the Yugoslav Communists, Stalin did not allow ideological preferences to determine his policies. He seems to have neither expected nor encouraged radical political and social changes in the Balkans. He remained sensitive, however, to other factors that might give him a head start in a future contest for influence in this and other parts of east central Europe.

The possibility of such a contest worried the British. They had drafted for the conference a declaration clarifying the controversial Eden–Molotov "gentlemen's agreement" about treaties with the minor Allies.[20] Anticipating difficulties with the Russians, the Foreign Secretary had devised a plan of action which the War Cabinet had approved before he left for Moscow. He would try to induce them to accept a general "self-denying ordinance" against bilateral treaties with small countries and would particularly oppose "the early conclusion of any bilateral Soviet–Czechoslovak arrangement."[21] If pressed, Eden was ready to consent to a tripartite arrangement that would include Poland, but only if the discussion about the Polish question was progressing well. He had specifically ruled out the alternative of merely keeping the prospective treaty open to eventual Polish adherence.

Before Eden's departure for Russia, however, the Poles in London confounded his plan by asking him not to enter into any major discussion about their country. He agreed but neglected to adapt his strategy accordingly.[22]

When the "self-denying" ordinance came up for discussion on October 24, Eden grasped readily enough what was at stake. In a handwritten note passed to Hull, he observed that "behind all this is a big issue: two camps in Europe or one."[23] Yet, despite his original plan, he stated at the onset that "there would have to be some exceptions to this general rule," and that the proposed Soviet–Czechoslovak pact was one.[24] Molotov later confided to Beneš that he had expected a debate and had been very much surprised when none took place.[25] Nevertheless he promptly put his foot in the door and demanded that the British formally withdraw their previous objections to the pact.

Eden replied that "he now had a draft of the proposed treaty which he had not had at the time Dr. Beneš suggested his visit in July and that after examination he felt that there would be nothing objectionable from the point of view of his Government to the signature of this treaty." He had evidently acted on the spur of the moment for, when Molotov proposed that he would notify Beneš immediately, the Foreign Secretary requested a delay of "24 hours to inform his Prime Minister of the opinion he had just expressed in regard to the Soviet–Czech treaty, so that he would not learn this for the first time from Dr. Beneš."[26]

The reasons for Eden's unexpected change of mind have never been sufficiently explained. Philip Mosely, who attended the conference as an adviser to the American delegation, later reported that Molotov's "abrupt riposte" had confused the Foreign Secretary's presentation, but there is no evidence of any such riposte in the minutes.[27] In a message sent to London immediately after the meeting, Eden stressed the importance of a "Protocol" which the Russians had appended to the text of the treaty at the last minute. The appendix, though not mentioning any particular country by name, was so phrased as to allow for the possi-

115

ble later accession of Poland. According to Eden's own explanation,

It was clear to me that by the addition of Protocol and by the general tenour of the Treaty the Soviet Government have made a serious attempt to meet the spirit of our requirements. It was equally clear that they felt resentment at delays which we had caused them. We have further examined the treaty here. I am convinced that it is the best we could hope to get and that, together with Protocol opening it for signature by Poland, it is unobjectionable from [a] general point of view.[28]

The Foreign Secretary thus contradicted his earlier opinion that a clause allowing for Poland's adherence would not do. He was obviously at pains to justify himself before his colleagues in London, some of whom, particularly Cadogan, immediately questioned his less than precise reasoning.[29] But Eden omitted what seems to have been a more important motive for his change of mind, possibly because that motive was unrelated to the merit of the case. In another message on the same day, he referred to a "good prospect" for establishment of an Allied commission on Europe, emphasizing that this particular achievement would alone suffice to qualify the conference as a success.[30] He meant the commission that the British had first proposed in July; its planned location in London no doubt enhanced its worthiness in Eden's eyes. In order to obtain the necessary Russian approval, he must have been strongly tempted to abandon the Czechoslovak issue as a lost cause. He had been fighting an uphill battle ever since the Czechs, in a special press communiqué on October 2, had impatiently proclaimed their determination to sign the treaty with the Russians anyway.[31]

Whatever Eden's reasons, and he may not have sorted them out at the moment he made the decision, his reversal marked the turning point of the conference. Molotov quickly consolidated his gains, and from now on he kept the upper hand in the negotiations. He read a prepared statement which in effect annulled the

116

1942 "gentlemen's agreement" by asserting the right of both governments

to conclude agreements on post-war questions with bordering Allied states, without making that action dependent on consultation and agreement between them, in so far as agreements of such a character concern questions of the direct security of their boundaries and of the corresponding states bordering on them, as, for example, the U.S.S.R. and Czechoslovakia.[32]

The ministers then appointed a small British–Soviet committee to consider the question further, but the committee never met. Thus the British proposal was rejected by default, while Eden's consent to Beneš's controversial treaty implied acceptance of the principle embodied in Molotov's statement. The Foreign Commissar could derive additional comfort from the failure of his Western counterparts to contest its last sentence, for a common border between the Soviet Union and Czechoslovakia presumed recognition of Moscow's territorial claims against Poland.

The right of the great powers to seek client states was the subject of yet another British document, which proposed a declaration against spheres of influence and in favor of regional associations. According to the draft, introduced at the session on October 26, "all States are . . . free to associate themselves with other States in order to increase their mutual welfare" and the Big Three "regard it as their duty and interest" to assist in this endeavor.[33] The Russians were certain to object, and their opposition was made easier by Eden's having expressed his government's opinion which in effect excluded three eastern European countries from the benefits envisaged in the declaration. On October 25, he had stated that the Soviet Union alone was entitled to decide under what conditions armistice should be granted to Hungary, Romania, and Finland.[34] On the next day, Molotov therefore had little difficulty in steering the debate away from the British draft and pressing instead a memorandum forcefully reiterating the familiar Soviet arguments against any associations of small nations. The memorandum received sanction by the conference and was embodied in its final protocol. [35]

The American-sponsored declaration on general security led to squabbles with Molotov and his deputy, Andrei Ya. Vyshinskii, over details of the wording. At first sight, the issues involved might seem purely formal and therefore hardly worth quarreling about—as indeed they were not to the Western representatives. The Russians, always alert to the value of formalities, insisted on changes conducive to their long-term interests. They deleted the phrase obligating the signatories to act together regarding "any occupation of enemy territory and of territory of other states held by that enemy." [36] They also refused to assume the commitment to consult with their allies before raising any demands for military bases abroad. [37] The thrust of their revisions was to preclude anything that might tie their hands in a future sphere of Soviet influence. As far as the rest of liberated Europe was concerned, they consented to an advantageous compromise.

The compromise, reached after lengthy discussions, entailed the creation of two new tripartite agencies: the general European Advisory Commission (a brainchild of the British) and a special Allied Advisory Council for Italy that was reminiscent of the Military Political Commission proposed by Stalin in August 1943. [38] This meant that the Russians limited to Italy their original bid for joint supervision of all territories liberated by the Anglo-American forces. [39] They did agree to an agency with jurisdiction over the whole of Europe, but only after having restricted its frame of reference to little more than technical questions related to the surrender and administration of the enemy countries. Rather than letting a collective body consisting of subordinates handle any substantive issues, Stalin preferred to discuss and decide such issues with his two peers behind closed doors. Eden's hope that he would win the Russians for the European commission was vindicated, but his high estimate of its value was not. [40]

On behalf of the United States, Hull submitted an elaborate

118

draft about the postwar treatment of Germany.[41] The document foresaw joint occupation by the three Allies, extradition of all suspected war criminals, liquidation of German armed forces, thorough decentralization of the country, and the diminution of its territory. The Russian reaction was evasive. Molotov hastened to assure Hull that "the Soviet Union gives its full approval of all measures which would render Germany harmless in the future" but apologized that his "Government was somewhat behind in its study of the post-war treatment of Germany."[42] Understandably he did not expand on the probable cause of the delay, namely, his government's recent probes toward accommodation with Germany.

At the end of the conference, Stalin saw fit to reassure his guests about this awkward matter. During the farewell reception, he came over to Hull to deny "in the most sarcastic terms . . . reports . . . that the Soviet Union and Germany might agree on peace terms."[43] And when General John R. Deane, the recently appointed chief of the United States Military Mission, proposed a toast to the day when Western and Soviet spearheads would meet each other in Berlin, Stalin animatedly walked all the way around the table to click glasses.[44] Even if still undecided about what to do with Germany, he made it clear that he preferred a solution with rather than without his Western allies.

The evanescence of prospects for a negotiated peace led the Russians to commit themselves to supporting the independence of Austria. They endorsed a declaration the British had introduced in favor of its restoration, subject only to the significant addendum that "Austria . . . has a political and moral responsibility which she cannot evade for participation in the war on the side of Hitlerite Germany."[45] The wording, reminiscent of the notorious "war guilt clause" of the Versailles treaty, was intended to serve the same purpose—establishing liability to pay reparations. Thus Austria's sovereignty was to be recognized, but the material foundations of its independence were to be impounded. In the end, the Soviet insert became part of the declaration,

119

though without the qualifying adjectives "political and moral."[46]

Only the future could reveal how much all these subtle understandings would affect the postwar order. Yet even before the conference adjourned Eden had apparently begun to feel that the West had ended up with the worse part of the bargain. Trying to reopen the question of spheres of influence, he suggested at the last session that at least two principles expressed in the discarded British draft "would be a valuable addition to the work of the Conference if they could be published."[47] These concerned the confirmation of the peoples' right to choose their governments and the repudiation by the great powers of any claim for areas of responsibility.

The Russians parried with aplomb. Molotov replied that he thought Eden had withdrawn his proposal earlier, and Litvinov seconded with the shrewd remark that both principles

were already embodied in the Atlantic Charter, and since there was no evidence that any of the three powers here was seeking special areas of responsibility or influence he felt that to make a special declaration denying this would give rise to the belief that there had been some such intention on the part of one of the three countries here represented.[48]

The foray failed when the Foreign Secretary gave up, saying that "he did not feel he could press the point if there was any objection."

The outcome of the conference was generally regarded as a success, although opinions about its significance differed. Hull proved his innocence when, elated by Russia's and China's adherence to the American-sponsored "Declaration of Four Nations on General Security," he saw the advent of a new millennium. He described it in almost lyrical terms in his speech to the Senate on November 18:

As the provisions of the four-nation declaration are carried into effect, there will no longer be need for spheres of influence, for alliances, for balance of power, or any other of the special arrangements through

120

which, in the unhappy past, the nations strove to safeguard their security or to promote their interests.[49]

More to the point, several comments in the American press grasped that the decisions of the conference meant acquiescence to future "leadership asserted by the Russians in eastern Europe."[50] In particular, Soviet "territorial demands were either tacitly granted or left in abeyance."[51]

The public reaction in Britain, though favorable, was more restrained, and doubts continued to linger in Eden's mind as well. He seemed retrospectively uneasy about his handling of the Czechoslovak question especially, as Poland's new Premier Stanisław Mikołajczyk noticed in a conversation with him shortly after Eden had returned to London.[52] In his postwar memoirs, Eden conspicuously omitted any mention of this particular topic from his account of the Moscow discussions.[53] He did note, however, that during those discussions he had first become apprehensive that the goal of Soviet policy was a weak Europe.[54]

As far as the Russians were concerned, they had qualified praise for the actions the conference had taken on their military desiderata. Their public comments dwelt on the continued uncertainty of the Second Front. A keynote article in *Voina i rabochii klass*, for example, stated obliquely that although the decisions reached were sound, everything now depended on their implementation, particularly the scope and speed of the Anglo-American operations.[55] A week after the ministers left for home, in a conversation with Harriman and Deane Molotov charged that insufficient Allied pressure in Italy had enabled the Germans to transfer troops from the Mediterranean theater to the eastern front.[56] On November 11, Marshal Klimentii E. Voroshilov expatiated on the same theme in a conversation with Deane.[57]

Soviet spokesmen extolled the political results of the conference, however, without reservations. They gave particular prominence to the outcome of the controversies about regional associations and about the "self-denying ordinance," rightly stressing that the Soviet views had prevailed.[58] An editorial in *Izvestia* dismissed speculation in the British press that Russian support for Austria's independence implied approval of its membership in a confederation of small states that might be created in east central Europe.[59] The Soviet Union left no doubt that it now regarded this annoying project as safely dead.

Among the great tripartite gatherings of the war, the Moscow meeting stands out as the only one where issues were clearly defined, systematically discussed, and disposed of through genuine bargaining. No foreign conquests by the Red Army had as yet cast a shadow over the deliberations. Instead, the Western powers were the ones who had achieved such conquests in Italy—and these, significantly, enabled them to elicit the only important Soviet concessions. The Russians played a weak hand, but they played it well. Molotov was at his very best at Moscow, a compliment that can hardly be made about his British, much less his American, counterparts. It was thanks to superior Soviet diplomacy, despite inferiority in power and resources, that Stalin could look forward confidently to the impending Teheran talks with Roosevelt and Churchill.

The Big Three at Teheran

Compared with Moscow, Teheran was a shambles. No formal agenda had been prepared. The Western participants thought that unstructured discussion would be more conducive to agreement, and Stalin did not oppose the idea. The experience with the foreign ministers had shown him that nothing was to be lost and much to be won by letting his partners take the initiative. The ensuing conviviality inevitably impaired clarity; even today, with most of the documents at hand, it is all but impossible to unravel exactly what was said during those rambling conversations.

The very setting of the conference was bizarre. At Stalin's in-

122

sistence, the Big Three met in one of the less accessible parts of the world, in a swarming oriental city with formidable security problems. Yet these were more manageable for him than for the Western visitors; the Russians, having occupied half of Iran in 1941, had huge military and police forces in its capital.[60] Before the conference opened, Stalin had warned Roosevelt that, despite all the precautions, there were Nazi assassins at large in town.[61] For protection, he offered the United States delegation hospitality at the Soviet Embassy, an invitation which was accepted after some hesitation.[62] The Americans then moved into the new quarters, which undoubtedly were thoroughly wired with listening devices. Since there is no evidence that the President and his party worried about this special feature of the premises, Stalin very likely could eavesdrop on their most intimate conversations.[63] It was "open diplomacy" of a new type.

On November 28, just before the three leaders began their official talks, Roosevelt and Stalin met for the first time. The subsequent confusion about who else was present at this historic meeting conveys the authentic flavor of Teheran. Soviet interpreter Valentin M. Berezhkov has claimed that he was the only other person there.[64] But Roosevelt reportedly told his son Elliott that the only other person had been Stalin's interpreter Vladimir N. Pavlov.[65] And Charles Bohlen, then the chief of the Soviet section in the State Department, later identified the other participants as both Pavlov and himself.[66] In any case, the Russian (whoever he was) and Bohlen agree substantially in their written accounts of the conversation, during which Roosevelt strove to establish close rapport with the Soviet leader.[67] He used the deplorable technique of stressing, and exaggerating, the differences between his and Churchill's views on the world's problems, such as the colonial question or recognition of the Free French movement of General Charles de Gaulle.

Although Roosevelt's approach did not elicit a congenial response on Stalin's part, it did alert the dictator to disagreements between his capitalist partners. Their lack of coordination then became painfully evident when the conference began with a discussion of where the Second Front should be established.[68] Eden captured the atmosphere in his subsequent report to the War Cabinet:

The Conference at Teheran had opened with a request from Marshal Stalin that our plans should be unfolded. . . . The Anglo-American plans not having been agreed, we were placed in the unfortunate position of having to discuss matters with the Americans in front of the Russians, and of having to express our dissent from an American proposal that OVERLORD, ANVIL and BUCCANEER should all be carried out in the spring of 1944. The Prime Minister displayed great patience in these awkward circumstances.[69]

In a similar vein, Cadogan commented in his diary that the "President promises everything that Stalin wants in the way of an attack in the West, with the result that Winston, who has to be more honest, is becoming an object of suspicion to Stalin."[70] The contrast between Moscow and Teheran could not have been greater. After having been the Western standard-bearers, the British were now reduced to the uncomfortable role of a somewhat difficult junior partner.

Stalin was not a person to overestimate the British–American rift; he more likely suspected a mean trick. But neither was he disinclined to exploit it for whatever it was worth, particularly since the all-important Second Front was at stake. He pressed for its launching as hard as Molotov had done a month earlier in Moscow. In the interim, however, his opinion about the relationship between a campaign in the Mediterranean and a landing in northern France had evidently changed. Whereas previously he had not suggested that the former would necessarily endanger the latter, now he insisted it would.[71]

This reflected a fundamental change in the Russian strategic thinking. Herbert Feis, one of the few authors who have taken note of it, attributed the change to a suddenly increased Soviet need for Western help as a result of heavy fighting in the Ukraine during the period between Moscow and Teheran.[72] But this explanation misses the main point; the Russians' insistence on the Second Front remained constant, while their views about where Allied forces should or should not be deployed became more definite. What actually happened at Teheran is that Stalin, given a full view of the Anglo-American dispute, joined the side that seemed to offer a better guarantee that the cross-Channel operation would indeed take place and soon. His pressure led the conference to endorse the American concept of using all available resources for this operation and to finally discard Churchill's southern option.[73]

If previously the Russians had made no effort to divert Western attention from the Balkans, they began to show more interest in the area now that Churchill's option had been abandoned. At Teheran, Stalin no longer favored Turkish belligerence, with its likely result that the Turks would be entitled to share in the fruits of victory. Rather, at the November 30 session he raised the question of revising at their expense the agreements governing the passage through the Black Sea straits.[74] By coincidence, on this same day, in the mountains of Yugoslavia the Communists took the decisive step toward the seizure of power in their country. Their "Anti-Fascist Council of National Liberation," meeting in the Bosnian town of Jajce, proclaimed itself the national parliament, repudiated the authority of the king, and established a committee to function as a provisional government.[75]

Stalin had not been informed about the coup in advance, an indication of Tito's growing readiness to act independently and present him with *faits accomplis*. When he learned the news from Tito's message the next day, he was furious.[76] He charged a "stab in the back"; in its broadcasts to Yugoslavia, Moscow tried to ignore the Jajce decisions. When no Western objections were forthcoming, the Russians acquiesced two weeks later; they still refused to acknowledge the dethronement of the king.[77] Tito's successful "revenge" for their failure to bring his demands for rec-

125

ognition before the foreign ministers' conference also forced at least the dispatch of a Soviet military mission to his headquarters. Drawn into the Balkan imbroglio by Communist action and Western inaction, Moscow would soon begin maneuvering for positions of influence in Bulgaria and Greece as well.

It has been argued that by this time "military necessities had already created spheres of responsibility, precursors of the postwar spheres of influence."[78] East Europeans in particular have often suspected that a secret deal was made at Teheran, assigning their countries to the Red Army as its area of operations while banning Western military activities there.[79] In reality, no such exclusive rights and restrictions were involved. The British steadfastly opposed the idea and the Americans disliked it, too, even though the United States Chiefs of Staff later "appeared to waver for a moment."[80] The Western powers were not inhibited, except by logistic reasons, from continuing to send arms and agents into the Balkans as well as into Czechoslovakia and Poland. Nor did they hesitate to fly bombing missions in the region without advance notice to the Russians. Thus, if a decision about zones of operational responsibility had been reached, implicitly rather than explicitly, its outstanding feature was ambiguity about the extent of both the zones and the responsibility.

Moscow did not link its new involvement in the Balkans with preparations for military conquest. According to General Sergei M. Shtemenko, the leading Soviet authority on wartime military planning, the Teheran meeting resulted in no new directives for the Red Army's General Staff.[81] Incredible though it may seem, Stalin so mistrusted his allies that he still continued to regard the Second Front as uncertain. Two weeks after the conference, the normally well-orchestrated Russian leaders made a curious slip in front of Beneš, who visited Moscow at that time. On one day, Molotov told him that the question had been settled at Teheran "to our complete satisfaction." But on another day, Stalin quizzed the guest "whether Great Britain and the United States intended to pursue this war to the end with all its consequences and what were their intentions concerning the invasion of the European continent."[82] Thus, in Stalin's mind, the military outcome of the conference did not determine with any finality the future power alignment in Europe; it was the discussion on the political issues that did.

Among these issues the question of Germany figured prominently. The Russians had prepared themselves well to discuss it at Teheran, unlike the situation at the foreign ministers' meeting the month before. They had also taken a further step to clear themselves of the suspicion of shady dealings with the Germans. On November 12, Molotov had gone as far as disclosing to Harriman and Clark Kerr the names of Clauss and Kleist, the intermediaries involved in the abortive Stockholm peace feelers, which the Foreign Commissar naturally laid to German initiative.[83] Having burned that bridge (not to mention his toes), Stalin could now pose as an implacable foe of all things German.

At dinner in Teheran on November 28, Stalin expressed the alarmist view that in fifteen or twenty years Germany would revive and threaten peace again. He asked what, if anything, could be done to avert the threat.[84] Three days later, Roosevelt and Churchill outlined to him their respective variants of a plan for the dismemberment of Germany: the former providing for five self-governing states and two territories to be ruled by the United Nations, the latter anticipating the separation of Prussia and a loose grouping of southern and western German states. Stalin seemed to prefer the more radical American plan but was not entirely satisfied with either. He agreed with Churchill that Prussia was the main source of militaristic contagion and must be destroyed, but he did not think that Germans elsewhere were any better than the Prussians. He warned that dismemberment would generate an aggressive desire for reunification, making it more difficult to keep Germany subdued.[85] He favored instead strict supervision of the country by the victors through a system of strategic "strong points." But the safest way, he remarked casually, would be to take 50,000 or more of the German "Commanding

127

Staff" and simply shoot them at the end of the war, a remark that shocked Churchill and embarrassed Roosevelt.[86]

Stalin also mentioned "strategic points" in relation to France. He argued that no such points, whether in Europe or overseas, ought to be left to a nation which deserved punishment for helping the Germans and whose ruling class was "rotten to the core."[87] He introduced, and Molotov further pursued, the idea that the British and Americans should take away from the French the control of Dakar and Bizerte. France must not get back its colonial empire or be allowed to become a great power again; it might still be a charming place to visit but little more.[88]

Stalin's harshest statements thus concerned the only two nations on the Continent that were potentially powerful enough to inhibit Soviet hegemony. Yet his flamboyant rhetoric, which so impressed Roosevelt and Churchill, actually misled them. As Bohlen observed,

in regard to German and French questions Stalin was obviously trying to stimulate discussion and to ascertain the exact views of the President and Prime Minister on these questions without, however, stating clearly what solutions he himself proposed.[89]

Although Stalin wanted a weak Germany, he did not know how best to achieve it; while encouraging his partners to be tough, he was testing their willingness to be his hatchet men. For himself, he kept the more rewarding option of leniency, although he did not commit himself either way. He never clearly endorsed the principle of dismemberment; in practice he worked instead toward the amputation of the Reich's outlying parts, particularly Austria and eastern Germany.

Once the Moscow conference had recognized Austria's right to independence, at British initiative, the Russians took positions on various issues relevant for its political future. They singled out for condemnation both Otto von Habsburg's right-wing Free Austria movement and the left-wing Revolutionary Socialists, the

Communists' chief ideological rivals.[90] They praised the country's allegedly impressive, but in fact feeble, resistance movement, promising Austrians rewards for their contribution to Hitler's defeat. While Soviet propaganda was playing up differences between them and the Germans, Stalin observed at Teheran that Austrian soldiers were fighting less willingly than their German comrades, an estimate questioned by at least one prominent Austrian Communist in Russia, Ruth von Mayenburg.[91] In short, Moscow was preparing to assume the role of Austria's benevolent though stern protector in postwar Europe.

Although the Russians were thus manifesting a keen interest in different aspects of the German question, they did not press for any particular solution other than the territorial changes that linked it with the Polish one. Announcing a desire for at least "a bite of Germany," the Baltic port of Königsberg with a portion of East Prussia, Stalin professed a willingness to leave the rest of this German land to Poland.[92] Actually, by suggesting this, he contradicted both his previous public assurances denying any Soviet wish for foreign territory and his earlier statement to Sikorski that the whole of East Prussia should become Polish, a proposition Maiskii had confirmed to Eden as late as March 1943.[93] Stalin made the disturbing hint that his aspirations might increase with expanding opportunities: "There is no need to speak at the present about any Soviet desires, but when the time comes, we will speak."[94]

It was not the elusive German question but rather the more tangible Polish one that Stalin regarded as the key to Russia's security. To be sure, the Polish question was, if anything, more intractable; significantly, even the Polish Communists (including Moscow's own man on the Warsaw central committee, Finder) considered Soviet concessions on the eastern frontier imperative.[95] At the same time, the idea of compensating the Poles in the west was very much in the air; it was Churchill, rather than Stalin, who brought it down to earth at Teheran.

The debate about Poland, as recorded in the full British

transcript now available, was not Churchill's finest hour. After dinner on November 28, when Roosevelt had already retired to his room, the Prime Minister first broached the topic with Stalin. The dictator was initially reluctant but warmed up at the suggestion that a settlement should be reached without the Poles and imposed upon them. He asked derisively whether Churchill thought that he would "swallow them up"—not a clear option for Stalin so long as his military advance into Poland remained an open question in his mind. Then the Prime Minister illustrated, with the help of three matches, how the troublesome nation could be shifted westward.[96]

Roosevelt, too, discussed Polish affairs with Stalin separately, having sought him out on December 1. The several records of their meeting differ in exactly what opinion the President expressed on Poland's eastern frontier, particularly the future of Lvov. According to the most complete account, he said that

personally he agreed with the views of Marshal Stalin as to the necessity of the restoration of a Polish state but would like to see the Eastern border moved further to the west and the Western border moved even to the River Oder.[97]

Roosevelt added, however, that he "could not participate in any decision" because of his concern for the Polish-American vote. He did not give Stalin an impression of feeling very strongly about the territorial dispute; in fact, he seemed eager to wash his hands of it.

Churchill returned to the subject of Poland at the last session on December 1, but the moment was inopportune. The conversation took place in the final rush of the conference, as its participants were getting ready to leave. Roosevelt repeatedly tried to steer the discussion toward the German problem, eliciting Churchill's protest that he, for his part, was "still living at Lvov." Stalin finally consented to talk about Poland. There was a tense moment when he insisted categorically upon the Curzon line, implying that Lvov must be Soviet. But the air cleared after Churchill said that cession of Lvov or of any German territory would not "break his heart." He further stated that he would present this solution to the London Poles as a fair deal, and tell them that if they did not agree he could not help it. He added the gratuitous remark that they were the type of people who would never be satisfied anyway. [98]

The critical Polish question was thus disposed of with unseemly haste in a manner liable to criticism on both moral and practical grounds. Equally deplorable, though never adequately noticed, was the glaring discrepancy between what the two Western leaders had intended to do and what they actually did. Eden, more than anyone else familiar with Churchill's thinking, had summarized the British strategy for Teheran clearly enough: Britain was to agree in principle to the Curzon line and a compensation for Poland in the west but was to demand Russian concessions in return. These were to include especially guarantees that the Polish government could safely return home and that the Polish people would be free to decide their political future. [99] Not only did the Prime Minister fail to make any bid for such concessions, but he also acted as if he did not really care how the Poles would fare at Soviet hands—a behavior all the more unfortunate since it did not correspond to his true feelings.

Similarly, Roosevelt had told the inner circle of his advisers on October 5 that when he met with Stalin he would "appeal to him on grounds of high morality" to respect the east Europeans' right to self-determination. Concerning the Poles in particular, he thought "that the new boundary should, in any event, be somewhat east of the Curzon line, with Lemberg [Lvov] going to Poland, and that a plebiscite should take place after the shell-shock of war had subsided." [100] And yet, like Churchill, he conducted himself very differently when facing the Soviet leader. It seems futile to look for a political rationale to account for the conduct of the Western statesmen. The spell of Stalin's personality (which they both admitted fascinated them) [101] may well have proved stronger than any such rationale. Soon after his return to London, Churchill wrote to Eden about "the new confidence which has grown in our hearts toward Stalin."[102]

Not surprisingly, the official Russian assessments of Teheran were uniformly exuberant, free from even the undertone of caution that had been evident after the Moscow meetings. Although Stalin proved by his behavior that in the depths of his suspicious mind he still held doubts about the Second Front, he did not allow them to be publicized. The Soviet press and radio acclaimed the new spirit of Allied cooperation, emphasizing pointedly the contrast between the emerging concert of the great powers and the "falsely democratic attitude toward small states" which had failed to secure peace in the past.[103] The apparent ease with which the Western statesmen seemed ready to shed such an attitude may have astonished but otherwise only gratified Stalin. Molotov later recalled with irony and satisfaction the moment when they had unfolded their maps of Poland with the Curzon line already drawn as the future frontier.[104] Indeed, as a Soviet diplomat privately put it, the Russians perceived the outcome of Teheran as giving them "the right to establish friendly governments in the neighboring countries."[105]

Two weeks after the conference, Bohlen wrote an assessment of the emerging Soviet aims which has often been quoted but seldom fully understood:

Germany is to be broken up and kept broken up. The states of eastern, southeastern and central Europe will not be permitted to group themselves into any federations or association. France is to be stripped of her colonies and strategic bases beyond her borders and will not be permitted to maintain any appreciable military establishment. Poland and Italy will remain approximately their present territorial size, but it is doubtful if either will be permitted to maintain any appreciable armed force. The result would be that the Soviet Union would be the only important military and political force on the continent of Europe. The rest of Europe would be reduced to military and political impotence.[106]

132

Apart from the alleged Soviet preference for the dismemberment of Germany (a dubious assumption at variance with Bohlen's own earlier estimate) the American diplomat grasped admirably Moscow's rising expectations. With rare insight he separated its drive for political influence from actual physical conquest. Significantly he put Poland and Italy into the same category, although the former was likely to be eventually liberated by the Red Army, the latter by the Western powers. Stalin's still indefinite military plans were the true measure of his Teheran gains, and his gains were to continue with the signing of the alliance with Czechoslovakia before the year's end.

The Czechoslovak Model

The long-hidden details that constitute the story of Beneš's treaty with the Russians illuminate in quite an unexpected way the state of Soviet aspirations at the end of 1943 and the central role Czechoslovakia unwittingly played in fostering them. Having been the one who suggested an alliance to the Russians, the Czech leader had also drafted its text. He had originally submitted his draft (modeled after the British–Soviet treaty of May 1942) to Bogomolov on August 22, 1943.[107] When no reply was forthcoming other than continued Soviet proddings that the signing must not be delayed, Beneš became worried that "Moscow is playing a game with us . . . wishing to weaken our republic and make it into a pliable tool."[108] When the draft finally came back from the Foreign Commissariat at the beginning of October, the Russian amendments lent support to this estimate.[109]

Although trivial at first sight, the proposed changes were aimed at transforming a fairly straightforward mutual defense pact into a primarily political treaty, loose and tight at the same time. The Russians defined only vaguely the conditions under which

133

the military clauses would become operative. They alluded to danger from "states allied with Germany directly or in any other form," a phrase bearing ominous resemblance to the "indirect aggression" formula they had advanced during their abortive negotiations with the British and French on the eve of the war in 1939.[110] That formula had been devised to give the Soviet Union the right to intervene in neighboring countries if a situation arose which, according to Soviet interpretation, constituted a threat of aggression.

At the same time, a proviso prohibiting either signatory from taking part in any "directly or indirectly" hostile combinations was inserted into the text, thus restricting Czechoslovakia's freedom to seek other friends for protection. Without explanation, the Russians also deleted the adjectives "full international" in referring to the sovereignty of their junior partner that they would pledge to respect. Finally, they specified that the document become effective immediately upon signature by government plenipotentiaries, that is, prior to ratification by any representative bodies, and remain effective for twenty years, with an automatic renewal clause. To sum up, they tried to make the most of the two nations' asymmetry of power by securing prerogatives without commitments while saddling the weaker party with obligations and no safeguards against abuse. It was to be one of those grandiloquent instruments, favored by Soviet diplomacy, that could be rendered meaningless if the weaker party maintained its distance (or if Moscow itself for some reason ever wished to do so) but that under other circumstances could be turned into an effective tool of compulsion in Russian hands.

Incredibly enough, the amendments did not stimulate among the Czechs the circumspection they deserved. Beneš had been under mounting pressure from his entourage to go ahead with the treaty "even if it were to lead to a complete break with England and America."[111] In 1943 none of the London-based liberation movements was as uncritically pro-Soviet and anti-British as the Czech one. As the President's perceptive *chef de cabinet*,

Smutny, sarcastically remarked, "people of impeccable bourgeois credentials now honor the Communists by sitting together with them and debating with them as equals"; at the same time, they "cannot even swallow a spoonful of soup without crying 'Munich' if they think the British did not put enough salt into it."[112] Foreign Minister Jan Masaryk was aware of having in his office "people who immediately leak everything to the Communists and the Soviet Embassy"[113] but did not know what to do about it. The rash communiqué on October 2, insisting that Czechoslovakia would sign the pact regardless of British objections, had actually been pushed through by his deputy, Hubert Ripka, without clearance.[114]

Beneš himself was too shrewd a politician to succumb easily to the crude emotions that had swayed his impatient followers. But neither had he earned his reputation by calculating accurately the motives of dictators, as his Munich debacle had shown. In any case, having himself initiated the project, he would have found it difficult to back out. So he convinced himself that the treaty as such mattered more than the ostensibly trivial Russian amendments to it. The Russians evidently thought the same, for they obligingly withdrew most of those amendments after the President had suggested that these might provide ammunition to its critics.[115] The last-minute Soviet addition of the special proviso to facilate Poland's adherence, which Eden cited as the main reason for giving up his opposition at the Moscow conference, further reassured Beneš about his course.[116]

The British remained uneasy, however. In conveying his misgivings about Eden's turnabout, Cadogan predicted that the trip to Moscow would "increase Dr. Beneš's already exaggerated idea of his own importance and political wisdom, and will make him very hard to manage in the future."[117] The Czech leader seemed eager to mediate in his own way between the Russians and the Poles. Before his departure, he met Mikołajczyk and other Polish politicians at his home for conversations which he said they had requested but which they said he had proposed

135

himself.[118] Although the interview remained inconclusive, Beneš assured the British that he would press the Russians to resume diplomatic relations with the Poles and would also "make it quite plain to the Russians that he is in favor of a confederation with Poland." On hearing this, Eden wondered whether "Dr. B. will in fact behave in Moscow as he envisages."[119]

As at Teheran earlier, the external circumstances influenced substantially the character of Beneš's Moscow talks. On his way, the President became stranded for several days at the Royal Air Force base of Habbanyia in Iraq, a delay suspected as being a last-ditch British effort to thwart the trip but in fact necessitated by the actual or pretended bad weather which the Russians claimed prevented flying over Soviet territory.[120] While Stalin was thus given enough time to get home from Teheran by rail and take stock of his recent gains, he had his Deputy Foreign Commissar Korneichuk keep Beneš company in the desert. The jovial Ukrainian shared with the visitor amazing confidences. With unusual candor, he mused that "every German, even a Communist, looks at the Slav with contempt." He also hinted that if "they [presumably the remaining diehards in the Soviet hierarchy] don't give us a bigger share in national policy we shall take it one day."[121]

Having finally proceeded the slow way, by train, on December 11 the Czechoslovak statesman reached the Soviet capital in a state of elation, fueled by the elaborate reception his hosts extended to him wherever he came. On the following day, Molotov and Ambassador Fierlinger ceremoniously initialed the treaty. But the informal conversations, on which Smutný took copious notes, mattered even more than this formal act. His record of the talks is a devastating document of shoddy statesmanship, even more startling in view of Smutný's profound devotion to the President. Although the assistant by no means intended to make his boss appear in a bad light, the notes fully substantiate charges by Beneš's wartime critics that Czechoslovakia was in effect offering itself as an instrument of Russian expansionism.[122]

136

The "discussions" with Stalin and Molotov actually consisted largely of Beneš's monologues, ranging from various future aspects of mutual relations to details of the postwar settlement in east central Europe. In contrast to the tight-lipped Russians, the visitor not only asked questions but usually offered the answers and the commentary as well, at times visibly annoying Molotov with his loquacity. No other contemporary statesman spoke to the Soviet leaders with the same mixture of studied informality and eager subservience and to no one else did they extend the same condescending benevolence. The conversations testified to the plight of diplomacy in the era of Hitler and Stalin.

At the beginning of his first talk with Molotov on December 14, Beneš volunteered the promise that "in regard to issues of major importance [Czechoslovak officials] would always speak and act in a fashion agreeable to the representatives of the Soviet government." He explicitly pledged "loyal collaboration and concerted action in all future negotiations."[123] Indeed, he encouraged Moscow's interference in his nation's internal affairs as well. He invited the Soviet government to "put pressure to bear on ours, demanding the punishment of all those people in Slovakia who have been responsible for the war against the Soviet Union." With Russian help, he hoped to impress his authority on the Slovaks by meting out punishment for their anti-Soviet activities. So sweeping was his indictment that Molotov himself observed that "we cannot very easily throw the Slovaks into the same bag as the Germans and the Hungarians."[124] Similarly, when Beneš, having elaborated on his plan to expel the Sudeten Germans and confiscate their property, added that his government would press for the expropriation of big Czech capitalists, Stalin's aide reacted with incredulity.[125]

Beneš further tried to out-radical Molotov by lecturing the Bolshevik about the necessity to uproot "feudalism" in Hungary and Poland. To assure that the hated neighbors would be crushed brutally enough, he went so far as urging the Russians to share in the occupation of Hungary rather than leave it to the responsi-

137

bility of the lenient British and Americans.[126] Whatever the need for reform in those countries (and need there certainly was), such outpourings of chauvinism ill suited the leader of a nation whose fatal weakness had been its inability to establish good enough relations with its neighbors. He adopted a patronizing attitude toward Austria, and did not spare even the Romanians and Yugoslavs, Czechoslovakia's only friends in east central Europe between the wars. As far as Germany was concerned, he asked that Czechoslovak forces be allowed to participate in its occupation—an irritation certain to keep passions aflame.[127]

In contrast to this loose and rambling talk, Stalin introduced in a calculated fashion the one topic that was foremost in his mind. Having unexpectedly appeared at the gala performance given at the Bolshoi Theater in honor of the Czech guests, he cornered Beneš during the intermission and opened the conversation with the blunt statement: "We want to reach an agreement with Poland; tell me how to do it and whether it is possible." With a touch of sarcasm, he complimented the President's intimate knowledge of the Polish milieu in London. Then, taking up the names of one Polish politician after another, he seemed to be searching almost desperately for a Beneš among them. He asked the rhetorical question: "Where can one find any Poles one could talk to?"[128]

As Eden had feared, the Czech leader proved of little help. Although he spoke more charitably about Mikołajczyk than about others, he did so only after Stalin had indicated his own preference for this particular politician, and even then he did not recommend the Premier with any zeal. Beneš's aspirations were of a different sort: he was anxious to convince the Russians that he was no longer tainted by any association with the Poles. At variance with the intentions he had expressed before his departure, he repeatedly emphasized that the confederation project was dead. And, referring to the prospect of the Red Army occupying Poland, he suggested that only this would settle the Polish question: "In some time, a new government will be formed in the territory of Poland which will have nothing to do with the government in London."[129] In this respect, Beneš may have seen the future more clearly than Stalin did.

The President's statements to the Czech Communist leaders resident in Moscow, whom he met from December 13 to 20, had a quality of self-fulfilling prophecy. Alluding to their political rivals back in London as a thoroughly demoralized "terrible lot," he predicted that after the war the Communists would emerge as the strongest party and that he would then appoint one of them as Premier.[130] Although Beneš detested Communism, he confidently believed that he could "swallow and digest" them by absorbing their program and "engaging" them in positions of responsibility.[131] Above all, he was certain that he could retain the upper hand by keeping on intimate terms with their Soviet masters. In the absence of any true intimacy, however, his tactics were singularly liable to produce the opposite effect. Significantly, the Communists' own record of the conversations shows contempt rather than respect for the political acumen of this "bourgeois radical."

In retrospect, the Moscow performance of a statesman reputed for both diplomatic skill and devotion to democracy might be mistaken for an effort to make the best of a desperate situation, predetermined by the impending Russian domination of east central Europe. Yet rather than seeing the situation as desperate, in 1943 Beneš saw it as replete with exciting opportunities, some of which he described in memoranda he handed to Molotov and Stalin. One of the memoranda extolled the benefits to be derived from a reorientation of his country's foreign trade from the West to the East; another described in detail the planned expulsion of the German minority; a third requested Soviet aid to equip a 50,000-man underground army in Czechoslovakia before the end of the war.[132]

The circumstances of this last request again show no simple correlation between the military developments and the impending division of Europe into spheres of influence. In July 1943, the

British had rejected a similar demand by the Beneš government not because they deemed Czechoslovakia part of the Russian sphere but because they thought the project was not technically feasible.[133] It was likewise on purely military grounds that two months later the Anglo-American planners in charge of the cross-Channel invasion had ruled out any Western advance as far as Czechoslovakia or Poland and had informed the respective governments accordingly.[134] But the Czechoslovak government preferred Soviet to Western aid anyway, for political reasons. As noted in the December 1, 1943, entry in the "War Diary" of the Czechoslovak General Staff in London,

The President of the Republic has ruled as follows: We want to create our own army at home as quickly as possible. Its main task will be to purge the nation from the Nazis (Germans). In this action, we rely upon Soviet help. It is desirable that the British and Americans do not participate in this internal action of ours because of the probable disapproval on the part of a portion of their public.[135]

In the retrospective judgment of Ladislav Feierabend, one of Beneš's wartime collaborators and later critics, "it was through our own contribution that we became part of the Soviet orbit in the military sense—as we had done already . . . in the political sense."[136] The Russians, to be sure, did not fund the projected underground army either, despite their professed readiness to do so. But they supported all the more willingly the Czechoslovak army corps which they had nurtured on their soil and which they had by then brought under control with the help of their Communist confidants.

The Russians actually failed to act on any of the three memoranda or on the remarkable "Protocol" that Smutný had drafted, on Beneš's instructions, at the end of the talks to summarize their results.[137] While this document therefore cannot be regarded as reflecting the Soviet views, it conveys in the tone of supreme satisfaction what the Czechs believed they had accomplished. It dwelt especially on Moscow's presumed endorsement of the transfer of the Sudeten Germans, although neither then nor afterward did the Soviet government formally approve the drastic plan, letting the Czechoslovak Communists pursue it instead.[138] Otherwise, the summary exalted Czechoslovakia's prospective status as Russia's pet ally in east central Europe, contrasting this privileged condition with the different remedies to which the other nations in the area were to be subjected in order to become reformed.

In view of the obvious reserve the Russians maintained except for the resounding generalities of the treaty, Beneš was hardly justified in eulogizing the pact as a firm safeguard of "our full sovereignty and mutual noninterference in internal affairs."[139] Nor did anything in the Soviet behavior warrant the opinion he subsequently stressed in conversations with such prominent foreigners as Harriman, De Gaulle, Churchill, and Mikołajczyk, namely, that there could be no doubt about Moscow's sincere respect for the rights of small nations.[140] Nevertheless, to his government colleagues back in London, the President elaborated in glowing terms on the many advantages presumably accruing from a particularly close association with the Soviet Union.[141]

Five years later, following a Soviet-backed Communist seizure of power in Czechoslovakia, Beneš would charge that "Stalin lied to me cynically . . . and that his assurances to me . . . were intentional deceit."[142] Yet the true story was one of self-deception. It was Beneš, not Stalin, who first interpreted the treaty as implying subordination to Soviet wishes. For his part, Stalin need not be suspected of having concluded this, or any other, treaty with the intention of violating it in his own terms. Of course, as a Marxist he regarded any contract with a capitalist partner as mere formalization of an intrinsically antagonistic relationship and valid only as long as the conditions that had originally created the relationship lasted.[143] At the same time, his willingness to conclude the contract implied a belief in the relative permanence of the relationship and in its positive benefits for the Soviet Union.

141

Hints of the benefits the Russians expected from the treaty with Czechoslovakia began to appear within a few weeks after Beneš's departure from Moscow. In the last analysis, they all concerned the exercise of political power in the country after the war. First, the authoritative *Voina i rabochii klass* urged that Czech "capitalists" be punished for helping the Germans.[144] Then the émigré Communist leaders demanded specifically that the conservative Agrarian party, the nation's largest, be banned after the war as tainted by collaboration with the enemy.[145] Finally, they put pressure on the London government to authorize the "national committees" as substitutes for the regular administration, presumed to be similarly discredited.[146]

Thus the Russians used their special relationship with Czechoslovakia to spur internal changes there that would assure its obedience in case its readiness to heed their wishes ever faltered. Beneš had gone too far in insisting on the presumed identity of Czech and Soviet viewpoints in all matters of substance, to be able to resist the pressure successfully; this tactical error foreclosed many options. So he yielded to the demands, thus encouraging more to come, with no end in sight. It has always been the sad but inevitable plight of weak nations, and those of eastern Europe especially, that they are sure to pay a higher price for their follies than the stronger ones are for theirs; what the strong might eventually correct, the weak find irreversible.

The Soviet Union brought forth its arrangement with Czechoslovakia as a model for the London Poles. It called their attention to the clause that the Foreign Commissariat had providently appended to the treaty to facilitate their country's accession.[147] Such an invitation might seem to have squared poorly with Moscow's increasingly vicious attacks on the Polish leaders as hopeless reactionaries. But it was sometimes typical of Stalin, as of Hitler, to try by his very arrogance to impress on others the desirability of reaching an accommodation with him. Polish Communist sources confirm the essence of the Bolshoi Theater conversation reported by Smutný, namely that Stalin would have

142

wanted a "Czechoslovak solution" for Poland.[148] In resisting that solution, the London Poles rightly perceived it to be a precept for subservience. It was their tragedy that regarding Poland, unlike Czechoslovakia, Stalin would never be satisfied with less.

On February 1, 1944, in a major speech before the Supreme Soviet, Molotov extolled the relationship with Czechoslovakia as a model for other countries.[149] Later that month, Moscow invoked it during secret negotiations with Italy's Badoglio government and subsequently during preliminaries for a friendship treaty with De Gaulle's France as well.[150] Although there was hardly any way of applying the model to France, an interesting parallel existed between what the Russians had accomplished in regard to Czechoslovakia and what they apparently hoped to achieve in Italy by their sensational recognition of its ex-Fascist Premier in March 1944.

In a lengthy memorandum for London and Washington, Moscow discoursed on the rationale for the gesture toward a government which many Italians, as well as the United States, viewed as too compromised to rule.[151] The Soviet Union justified the recognition as being conducive to "a certain reorganization and improvement" of the regime which, by making it more responsive to "popular wishes," would benefit the Allied cause. What really mattered, however, was the potential benefit Moscow could derive from serving as an indispensable intermediary between the weak government and those popular wishes, which would be articulated by the Italian Communists. Accordingly, their exiled chief, Palmiro Togliatti, came back home from Russia at the same time to take charge. The fact that the actual developments soon defied the Soviet scheme alters nothing about the scheme.

There was a certain amount of snobbery in the preference that Stalin, the revolutionary upstart, showed for dealing with established leaders. But this preference had practical advantages, too, provided his loyal Communist lieutenants could be used to make those leaders more pliable. Ideally, he wanted Communists to become powerful enough to be influential, but not so powerful that they would develop ambitions of their own. Rather than holding the power in their countries, they were to hold the key to its balance, which could then be manipulated conveniently from Moscow.

The flurry of diplomatic activities at the end of 1943 had shaped Stalin's outlook in a curious way. There was an irony in the relationship between his original expectations and the results of Moscow and Teheran. He had sought, above all, Western military commitments that would shorten the war, and only secondarily looked for political gains to facilitate the growth of Soviet power and influence in postwar Europe. On his first priority he believed he had accomplished less, and on his second priority more, than he had been bargaining for. In reality, his gains were the opposite: the promise of the Second Front was definite whereas the Anglo-American recognition of his freedom of action in eastern Europe was not. Nor could Czechoslovakia's willing subordination, a windfall rather than a viable precedent, provide the desired model for other countries. Nonetheless, Stalin's peculiar illusions and misperceptions continued to shape his view of the relationship between military and political affairs for several more months.

chapter five

From Teheran to Lublin
December 1943 – July 1944

The Conditions of Unconditional Surrender

Τhe ambivalent Soviet attitude toward the Western notion of "unconditional surrender" has been a curiously unexplored aspect of wartime Russian policy. In January 1943, Roosevelt and Churchill had enunciated the formula at Casablanca in the hope of "assuring Stalin that the United States and Great Britain would continue on until they reached Berlin."[1] But the Soviet leader remained unimpressed and aloof, even after his own prospects for a separate peace had vanished. Only at the Moscow conference in November did Molotov add his signature to the American text of the four-power declaration that envisaged the unconditional surrender of all Axis powers.[2] At Teheran Stalin still criticized the formula as "bad tactics."[3] He made his Western partners believe that he would prefer to enumerate specific conditions of surrender. Soon after the conference, the British Foreign Office therefore proposed that the recently constituted European Advisory Commission (EAC) tackle the question with urgency.[4]

In early January 1944, Molotov approached Harriman to sound him out about what unconditional surrender really meant and especially how it was to apply to Germany's satellites.[5] Unsure himself, the ambassador checked with Washington but received little satisfaction, for Roosevelt was apparently unable and Churchill unwilling to clarify the concept. The President drew the misguided analogy with Grant's chivalrous treatment of Lee at Appomattox at the close of the American Civil War.[6] For his part, the Prime Minister thought that in dealing with the Germans the "vaguer terrors" of the formula were preferable to any

145

specifics, since these would necessarily be so harsh as to make a worse impression.[7] Regarding Hitler's European allies, the British favored a modification of the stiff demand, as had already been done the previous summer when the Allies accepted Italy as co-belligerent.

In conformity with Stalin's Teheran proddings for a harsh treatment of the main enemy, Moscow soon gave a new twist to the propaganda of the Free Germany Committee. It ceased to lure the German generals with the suggestion that an armistice could be arranged if they pulled their forces back to the Reich frontier. On January 5, the organization instead adopted a new slogan calling for "immediate cessation of hostilities and adherence to the Free Germany Committee."[8] This simple call for desertion was no longer addressed to the top military but rather to the troops. Having drawn the appropriate conclusion from the generals' failure to act, the Russians now envisioned a plain surrender rather than any give and take; even so, in trying to induce it, they used only sparingly the offensive adjective "unconditional." In contrast to the doctrinaire Western approach, they proceeded pragmatically.

Simultaneously with the propaganda twist, in deepest secrecy Moscow set into motion the preparations for a "solution of the political tasks in Germany after the war." This was the subject of an important briefing by Dimitrov on January 13, as a result of which the official German party head, Wilhelm Pieck, appointed a team of twenty comrades to elaborate a comprehensive plan of action.[9] Significantly, according to Ulbricht's subsequent confidential remarks, the Communists' tasks in postwar Germany would not differ fundamentally from those of their counterparts in Italy or even France, the country's special status as the chief aggressor notwithstanding.[10] Indeed, the preparations disregarded not only the implications of unconditional surrender but, even more astonishingly, also the prospect of Germany's subjection to the victors' military rule. Either Stalin was not entirely candid with his German confidants, or he himself had not yet made up his mind, or most likely, both.

At the EAC's first meeting for business, in London on January 14, the Soviet delegation was unprepared to discuss the British proposals about the treatment of Germany. One of them was the draft of an instrument enumerating both military and political requirements of a surrender, including complete disarmament, punishment of Nazi wrongdoers, and tight control of German politics. The other was a scheme to divide the defeated country into three occupation zones. Although Berlin was to be administered jointly by the three victorious powers, the Soviet Union was to occupy all of eastern and most of central Germany, Great Britain the area farther west, the United States southern Germany and Austria.[11] Thus the British, fearful lest they be left with the main burden of enforcing the punitive peace they desired, were the first to outline the zonal boundaries in a fashion that placed a major portion of Germany under Soviet control.

Testifying to the still indefinite nature of their plans, the Russians failed to grasp readily what in retrospect might seem a golden opportunity to secure a foothold in the heart of Europe. Indeed, they kept inventing excuses to block further EAC debate on the subject for another month.[12] Moreover, in the meantime they gratuitously provoked a crisis with the very government that had provided the opportunity. Three days after the London meeting, *Pravda* printed a report, allegedly by its Cairo correspondent, asserting that two prominent Englishmen had discussed a separate peace with Ribbentrop's agents somewhere in the Iberian Peninsula and that their talks "had not been without results."[13] The story was an invidious fabrication. The paper had no correspondent in Cairo, and no such report had cleared the British censorship in Egypt, as would have been required by the regulations.[14] Even the otherwise civil Cadogan was moved to write in his diary that the Russians "*are* swine," and Churchill lodged a vigorous protest with Stalin.[15]

The Soviet reasons for so mistreating the goose just when it was laying a golden egg have been a mystery. It has been suggested, though not documented, that the hoax may have been relayed to Stalin by the surviving members of the "Red Orchestra" performing in Paris under Gestapo supervision, and that he genuinely believed it.[16] The question remains why he saw fit to publicize this rumor among the many that were circulating. Besides, the Soviet government, having perfunctorily given the British satisfaction by printing their (but not its own) denial of the alleged peace feeler, proceeded to publicize other variations on the same theme.

On February 3, Moscow informed London and Washington that agents of Werner Best, the German administrative chief in Denmark, had recently approached Soviet personnel in Sweden with an offer of negotiations and had been rebuffed. Best, however, has assured me that no such initiative ever took place.[17] A few days later, *Voina i rabochii klass* published an article pointedly entitled "The Peace Maneuvers of German Imperialism," dwelling on the resemblance of alleged current maneuvers to those at the end of World War I and urging vigilance.[18] Radio Free Germany seconded with similar warnings against drawing an analogy between 1918 and 1944.[19]

The analogy must have weighed heavily on Stalin's mind, for the common denominator of all these Soviet moves was an apparent desire to discourage the West from responding to expected enemy peace feelers behind his back. Unwittingly, the British may have given him the idea; at the end of 1943 they had notified Molotov that pro-German Swedish businessmen had approached the British Minister to Stockholm to alert him about the alleged readiness of several leading Nazis, including Heinrich Himmler and Martin Bormann, for armistice talks with London.[20] Since the Russians had not received any such interesting offers, they had to at least pretend they had, so the West would think they could retaliate in kind against any attempted deal with the Germans. That Stalin could entertain such thoughts, so soon after Teheran, showed how little he reciprocated the "new confidence" that Churchill felt for him—as the Prime Minister confided to Eden on the day before the Cairo affair wrecked it.[21]

Only after having taken these redundant, but in Stalin's eyes quite indispensable, precautions did the Soviet Union respond to the British draft of a surrender instrument by submitting one of its own at the EAC's February 18 meeting.[22] Unlike the British text, the Russian one was relatively short, consisting of military provisions only. Commenting on the reasons for omitting political items, Fedor T. Gusev, the chief Soviet delegate who was also Maiskii's successor as Ambassador to Britain, explained that

if a comprehensive document was presented to the Germans, it would be more difficult to avoid discussion of its terms. . . . And if the Allies were to enter upon discussions with the Germans on the various political and economic points which would arise, it would be an indication that the general principle of unconditional surrender had not been completely applied.[23]

The document was a revealing product of Moscow's preoccupations at a period when the exact time and circumstances of Germany's demise were still anybody's guess. Haunted by the fear that the Germans might try to surrender in the west but not in the east, the Russians strove to exclude any terms that might provide enemy negotiators with an opening to drive a wedge between the victors. Thus, nothing was to be said about war criminals who, as Gusev appropriately observed, might well be the only Germans available to arrange a cease-fire. And since there was no guarantee that they would accept the terms so long as the German army remained capable of fighting, he insisted that everything possible be done to prevent a rejection which would needlessly prolong the war.[24]

The draft incorporated a detailed description of the occupation zones along the lines of the British proposal, except that the Russians envisaged tripartite control not only for Berlin but also Austria. Their willing acceptance of the allotments drawn up by the British, especially the awkward status of the capital city deep inside the prospective Soviet zone, suggests that at that time they did not consider such details to be important. Like their Western partners, they regarded the whole arrangement as temporary. They distinguished it from Germany's possible permanent dismemberment—a more sensitive subject to be tackled by the heads of state rather than the underlings sitting on the London commission.[25]

What really mattered to Stalin at this point was the principle of joint occupation, which would make it more difficult for the Germans to get away with a separate surrender. Gusev therefore tried to make the zonal provisions part of the text to be presented to any German armistice delegation. But the zones seemed less important in the long run than other objectives, so he eventually agreed to consider the surrender terms first. High among those objectives was the victors' right to exact reparations. The Soviet document followed the Versailles model by including a "war guilt" clause to justify the Germans' responsibility to pay for the damage they had caused. In particular, they would surrender immediately

all research institutions, drawing and planning offices, laboratories, testing stations, and ranges, factories and industrial undertakings, together with all records, technical data, patents, plans and inventions belonging to the military, naval or air Departments.[26]

In addition, all German armed personnel were to be declared prisoners of war, thus placing "under the control and at the immediate disposal of the Allies the most active, compact, militarily trained and organised part of the German population."[27] This was supposedly desirable to prevent the nation's job market from being flooded by demobilized soldiers but in reality would facilitate use of the prisoners as forced labor in the Soviet Union. Gusev hinted ominously that the length of their detention would be entirely at the victors' discretion. As far as their treatment was concerned, he said that the Hague and Geneva conventions, to which Washington and London were parties but Moscow was not, would not apply.[28]

The Soviet text further stated that "additional requirements on political, economic, military and all other questions connected with the surrender of Germany" might be imposed at any time after the event.[29] Such a blanket provision would make the instrument more flexible than the proposed British one, with its enumeration of the particular measures the Allies intended to enforce. The Russians also wanted to assure that this document would be used specifically for concluding an armistice with "the German government and the Supreme Command of the German Armed Forces."[30] In the not unlikely case that these institutions no longer existed at the end of the war, Moscow would have an excuse to discard the text altogether and look after its interests in whatever manner best suited the prevailing circumstances.

Loath to commit themselves in an unpredictable situation, the Russians did not press for an early agreement. Gusev and his assistants haggled for weeks over such trivial issues as whether the Baltic island of Fehmarn should belong to the British or the Soviet zone. Meanwhile, pending a decision about the surrender terms, they refused to tackle any other aspects of the postwar treatment of Germany.[31] The American delegation had its hands tied by a lack of instructions (indicative of the low priority its Washington superiors assigned the subject) and did not press matters. The EAC therefore was unable to accomplish anything constructive for almost half a year.[32]

The Russians posed as avenging angels behind the closed doors of the EAC while trying to cultivate a public image of moderation. They sought to dispel the common belief that they intended to treat the Germans with particular ferocity. On March 15, in a special statement Tass denied that Stalin favored the "peace terms" attributed to him in a highly laudatory article recently published in the London *Sunday Express*.[33] These allegedly included summary punishment of all Nazi culprits and wholesale expulsion of German minorities from eastern Europe. The denial was all the more necessary to enhance the credibility of the "Twenty-Five Points for the Termination of the War," which Moscow had enunciated on the Free Germany radio five days before—without any consultation with Washington or London.[34]

That document painted for the Germans the dark prospect of a new Versailles and perhaps dismemberment. But it implied that these horrors were of Western rather than of Soviet design, and urged the Germans to earn a claim to better treatment by overthrowing Hitler before it was too late. We may doubt whether Stalin seriously expected ordinary Germans to succeed where the generals had failed or, for that matter, really wanted them to earn a claim to anything. But neither were the "Twenty-Five Points" merely a propaganda trick calculated to weaken enemy morale. They conformed with the assumptions underlying the secret plans that were being drawn up by the Communist task force supervised by Ulbricht. These envisaged a popular upheaval at the end of the war, not a "revolution of the proletariat" but a patriotic uprising spearheaded by "illegal anti-Fascist interest groups" representing different segments of the German society. On these foundations the nation's future "militant democracy" was to be built.[35]

Stalin's emerging long-term goals could not be easily reconciled with his short-term aspirations. On the one hand, he wanted harsh enough surrender terms to discourage the Germans from capitulating to the West alone. On the other hand, those terms were not to be so harsh as to delay any surrender. The moderate Soviet public posture, though deliberately exaggerated, was not entirely deceptive. To its Western allies Moscow had expressed the intention to exact a high price from the vanquished, yet it had also asked its German confidants to prepare plans that would mitigate the economic rigors by relative political leniency. Such a policy was no doubt a step forward compared with the previous lack

152

of any policy on the German question, but it was still far from a clear precept for its solution.

In the matter of armistice with Germany's satellites, the Russians readily accepted the British suggestion to modify the principle of unconditional surrender. In a memorandum handed to Clark Kerr on March 29, the Soviet government agreed that this was desirable to speed up the Axis' disintegration but maintained that each Allied government should consult with the others before deciding on the actual terms.[36] However, more than once Moscow proffered terms to Hitler's wavering accomplices without such consultation, a practice condoned by the West in conformity with the position that Eden had taken at the foreign ministers' conference. The Russians developed a distinction between preliminary and final armistice; the former, the actual cease-fire, they would try to hasten by various inducements that they might or might not honor in the latter agreement, which would be mainly political.

Suggestive of Stalin's uneasiness in dealing with the Finns, peace initiatives had emanated more often from Moscow than from Helsinki. In November 1943, the Finnish government finally responded, and secret talks were scheduled for the next March in the Russian capital. The Finns were led to believe that the terms would be generous, a belief strengthened on the eve of the talks by a Soviet broadcast stressing that they would not be required to surrender unconditionally.[37] Once in Moscow, their negotiators did not find the terms as lenient as they had hoped, though still more lenient than they could have been.

The Russians insisted on reannexation of all the parts of Finland that they had taken in 1940 but not on military occupation of the rest. Molotov proved willing to retreat from his original stiff demand that the Finns should disarm and intern their former German comrades-in-arms on their territory; instead, the Germans were to be allowed to withdraw. Much like the proposed surrender instrument for Germany, the Soviet terms for Finland

153

dwelt on economic matters: reparations in the steep amount of $600 million and the cession of the nickel-rich district of Petsamo. These were the demands that the Finns found excessive. They preferred to let the war go on—to Moscow's chagrin and their own later sorrow.[38]

By contrast, Hungary kept extending feelers to the Russians, who stayed aloof. In December 1943, Stalin complained to Beneš that the Hungarians behaved even worse in occupied Soviet territory than did the Romanians.[39] There was no substance in this allegation, which was perhaps intended to help justify the award of Transylvania to Romania. Stalin had no reason to harbor any special grudge against Hungary, which by 1944 had withdrawn most of its troops from the eastern front and with which the Soviet Union did not even have a common frontier. Moscow's aloofness to Budapest's efforts to get out of the war probably stemmed from the justified apprehension that these efforts might backfire and provoke the Germans to occupy the country, which they did in March.

True to their preference for established politicians, the Russians kept the door open to a possible understanding with the Horthy regime. In the spring of 1944 they vetoed the plan, favored by Hungarian Communist exiles, to organize prisoners of war into a "Kossuth Legion" dedicated to its overthrow.[40] Meanwhile in Stockholm, Ambassador Kollontai assured Horthy's envoy, Antal Ullein-Reviczky, that the Soviet Union had no intention of interfering in his country's internal affairs and was even ready to guarantee its existing frontiers provided that Hungary changed sides and declared war on Germany.[41] This intimation that Hungary might be allowed to keep Transylvania rang increasingly hollow as inducements to Romania took priority for the Russians.

With the Red Army already in Bessarabia and Bukovina, emissaries of Iuliu Maniu (the respected leader of Romania's semiclandestine liberal opposition) pressed urgently for Western mediation to extricate their country from the war. They stressed his

154

willingness to engineer a coup d'état against the Antonescu regime.[42] Referred invariably to Moscow, they found the Russians to be neither opposed to Maniu nor interested in negotiating with him. Apart from his pro-Western orientation, his very respectability was a handicap in Stalin's eyes.

Fishing in the large pool of prominent Romanians with a tarnished past, the Russians approached individuals linked with the prewar royal dictatorship, such as former Prime Minister Gheorghe Tătărescu, and did not rule out an understanding with the faltering Antonescu himself.[43] In December 1943, Soviet diplomats indicated to Bucharest's official representative in Sweden, Frederic Nanu, that their government was willing to discuss an armistice.[44] Antonescu was still dilly-dallying on April 2 when the Red Army first crossed the pre–June 1941 frontier and entered Romanian territory in Moldavia.

On this momentous occasion, Molotov issued a press release saying that the Soviet Union did not aim to alter Romania's political or social system. In view of later developments this assurance seems hardly worthy of serious attention;[45] it did conform, however, with the confidential instructions given to the commanders of the invading troops.[46] The invasion of Moldavia was not necessarily intended to inaugurate the occupation of all of Romania. In fact, the troops detailed for the operation were so weak that further advance had to be halted after two weeks.[47] Conceivably the Russians had wanted mainly to administer a shock and force a surrender. It was during the short-lived campaign that they finally abandoned their reserve, revealing the price of an armistice to those intent on overthrowing the Antonescu regime.

On April 12, Ambassador Vladimir Novikov announced the terms to Maniu's representative, Prince Barbu Ştirbey, in Cairo.[48] Romania was to switch sides, allow the Red Army free movement on its territory, pay a still unspecified amount of reparations, and recognize the loss of Bessarabia and northern Bukovina. In return, the 1940 Vienna Award of northern Transylvania to Hungary would be annulled, making the province revert to

Romania. These were fairly stiff terms, but when Antonescu's enemies hesitated to act, the Russians offered a better deal to him. In Stockholm, their confidants hinted to Nanu that Romania would be allowed to remain neutral provided the German troops vacated the country within fifteen days.[49] In that case, which admittedly was not likely, the Red Army would confine its movements to designated areas and the reparations would be moderate. But the Bucharest strongman was still unwilling to execute an armistice, and his domestic adversaries were unable to do so. Thus the Soviet efforts to elicit a surrender before overrunning the country by force came to naught.

In handling the various issues related to the possible surrender of Germany and its allies, the Russians revealed the supreme priority they assigned to winning the war as quickly as possible. To this overriding goal Stalin still subordinated all his other objectives, thus betraying a self-perception of weakness rather than any eagerness to flex his military muscle for political gain. For the time being, his nagging doubts about the Second Front inhibited him, and in important ways the inhibitions shaped the geographical pattern of the Red Army's advance following Teheran.

The Second Front at Last

The progress of the Soviet army during the first half of 1944 was as notable for its speed as for its limitations. The Russians entered the disputed parts of Poland on January 4 and the former Baltic republics two weeks later; by the middle of the year they had regained almost the entire area that they regarded as their home territory. Yet nowhere, with the awkward exception of Romania, did they advance beyond the frontier of June 1941 in any depth. In particular, they abstained from crossing the magic line into the rest of Poland, as well as into Finland or East Prussia. On April 8, they reached the border of Czechoslovakia but stepped across it

156

only symbolically, and the *Pravda* article hailing the event contained no hints about further advances.[50]

It is possible but not probable that these limitations were accidental or determined by the pattern of enemy resistance. One can hardly avoid concluding, however, that Stalin in fact had the option of pushing forward but deliberately waived it. With hindsight it is easy to say that he could well afford to wait; the real question is why he did so.

In early 1944, the prospect of fighting all he way to Berlin did not seem the only possible, or even the most desirable, road to victory. The greater the setbacks the Germans suffered, the greater the chances that they would surrender rather than struggle to the bitter end. Should they keep on fighting, however, then campaigning on hostile foreign soil would make the Russian advance that much more difficult. According to estimates by German generals, the Red Army needed a superiority of at least 3:1, and sometimes as much as 12:1 or even 18:1, in order to push on.[51]

At a conference with his top commanders soon after the premature end of the Moldavian operation, Stalin reportedly reflected on the political problems of waging war abroad.[52] Although we do not know exactly what he said, it is not hard to deduce what these problems were. One was the adverse effect that exposure to better ways of life might exert on the morale of Soviet citizens in uniform—citizens whom he had been elaborately sheltering from any foreign contagion. Another was the strain that Stalin's crude methods of controlling hostile populations might put on his relations with the West. From his point of view, too vivid a demonstration of those methods might well lead to further delays of the Second Front, if not to the nightmare of a Western–German rapprochement. In any case, Stalin had good reasons to pause before committing his troops abroad on a large scale.

In March, the Russians rehashed the polemics about the Second Front. Writing in *Voina i rabochii klass*, General Mikhail R.

Galaktionov pointedly raised the question of whether the West was really determined to deal a "crushing blow to Germany" or was rather pursuing a strategy of attrition.[53] A contemporary analyst in the American War Department appropriately concluded that

the Soviets will not attempt to go beyond the 1941 boundary except in case of a successful cross-Channel operation and/or a German collapse. In the former case, they will continue their offensive. In the latter case, they will move rapidly into Germany.[54]

Whether Stalin took this latter course for granted or, more likely, made it contingent on circumstances, the situation changed suddenly with the news that the Second Front was imminent.

On April 7, 1944, the chiefs of the British and American military missions in Moscow delivered the official confirmation that the landings in Normandy would take place seven weeks later, as promised at Teheran.[55] At the same time, they requested details about the Soviet offensive which Stalin had told Roosevelt and Churchill would coincide with that operation. The shoe was now on the other foot; the Russians had not yet drawn up the necessary plans, and Deputy Chief of Staff General Aleksei I. Antonov therefore had no answer ready. Nor did another Anglo-American inquiry two weeks later succeed in pinning him down. The general merely reaffirmed that the offensive would start simultaneously with the invasion of France but otherwise was so indefinite that the Western representatives finally gave up trying to extract more from him.[56]

Only after the British and Americans had reassured Stalin that they would do their part did he set into motion the machinery that would eventually dispatch his troops *en masse* beyond the confines of their homeland. The plans were drafted during the first half of April and approved by the end of the month.[57] Equally significant, only now did the Kiev partisan-training center launch a crash program aimed at sending commandos and arms into the countries on the Red Army's prospective path, especially Poland, Czechoslovakia, and Hungary.[58] Composed of Soviet instructors and native Communist émigrés, the groups were to organize guerrillas in cooperation with the local Communist undergrounds. This was a radical change from the long-standing Russian policy of supplying those movements with much advice but little material help.

As the great offensive drew near, Stalin must have often reminisced about the experiences of 1920, when the Bolsheviks had attempted to "liberate" Poland in conjunction with the local Communists. Admittedly, the new situation was different—but merely because the Red Army had achieved military superiority rather than because the neighboring peoples held a different opinion of its liberating mission. It was fairly predictable that the reception given to the Soviet army would contrast glaringly with that extended to the troops of Stalin's capitalist allies on their road to victory. And the demoralizing impact of such a reception on the Soviet soldiers themselves might prove equally embarrassing.[59]

The political preparations for the attack were therefore designed to minimize the embarrassment. On the domestic front, the Soviet authorities launched an indoctrination campaign to buttress party discipline and prop up the citizens' belief in the superiority of their own political and social system.[60] Abroad, the Russians played up the theme of great-power solidarity against troublesome small nations. They vetoed the Western suggestion that some of the minor Allies be invited to share in the deliberations of the European Advisory Commission.[61] Meanwhile the Soviet press floated the spurious thesis that the recent military developments had rendered the Atlantic Charter (and its provisions about self-determination) obsolete.[62]

Stalin's May Day address sounded another new. note. His metaphor that "the wounded German beast must be pursued close on its heels and finished off in its own lair" gave the first authoritative confirmation that the Red Army was ready to march all the way to Berlin.[63] But this was not to be understood as a signal

159

that the Western powers could relent in doing their share. When the Soviet leader proclaimed that "our tasks cannot be confined to the expulsion of the enemy troops from our Motherland" but must include the liberation of "the Poles, the Czechoslovaks, and the peoples of western Europe," he added that this was a task to be accomplished hand in hand with Britain and the United States.

Even while they proceeded with their military preparations, the Russians still avoided whatever others might regard as an irreversible commitment on their part, just in case the Second Front failed to materialize at the last moment. They had been dragging their feet on an agreement proposed by the Beneš government in anticipation of the Red Army's entry into Czechoslovakia and intended to establish the procedure for transferring power in the liberated territory to the local authorities. The Soviet Union finally signed the agreement on May 8, but only after changing all references to the liberating forces from "Soviet" to "Allied (Soviet)."[64] If such nit-picking had a meaning (and the Soviet phraseology, no matter how esoteric, has seldom been meaningless), it conveyed a reluctance to assume unequivocally the exclusive responsibility for the job to be done in Czechoslovakia until the Western powers had started doing theirs in France. So, too, the commandos who were being groomed at Kiev for assignments in that country and others did not actually depart for their destinations until after this essential precondition had been met.[65]

By May the Soviet media hailed the prospective Second Front as a foregone conclusion, but General M. B. Burrows, the chief of the British military mission, noticed more uneasiness than joyful anticipation among Soviet officials.[66] That uneasiness surely increased after May 24, when Moscow received a communication from the United States government saying that emissaries of the German opposition had recently approached American representatives in Switzerland.[67] According to the message, they had revealed a plan to overthrow Hitler, whereupon Germany's new government would not resist the Allied advance through France. The emissaries had further indicated a desire to discuss peace

160

with the West, but not with Russia, citing as a precedent the Finnish armistice talks which the Russians had conducted on their own. Even though the Americans stressed that the approach had been flatly rejected, the fact that it could have taken place was worrisome.

The closer the date of the long-desired Second Front, the more the Russians seemed to worry about whether they had taken care of everything that might go wrong. At the end of May, *Voina i rabochii klass*, that compendium of their hopes and anxieties, assaulted "reactionary circles" in Britain for advocating a policy of "balance of power," conducive to a "compromise with the German bandits."[68] It was perhaps with this contingency in mind that three days after the American message arrived the Soviet High Command abruptly changed the orders for the troops of General Vasilii I. Chuikov, which were poised for further advance into Romania. To his surprise, they were instead redeployed farther north, along the shortest route to Berlin.[69]

When the news of the Normandy landings first flashed on June 6, the official Russian reaction was subdued. Stalin curtly congratulated Roosevelt and Churchill and for several days the Soviet press confined itself to factual reporting about the battlefield developments.[70] A *Pravda* article on June 11 by the well-known author Ilya G. Ehrenburg actually glorified the French people's own liberation effort while completely ignoring the Anglo-American contribution.[71] Later, at the height of the Cold War, Soviet spokesmen would further denigrate the value of the Second Front, attributing its establishment to motives no less sinister than those allegedly responsible for its previous delays. In 1959, Khrushchev charged that "our allies hastened to open the second front in order not to let the nations of Western Europe defeat the Germans themselves with the help of the Red Army."[72]

At the time, however, the initial Soviet reserve indicated not disapproval but rather anxiety about whether the operation would succeed, and if it did, whether it might prompt the Germans to try for a separate peace in the west. The more reassuring the developments on both counts, the more the Russians warmed up; the Ehrenburg article was already out of place when it appeared. On the same day, *Pravda* first published the figures on the massive material aid the Soviet Union had been receiving from the West, an unprecedented gesture of appreciation.[73] Two days later, Stalin paid an effusive tribute to his allies' military prowess by declaring publicly that "one cannot but recognize that the history of warfare knows of no other similar undertaking in the breadth of its conception, in its giant dimensions, and in the mastery of its performance."[74] On June 27 he went so far as suggesting to Harriman that the three powers establish a joint staff to coordinate their further operations.[75] Never before had the Soviet leader displayed such obvious satisfaction with the alliance.

No sooner did the Second Front enhance dramatically the prospect of the enemy's collapsing under simultaneous blows from east and west than the Russians also got down to business in the European Advisory Commission. On June 9, they added their endorsement to the final text of the German surrender instrument, which incorporated the principal features of the Soviet draft. With this item satisfactorily settled, they agreed to tackle other subjects made urgent by the quickening pace of the war, such as the administration of Austria and of Berlin.[76]

In the meantime, the inauguration of the Russian offensive reflected the same careful attention to proper timing. On June 6, Stalin confirmed to Churchill that the promised "summer offensive of the Soviet troops . . . will begin in mid-June in one of the vital sectors of the front."[77] He explained that it would "develop by stages, through consecutive engagement of the armies in offensive operations." Yet, to everyone's surprise, when the troops began to move four days later, they did so not in any "vital" sector but rather against peripheral Finland, the adversary that could be expected to succumb with the least effort.[78] Indeed, the Finns promptly sued for an armistice, although Stalin would not grant them one until September—on terms not significantly worse than those they had turned down in the spring.[79]

By his choice of an area where the war could not be decided but where instant success beckoned, Stalin showed how the Second Front changed his outlook. With his allies safely locked in combat in the west and with Germany's ability to resist eastern pressure reduced accordingly, he was no longer eager to win the war quickly. He had little to lose and much to gain by letting the current offensive run its course before taking stock of the situation again. When Roosevelt, seeing victory within reach, proposed another meeting of the Big Three to compare notes and prepare for the postwar settlement, Stalin responded evasively; on June 10, he told Harriman that there was no urgent need for the three to meet. By the time he surveyed the results of the Red Army's incipient advance,he would be able to deal with his partners from a stronger position than now, when the military initiative was in their hands—unless, of course, the developments at the western front suddenly precipitated the war's finale. So he added that he would be ready to meet "on quick notice if events should make it desirable."[80]

As the forces of the anti-Hitler coalition were advancing on all fronts, many signs suggested events in the making which might indeed bring the war to a sudden end. The great idea that had inspired the launching of the Free Germany movement a year ago seemed to bear fruit belatedly: Hitler's nationalist enemies were at last getting ready to act, when Moscow no longer needed them. One of them, Adam von Trott zu Solz, traveled in June to Stockholm, where he tried to meet with Kollontai. He apparently wished to sound her out about the Soviet attitude toward their plans, but the meeting never materialized.[81] However, the Russians may have learned about those plans from their notorious British spy Kim Philby, who is said to have been informed at that time by the German defector Otto John.[82]

Moreover, the indomitable Kleist, although he was not involved in the plot, also lingered about Stockholm, again cultivating lines of communication with the Soviet Embassy.[83] And confidants of the German General Staff, with Japanese prodding and perhaps with Hitler's own consent, were gingerly exploring possible mediation services by the Swedish government.[84] The Russians became sufficiently aware of these matters to urgently request the British government to inform them of any peace feelers that might reach London. But in their usual disingenuous manner, they failed to reciprocate by sharing the information they themselves possessed about Kleist's recent scheming, so the British had to find out about this from their own sources.[85]

Although forewarned in a variety of ways, Moscow seemed at a loss when the news of the attempt on Hitler's life first spread on July 20. The immediate Soviet reaction was overwhelmingly positive. This ranged from unrestrained enthusiasm voiced by Radio Free Germany to the more measured approval conveyed by other Soviet media. The July 22 "Appeal of the National Committee for a Free Germany to the People and the Armed Forces" rejoiced that "the heart of every honorable German is with the men who challenged him" and pleaded passionately: "Don't leave them in the lurch!"[86] *Pravda,* alluding to the historic Russophile tendencies among the German military, commended the "realistic" generals of the "Seeckt school" for trying to rid the country of the tyrant. As late as July 24, when their failure had already become evident, the newspaper still expressed the hope that similar efforts would continue.[87]

On July 22, a sudden euphoria seized the Moscow populace as the city was swept by a rumor that peace was imminent.[88] This uncontrolled reaction may have been the decisive factor that prompted the authorities to suddenly reverse their position and take steps calculated to make it more likely that any similar efforts to overthrow Hitler would *not* continue. Moscow began to discourage the notion that peace might come if there were a change of government in Berlin. It hammered on the thesis that the war would be decided not by any German schemes to dispose of

Hitler but solely by the force of Allied arms. On July 30, *Pravda* was already depicting the conspirators as inveterate reactionaries who were striving to salvage German capitalism and militarism.[89] Although Radio Free Germany was still allowed to pay respect to their motives, its broadcasts no longer ended with the familiar exhortation: "Germany must live, therefore Hitler must die. Fight with us for a free and independent Germany!"[90]

The July 20 events demonstrated to Moscow how dangerously it had been playing with fire by encouraging nationalist resistance in Germany. Despite all the subtlety of the Soviet blandishments, and all the crudeness of the Western unconditional surrender propaganda, the conspirators had still pinned their hopes on accommodation with the West rather than the East. Stalin must have shuddered at the thought of what might have happened if the plot had succeeded—and Hitler had escaped death by a hair's breadth! It can only be conjectured how the Russians would have behaved had the revolt been a success. But its failure made them stiffen their attitude in important ways.

To begin with, the Soviet enthusiasm for the recent Anglo-American military accomplishments, whose crushing impact had been responsible for forcing the conspirators' hand in the first place, diminished. There was wishful thinking in the press comments denigrating those accomplishments and instead lionizing the Red Army as the only decisive force in the war.[91] In any case, when Harriman returned to Stalin in mid-September with a positive reply to his earlier proposal for creating a joint military staff, Stalin was no longer interested.[92]

The abortive conspiracy reduced drastically the usefulness of the Free Germany movement, and especially the League of German Officers, in Russian eyes. Ironically, the movement degenerated into a propaganda tool pure and simple just when hundreds of thousands of new prisoners of war were swelling its ranks.[93] Among the generals who joined was Field Marshal Friedrich von Paulus of Stalingrad fame, and on December 8 he and 49 others issued a sensational appeal for Germany's surren-

165

der. But the manifesto was the League's swan song.[94] For his political purposes, Stalin no longer needed Germans other than the servile Ulbricht group.

In August, after a long pause Moscow again dispatched Communist agents into Germany. Like their counterparts sent recently to Czechoslovakia and other neighboring counties, they were to organize guerrillas in cooperation with the party underground. The Russians evidently did not know that by then the German Communist underground had been effectively liquidated; the agents themselves were either captured or forced to abandon their efforts.[95] With no further chance of a Soviet-sponsored resistance movement in Germany, the way was open for a policy of summary punishment. Having quietly shelved the "Twenty-Five Points for the Termination of the War," Moscow at last embraced with gusto the unconditional surrender formula and the doctrine of the Germans' collective guilt.[96]

Understandably enough, such a situation offered no promise for the peace soundings that Kleist resumed in Stockholm in September, this time backed not only by Ribbentrop but also by high-ranking figures in the SS hierarchy.[97] The unequivocal Russian rebuff precipitated in November the German launching of a volunteer army of anti-Soviet Russians under General Andrei A. Vlasov.[98] This belated Nazi counterpart of the Free Germany movement proved of little consequence militarily but sealed the fate of those Soviet citizens unfortunate enough to have fallen into enemy captivity. The Vlasov undertaking aroused Stalin's vengeance to such a high pitch that after the war he punished indiscriminately all the returning prisoners of war, tainted in his eyes with guilt by association. From Hitler's concentration camps, they were shipped directly to Stalin's.

In its wider consequences, the Second Front altered profoundly Stalin's attitudes toward the West and the Germans, affecting in a perverse way his treatment of his own people as well. Most importantly, and ironically, the Western military feat finally opened the door to the Soviet conquest of east central Europe.

"Until June 1944," observed George Kennan (Harriman's deputy at the American Embassy in Moscow), "Russian aims had to await the exertion of a real military effort by the Western powers. Without that effort, not even Russian victory was assured. The second front was a paramount requirement of all Russian policy."[99] With this requirement fulfilled, Stalin could more easily afford to disregard his allies' sensitivities, and within six weeks of the Normandy landings he showed unequivocally his readiness to do so. He gave his blessing to establishment of a de facto Polish government to replace the one in London. Disguised as the "Polish Committee of National Liberation," it was inaugurated on July 22 near Lublin, the first sizable city west of the Curzon line to be captured by the Red Army.

The Poles That One Could Talk To

A straight road seemed to have led from Katyn to Lublin. Having severed diplomatic relations with the London Poles in the wake of Katyn, Stalin had proved impervious to Britain's assiduous efforts to restore them.[100] In addition, he had been nurturing in Moscow the Union of Polish Patriots (*Związek Patriotów Polskich*, ZPP) as a possible substitute government, and also a separate Polish army. Inflexible in his claim for Poland's eastern lands, he had simply had his troops take them by force. And now that the troops had entered the indisputably Polish part of the country as well, he had ushered his protégés into power there.

This seemingly neat design does not necessarily mean that Stalin had planned it that way or, for that matter, welcomed the outcome. The evidence that has filtered out of the Warsaw archives suggests that he got something he had not originally bargained for. That evidence, with its fascinating details about the unexpectedly complex and turbulent relationship between the Soviet ruler and those whom he eventually placed in power, puts the whole Polish question in a different light than has been customary in Western accounts.[101]

To begin with, neither the ZPP nor the Soviet-based Polish army had originally been commissioned by the Russians; pro-Soviet Polish émigrés had promoted both. The moving spirits behind the former had been Wanda Wasilewska, a left-wing Socialist turned Communist, and Alfred Lampe, one of the Polish Communist party's few prewar leaders who survived Stalin's decimation of its leadership. The two had proposed the establishment of the organization in a memorandum for Molotov on January 4, 1943.[102] The initiative for the creation of a military force independent of London came a month later from Colonel Zygmunt Berling, the maverick officer who in 1942 had refused to join other Polish survivors of Soviet internment camps in their mass exodus to the West.

Although Stalin had already approved the ZPP before his rupture with the London government, he only gave a green light to the military project afterward.[103] It is not surprising that this idea was anathema to London. But, according to Berling's later testimony, some of the Moscow émigrés as well, eager to "introduce Socialism into Poland on the bayonets of the Soviet army," apparently regarded a separate Polish army as redundant for the purpose.[104] In the range of possible options, Stalin's preferences were not the most extreme.

Far from freeing Stalin's hands by providing a convenient excuse for rejecting the London government in favor of a pliable substitute, the Katyn scandal narrowed his choices. Having rekindled the Poles' worst suspicions of Muscovite treachery, he faced the dismal prospect of having to solve the Polish question exclusively with the help of the country's despised Communist minority—something that his guidance of the party leaders had been calculated to prevent. So bad was the situation that when the Berling army was organized there were very few recruits and Soviet officers masquerading as Poles had to be commandeered to fill in.[105]

The intractability of the Polish question, as viewed from Moscow's perspective, was described vividly in a confidential paper Lampe wrote in September 1943. In this document of rare candor and unmitigated pessimism—published only after being smuggled out of the Warsaw archives three decades later—the exiles' chief ideologist posed the vital question: "What kind of Poland would not be anti-Soviet?" [106] He proceeded to analyze different alternatives, only to dismiss them one by one. At last he concluded that the nation's traditionally anti-Russian upper classes must be deprived of power; in theory he thought this was possible without using force, but he also realized that in practice the Communists were too weak and suspect in the people's eyes to perform the job. Lampe did consider the obvious solution—Soviet intervention—but ruled it out as detrimental to both Soviet and Polish interests. Having died at the end of 1943, he suffered posthumous disgrace once the Russians had resorted to that very solution. Yet at the time he wrote, his reasoning probably reflected quite accurately Stalin's own.

If Stalin, curiously inhibited by his self-induced doubts about the Second Front, still refused to regard his conquest of Poland as a foregone conclusion, most Polish Communists did not suffer from such inhibitions. They counted firmly on the Red Army's eventual presence in their country; it was their only hope of gaining power. Those in Warsaw, among whom the more radical "natives" had prevailed over the more cautious "Muscovites" by the end of 1943, leaned more and more toward open defiance of London; they wanted to create a new authority inside Poland that eventually would be upheld by Soviet fiat. [107] By contrast, the Moscow émigrés tended to play down any active political role for their homeland; the original ZPP platform of October 1943 anticipated a new regime to be imposed from the outside by the Berling army. [108] Although both groups relied on decisive Soviet help, there was a significant difference in outlook and in strategy between the men in Warsaw and those in Moscow. [109]

For all his distaste for the London government, Stalin was

notably reluctant to grant the wishes of those eager to replace it. The "Patriots" had to rewrite their platform and downgrade especially Berling's mission; the general was a difficult man who, among other shortcomings, "failed to appreciate the role of the political apparatus and showed a lack of understanding for its work."[110] Toward the end of 1943, Stalin's Polish confidants prepared to launch a new organization, to be called the Polish National Committee, that would both outshine the ZPP and preempt the formation of any shadow government by the comrades in Poland.[111] It was symptomatic of the evolving scheme that at the end of October the ZPP leadership suspended its regular meetings for two months. At about the same time, by coincidence, all contact with Warsaw ceased; on November 14, the Gestapo captured party secretary Finder and his associate, Małgorzata Fornalska, who alone possessed the codes needed for radio communication.[112]

Stalin was referring to a genuine problem when he asked Beneš the rhetorical question: "Where can one find any Poles one could talk to?"[113] That the problem was very much of his making did not make it any less intractable, particularly if he still refused to admit that he had no choice except using force. He indeed acted as if he believed that other Poles, more respectable than the Communists, could somehow be found to help him run the country if only he could impress upon them brutally enough that *they* had no choice; hence he insisted stubbornly on unconditional acceptance of his territorial demands as a proof of their pliability. There was nothing particularly clever or devious about this policy, if such a mixture of arrogance and wishful thinking deserved the name. As Clark Kerr noted,

Soviet Russia genuinely favors the revival of an independent Poland, but at the same time expects so much from the Poles in the way of exemplary behaviour that it would require a miracle for them to live up to the standard demanded of them without complete subservience.[114]

After Teheran, events first began to unfold in Warsaw, which remained cut off from Moscow. It is not clear whether the crucial decision to finally repudiate the government-in-exile (a decision that the Polish central committee had reached one week before Finder's arrest) had been approved by or at least communicated to Moscow at that time. But Finder's successor, Władysław Gomułka, definitely masterminded its subsequent implementation on his own responsibility. Prompted to action by rumors that London intended to sponsor a Council of National Unity as a broad coalition under its own auspices, he countered on December 31, 1943 by organizing the "National Council of the Homeland" (*Krajowa Rada Narodowa*, KRN).[115]

In a manifesto published in the underground press, the Council rejected the nation's constitution of 1935, from which the London authorities derived their legitimacy, and arrogated to itself the exclusive right to form a new government at the nearest suitable time. It not only announced the formation of its own "People's Army" but also claimed, somewhat extravagantly, command over all Polish armed forces, east and west.[116] Gomułka later accurately described his act as a coup d'état.[117] Nowhere else in Europe—except for Yugoslavia, where the Jajce resolutions had been passed exactly one month earlier—had Communists challenged so boldly the concept of constitutional continuity in their countries. And in both cases they presented Moscow with *faits accomplis!*

Unlike their Yugoslav comrades, however, the Polish Communists had a serious credibility problem. Apart from a small, left-wing Socialist splinter group, led by Edward Osóbka-Morawski, they had been unable to win any genuine partners. Although the KRN posed as a broad coalition between the Communist party and a dozen other groups, these were either Communist subsidiaries or (as Gomułka himself later admitted) mere inventions.[118] On one "National Initiative Committee" the sole member was its founder. Moreover, twelve of the expected

171

thirty-two participants in the KRN's inaugural conference failed to appear, either because they were unable to get to Warsaw or because they had second thoughts about taking part in such a dubious venture. In any case, the meeting was not really a conference but rather an occasion for the delivery of statements prepared by its Communist stage-managers. [119]

Thus the council, quite unlike its Yugoslav counterpart, began more as a phantom than a living body. Its membership included prominent Communists, but otherwise no truly representative personalities. Among the Communists was the council's chairman, Bolesław Bierut. The vice-chairmanship went to Osóbka-Morawski, a little-known figure in Polish politics; the command of the People's Army went to Michał Rola-Żymierski, known only too well in connection with shady dealings involving army contracts before the war. [120] Less authentic spokesmen for the nation could hardly be imagined, but they rightly trusted their ability to earn a place for themselves. [121]

At the beginning, the Russians as well as the Poles balked at the KRN. No sooner was the radio link with Warsaw restored in mid-January than Moscow took Gomułka to task for neglecting the principles of the national front. [122] The party secretary defended himself by trying to impress on his critics that no such front was feasible in Poland. He tactfully, though unequivocally, reminded the Russians that they were not innocent in this unsatisfactory state of affairs. He noted that it was not so much the Communists' social radicalism as their obligatory endorsement of the extreme Soviet territorial claims that hung like a millstone around their necks. [123]

Outflanked, Moscow dropped its plans for the Polish National Committee. Instead, it created a "Central Bureau of the Polish Communists in the USSR" as a watchdog agency designed to better coordinate the party's policies inside and outside Poland. [124] Meanwhile, in dealing with the London government, the Russians ignored the Warsaw group that had recently stripped it of any authority. In fact, regardless of their hostile rhetoric, their persistent appeals for Poland to join the Soviet–Czechoslovak alliance in effect upheld that authority.[125]

Nor did the Red Army's initial encounters with the pro-London resistance forces in eastern Poland indicate that Stalin had given up on achieving his coveted "Czechoslovak solution." On March 22, 1944, the chief of those forces in Volhynia reported to his London superiors that "the regular Soviet troops have behaved up to now in a correct manner, they are willing to accept all help and try to win the confidence of the Polish population."[126] The Soviet commander even proposed the conclusion of an agreement on joint operations against the common German enemy. The Russians also avoided aggravating relations with the legitimate Polish government by postponing the introduction of their civil administration in the disputed territory.

In order to secure the indispensable Soviet backing, Osóbka-Morawski and three other KRN members left for Moscow on March 16.[127] It is not certain whether the two-month interval between their departure from Warsaw and their arrival in Moscow should be attributed entirely to the difficult logistics of the trip or partly to deliberate Russian obstruction as well. What is certain is that while they were on their way Stalin engaged in last-minute machinations which, if successful, might well have frustrated their mission. He intensified his search for an acceptable non-Communist leadership, a task made more urgent because the reconfirmation of the Second Front had already prompted him to set into motion preparations for the Red Army's crossing into ethnic Poland.

It was a striking testimony to Stalin's predicament that he solicited assistance from so pathetic a figure as Stanisław Orlemański, who was a parish priest from Springfield, Massachusetts, and the organizer of the Kościuszko League of pro-Soviet Polish-Americans.[128] On April 28, the Kremlin became the scene of a most unusual spectacle as the mighty Russian ruler received this lowly and confused man with elaborate attention.[129] He devoted a considerable amount of time to conversation with the visitor, the

173

upshot of which was that the Polish-Americans should take a prominent part in Poland's future government. But if Stalin counted on this solution, perhaps hoping that the United States would underwrite it, he was soon disappointed. Orlemański's bishop promptly reprimanded him after he had returned from his escapade, and Roosevelt shunned any contact with him.[130]

Stalin again pursued the American connection on May 17, when he received a visitor of higher caliber: the Polish Marxist economist Oskar Lange of the University of Chicago. Stalin spoke favorably about Mikołajczyk and encouraged Lange to sound out other London politicians about possible cooperation. But although time was running short, he could not bring himself to offer even the slightest incentive. In particular, he turned a deaf ear to his guest's very sensible suggestion that at least Lvov be left to Poland for, as Lange stressed, Stalin surely could better afford to hurt the Ukrainian than the Polish feelings.[131]

By this time the Warsaw emissaries were already in Moscow, waiting. When Stalin finally received Osóbka-Morawski and his companions on May 22, their first anxious question was whether the Soviet Union was going to come to terms with London. He reassured them on that score, but he did not meet their demand for recognition of the KRN.[132] He failed to tell them that two days earlier, in deepest secrecy, his agents had initiated an attempt to restore relations with their hated rivals. On May 20, Soviet diplomats in London had surreptitiously arranged a meeting with Mikołajczyk's associate Stanisław Grabski; from a spot in Kensington Park they whisked him through the back door into the residence of Viktor Z. Lebedev, Bogomolov's successor as ambassador to the exiled governments domiciled in Britain. A series of conversations followed this first meeting, several of them with Mikołajczyk participating. In a businesslike manner, the two sides examined the possible ways of resolving the main issues that separated them.[133]

On May 23, Moscow made public the presence of the Warsaw group and its reception by Stalin.[134] But while the message to London implicit in the announcement was clear, the Russians played it down and continued to negotiate secretly with Mikołajczyk. Three days later, Gusev sought out Eden and explained that his government was investigating the emissaries' claim that the KRN represented all Polish resistance. He promised to keep the British informed; Eden merely took note of the news.[135] There were no further developments in this matter until after the Second Front was launched; even then, it was not Stalin but ironically the Americans who touched off the chain of events that culminated in the establishment of the Lublin committee.

On June 10, during his first interview with Stalin after the Normandy landings, Harriman remarked that the Soviet leader did not like to talk about the Poles but "Stalin smiled and said that there were many good Poles." After Stalin mentioned the four KRN delegates he had recently met, the ambassador rejoined that "if they desired to see me I was authorized to receive them unofficially, although of course I would not seek such an interview. I inquired whether the Marshal thought such a meeting would be useful." Stalin hardly ever spoke more truthfully than when he replied that "the meeting would be very helpful."[136] Harriman's interview with the KRN delegation was then arranged at the American Embassy the next evening.

During the interview the visitors rather sheepishly tried to conceal their true identities.[137] One of them, Marian Spychalski, using his *nom de guerre* Turski, first identified himself as a member of a "Left" party and only upon further inquiry admitted that he was in fact a Communist. Osóbka-Morawski also avoided divulging the name of the KRN's chairman, Bierut, referring to the old Comintern hand as "formerly the head of a large cultural institution in Poland." The Poles felt more at ease in denouncing their London adversaries. Pleading for Western recognition, they boldly suggested that the United States send observers to Poland to verify their claim to popularity. They even requested American

175

military aid; as Gomułka revealed many years later, the assistance that the People's Army had received until then from the Russians had been "rather minute."[138]

Harriman concluded that the Warsaw emissaries were sincere people and not simply Soviet agents—the first surely an erroneous estimate but the second quite a correct one.[139] On June 13, he gave Molotov a favorable account of the meeting, commenting how much he "was impressed with their earnestness." When Molotov rejoined that "they were real representatives of Poland," Harriman did not challenge this patent untruth.[140] The surprisingly benevolent American attitude toward the new candidates for power dramatically enhanced their acceptability to the Russians.

The Harriman–Molotov conversation of June 13 may well have been as important for Poland's future government as Churchill's intervention at Teheran had been for Poland's frontiers. On June 22, on the eve of the Red Army's great offensive into Poland, Stalin summoned his Warsaw clients for another interview. He first made the shocking revelation that he had been negotiating with their London rivals behind their backs. However, he then gave them the signal they had been waiting for: he invited them to "prepare the names and composition of a new government."[141]

The other pieces now fell logically into place. The next day in London, Mikołajczyk suddenly found the Russian negotiators difficult. They confronted him with new demands that they knew would be unacceptable (particularly unconditional removal of enumerated "reactionaries" from his government), thus forcing the talks to collapse.[142] Also on June 23, the ZPP formally disowned the London government and proclaimed its allegiance to the KRN.[143] The following day, Stalin replied negatively to Roosevelt's request that he invite Mikołajczyk to Moscow for discussions, giving the plausible reason that he found "it hard to express an opinion about a visit to Moscow by Mr. Mikołajczyk."[144] A week later, when the Warsaw delegates paid visits to Clark Kerr, they already showed that "they felt themselves strong in the knowledge that they enjoyed the full confidence of the Soviet Government." Unlike at the meeting with Harriman before, they "comported themselves with dignity"; also, whereas the American ambassador had asked them questions, this time they questioned their British host, particularly about his government's support of the London Poles and the possible British recognition of their own organization.[145]

While the stock of the exiled government went down in Moscow, it surprisingly rose in Warsaw, a further evidence of the imperfect coordination between the Communist establishments in the two cities. In conformity with the earlier Soviet proddings to widen his base of support, Gomułka had his associate, Władysław Bieńkowski, publish in the underground press on July 1 an important article that included kind words about Mikołajczyk and inducements to his followers.[146] The Communist chief made special overtures to the local leaders of Mikołajczyk's peasant party but received only the predictable, contemptuous reply: "When the Red Army enters the Polish lands we shall come to welcome it under our green banners. We shall talk with its commanders as with the lords, but we don't want and aren't going to talk with their henchmen."[147]

Four years later, the Bieńkowski article served as the crowning piece of evidence during a party trial that was staged to condemn Gomułka as a traitor. In reality, he was being tried for having pursued Stalin's own policy but too late; as he subsequently explained, he had realistically taken into account both Moscow's possible understanding with London and the Red Army's imminent arrival in Poland.[148] It was his misfortune that the Soviet position shifted during June and that Stalin did not want to be reminded of his unsuccessful effort to elicit the non-Communist Polish leadership he would have preferred. So the dictator, as was his custom, sacrificed a loyal subordinate as the scapegoat for a policy that failed. (Gomułka had his revenge, when he compelled Stalin's successors to accept his own manner

177

of controlling his restive countrymen in 1956; but so, in turn, did the Russians, when fifteen years later they let him fall after his authoritarian methods proved no longer workable.)

In July 1944, Soviet behavior in Poland took a decidedly sinister turn. Having ended their honeymoon with the pro-London Home Army, the Russians embarked on its systematic destruction, displaying some of their worst traits in the process. At Wilna, General Ivan D. Cherniakovskii at first let the Home Army share in the liberation of the city and even asked its officers to his headquarters afterward, only to have them arrested on the spot and their troops disbanded.[149] What happened at Wilna heralded worse things to come.

It was at this somber hour for Poland that the main negotiations between Stalin and his prospective Polish lieutenants opened in the Kremlin. This followed the arrival on July 5 of a second delegation from Warsaw, led by Rola-Zymierski. His later interviews and Osóbka-Morawski's memoirs (which, like Berling's, have been written but never published in their entirety) offer important glimpses of what happened on that momentous occasion. The startling features of the talks are that they entailed some genuine bargaining rather than mere Soviet *Diktat*, and that the few non-Communist delegates present were the ones who dared to bargain—enough reason for Stalin to appear "in the worst possible mood."[150]

Among the items that annoyed the Russian ruler were the Poles' demands for all of East Prussia and for the Forest of Białowieża, a sparsely populated wilderness east of the Curzon line. According to Osóbka-Morawski's account, in the end Stalin angrily drew a straight line across the map, thus dividing East Prussia between the Soviet Union and Poland, and grudgingly conceded the other demand. But the main point of contention was the compensation Poland was to receive in the west.[151]

At Teheran, Stalin had agreed with Churchill that Poland should expand to the Oder, but nothing had been said about the two major cities located on both banks of the river. Six months later, he had told Lange that Stettin should be Polish but had remained vague about Breslau.[152] Now the men from Warsaw demanded not only the Oder but also the Western Neisse, that is, both Upper and Lower Silesia. Rola-Zymierski especially pressed the issue, citing the desirability of a favorable strategic border against Germany.[153] But it was even more desirable for an unpopular regime to bolster its position by a territorial gain exceeding most Poles' wildest dreams. In this respect, Stalin's clients had leverage to get what they wanted; they needed him, but he also needed them.

Stalin required a last jolt before approving the creation of the Lublin committee. On July 15, Osóbka-Morawski and Wasilewska implored him on behalf of the KRN and the ZPP not to delay the formation of a provisional government any longer. In their memorandum, they reminded him how important it was to avoid the impression of a "Russian occupation" of Poland and warned especially that "the establishment of a Soviet administration in the territory west of the Curzon line . . . would threaten to weaken the democratic camp, and undermine Polish confidence in the Soviet Union."[154] Two days later, Stalin gave his assent. Conveying the news to the comrades in Warsaw, a secret Moscow message emphasized two tasks of the forthcoming "Polish Committee of National Liberation": winning to its side the majority of the people, and pursuing "a policy designed to preserve the unity of the Allied nations in the spirit of Teheran."[155]

The message betrayed Stalin's continued concern about both the new regime's credibility and the Western reaction. In particular, he had reason to be uneasy about his clients' territorial ambitions, which his allies might ask him to account for. Accordingly the committee's inaugural manifesto on July 22 shunned not only the word "government" (reserved perhaps for the unlikely contingency that some London politicians would eventually cave in, thus allowing its reorganization into a body more worthy of that name) but also any reference to Poland's western frontiers.[156] The first draft of the document had referred to Stettin as a Polish city,

179

but the final version mentioned neither Stettin nor Breslau, much less the Western Neisse. [157]

The omission of western frontiers reflected the fact that Polish and Russian negotiators in the Kremlin were still wrestling with the problem of where the line should be drawn. On July 27 they reached a secret agreement, but it did not settle the matter with any finality. The Poles formally endorsed the Curzon line, slightly modified in their favor, in return for an Oder–Neisse boundary, but the text did not specify whether the Neisse in question was the Western or the Eastern one. [158] This was not a detail the punctilious Russians could possibly have overlooked, for at issue was possession of the vast and rich territory between the two streams.

In all probability, Stalin did promise his difficult customers what they wanted but only, so to speak, at their own risk. The next day, Osóbka-Morawski announced the Oder–Neisse claim at a press conference, without making clear which Neisse he meant. [159] The Russians did not publicly commit themselves to either one, pending the Anglo-American reaction; with none forthcoming, the question remained open. When Mikołajczyk was finally allowed to visit Moscow at the beginning of August, Stalin mentioned to him the unspecified Neisse as Poland's future frontier. [160] But in October, during talks with Churchill, the Soviet leader registered no objections to the draft of a joint declaration which again referred only to the Oder. [161] (The declaration was not adopted because of the London Poles' opposition to its provisions favoring the Curzon line.)

Stalin kept not only his Poles but also his Ukrainians in the dark about how much territory they would get. As late as November 1944, Khrushchev (then the Ukrainian party boss) was overheard saying in Lvov that he did not know to whom the city would ultimately belong. [162] He confirmed his uncertainty in his later memoirs, where he portrayed Stalin as "going out of his way to court" Poland's new rulers and being ready to make "major concessions to them." [163] This is overdrawn, but otherwise it agrees with the retrospective view of Osóbka-Morawski (a person well-qualified to judge), that Stalin had no "preconceived plan in regard to Poland which he implemented with iron consistency."[164]

How does the new evidence illustrating the tortuous course of Soviet policy alter the conventional view of the Polish question? Certainly, until the Second Front changed his premises, Stalin would have been quite willing to frustrate the Polish Communists' power ambitions if only their London rivals had given him proof of the pliability he required. This is not to say that later on, once his relations with the West had deteriorated, he would have hesitated to impose a Communist regime in Poland. Yet it is also true that nothing contributed to that deterioration more than his inability to obtain his desired alternative of a subservient non-Communist one. Does it follow, then, that the London Poles held the key to saving their country from Communist rule and perhaps Europe from the Cold War? The question is contrived, for by their nature they were not prepared to pay the humiliating price Stalin required; in refusing to pay it, they were as obstinate as he was in demanding it. The deadlock was complete. As a result, the old Poland was moving irresistibly toward its doom, bound to lose everything but its honor.

Honor was one motive that seemed singularly lacking as inspiration for Poland's new rulers, men who struck Churchill as "the greatest villains imaginable."[165] In their unscrupulous drive for power, they were ever ready to use trickery, flattery, and deceit. Yet they had redeeming virtues that were particularly timely in their country's dire predicament: a devotion to its national interest as they understood it and a readiness to uphold it even to Stalin. Rather than being his eager stooges, they were harbingers of a Poland that in the end would reemerge from its travails, not an independent nation to be sure but still Moscow's most difficult, as well as most respected, satellite.

Stalin's grasping for a unilateral solution to the Polish question highlighted the profound change in his outlook that had been brought about by the advent of the Second Front. In shaping his long-term aims, the Normandy landings proved an even greater landmark than Stalingrad. After the elaborate Soviet blandishments to induce the enemy to surrender had come to naught, the compelling Anglo-American commitment to further struggle at last prompted Stalin to order his armies beyond the frontier of June 1941 and conquer the lands that would eventually become components of his new empire. With the Rubicon crossed, any premature end to hostilities now would only serve to reduce the potential rewards of the conquest. For the first time since the war began, concern for those rewards started to outweigh Soviet military considerations. It was at this moment that the uprising in Warsaw posed starkly the dilemma between political and military imperatives, with all its grave implications for Stalin's nascent empire.

chapter six

The Birth of an Empire
July – November 1944

The Doomed Uprisings

The long-planned insurrection of the Polish Home Army in Warsaw began on August 1, 1944, a week after the installation of the Lublin committee. Militarily the revolt was a potential boon for the Russians, because it promised to ease their drive to the heart of the Nazi Reich along the most direct route. The question of why the opportunity went unexploited involves not only the Red Army's *ability* to push forward by joining forces with the Poles but also Stalin's *willingness* to do so. In a larger sense, it illustrates what, if any, role he assigned to uprisings behind the enemy lines in pursuing his political goals.

By launching the insurrection, its anti-Soviet leaders took a grave but calculated risk. They believed that if they succeeded in seizing power in the city before the Russians arrived, Stalin would not dare to prevent the London government from taking charge of the liberated country. Alternately, if he tried to dislodge them by force, this would prompt the West to counteraction, and because of its superior strength the Russians would be compelled to yield. There was, of course, the risk that the Poles' own resources would prove insufficient for coping with the Germans, but this had to be discounted because of the people's almost irrepressible urge to settle accounts with the oppressors. Besides, even Poles found it hard to imagine that, if worst came to worst, Stalin would not do his best to rescue them—for the sake of Allied unity if not for any love of them.

General Tadeusz Bór-Komorowski, the Home Army's commander-in-chief, acted on the premise that Stalin's design for

Poland was still flexible.[1] The premise was wrong though barely so, considering how long Stalin had been delaying the green light to his Communist clients. In fact, the July 22 inauguration of the Lublin committee coincided almost to the day with Bór's decision to launch the uprising, although it did not trigger that decision.[2] At the very least, until July 22 Stalin would have had more inducement to come to terms with a leadership presiding over a massive popular upheaval aimed at liberating the capital of an Allied nation. Admittedly, this is a hypothetical situation, for Bór could not have given the signal for the rising earlier than he did; the front would have been too far away and the German power impregnable. He was indeed a prisoner, not so much of illusions as of time.

The Russians had already started an offensive in the Warsaw area on July 18, but it is not clear whether the city itself was their target. Although Stalin would later assert that it was, their actual military movements indicate the opposite.[3] Even so, he was unlikely to have ruled out taking Warsaw if a favorable opportunity arose, and such an opportunity seemed to appear when the Germans began evacuating the city at the end of July. On August 2, a *Pravda* article suggested that its liberation was imminent.[4]

The possibility of seizing the capital quickly would have been all the more attractive to Stalin because this would have enabled him to relocate the fledgling Lublin committee, giving a much-needed boost to its prestige. For this reason, the Soviet radio exhortations urging the people of Warsaw to take up arms may have been aimed at encouraging acts of resistance for which the committee could then claim credit.[5] The Russians, having again lost contact with the Warsaw party headquarters at the end of July, hardly realized (any more than the Germans did) how little encouragement the people really needed.[6]

The uprising was both a surprise and an embarrassment to Stalin. To compound the embarrassment, the Red Army's offensive had run out of steam; the enemy had brought in reinforcements and had even managed to roll the front back.[7] However,

184

from Stalin's point of view, one embarrassment had the potential of ridding him of the other. The resurgence of Nazi strength might well cause the uprising to collapse before he had to face the dilemma of whether to help the Poles or not. His disparaging remark to Mikołajczyk on August 5 that the Home Army, lacking heavy weapons, was no match for the Germans, expressed his main hope.[8] But Warsaw kept holding out against formidable enemy pressure, which the Anglo-American air drops alleviated but could not decisively alter. On August 9, Stalin told Mikołajczyk that he, too, was prepared to do everything possible to help, implying that something could indeed be done.[9]

True enough, the preceding day the staff of Marshal Konstantin K. Rokossovskii's army, which was facing the embattled capital, had reported to the supreme commander that the troops would be able to resume their advance by August 25.[10] But Stalin failed to give the necessary orders. Instead, in an unprecedented departure from the Soviet practice, he had the press and radio publicize the setback that had occurred more than two weeks earlier.[11] On August 13, Tass issued a special statement condemning the Warsaw revolt as a reckless adventure and disclaiming any Soviet responsibility for it.[12] In his messages to Churchill, Stalin saw fit to describe its leaders as a "handful of power-seeking criminals."[13]

Not only did Stalin begin to abuse the insurgents verbally as soon as they had demonstrated their staying power; he also took active steps to assure their defeat. On August 15, the Soviet government ignominiously refused to allow Anglo-American aircraft, which had been flying supplies to Warsaw from as far as southern Italy, to land on Russian airfields near the city for refueling and treatment of wounded crewmen.[14] In a further effort to sabotage the revolt, on August 24 the Lublin committee decreed the dissolution of all "secret organizations," which meant particularly the Home Army.[15] On the same day, Soviet troops received orders to prevent any movement of Home Army detachments from the provinces to the capital.[16] Since the city was thus to be sealed off to die, no attempts were even made to restore liaison between Lublin and the Warsaw Communists.[17]

Survivors of the uprising have testified that if the Russians had acted to save Warsaw at this time of ordeal, "bygones would have been bygones" and they would have been greeted as liberators.[18] It may be questioned whether the Red Army, smarting from the recent German counterattack, was fully up to the task, although the officers of Rokossovskii's staff (who were in the best position to know) thought it was. What is beyond doubt is that Stalin did not want to give a possible Soviet–Polish reconciliation a chance. This was the situation for the remainder of August.

Matters could have been different if the Western allies had put pressure on Stalin early enough. But they even hesitated to contest the scandalous banning of their planes from the Soviet airfields.[19] Churchill was shocked at the "strange and sinister behavior of the Russians" and also puzzled why that behavior was receiving so little publicity in the British press. However, as his Minister of Information Brendan Bracken explained to him, the press had no confidence in the Poles and was rather inclined to accept the Russian version of events. In Britain as well as in America, the makers of public opinion abhorred striking a discordant note at a time when excellent news was coming in from all the other battlefields.[20] As in the case of Katyn, the British and Americans did not come to grips with what was happening in Warsaw because they did not want to.

While the Warsaw events were taking their "strange and sinister" course, another revolt was brewing in neighboring Slovakia. There were significant, as well as confusing, differences between the two, a reason why the Slovak revolt has remained little known or understood.[21] Unlike Poland, Slovakia was Hitler's ally, and the men behind the insurgency were its regular army officers who, in contrast to their Polish counterparts, wished eagerly to coordinate their plans with the Russians.[22] Communists not only took an active part in the preparations but also were a prominent component of the Slovak National Council (*Slovenská národná rada,* SNR), the political arm of the conspiracy.[23] Moreover, Beneš's government-in-exile enjoyed full acceptance by Moscow—though not so much by the Slovaks, many of whom resented the preponderance of Czechs in it and the President's theory denying the existence of any separate Slovak nationality.[24] Finally, the Russians knew in advance what was in the offing, having been informed by London though not directly by the SNR or the Slovak Communist leadership, whose only lines of communication with Moscow had been through the Beneš government.[25]

The conspirators' attempts to communicate with Moscow directly had a touch of comedy only too lacking in the Warsaw tragedy. At the beginning of August, the two aircraft that were to spirit emissaries to the other side of the front carried several persons who were not supposed to be there at all, while some of the designated ones missed their flight by mistake. Among those who did make the trip was Karol Šmidke, the agent whom Moscow had dispatched into Slovakia in mid-1943 but from whom it had heard nothing since then.[26] Now he was returning as a leading member of the SNR and also as the bearer of a most curious letter. Its author was Slovakia's Minister of Defense, Ferdinand Čatloš, who had supplied Šmidke's plane. He proposed engineering a military coup to detach Slovakia from Germany, whereupon the country's new regime would cooperate with the Red Army in return for guarantees of its independence.[27]

The Russians seemed interested in the offer. After all, the man who had been presiding over Slovakia's war against the Soviet Union was sufficiently compromised to serve as a potential Russian puppet. While treating the other emissaries as captives rather than as negotiating partners and while obstructing the attempts of Beneš's Moscow representatives to gain access, Soviet officials interrogated Šmidke in deep secrecy, a mode of behavior which greatly disturbed the Czechoslovak government.[28] But in another two weeks Šmidke performed the triple feat of reassuring his interrogators about his personal loyalty, checking any temptation on their part to pursue the Čatloš offer, and convincing them about the merits of the SNR's own plan for an army revolt. (Still, Čatloš received his reward when, after the war, he was merely sentenced to a prison term rather than death, as he would have otherwise merited by Soviet standards; eventually he finished out his life in comfortable retirement.[29])

Although on August 23 the émigré party leadership adopted a secret resolution endorsing the SNR plan, the Russians still preferred to avert the revolt.[30] They made no attempt to communicate the resolution, or any other message, to the SNR. Instead, the central staff for partisan warfare in Kiev, which had recently been planting commandos in Slovakia, alerted their members that any "provocation of an uprising is strictly forbidden."[31] As if to further discourage the Slovaks, the Red Army also rescinded its plans to strike on August 28 in the direction of Mukachevo and Uzhgorod, towns in the Carpathian Ukraine very near Slovakia.[32]

Thus it was against Soviet wishes that the Slovak insurgency started on August 29, having been triggered by German military intervention to stamp out the partisan activities that the Russians had belatedly tried to curtail. Almost immediately Moscow received pleas for assistance from two different quarters. The Beneš government, presenting the revolt as its own enterprise, approached Vyshinskii on August 31.[33] Two days later, the émigré Communist leaders wrote to Molotov that the uprising was directed by their Slovak comrades and eminently worthy of support on that account.[34] There was some truth in both claims: Beneš's followers had dominated the scene at the onset, but they had soon been overshadowed by the SNR, whose most active members were the Communists.[35] The Russians kept both groups of supplicants in suspense while trying to find out for themselves what the real situation was. On September 4 they flew Šmidke, along with some thirty planeloads of arms and supplies, to Banská Bystrica, the center of the liberated territory.[36]

The Soviet response to the Slovak uprising thus differed from its response to the one in Warsaw. However, at this time the premises of the Polish affair, too, began changing for Stalin. On September 5, Clark Kerr at last delivered to the Russians a spirited protest against their obstruction of the Western air drops. Churchill would have gone even farther, particularly by ordering British airmen to land on the airfields near Warsaw anyway or by suspending the monthly British convoys to the Soviet Union. But Roosevelt, when consulted about these measures, disapproved for fear of antagonizing Stalin.[37]

The outrageous Soviet behavior all but wrecked the Lublin committee. According to the fragmentary information available on this exceedingly sensitive subject, various members of the group saw Stalin on no less than thirty occasions during the uprising. Some of them pleaded for his help to save their compatriots from being massacred by the Germans. Others solicited his arbitration between those members of the committee who favored such help and those who preferred to let the insurgency take its course. This seems to have been the position especially of Rola-Żymierski, who nurtured a great ambition to become Poland's supreme military chief.[38]

The British diplomatic intervention and the unrest among Stalin's Polish lieutenants called for a reconsideration of Soviet policy. On September 9, Moscow reluctantly granted the desired landing rights to Western aircraft; moreover, the Russians themselves began parachuting matériel into Warsaw, and the Red Army finally started to move.[39] On September 14, it reached the city's suburbs on the eastern bank of the Vistula. The Lublin committee greeted the event by issuing a rousing manifesto which proclaimed that "the hour of liberation for the heroic Warsaw is approaching. Help is coming. Victory is near. Fight on."[40]

But the help was not coming, certainly not enough to secure victory, although the city did fight on. On September 16, in what can best be described as a bogus operation, the Soviet command sent Berling's troops, though not any Russian troops, across the Vistula. Once his gallant but outnumbered men had been, predictably, repelled and then withdrawn after considerable losses, Stalin sheepishly explained to Clark Kerr that "they could not be of much service to the underground movement because their uniforms made them conspicuous amongst the people who emerged from the sewers to fight and went back to them when things got too hot."[41] Nor were the Russian air drops of greater help, because they fell into German-controlled parts of the city or because they were made without parachutes.[42]

The net result of such rationed assistance was to prolong the city's agony, a calculated rather than accidental effect. Stalin had reversed his policy of total boycott only after the leaders of the uprising had begun negotiating for a surrender, which was to take place on September 10. The hope of deliverance, kept alive by the token Russian help, had made them break off the negotiations and keep fighting on until October 2, with devastating results.[43] They had every reason to charge later that they had been "deceived. We did not receive proper help. . . . We have been treated worse than Hitler's allies."[44] As a matter of fact, Stalin's policy was even more dastardly than it appeared; only joining the Germans outright in their systematic extermination of Warsaw's population would have been worse.

The Soviet aid to Slovakia also left something to be desired.[45] The Czechoslovak troops fighting alongside the Red Army bore the brunt of the difficult assault on the heavily fortified Dukla Pass in the northern Carpathians. Without adequate artillery cover, they inched their way forward, suffering enormous casualties and taking the pass only on October 6—much too late to be of use to the insurgents.[46] Nor did the Red Army's advance into the Carpathian Ukraine alleviate their plight. It was canceled at the end of August and not resumed until seven weeks later, although enemy resistance was light.[47] The Soviet-organized transfer of a Czechoslovak airborne brigade into the liberated territory took four weeks to complete, allegedly because of inclement weather; this was also the Russians' explanation for not bringing in the representatives of the Beneš government. Yet while the latter were kept waiting in Galicia, unable to communicate with the SNR, the weather was benign enough to fly in Šmidke and several other Soviet confidants, including a special emissary of the exiled party leadership, Jan Šverma.[48]

Stalin's objectives in Slovakia were less transparent than in Poland. He had little patience with Slovak nationalists (whether Communist or not), whose aspirations complicated the blueprint for the unified Czechoslovakia that Beneš sought and he endorsed. The true purpose of Šverma's mission in Banská Bystrica was therefore to assure that the wayward local comrades would not openly challenge the President's authority and that the SNR would not push its demands for Slovakia's self-government.[49] Similarly, to the Communists' dismay, Soviet Marshal Ivan S. Konev decreed that Slovak partisans be subordinated to the command of the London government rather than the SNR.[50]

So it was largely thanks to Russian groundwork that the London representatives, finally airlifted to Banská Bystrica on October 7 (a full six weeks after the uprising began), received a correct, though hardly enthusiastic, reception. The Communists continued to pursue, with Soviet encouragement, the familiar policies calculated to weaken the "bourgeois" authority, masterminding "spontaneous" national committees and summary measures against presumed collaborators with the enemy.[51] Thus Moscow upheld the Czech-dominated Beneš government against the Slovak dissidents while at the same time promoting its dependence on Communist good will.

Nonetheless, Stalin did not save the uprising. On balance, he probably preferred the insurgents to be defeated, not because their victory would have seriously hindered his future domination of Czechoslovakia but because it would not have significantly facilitated that goal either. Therefore, an all-out effort to save them simply did not seem worth the trouble, especially since the physical obstacles were much more formidable than in Warsaw and the potential military rewards substantially smaller. Thus Stalin's reasons for not helping as much as he could have, while pretending

191

that he was doing his best, were basically military. In contrast, the motives behind the West's aloofness were essentially political.

For the British and Americans, Slovakia was easier to reach than Warsaw. And yet, faced with a request for aid by the Beneš government shortly after the uprising began, the British Chiefs of Staff decided (and their American counterparts concurred) that they would "proceed with caution until more is known of Russian intentions, observing that Slovakia is in Russian sphere of operations."[52] The Foreign Office inquired in Moscow about those intentions, but since no reply ever came, British help remained limited to a shipment of medical stores in a plane bringing in an observer mission. The United States also sent observers, along with eight bombers loaded with arms and ammunition as a token of support.[53]

But Slovakia was not any more in the Russian sphere of operations than Warsaw, where the Western Allies were then sending hundreds of aircraft with supplies.[54] The real reason for their not trying as hard in Slovakia was their fear that the "Polish pitfalls"[55] would be repeated, although Czechoslovakia's pro-Russian orientation did not make the parallel readily applicable. Apart from its failure to answer the Foreign Office inquiry, Moscow actually never indicated any strong feelings about the matter. Thus it was by unilateral decision, rather than by any arrangement with the Russians, that as a result of the Warsaw experience the Western powers adopted a policy of abstaining from anything beyond token aid to resistance movements in areas they arbitrarily defined as being within the Soviet sphere of operations.

With both the East and the West curtailing assistance, albeit for different reasons, nothing could save the Slovaks from finally succumbing to the Germans on October 28. Yet even before this predictable outcome, the Russians had begun to instigate another uprising in the Czech Protectorate. Admittedly, the call to arms authored by the Czech Communist exiles and broadcast over the Moscow radio on September 16 was not very likely to be heeded in a country where the necessary preconditions were lacking.[56] But neither was the appeal merely academic, for within a fortnight the Russians began flying in their commandos (as usual, Soviet instructors and native Communists).[57] And precisely because they were unlikely to meet any significant competition from the home-grown underground, as had been the problem in both Poland and Slovakia, the Czech situation is instructive about the kind of resistance Stalin really wanted.

Until the Soviet partisans arrived, the Protectorate had been almost exclusively the domain of the British Special Operations Executive (SOE). Its agents had been providing the vital communication between London and the main resistance organization that had emerged by 1944, code-named the Council of the Three.[58] So successful had they been that in October the Foreign Office became worried lest the SOE had exceeded its original instructions, which had called for no more than "day to day sabotage," and had consequently given rise to exaggerated hopes about the extent of the British commitment.[59] By then, London had come to assume that not only Slovakia but also the Protectorate belonged to the sphere of Soviet military operations, little though any Russian action had yet justified such an assumption. On November 13, Chief of Imperial General Staff Sir Alan Brooke ruled that all Czechoslovak requests for resistance aid must henceforth be addressed to Moscow.[60]

Shortly afterward, the Council of the Three first made contact with the newcomers from the east, only to become puzzled about the true purpose of their mission. Unlike the Moscow radio appeals, the Soviet partisans stressed intelligence work rather than armed struggle, showing little interest in recruiting guerrillas among the local population. Nor were they eager to join with the Council in fighting the Germans, although they promised its members Russian medals and other certificates of valor once the war was over.[61] Nevertheless, their presence prompted the SOE agents in the Protectorate to observe in a message to London that

if Partisans are to be armed and supplied with materials from the East only, as is the case to-day, the influence of the East will be absolute.

The mob and the former Communists will gain influence in creating National Committees, and through them will direct future political developments.[62]

Having received the message, the Foreign Office noted that what was happening was regrettable but already foreseen. By contrast, the British Chiefs of Staff sensibly recommended sending arms to meet the challenge in kind though not to encourage a general insurrection. But their recommendation was never implemented to the extent necessary to forestall the development that the agents in the field had predicted.[63]

There was a distinct pattern in Stalin's attitude toward resistance movements anywhere on the Red Army's prospective path of advance. The Soviet Union would withhold material support until the advance became imminent; even then, the gathering of intelligence and sabotage activities would take precedence over any mass action. Striving to prevent the emergence of any power unaccountable to Moscow, the Russian-sponsored partisans would try to organize a political underground that could subsequently function as a Soviet arm in the liberated country. In 1944, the defeat of the Polish and Slovak insurgencies therefore served Stalin's purposes as much as did the absence of a similar upheaval in the Czech lands. At the same time, the doomed uprisings influenced in crucial ways the attitudes of the peoples concerned and ultimately their status within the Soviet orbit as well.

In the ruins of Warsaw, the romantic Polish propensity for gallant but hopeless resistance succumbed along with the elite of old Poland, and a new pragmatism was born. The dual experience of Soviet cynicism and Nazi barbarity proved a sobering lesson for the nation in general and its new ruling elite in particular. Nowhere in Soviet eastern Europe would the veneer of the Communists' devotion to their official creed be as thin as in Poland, and nowhere would the abuses of Stalinism be more effectively mitigated by leniency. The frightful memories that the Communists shared with the rank and file of their compatriots sealed an unwritten compact between the rulers and the ruled: to make life livable again, certain minimum standards of civility had to be maintained.

In a different sense, the Slovak revolt marked a formative second stage in the coming of age of one of Europe's youngest nations, after the first stage of its flawed yet not meaningless statehood under German sponsorship. Here the dual experience finally helped to create the necessary prerequisites for a genuine, though far from mutually relished, partnership between the Czechs and the Slovaks in the same state. In 1968, the memory and myth of the uprising would provide a vital inspiration for the Slovak drive for the state's federalization, one of the few lasting achievements of that year's reform movement cut short by Soviet intervention.

In 1944, of course, not even Stalin, for all his fabled prescience, could anticipate these consequences. What mattered at the moment was the fact that the Russians, having found it politically advantageous to curtail their military operations on the northern tier of the front, were now free to turn to the Balkans instead.

The Balkan Machinations

Even before events in Poland and Slovakia sealed the decision, the Russians had considered turning south. As reported by Chuikov, on the eve of the Normandy landings they had canceled their plans to advance into Romania. Although the subsequent launching of a general offensive had again revived the option, the Soviet High Command made the decision only on July 31. Two days later, it scheduled an attack on the Romanian front for August 20.[64]

As the stage was set for a massive Soviet thrust into Europe, Churchill became increasingly worried about the Red Army

195

"spreading like a cancer from one country to another."[65] With Germany's defeat assured, he therefore sought to check the spread; now his continued advocacy of a Western attack through Europe's "soft underbelly" in the south acquired the overwhelmingly political rationale it had not had before. On May 5, 1944, Eden suggested to Gusev that Britain and Russia let each other take the lead in different parts of the Balkans—the former in Greece, the latter in Romania.[66] The Russians were not averse to the idea, but they delayed action while professing concern about American disapproval of an arrangement smacking of spheres of influence. In the meantime, they pursued their own intricate machinations in different parts of southeast Europe.

As far as Romania is concerned, for their separate reasons both Soviet and Romanian authors have been notably uninformative about the extent to which Moscow manipulated the country's feeble Communist underground. The former have been too uneasy about the difficulties inherent in the effort, the latter overly eager to downgrade any foreign influence. It is known, however, that in the spring of 1944 the Russians sent in their trusted man, Emil Bodnăraş, a former Romanian army officer of Ukrainian parentage who had later become a Soviet citizen and secret police operative. Shortly after he made his appearance, the party leadership was purged. The victims included especially Ştefan Foriş, a dark figure reputed to be its liaison to the Antonescu regime.[67]

The purge followed Moscow's abortive efforts to elicit Antonescu's surrender and coincided with its offer of armistice terms to the Cairo representatives of his domestic opponents, at the time of the Red Army's incursion into Moldavia. Under Bodnăraş's watchful eye, and thus presumably with full Soviet blessing, the party then embarked on a policy aimed at securing substantive influence in the government that would emerge after Antonescu was overthrown, which seemed more and more likely to happen. The Communists managed to establish a link with the royal palace, where dissident generals had been plotting a coup d'état with King Michael's support.

On June 13–14, Bodnăraş and several of his comrades took part in the formation of a secret military committee entrusted with the preparations. A week later, they also concluded a political agreement with Maniu and other opposition politicians. This provided for a "National Democratic Bloc," one of those embryonic "national fronts" that finally started cropping up in eastern Europe as the Russian shadow approached. No understanding had been reached, however, about the form of the prospective government. The Communists wanted a civilian coalition, in which their party would be strongly represented as one of four; their partners preferred a "non-political" military regime. [68]

No doubt capitalizing on the king's need to improve the tarnished image of the monarchy in Soviet eyes, the Communists acquired an influence far beyond that warranted by their numbers. At the end of July, they pressed their partners to carry out the coup without further delay, or else they would go ahead independently. [69] Although this was no more than an empty threat, their chief ideologist, Lucreţiu Pătrăşcanu, was then entrusted with the important task of drawing up the royal proclamations the conspirators intended to issue after Antonescu's downfall. [70]

Nevertheless, Communist representatives were excluded both from the final decision that set the date of the coup and from its actual execution on August 23. Prompted by the Soviet offensive launched three days before, the overthrow of Antonescu was mainly the king's work. [71] Only afterward did the Communists support his action, and Pătrăşcanu joined the new government directed by the military. However, the Russians unmistakably disapproved; for many years, Stalinist historiography would pass over the August 23 events in studied silence. [72] And Pătrăşcanu, hunted down by Stalin's stooges, would eventually pay with his life.

From the Soviet point of view, what went wrong in Romania? Although Bodnăraş, Moscow's man on the scene, had been intimately involved in the party's policy during all the critical stages, nothing is known about his ability to communicate with the Russians, and circumstantial evidence indicates rather imperfect coordination. According to a report that American intelligence agents received from a supposedly reliable Romanian source in May, the Russians were readying an alternative Communist government in the town of Ştefăneşti in occupied Moldavia;[73] if they were, the Communist participation in the Bucharest conspiracy would not have fitted their plans. Nor is the *ex post* projection of a putative conflict between "nationalist" and "Muscovite" Communists a plausible one; the contemporary evidence shows no traces of such a conflict. And significantly, Bodnăraş remained in the good graces of not only the Stalinists but their nationalist successors as well.

In all probability, Moscow, having originally guided the Communists toward sharing power with the anti-Antonescu conspirators, later discarded the scheme. Stalin may have doubted all along the Communists' ability to gain influence in any regime that was not Russian-made. Or, more likely, he changed his mind when he decided to overrun the country by force, after its failure to surrender in the spring of 1944. By July 31 at the latest—the day the Red Army's offensive was scheduled—he must have concluded that he should not owe anyone gratitude for assistance, certainly not the king, but not the Communists either. Possibly he wanted to install a Soviet military administration without tolerating any Romanian government whatsoever; the Russian chauvinism and condescension toward Romanians, evident in Moscow's propaganda at that time, would seem to support this conclusion.[74] Yet in the end, though the king's action thwarted the apparent design, both Moscow and the local Communists benefited handsomely; perhaps that is why Bodnăraş, the central figure in all these happenings, survived so well.

Having ordered the Romanian army to cease resistance, the king enabled the Russians to sweep through the country to the borders of Bulgaria, Yugoslavia, and Hungary. The Romanians then joined the Soviet side and fought the Germans for the rest of the war. Cooperation by the royal authorities further spared the

conquerors the necessity of relying either on a military administration or on the services of the 1,000 or so Communists available
for the job (according to an authoritative party estimate). But the
Communists, thriving on Romania's endemic corruption and nep-
otism, quickly increased their numbers.[75] This helped to set the
traditionally misruled country on the way to becoming the Soviet
dependency that Stalin desired and they hoped to run on his
behalf.

If Stalin had originally found it difficult to manipulate the
politics of a hostile Romania by remote control, with only a tiny
fifth column, in Bulgaria the task was easier. Besides the people's
pro-Russian sentiments, he could rely on an influential, though
hardly formidable, Communist party. Having recovered from the
calamities it had suffered two years earlier, by 1944 the party
had built up a force of some 10,000 guerrillas who were a nuisance,
even if not a serious threat, to the government. The Communists
also dominated the Fatherland Front, formed the previous September and now the most important grouping of clandestine political opposition. Kept in line by numerous Moscow emissaries, the
Bulgarian Communists offered the Soviet Union a leverage unparalleled anywhere in Europe.[76]

Soon after Teheran, the Russians had adopted a hard line
toward the Sofia government, ignoring its efforts to placate them.
Charging collusion with Germany, they demanded that Bulgaria
allow them to establish additional consulates in the country as a
proof to the contrary.[77] They also proved singularly unhelpful in
dealing with Anglo-American requests to mediate a termination of
Bulgaria's state of war with the Western powers. Disingenuously,
Vyshinskii argued that the Soviet Union could be of no assistance
since it was not at war with Bulgaria.[78] Publicly drawing a distinction between a bad government and a good people, Moscow appeared to wish to be regarded by the Bulgarians as a savior—
without prejudice to claiming substantive rewards, such as military bases, in return.[79]

Because of the Bulgarian Communists' special role as Soviet

agents, their relationship with the government may be regarded as a fairly reliable barometer of Moscow's designs in the country. In June, the new Premier Ivan Bagrianov appointed as Minister of Agriculture Doncho Kostov, who had been educated in the Soviet Union and had only recently returned home. The Communists, though not the Moscow radio, immediately stopped attacking the regime. But after a mere two weeks, Kostov was dropped from office just as mysteriously as he had ascended, whereupon they turned hostile again.[80] If, as the sequence of events suggests, there had been a deal in the making between Bagrianov and the Communists, then Moscow was not unequivocally bent on removing the government with their help. Even after the presumed deal had failed, the Soviet effort to block discussion about armistice terms for Bulgaria in the European Advisory Commission shows that Stalin was biding his time.[81]

Only the Romanian coup of August 23, by suddenly opening the road toward Bulgaria, prompted the Russians to act; even so, their action seems to have been not premeditated but improvised, and brilliantly so. Three days after the Bucharest events, Molotov informed Harriman and Clark Kerr that he had been recently advised by the Sofia government about its intention to disarm all German troops on Bulgarian territory. He added approvingly that this gave substance to its recent declaration of neutrality, a judgment seconded by the Soviet press.[82] On the same day, Bulgarian party liaison men took off from Russia for their homeland (they never arrived, because their plane crashed en route).[83] And on August 29, in the EAC, Gusev stated categorically that he could no longer "take part in the discussion of the terms of Bulgarian surrender."[84] The apparent common denominator of all these moves was a desire to take Bagrianov under the Soviet wing, presumably in return for concessions that would assure his government's subservience.

However, if the Russians were satisfied with the declaration of neutrality, the British were not. Since the Balkan War of 1913, Churchill especially had been harboring an extraordinary grudge against the Bulgarians, as he again proved by the tirade he delivered in the House of Commons on August 2, 1944:

Thrice thrown into wars on the wrong side by a miserable set of criminal politicians, who seem to be available for their country's ruin generation after generation, three times in my life has this wretched Bulgaria subjected a peasant population to all the pangs of war and chastisements of defeat. . . . What would be the place of Bulgaria at the judgment seat, when the petty and cowardly part she has played in this war is revealed . . . ?[85]

Accordingly, on August 29 Clark Kerr handed Molotov an urgent note asking that Moscow take a clear position against the Bulgarian declaration of neutrality.[86]

The Russians complied only too readily. In a striking reversal of Molotov's previously expressed opinion, on August 30 they charged in a Tass statement that the declaration was "completely inadequate."[87] More important, two days later they demanded that the Bagrianov government allow Soviet troops to enter Bulgaria in pursuit of the Germans, a demand which the Premier's resignation left unanswered. Finally, Soviet planes dropped arms to the Communist partisans (for the first time since the beginning of the war), thus encouraging them to act.[88] In short, on or about August 30 Stalin had changed his policy, and the British intransigence toward Bulgaria's quest for neutrality had triggered the change.

Soviet sources, usually so emphatic in their insistence on Moscow's accurate anticipation of events, make no mention of military preparations against Bulgaria before September; in fact, the Red Army had even been under orders to abstain from reconnaissance across the border.[89] Only in the first days of September was an invasion plan hurriedly drawn up at its command post at Cèrnavoda in Romania.[90] On September 5, the Russians abruptly declared war, on the pretext of Bulgaria's failure to do the same against Germany. Taken by surprise, the British and American ambassadors nodded their approval when informed by Molotov half an hour beforehand.[91] Although London and Washington subsequently resented the peremptory conduct of their Soviet ally, by then they had little choice but to acquiesce.

Timely moves by the Communists assisted the bold Soviet improvisation. On September 2, the day the Russians first demanded entry into Bulgaria, the Sofia party leaders started preparing to seize power in the name of the Fatherland Front. In doing so, they certainly were encouraged although not, as far as can be ascertained, actually directed by Moscow. They had confederates within the new government of Konstantin Muraviev, and one of them, Minister of War General Ivan Marinov, sabotaged the Premier's decision to break relations with Germany. Since Muraviev only managed to implement the decision on September 7, the Communists had an excellent pretext to insist that he quit.[92]

As in Romania, the Russians may not have wanted the government to be overthrown from within, for on September 8 they surprisingly agreed to an armistice request by the very regime the Communists were planning to topple the next day.[93] It is also possible that Stalin doubted whether the Communists were strong enough to carry out the job. In any case, while Moscow seemed to falter at the last minute, the conspirators demonstrated their competence by masterminding on September 9 a classic palace revolt, if not any popular insurrection.

Without bloodshed, the Communists and their associates seized the government buildings in Sofia after they had been unlocked from the inside; the partisans appeared in town only afterward.[94] The swift operation immobilized the otherwise respectable Bulgarian army, which under different circumstances would very likely have resisted the invaders.[95] Proving that nothing succeeds like success, the populace even extended the Russians a moderately enthusiastic welcome. Moscow promptly endorsed the new Fatherland Front regime, which committed the country to fighting against Germany together with the Red Army, and Bulgaria soon became Europe's first Communist-controlled nation outside the Soviet Union.

Bulgaria's sudden metamorphosis from an enemy into an ally had stunned the Yugoslav Communists. It abruptly redefined the terms of both the ancient Serbian–Bulgarian feud over Macedonia, which the Yugoslav and Bulgarian Communists had inherited from their countries' old regimes, and Tito's cherished project of a Balkan union. Substantive differences in outlook surfaced during negotiations between the two parties in Sofia in the fall of 1944: The Yugoslavs pressed for a close federation in which Bulgaria would be one of seven constituent units, the other six being parts of Yugoslavia, among them a unified Macedonia; the Bulgarians preferred a loose bilateral confederation with Yugoslavia as a whole, and Macedonia divided between the two but accorded a measure of autonomy. Despite the differences, a compromise was not out of the question, particularly since the Russians apparently favored it. While expressing a preference for neither variant, they did not discourage the project at that time.[96]

To Stalin, the proposed merger offered an opportunity to employ his staunchly subservient subordinates in Sofia to keep a tighter rein on the disturbingly freewheeling Yugoslavs. When Tito came to Moscow in September 1944, Stalin repeatedly put him down. Presumably because "the bourgeoisie in Serbia was very strong," he urged Tito to come to terms with the royal government by letting some of its supporters share power; the Communists subsequently complied, but without yielding any of their own. With Molotov's assistance, Stalin further played the devious joke of pretending that the British had just landed in Yugoslavia—only to hear with consternation Tito's vow that the partisans would fight them if this ever came true. Without enthusiasm, Tito at least bowed to the Russian wish that the freshly allied Bulgarian troops enter Yugoslavia side by side with the Red Army.[97]

The dread of an Anglo-American landing also haunted the Albanian Communists, whose party was a subsidiary of the Yugoslav

203

one. Upon Tito's prodding, they tried to preclude any adverse consequences of a possible Western military presence by proclaiming, in May 1944, a provisional government patterned after the Yugoslav model. In the Yugoslav scheme of things, Albania, too, was to be integrated in the prospective Balkan union, and the preparations gained momentum after Bulgaria switched alliances. Since July, a Soviet mission had been present but apparently not very active in Albania. Stalin, whose contempt for the Albanians resembled Churchill's for the Bulgarians, was quite content to let Tito treat the country as his own fiefdom.[98] Little did he suspect that in the course of time its resourceful leaders would defy successfully both its Yugoslav and its Russian overlords, only to cling tenaciously to the purest Stalinist regime of all.

Among the Balkan nations where Communists earned a prominent place during the war, Greece is the one where their role has been most distorted by self-serving polemics either exaggerating or minimizing their actual power base. In March 1944, their front organization EAM, the largest and best run of the nation's competing resistance movements, formed a "Political Committee of National Liberation" as its executive arm. But this ambiguous entity, unlike its counterparts in Yugoslavia and Poland, never repudiated the government-in-exile; the Greek comrades were neither strong enough to be that self-assured, nor so desperately weak as to be that reckless.

Responsive to Soviet wishes, conveyed to them through Tito's headquarters, the Greek Communists sought instead to penetrate and eventually dominate the lawful government.[99] In this effort, they were aided by its obvious unpopularity in its present composition, as well as by Soviet diplomacy and propaganda. Shortly after the establishment of the Political Committee, the Russian ambassador to the Greek government in Cairo, Novikov, offered to Vice Premier Georgios Roussos the unsolicited advice that he and his colleagues should free themselves from British tutelage by moving from Egypt to the Communist-held portion of northern Greece and forming a new coalition regime with EAM.[100]

The British proposal about areas of responsibility and the subsequent Soviet thrust into the Balkans posed the issue with urgency. In July, the Russians recalled Novikov from Cairo without appointing a successor, thus indicating that they might shift recognition to EAM. And indeed, later that month they dispatched their mission under Colonel Grigorii Popov to its mountain headquarters. But to everybody's surprise, soon afterward EAM abandoned its long-standing demand for a thorough reorganization of the exiled government, consenting instead to join it in a distinctly inferior status. Popov can plausibly be given credit for browbeating the Communists to cave in, although it is uncertain whether this had been the purpose of his mission all along or whether he had discovered only on the spot the inadequacy of their resources.[101] In any case, their *volte face* signaled a fundamentally negative Soviet assessment of their chances in an area where Britain left no doubt about its determination to back the government.

The Soviet entry into Bulgaria stirred the imagination of Greek Communists, evoking visions of the Red Army's rolling on farther south.[102] Yet the visions failed to materialize; in fact, Moscow toyed with the idea of letting its new Bulgarian friends keep some of the Greek territory they had seized as Hitler's accomplices.[103] Thus the traditionally pro-Russian Bulgaria emerged as the main stronghold of Soviet influence in the Balkans, much as the pro-Russian Czechoslovakia was slated to in central Europe.

In the military sense, however, Hungary was the country "in the center of our interests," as Stalin stressed to his generals in the late summer of 1944.[104] After the collapse of Romania, Hungary held the key to Germany's back door in the south while the front door in the north remained temporarily unusable because of the Warsaw events. In mid-September, the Russians at last delivered their armistice terms to the Hungarians, or so at least the Hungarians thought. Admiral Horthy's confidant Count Vladimir Zichy believed he had received terms approved by Stalin from a Russian colonel who identified himself as Makarov, in the then-liberated part of Slovakia.[105]

According to Zichy's account, the Russians promised to abstain from interference in Hungary's internal affairs and recognize its existing frontiers, provided Budapest would break off with Berlin and allow Soviet troops freedom of movement on Hungarian territory. Makarov supposedly also specified that even if his government temporarily assigned Transylvania to the Romanians, at the peace conference it would still favor conducting a plebiscite there—a credible assertion, as the Red Army barred Bucharest authorities from the area.[106]

When the Hungarians had proved their good faith by sending an armistice delegation to Moscow on October 1, the Russians cast doubt on their own by denying any knowledge of a colonel named Makarov and by presenting much harsher terms than he had spelled out. They particularly insisted that Hungary turn its arms against the Germans at once and withdraw to its prewar frontiers within ten days. But the idea of stabbing an ally in the back was more abhorrent to Horthy, with his old-fashioned sense of honor, than it had been to the Romanians or the Bulgarians, and he hesitated. The Russians had all the power, however; they first applied pressure by invading the country, then released it by agreeing to suspend hostilities, then applied it again by threatening to resume fighting if all their demands were not met within forty-eight hours. By the time this last Soviet ultimatum reached Budapest on October 14, Horthy had decided to yield on all points although in his later memoirs he was too ashamed to admit that he had in fact done so.[107]

In December 1944, Stalin confided to a delegation of Hungarian Communists that if only Horthy had succeeded in disengaging himself from the Germans, he would have kept the admiral in office.[108] This would have made sense, considering the shortage of suitable substitutes. Certainly Stalin could not hope for much from the tiny and inert Communist party. In May 1944, its leaders had made a compact with a few politicians from other parties to form a "Hungarian Front."[109] But there was every reason to deprecate the actual influence of this creation, if indeed the news about it had reached Moscow. By contrast, Horthy (unlike Antonescu and much like Beneš) still enjoyed among his countrymen unmatched, though hardly deserved, prestige as a skillful and wise statesman. Having finally accepted the Soviet armistice terms despite great reluctance, he could be expected to perform quite satisfactorily under Soviet command.

This was the open-ended situation at the time Churchill settled down for his October talks with Stalin to clarify the proposed areas of responsibility. The Prime Minister had come to Moscow reasonably optimistic, for "Uncle Joe has shown himself more forthcoming than ever before," although he believed that "we must strike while the iron is hot."[110] So on the first day, October 9, the two leaders forged the remarkable "percentages agreement" which the Prime Minister later described vividly in his memoirs.

According to that description, Churchill passed a slip of paper to Stalin, which the dictator quickly approved with a tick of his pencil.[111] It set the ratios of Soviet and Western influence as 90:10 in Romania, 10:90 in Greece, 50:50 in Yugoslavia and Hungary, and 75:25 in Bulgaria. Whether judged as a clever move to salvage some Western influence in the area or as a cynical scheme to decide its fate over the heads of the peoples involved, Churchill's initiative has usually been credited with striking a congenial note in Stalin because of its boldness and simplicity.[112] The facts of the episode, however, are not simple, and their reconstruction presents surprises.

To begin with, the official British minutes of the meeting do not mention the bargain.[113] Nor does the Russian record—at least according to a Soviet author who claims to have seen it and who maintains that Churchill merely offered Stalin a "rather dirty and clumsy document," which Stalin virtuously ignored.[114] Yet the notorious slip of paper is in the Prime Minister's files for anyone to see, complete with the penciled tick next to the figures for Romania.[115] Moreover, an early draft of the minutes, preserved among the papers of the British Embassy in Moscow although not in the main Foreign Office file, does include a passage that conforms with the account in Churchill's memoirs but was deleted in the final text.[116] And the Russians certainly knew what had happened, for the day after the Stalin–Churchill encounter, Molotov attempted to revise the percentages at a meeting with Eden. Though much less well known, this sequel is actually more revealing of Stalin's true aims than the original deal in which the Russian ruler had played only a passive role.

Molotov opened the meeting by invoking the Soviet military who, after all their sacrifices, might be disappointed if the shares of influence allotted to their country were not increased.[117] He particularly wanted the percentages in Hungary changed from 50:50 to 75:25 in the Russian favor. Startled, Eden tried to change the subject, but Molotov proceeded to demand 90 percent in Bulgaria. This touched on Britain's prestige as a belligerent of considerably longer standing than the Soviet Union, and Eden rejoined: "We must have more influence there than in Romania." Thus the stage was set for a horsetrading session, as Molotov had undoubtedly hoped from the start.

Delighted at having elicited a response, Molotov promptly proposed 75:25 for Bulgaria, Hungary, and Yugoslavia. When Eden refused, he offered an alternative of 90:10 in Bulgaria, 50:50 in Yugoslavia, with Hungary subject to amendment. Or, perhaps, 75:25, 60:40, 75:25. Then it was Eden's turn to throw in a few numbers: 80:20, 50:50, 75:25. Stalin's aide was ready to accept 50:50 for Yugoslavia, but only if Bulgaria were to be 90:10; or else 60:40 and 75:25 respectively. At this point, the meeting reached a deadlock and was adjourned until the following day, when Molotov returned with his final offer: 80:20 in Hungary and Bulgaria, 50:50 in Yugoslavia.[118] By then Eden had consulted with Churchill, and was no longer willing to bargain; the figures remained in limbo.

At no time did the negotiating partners agree on just what those percentages were supposed to mean. In fact, Churchill, who had started the numbers game, began to hedge as soon as the Russians demonstrated a tendency to take them seriously. On October 11 and 12 he composed two memoranda, one for Stalin and the other for his own government colleagues.[119] He argued, elaborately but tortuously, that the figures were to serve merely as a rough guide about the extent of the respective interests, that they showed how much these interests really coincided, and that in any case they applied for the period of the war only. But if Churchill wavered, Harriman disapproved unequivocally when shown the draft intended for Stalin—probably the reason why the document was never sent, thus perpetuating the ambiguity of the agreement *manqué*.[120]

The Russians did at least try to clarify some of the percentages. Thus Molotov explained to Eden that the 60:40 ratio in Yugoslavia would mean no Soviet interference along the Adriatic coast but a right to exert influence in the interior. As far as Bulgaria was concerned, he interpreted the 80:20 formula as allowing the establishment of a Soviet rather than joint Allied control commission; the Russians would wield effective power while the British and Americans would serve in a merely advisory capacity.[121]

The conversations not only revealed Moscow's different stakes in different countries but also influenced its further aspirations, despite the lack of a definite agreement. Of the countries in question, only Romania and Greece remained unaffected; there was never any discussion about the reciprocal 90:10 formula Churchill had proposed and Stalin readily accepted. There the issues had already been clarified: the British had long been displaying *désintéressement* in Romania, and the Russians had proved equally unwilling to be drawn into the Greek imbroglio.

Nor did the Russians attempt to bargain hard about Yugoslavia, claiming no more than 50–60 percent influence there. Their restraint contrasted with the zeal the Yugoslav Communists displayed in building a state closely fashioned after the Soviet model. To dampen that zeal, which inspired Tito to behave as his partner rather than his underling, Stalin did not mind letting the British try to exercise their share of influence; from his conversation with Tito a month earlier, he knew what was likely to happen. Little though an all-out British–Yugoslav conflict would have been in Soviet interest, any tension short of war promised to put Moscow into the enviable role of arbiter.

In attempting to revise the percentages, Molotov started with Hungary, whose armistice delegation had arrived in Moscow a few days earlier. If the Russians intended to keep Horthy in charge for any length of time, they also undoubtedly wished to retain maximum leverage over him; hence the 75 percent below which Molotov was not prepared to go. In his exchanges with Eden he was actually using the figures for Bulgaria as bargaining chips to obtain Western recognition of Soviet primacy in Hungary. As long as the percentage in Bulgaria remained decisively tilted in Russia's favor, the exact amount did not make much difference; the country was already under Moscow's firm grip anyway.

Before the British left for home, an important, though scarcely ever noticed, understanding had been reached about Hungary and Bulgaria. In effect, though not in so many words, the British professed indifference about the former in return for a promise of influence in the latter. The Russians agreed to Anglo-American participation in the control commission in Sofia and ordered their Bulgarian clients to vacate the territory belonging to Britain's Greek clients. These concessions made possible the conclusion of a final armistice with Bulgaria but in no way impaired the Soviet grip over it.[122] The British could hardly congratulate themselves on their accomplishment. For the sake of an ephemeral role in a country for which Churchill felt little but disgust, they resigned themselves to the status of passive bystanders in

210

Hungary, perhaps the most Anglophile nation in all of east central Europe.

The barter was all the more questionable as Stalin seemed prepared to share with the West the liberation of Hungary. On October 14, the day he dispatched his ultimatum to Horthy, he suggested to Churchill that the British land in the upper Adriatic and join the Red Army near Vienna.[123] This was the Prime Minister's favorite idea and also the one to which Stalin had alluded in the trick he had played on Tito. Since the operation would have involved the British in rather difficult fighting across rough terrain while the Russians were planning a quick advance through Hungary, Stalin's suggestion may seem academic. Yet if it had been, why would he have bothered to make it at all, and why would he have reiterated it even after the Russian advance had failed to materialize, as he did more than once?

While Stalin was playing host to the British visitors, news from Budapest foiled his plans. All along the Nazis had been aware of Horthy's Moscow gamble, and on October 15 they struck. They deposed him and installed Ferenc Szálasi, the leader of the Fascist Arrow Cross, who vowed to continue fighting on their side. The outcome forced the Russians to reconsider the fundamental strategic question of whether to direct their main thrust through Hungary or through Poland. It also heralded a prolongation of the war during which the true meaning of the percentages agreement would be tested.

The British and the Russians had played a curious diplomacy, resorting to arithmetic in the quest for an influence that neither wanted to define precisely. Although Churchill had taken the initiative, he abhorred a rigid partition of Europe and hoped to preserve Western influence in its eastern part; at the same time, his posture of a hard-boiled realist masked indecision about both the means and the nature of that influence. To Stalin, the figures did not make much sense either, regardless of Molotov's acrobatics in juggling them up and down; in the last analysis, he sought freedom of action without any agreed limitations no matter

211

how generous. It was not so much an open clash of interests as their dangerously indefinite and elastic nature that jeopardized the wartime alliance in the long run.

The Future of the Alliance

In his famous April 1945 conversation with Djilas, Stalin explained that "this war is not as in the past; whoever occupies a territory also imposes on it his own social system. Everyone imposes his own system as far as his army can reach. It cannot be otherwise."[124] There was much truth in the statement, but not the whole truth. While the war still continued the Russians had choices: Which territories should they try to occupy first and which should be possibly left unoccupied? How far should the Red Army try to reach? And wherever it did reach, to what extent should Stalin impose "his own system" there? These were important questions for him and for his coalition partners, too.

Soviet conduct in Poland and the Balkans bred in the West the suspicion that a fundamental change of policy had taken place in Moscow and fostered doubts about the future of the coalition. By September 1944, the top British military no longer held "the slightest faith in the Anglo-Soviet Alliance."[125] And Harriman, who had come to Moscow the year before with his mind wide open and had since been inclined to give the Russians the benefit of the doubt, now became one of the first American officials prepared to face the disconcerting realities.[126] In his ever more urgent dispatches to Washington he warned that the Soviet Union might become "a world bully."[127] "What frightens me," he wrote,

is that when a country begins to extend its influence by strong arm methods beyond its borders under the guise of security it is difficult to see how a line can be drawn. If the policy is accepted that the Soviet

Union has a right to penetrate her immediate neighbors for security, penetration of the next immediate neighbors becomes at a certain time equally logical.[128]

The question of how the Soviet leadership handled its choices was one of personalities and of issues. Eden believed that a great debate was under way in the Kremlin, pitting against each other adherents of "imperialist" and "collaborationist" schools, the latter "fortunately" including Stalin.[129] But Harriman thought that the dictator himself was "of two minds," undecided amidst conflicting advice about whether he should consolidate Soviet power in cooperation with the West or exploit whatever opportunities Europe's disintegration offered to expand that power.[130] And Kennan wondered whether the secluded tyrant might actually be manipulated by competing members of his coterie who used their control over the flow of information he received for pursuing their selfish interests.[131]

Focusing on those interests, later interpreters have tended to view the putative clash of opinions as one involving not personalities but groups, which the different protagonists presumably represented.[132] The war had played havoc with established relationships among the main pillars of Soviet society. The cadres of the party had been decimated and then diluted by an influx of newcomers, mostly young. The army had increased enormously in size and prestige. The formidable task of reconstruction had enhanced the prominence of the managerial establishment. And the police had become more necessary to keep all the changes from getting out of hand. But the question remains: Could these potential pressure groups have possibly coalesced under the conditions of Stalin's terror to effectively influence specific policy decisions?[133]

From what is known today about Stalin's style of decision-making, it appears that he seldom made up his mind in advance, or if he did he would not immediately reveal his choice even to his associates. His style was bizarre; he would sometimes handle important business during his extravagant nocturnal feasts with his cronies.[134] But he also held more conventional meetings, particularly with his generals, and sought advice in an orderly manner.[135] On foreign affairs he consulted Molotov especially, one of the few persons with whom he was on a first-name basis.[136] The pervasive fear that was the hallmark of the dictatorship hardly encouraged even his closest aides to speak their minds freely. Still, although he thus deprived himself of the full range of opinions, he did get the range he wanted, and within these limits there was room for debate as long as he remained undecided.

Among the issues to be decided, the possible annexation of lands beyond the June 1941 border must have arisen even before the Red Army crossed that line.[137] When the Russians first reentered the territories they had seized in 1939–1940, they took a step that would ease the eventual admission of new members into the Soviet Union. In February 1944, they ceremoniously passed a constitutional amendment which on paper granted the existing republics impressive privileges, including the right to conduct their foreign relations and to organize their defense.

Bestowing the paraphernalia of sovereignty on the hapless union republics was to make the then-imminent reannexation of the Baltic states more palatable to the West. In addition, the elevation of the Ukraine and Belorussia to pseudo-sovereign entities enabled Stalin to pretend that there were forces pressing him for incorporation of the parts of Poland that would be added to the two territories.[138] In front of Western representatives, he liked to invoke Ukrainian and other ethnic lobbies which he allegedly had to heed.[139]

Even if these phantom lobbyists were none other than Stalin himself, the upsurge of nationalism among the non-Russian peoples of his realm was very real, as was the decline of the Russians' numerical preponderance as a result of their higher war losses. These were matters of no small importance to such an ardent Russian nationalist as Stalin, and ultimately they ruled out the option of further annexations. Soviet imperialism took the pattern of subordinating nominally sovereign states.

An economic imperative reinforced that pattern: the need to exploit the conquered lands to alleviate the devastation that the Soviet Union had suffered. Opinions in the Kremlin apparently were sharply divided about the best course to take, specifically in Germany, which was the main prize. According to high-ranking Soviet defectors, Georgii M. Malenkov (who in 1944 headed a "Special Committee for the Economic Disarmament of Germany") urged Stalin to summarily strip the vanquished of their valuables. But Andrei A. Zhdanov and Anastas A. Mikoyan (respectively, Stalin's top ideological and foreign trade aides) are said to have disagreed on both political and practical grounds.[140] The split suggests that Stalin withheld decision, pending clarification of other aspects of the perplexing German problem.

The question of where the resources for postwar Soviet reconstruction were to be found inevitably affected the relations with the West, especially the wealthy United States—the only nation capable of satisfying Russia's vast needs. Was there a correlation between the American willingness to meet those needs and the Soviet disposition to squeeze the eastern Europeans? In January 1945, when Molotov told Harriman that the Russians desired a $6 billion American loan, with a low interest and easy terms of repayment, he astoundingly presented the request as something of a favor.[141] He implied that the loan would help the United States out of the economic trouble which, according to Marxist writ, was bound to follow the end of the war.

The request was not readily entertained by the Americans, but neither was it persistently pursued by the Russians, thus showing a curiously distorted practical effect of the Marxist theory about the primacy of economics over politics. In accordance with the doctrine, the Soviet leaders have always been acutely sensitive to economic dependence as a harbinger of political dependence. Yet precisely because of their economic weakness, they

215

would also do whatever they could to defy the dogma; so, too, in their relations with other countries they would take pains to act as if they labored under no economic constraints at all. In their quest for an empire, any expected material rewards were therefore a secondary benefit rather than a primary cause; accordingly, any Western belief that the Soviet conduct in that part of Europe could be substantially influenced by purely economic devices was an illusion.[142]

It was not the same with political devices, however, as suggested by the Russian alarm over the projected western European bloc that Britain began actively promoting in the summer of 1944. In the original concept, expounded by Belgian Foreign Minister Paul-Henri Spaak in his March 1944 memorandum for the Foreign Office, close association of the small states in the area was to counter the trend toward spheres of influence and eventually facilitate integration of Europe as a whole.[143] For their part, the British, particularly their top military, had embraced the project as a deterrent to Russian expansion rather than as a means to prevent partition of the continent, although the Foreign Office emphasized that every effort must be made to preserve Soviet friendship.[144] The Russians viewed with similar apprehension De Gaulle's alternative plan for western Europe's organization under French auspices.[145]

Did the Western integration efforts precipitate Stalin's regimentation of the countries under his own influence?[146] Having written off western Europe as a negligible quantity, he perceived any resurgence of its strength as a threat. Besides, by pitting the principle of voluntary association against that of forcible subordination, the western European example threatened to expose the fragility of the new order he envisaged for eastern Europe. But Stalin's regimentation efforts had antedated the Western project. In his mind, the project may have aggravated but it had hardly created the problems he encountered in his new domain; those problems were of local origin rather than imported.

The point at issue was whether indirect control—something

Stalin had never tried before—could work, and the docility of the Russian people may have made him overly optimistic. In the lands they overran, the Russians initially behaved as if they thought their time was limited. Not only did they carry away much of what they could. They also tried to enforce sufficient, but not excessive, internal transformation to prevent a later growth of hostile influences. While the Red Army was on the spot, they and their local helpers therefore pushed through measures calculated to break the back of the classes believed to be mainstays of such influences: punishment of individual "collaborators," land reform, partial nationalization of economy, the establishment of "national committees."

But despite massive Soviet support, the eastern European Communists often found it hard to prevail; they sometimes could not control even the institutions they had created. The Lublin regime, for example, soon decided to run Poland by using the old system of administration rather than the newly established local councils; a struggle for power occurred also in the national committees in Slovakia.[147] In Romania, the post-Antonescu government, though obedient to Soviet wishes, resisted pressure by the Communist party and frustrated its November 1944 bid for the crucial Ministry of the Interior.[148]

The comparison with Bulgaria, where the Communists already held the reins of power, is instructive. As early as the fall of 1944, the Sofia leaders with Soviet connivance went the farthest in introducing the methods of Stalin's "own system." This meant that those who dared to resist, often with a courage bordering on abandon, were ruthlessly crushed. Even before the war ended, more persons were executed in Bulgaria for alleged war crimes than anywhere else in Europe, despite the country's modest contribution to the German cause.[149] But how much terror could Stalin afford to apply in his dependencies before wrecking his alliance with Britain and the United States? Although the West saw its leverage as severely limited, he was far from oblivious of the linkage.

217

Stalin showed his concern in his response to the American plan for a world organization, the future United Nations. When Roosevelt first tentatively outlined it to him at Teheran, Stalin sought to clarify his freedom of action toward small nations in view of possible interference by the world body.[150] He was encouraged by the President's intention to have the concept of great-power "policemen" built into the structure of the organization. Still, like Churchill, he would have preferred a regional security system rather than a global one, because a regional system would entail fewer restrictions on the exercise of Soviet power in Europe. In the end, he went along with the American plan.

It has been fashionable to assume that Stalin the realist regarded that plan as little more than an amusing American folly, whose main value lay in enabling him to bargain with its obstinately idealistic sponsors for more substantive concessions in return for his adherence. But precisely because of the central role of this organization in the American scheme of things, the issue involved the entire pattern of future relations with the most powerful nation on earth—something on which the security of his expected war gains might well hinge. Indeed, the Soviet handling of the United Nations project gives the best insight into the question of how the men in the Kremlin managed their critical choices.

The person in charge of Russian postwar planning, with special responsibility for that project, was no less than Maxim Litvinov, the architect of Moscow's prewar collective security schemes and Ambassador to Washington from 1941 to mid-1943. Although his subsequent rank of Assistant Foreign Commissar was not high, his particular duties implied recognition of his expertise in a very important matter. By then, however, Litvinov had begun dissenting from his country's official policies. And since he was not only close to the center of power but also willing to share his dissent with outsiders, he is a unique inside source of information about the workings of the Soviet establishment.[151]

On May 7, 1943, shortly before his final departure from the United States, Litvinov had called on Under Secretary of State

Sumner Welles to express his anxiety about the future of the alliance he had helped to forge.[152] The Soviet diplomat complained that he was unable to communicate with Stalin, whose isolation bred a distorted view of the West and especially an underestimation of Western public opinion. He assured Welles that once back home he would do his best to improve matters but was not at all certain he could accomplish much. Litvinov gave vent to his frustration about the rigidity of the whole Soviet system and particularly about Molotov's tight grip on the Foreign Commissariat. He still abstained from any specific criticism of his superiors' policies.

Back in Moscow, Litvinov became intimately involved with the world organization project in the summer of 1944, when the Second Front and the ensuing Russian offensive had brought victory within sight. In July, Soviet ideas about the scheme that was expected to be a major product of victory were first publicized in an article in the Leningrad magazine *Zvezda* written by "N. Malinin."[153] Four weeks later, Litvinov confirmed the opinion prevalent in Moscow diplomatic circles that he was in fact the author.[154]

The salient points of the article, which was published ostensibly for the purpose of discussion, reappeared with the stamp of official approval in the August 12 memorandum the Soviet government prepared for the conference at Dumbarton Oaks, which was to lay the foundations of the future United Nations.[155] Acknowledging the urgent need to replace the anemic League of Nations with a more vigorous body, both statements stressed that the key to its success was in the proper application of the principle of unanimity. This meant that the ability of small nations to make the organization into a vehicle of their selfish interests would be effectively curtailed. The pursuit of such interests by the great powers, however, was to be dignified by their prerogative to veto any decisions they disliked. As Litvinov later explained privately, "this was our way of demanding a guarantee of equality, a guarantee against combinations, and a rejection of the balance of power system."[156]

Further concerns and aspirations permeated both the article and the memorandum. The Russians wanted the world body to limit its activities strictly to security matters, leaving economic and social issues outside of its purview. This would reduce the danger of exposing their rigidly controlled but disrupted economy to the potentially unsettling impact of the more robust free enterprise system of the West. Similarly, the exclusion of social questions from the agenda would help to shelter Soviet society from undesirable international scrutiny. It would also facilitate Moscow's manipulation of foreign Communist parties whose activities could be justified in Marxist terms as resulting from social tensions. But it was the issue of the veto that the Russians regarded as crucial and that eventually caused the Dumbarton Oaks conference to end in an impasse that was barely smoothed over by high-sounding generalities.

On August 22, when the conference was still in session but its breakdown was already visible, Litvinov in Moscow hinted at a disagreement between his recommendations and the official policy. He told Norwegian Minister Rolf O. Andvord that he wished the views he had expressed in *Zvezda* were those of the Soviet government but that unfortunately his government favored a looser international organization.[157] Six weeks later, he elaborated on the nature of those differences in a revealing off-the-record interview with the American leftist journalist, Edgar Snow.[158] Litvinov explained that his original plan had been discarded and that at Dumbarton Oaks Gromyko had instead pulled out of his pocket an altogether different scheme. Worse still, no attempt had been made to consult Washington and London about it in advance. These were, according to the veteran diplomat, the true reasons why the conference turned out to be such a fiasco.

Litvinov's explanation was not entirely fair. He may not have known that the memorandum had been forwarded to the two Western governments through diplomatic channels a week before the conference opened. Moreover, its contents were not all that different from the *Zvezda* article, and outsiders failed to notice any break in continuity.[159] But the August 12 document did omit one of Litvinov's original suggestions: that the world organization be reinforced by a special pact binding the Big Three particularly closely together. The omission might seem all the more surprising since Stalin was definitely attracted to the idea of a new *Dreikaiserbündnis*, which was congenial to Roosevelt's pet notion of "world policemen" as well. In a conversation with Mikołajczyk on August 9, Stalin praised the "sword" about to be forged at Dumbarton Oaks to safeguard future peace.[160] He was, of course, alluding to a prospective concert of the giants rather than to any cacophony of the dwarfs that would fill the halls of the United Nations by their sheer numbers. Nevertheless, the Russians failed to submit any specific proposal to institutionalize the concert.

Whether there had indeed been a shift of policy (as Litvinov suggested) or whether Moscow had merely vacillated (which is more likely), the Russian behavior underscored a dilemma: Should the Soviet Union anchor its relationship with the West in an institutional framework conducive to closer collaboration but implying also greater commitment? Or should it forego the benefits and responsibilities of such collaboration, seeking instead the greatest possible freedom from compulsion in a loose system built on the prerogative of the veto? Not only Litvinov but also other Soviet diplomats sensed that a watershed had been reached. Interpreter Berezhkov has recalled a long, anxious conversation he had at Dumbarton Oaks with Arkadii Sobolev, another member of the Russian delegation, concluding that "nothing good could come from a sharpening of the conflict."[161] Yet the conflict was already sharpening as a result of Stalin's policy of imposing in eastern Europe a political order to his own liking; the impact of the Warsaw uprising, which was nearing its melancholy end at that time, is a case in point.

Litvinov did not question that particular policy. He nourished no tender feelings for small nations, least of all the Poles, among whom he had grown up. He once told Harriman "it was unreasonable to consider that the interests of 30 million Poles should be given equal weight with those of 180 million Russians. Where the interests of the Russians conflicted with those of the Poles, the Poles would have to give way."[162] He astonished the ambassador by the intensity of his feelings against not only the Polish government but also the Polish people.[163] While Warsaw was dying of Stalin's neglect, Litvinov stressed to Edgar Snow that he might disagree with his "government on many things, but we are absolutely right about Poland. In fact we have been too lenient if anything." The Soviet statesman instead castigated what he regarded as the "revival of British traditional diplomacy in Europe . . . , this time fully backed up by America." In his opinion,

Britain has never been willing to see a strong power on the continent . . . without organizing a counterforce against it. The idea of collaborating with the strong power is alien to her thinking. She is at work in France and the Lowlands doing that already. She will want to use her occupation of Germany for the same ends.[164]

Litvinov was referring to the proposed western European bloc; he also was already predicting that "we won't be able to agree on a common program for Germany." But, cautioning Snow repeatedly that he was speaking merely for himself, he was by no means inclined to put all the blame on others. Admitting regretfuly that "we are drifting more and more in the same direction," he suggested that "diplomacy might have been able to do something to avoid it if we had made our purposes clear to the British and if we had made clear the limits of our needs, but now it is too late, suspicions are rife on both sides." Trying to account for this conspicuous negligence by his government, he singled out startling deficiencies of some of its leading representatives.

Among the most revealing passages of Litvinov's long chat with Snow was his lament that the Foreign "Commissariat is run by only three men and none of them understand America or Britain," namely Molotov and his deputies Vyshinskii and Vladimir G. Dekanozov. Deploring the trio's disastrously parochial outlook, he commented that Dekanozov, the former ambassador to Nazi Germany, "sat next to Ribbentrop for a year and that's all he knows about foreign countries." Although Litvinov did not mention Stalin by name, he hinted that the supreme leader also was prone to misconceptions, especially by reading too much into unfriendly statements in the free Western press. Implying that the responsibility for cultivating these misconceptions rested not so much with the dictator himself as with his entourage, he concluded that "absolutely the only way . . . to improve matters" was by direct talks between Stalin and Roosevelt.

Litvinov worried lest the President might be exposed to similar prejudicial influences from his respective aides. Giving proof that the gist of Harriman's recent alarming messages to Washington was no secret among Soviet officials, Litvinov implored Snow not to mention their conversation to anyone in Moscow, especially not to the American Ambassador. Snow complied. Only after his return to the United States two months later did he send the record of the interview to Roosevelt personally. The President replied graciously that he was "tremendously interested" but had the document filed without taking further action on it. [165]

To sum up the emerging trends in the fall of 1944, there was no quarrel between Litvinov and Stalin, both ardent devotees of power politics, about the axiom that the Soviet Union could and indeed should advance its international status by whatever means it saw fit. Neither saw anything wrong with twisting the arms of weaker nations except if relations with the stronger ones might suffer excessive damage as a result. The crux of the matter was not the desirability of an empire (that was now taken for granted) but rather the ways and means of its possible integration into an international order compatible with the Western notions. To Litvinov, Anglo-American support of any settlement his government would wish to enforce in east central Europe was indispensable for Russia's true security. Keenly aware of the depth of Western sympathy for his country's security needs, he was also convinced that such support could be obtained if only the limits of those needs were stated sensibly and clearly enough.

Nor was Stalin, a cautious tyrant despite all his excesses, rushing headlong to set his exhausted country on a collision course with its mighty coalition partners. Although inclined by nature and experience to expect the worst, he was not so reckless that he would ignore all opportunities to avert it. Eager to both have the cake of Western cooperation and eat his eastern Europeans too, he temporized in searching for a solution. Meanwhile it was in his paramount interest not to discourage subordinates from formulating their ideas on the subject, certainly not such knowledgeable ones as Litvinov.

This was all the more advisable since the men in the dictator's closer entourage, particularly Molotov and his assistants, had a vested interest in stressing obstacles to any long-term accommodation with the West. After all, they were the ones entrusted with the actual conduct of policy and, consequently, were vulnerable to being singled out (in conformity with Stalin's familiar habit) as scapegoats for its possible failure. As long as their taskmaster did not make up his mind, they were therefore the primary agents of that fateful drift which he abetted, to Litvinov's growing alarm.

The empire that Nazi folly and Western forbearance had prompted Stalin to seek was his triumph and his nemesis. By military action and inaction, he had by the fall of 1944 secured Russia's supremacy in all the countries he regarded as vital for its security, and beyond. However, on the issue of how the West could be persuaded to sanction that supremacy permanently, the Soviet ruler showed a disturbing reluctance to define the extent of his inflated security needs. Nor did the Western powers act with the necessary determination to clarify the extent of their tolerance, Churchill's elusive percentages deal notwithstanding. They would all have a further chance at another summit meeting, on whose success the future of the alliance now hinged.

chapter seven

The Hopes and Blows of Yalta
October 1944–April 1945

The Expectations

On October 19, 1944, the day Churchill left Moscow, Stalin at last responded favorably to Roosevelt's long-standing invitation to hold another meeting of the Big Three.[1] He was particularly attracted by Hopkins's idea that it take place on Soviet territory along the Black Sea coast. Although nearly four months were to elapse before the chiefs of state actually met at Yalta, in the meantime a whole new range of Russian policies showed Stalin's expectations after the failure of his Hungarian scheme had compelled him to improvise.

In his message to Roosevelt, the Soviet leader anticipated holding the conference as early as the end of November. At that time, he still hoped to reverse the verdict in Hungary. On October 28, he ordered an immediate capture of Budapest "for political reasons," even though his commander in the field, Marshal Rodion Ia. Malinovskii, warned that this was not feasible.[2] Malinovskii was right. After the attempt had failed, operations on the eastern front slowed down in early November. Later that month, Stalin readily accepted Roosevelt's proposal that the meeting take place after the President's January 20 inauguration for a fourth term.[3] By then, the necessary readjustment of Soviet plans had already started.

Aside from the military slowdown, the last days of October and the beginning of November were filled with events. In the United States this was the time of the presidential election. The Russians had been anticipating it with obvious, though unnecessary, anxiety, only to be much relieved by Roosevelt's landslide victory.[4] Meanwhile in Moscow the top brass of the Red Army conferred on future strategy and the ambassadors to London and Washington, Gusev and Gromyko, were summoned for consultations. The German Communist émigrés, who had been working since January on the postwar plan of action in their country, finally completed the job.[5] Concerning Hungary and Czechoslovakia important decisions were reached, which had immediate and visible consequences.

On November 13, the Russians approved a request by Horthy's forlorn armistice delegation that a provisional government be formed in the liberated part of Hungary.[6] They directed the Hungarian Communists to prepare a program which envisioned a multiparty system, guarantees for private enterprise, and a land reform favorable to independent farmers—a program the Horthyist generals found quite congenial.[7] The ensuing provisional government, installed in Debrecen in December, proved a rather respectable body consisting of several men of the old regime, many moderates, and only two Communists. In organizing the provincial and local administration, however, the Communists exercised decisive influence as confidants of the Soviet occupation authorities.

The Red Army's advance into Hungary was marked by widespread mistreatment of civilians by the invading troops. Moreover, the final armistice agreement that Moscow imposed on January 20, 1945, was onerous. It saddled Hungary with crippling reparation payments and confined it to its narrow prewar frontiers.[8] But matters could have been worse if, for example, the Russians had heeded the Czechoslovak suggestion to insert in the armistice a clause providing for expulsion of Magyar inhabitants from the lost territories.[9] All things considered, Stalin did not seem intent on treating the Hungarians much more harshly than their Finnish "cousins."

If Soviet policy toward hostile Hungary was more restrained than expected, the opposite came to be true about Stalin's showpiece "friendly" state, Czechoslovakia. No sooner had the Red

Army overrun the Carpathian Ukraine at the end of October than mass rallies (supposedly spontaneous but actually masterminded by Soviet agents) began to clamor for its unification with the Soviet Ukraine. Radio Kiev promptly seconded the demand, and representatives of the Beneš government found it impossible to reassert their authority in the province.[10] Evidently Stalin now raised by proxy a new territorial demand beyond those already on record. What were his motives for doing so?

If the Soviet ruler wished to probe "soft spots," the Carpathian Ukraine was an ideal one. Although it had never belonged to Russia, its inhabitants were Ukrainians. When their homeland reverted to Hungary in 1939, thousands had preferred to escape into Soviet territory once this had been extended to their borders as a result of the Stalin–Hitler pact.[11] In the following years, the Carpathian Ukraine proved less hospitable to anti-Soviet nationalist guerrillas than were other Ukrainian-populated areas.[12] Even so, the majority of its politically unsophisticated population would have probably liked best to return to the paternalistic Czech rule; the Czechs, however, were not eager to resume it.

The Carpathian Ukraine was no prize. An economic liability to any owner, it seemed a convenient item to trade for Russian friendship. As early as 1939, Beneš had indicated to Maiskii his lack of strong feelings about the territory. In December 1943, he had hinted to Korneichuk that it might be for sale, though better after the war than immediately.[13] And during his subsequent Moscow visit, he had supposedly told Stalin that the Russians could have it if they wanted to. Although the evidence is inconclusive, the Soviet leader reportedly refused the offer at that time.[14]

Until the end of October 1944, the Russians behaved as if they wanted the area to remain with Czechoslovakia. They had let the Czechoslovak Communists plan on that assumption.[15] They had signed, in May 1944, the administrative agreement with the Beneš government envisaging the resumption of its authority

227

within the nation's pre-Munich boundaries. As late as October 26, the Soviet press publicized (with implied approval) the arrival in the Carpathian Ukraine of the Czechoslovak plenipotentiaries entrusted with the task.[16] The local party boss imported from the Soviet Union, Ivan Turianitsa, began to extoll in his public appearances the bright prospects of living with the Czechs and Slovaks in the same state.[17] The separatist activities only started on October 29—a timing indicating a sudden decision rather than premeditation.[18]

Although outright incorporation of a land which in 1939 had served as a potential "Piedmont" of Ukrainian nationalism had a symbolic value for Stalin, this can hardly explain the reversal of his policy. His true motives should instead be sought in his current imperatives. With the failure of the Hungarian armistice scheme in mid-October, he lost the last incentive to assign Transylvania to Hungary; if Transylvania were to go to Romania, the only direct Soviet access to Hungary would be through the Carpathian Ukraine. And if Stalin was ready to risk keeping in Hungary a regime in which the Communists would maintain a low profile, as the experiment with the Debrecen government indicates he was, such an access would seem all the more desirable in case the experiment subsequently did not work.

Another motive was inherent in the Polish situation. Since both London and Washington ignored the Lublin regime's overtures for recognition, the Russians wanted Czechoslovakia to take the lead. They pressed it by generating uncertainty about its territorial integrity: the trouble in its easternmost province had disturbing implications for the future of Slovakia, with its small but significant Ukrainian minority. Beneš, though quite prepared to get rid of the Carpathian Ukraine, grew uneasy about the Soviet behavior and tried to delay action on the Polish issue. But Fierlinger, his own ambassador to Moscow (who was much more Moscow's ambassador to him), reminded him unceremoniously that "in an alliance such as ours, it just would not do if the partners thought they could merely stay correct toward each other." [19] And *Voina i rabochii klass* pointedly censured the President's favorite concept of Czechoslovakia as a bridge between East and West. [20]

In January, Stalin forced the issue. He first elevated the Lublin committee to a full-fledged government. Then, after a conspiratorial meeting with the Czech party chief, Klement Gottwald, he wrote Beneš a letter that was a masterpiece of dissimulation. He feigned indignation at the Czechoslovak government's presumed (though never actually expressed) disapproval of Soviet conduct in the Carpathian Ukraine. Recalling the President's earlier readiness to cede the province, he denounced any interference with the aspirations of its people. The result was not only Beneš's obsequious protestation of good will but also Czechoslovakia's recognition of Lublin five days before the Yalta conference met. [21] (The formal cession of the Carpathian Ukraine to the Soviet Union half a year later only confirmed the already existing situation.)

Poland was the common element in Stalin's successful blackmail of Beneš and his attempted blackmail of De Gaulle. Like his Czech counterpart, the French leader had been seeking a special relationship with Moscow, both to bolster his status in the eyes of the British and Americans and to tame the French Communists. [22] But it was Stalin who went so far as to propose signing a formal alliance during the French leader's forthcoming Russian visit at the beginning of December 1944 (to Churchill, however, Stalin pretended that the initiative had been French). [23] De Gaulle welcomed the proposal and, again like Beneš, prepared a draft modeled after the British–Soviet treaty of 1942. No sooner did he reach the Soviet capital than Stalin demanded recognition of Lublin as the price of the pact.

Although the Soviet and French accounts of the ensuing talks differ in many details, De Gaulle's personality clearly made a great difference in the test of will. Rejecting the price out of hand, he merely consented to send a subordinate officer to Lublin to handle repatriation matters. When Stalin kept insisting, De

Gaulle was ready to go home, treaty or no treaty. But Stalin wanted the pact badly, to keep France out of the projected Western bloc. So in the end he yielded by agreeing to sign without any strings attached; much as he later tried to ridicule De Gaulle's great-power pretensions, he was impressed.[24]

A desire to thwart the irritating Western bloc project also permeated the Soviet attitude during the contemporaneous crisis in Belgium, the home of Paul-Henri Spaak, who most actively promoted the idea. The crisis itself, arising from the refusal of the Communist-dominated resistance forces to submit to a government controlled by politicians who had spent the war in London, was not of Soviet making. The Russians welcomed it, however, and offered propaganda support to the Communist program, in which the rejection of any "one-sided alliances" figured prominently. They singled out for criticism both the Belgian and the Dutch governments, the two in the forefront of the regional integration efforts.[25]

The crisis peaked on November 25 when the Communists marched their followers into downtown Brussels, threatening government buildings. Even though Moscow had not instigated the action, neither did it disapprove of their effort to topple the government—something it had expressly forbidden their French comrades to do three months earlier.[26] The effort failed, not only because the Belgian police forcibly dispersed the demonstrators and British troops stood ready to intervene if necessary, but also because the workers refused to heed the Communist call for a general strike.[27] Only after that sobering lesson did the Russians counsel restraint to the Belgian Communists; yet a few days later, the Greek ones made a similar attempt on a much grander scale.

As in Belgium, the Communist leaders in Greece could not entirely control their followers. Nor did they try very hard, once riots in Athens seemed to offer them a chance to bring down the government they detested. The bid collapsed after the British army intervened to uphold its client regime and Moscow proved both unable and unwilling to assist the Communists. Unlike their Belgian comrades, the Greek Communists would probably have succeeded if left alone, but more because of their ruthlessness than because of the size of their following. Significantly, the royal government reached the peak of its popularity immediately after the suppression of their rebellion.[28]

While considerably more violent and more widely publicized, the Greek situation resembled the Belgian one in three important ways. In both countries, the Communists challenged legitimate governments that were unpopular, though not nearly as much so as appearances suggested. They evidently acted without Soviet authorization, though not against any Soviet orders. They sought to install regimes in which they would exercise important, though not necessarily exclusive or even predominant, influence. For its part, Moscow was prepared to give more moral support to the comrades in Belgium, who sought to frustrate the Western bloc project, than to those in Greece, a country not slated for membership in any regional association. But once their failure became evident, Stalin preferred to stay aloof in both cases, thus building up his credit with the British, which might well be useful later in averting Western intercession on behalf of his own unruly clients.

Against the background of the Belgian and Greek events, another important article under the familiar pseudonym of "N. Malinin" appeared in *Voina i rabochii klass* in mid-December, concerning the subject of "regionalism."[29] The author again was most likely Litvinov, who two months earlier had hinted to Snow that this was a further issue on which he differed with those who stood between him and Stalin. He advocated the creation of regional groupings within the framework of the United Nations but under the aegis of the great powers that had paramount interests in the respective regions. He took pains to emphasize that he did not mean spheres of influence, in which "from the point of view of peace nothing alluring can be found." It was different with "security zones," which he insisted would entail only mutually beneficial military arrangements between the great and the small powers.

No matter how specious the distinction, it conveyed a genuine concern lest excessive preoccupation with security lead to unrestrained competition and ultimately to the partition of Europe into hostile blocs. The article pointedly warned that "by no means all states need enter one or another of the zones." While directed primarily against the prospective western European bloc, the warning was more immediately applicable to the Soviet Union. The Russians, increasingly heavy-handed in manipulating the politics of the rapidly expanding area under their military control, were far ahead in carving out the sphere of influence Litvinov loathed.

Surreptitiously, rather than recklessly, the Russians made further probes. On November 11, after the Red Army had liberated a small portion of northern Norway, Molotov announced a claim for two territories under Norwegian sovereignty: Bear Island and the Spitsbergen.[30] In mid-December, Stalin revealed to Harriman extensive territorial aims in the Far East. Two weeks before Yalta, Gromyko notified the State Department about Soviet interest in assuming "responsibilities with regard to Italian colonies."[31] And Moscow's increasingly overbearing treatment of such European neutrals as Sweden and Switzerland further seemed to indicate a desire, contrary to Litvinov's advice, to draw them too into some sort of a Soviet "security zone."[32] As Kennan observed in a private letter to Bohlen on the eve of the Big Three gathering,

we have consistently refused to make clear what our interests and our wishes were, in eastern and central Europe. We have refused to name any limit for Russian expansion and Russian responsibilities, thereby confusing the Russians and causing them constantly to wonder whether they are asking too little or whether it was some kind of a trap.[33]

Stalin still did not act as if he thought confrontation was inevitable. He chose the November 1944 anniversary of the Bolshevik revolution for his most eloquent public homage ever to the alliance whose foundation, he insisted, "lies not in chance and passing considerations, but in vitally important and long-term interests."[34] At the same time, by emphasizing that it would "certainly stand the strain of the concluding phase of the war," he was calling attention to the main potential source of strain during that critical period—the lack of agreement on how to deal with Germany. And he himself hardly knew the answer.

As far as we can tell, the only Soviet "master plan" for Germany was the "Action Program of the Bloc of Militant Democracy," prepared at the end of October by the Ulbricht group.[35] This was more radical than similar programs for other countries: besides land reform and a state-directed economy, it contemplated workers sharing in factory management and a thorough revamping of the educational system, conducive to instilling in the Germans a love for the Soviet Union. Above all, there was to be no multiparty system. The supplementary guidelines drawn up by Anton Ackermann, one of Ulbricht's associates, anticipated the "immediate formation of a Government of the Bloc of Militant Democracy" as the first step toward eventual "consolidation of power" (*Zusammenfassung der Macht*). The reference was unmistakably to a Communist-controlled regime ruling all of Germany on Moscow's behalf.[36] Remarkably enough, however, such a regime was not to be installed in defiance of the Western powers. As Ackermann stated in another formula intended for intraparty guidance, the new Germany would maintain both "an especially close relationship with the Soviet Union and friendship with the West, particularly France, England, and the U.S.A."[37]

The progress of Soviet planning for Germany reflected closely the course of military developments.[38] The slowdown first on the Polish front and then on the Hungarian one increased the chances that the British and Americans might enter Germany first. The Russians therefore moved to formalize the agreements that would secure their own future position in the country. This was the main result of the consultations Gusev had conducted in late October and early November 1944 in Moscow. Back in London, at the November 11 session of the European Advisory Commission he signed the agreements about the division of Germany into zones, the three-power status of Berlin, and the tripartite control machinery.[39]

Moscow still deferred final ratification, pending the Red Army's possible later gains, but it apparently assumed that the three-power system would be put into effect. The sentence about the immediate formation of an all-German government was therefore deleted from a revised version of Ackermann's guidelines.[40] And in mid-January 1945 Ulbricht explained a group of forty party activists, undergoing crash training for assignments in the prospective Soviet zone, that only the provincial and local (not the central) administration would remain in German hands if the war continued "till the bitter end."[41]

None of these plans foresaw Germany's dismemberment, although the Russians still kept the West confused about their preferences. Upon returning from his October talks in Moscow, Churchill informed Roosevelt that Stalin had indicated he would be "glad to see Vienna the capital of a federation of south-German states, including Austria, Bavaria, Wurtemburg [sic], and Baden."[42] The Prime Minister may have gained that impression, but the unpublished British minutes of the conversation show that the statement was Churchill's and that Stalin expressed no opinion.[43] Nor did Maiskii's statement to Harriman on January 20, 1945, favoring dismemberment, carry much weight;[44] three days earlier, Ulbricht had assured his group of activists that no dismemberment was contemplated, despite the impending loss of German territory to Poland.[45]

As the hour of reckoning drew near, Soviet policies were filled with contradictions. On the one hand, the Russians never endorsed the Morgenthau plan, a bizarre American scheme for

Germany's forcible pastoralization and an infallible way to perpetuate German resentment.[46] During the October talks, Stalin also surprised Churchill by taking an "ultra respectable line" in regard to war criminals, none of whom he wanted executed without trial; this line conformed with the Ackermann guidelines that only the highest Nazi party, SS, and police officials would be subject to arrest after the war.[47] By January, Harriman noticed that the Soviet press "published rather less than the usual amount of material against Germany."[48]

On the other hand, the Russians were contemplating the use of Germans as forced labor, a prospect referred to in the "Action Program of the Bloc of Militant Democracy" as "the obligatory participation of all members of the German national community in the work of restitution."[49] Above all, when the Red Army entered German territory in East Prussia at the beginning of January, its treatment of the civilians made a mockery of any talk about democracy, militant or otherwise. In view of the worse Nazi behavior earlier in Russia, the indiscriminate atrocities of the Soviet soldiery would not seem especially surprising except that they were officially tolerated and indeed encouraged. A January 8 order, read to the troops that were about to cross the border, stated unequivocally that everyone was free to take revenge as he saw fit.[50] With no coherent policy, emotions were allowed to run wild.

For Austria, the Communist exiles prepared a general program entitled "The Rebirth of Austria."[51] Unlike its German counterpart, this rather conservative document was made public, having been broadcast over the Moscow radio as early as June 1944. It ruled out any socialistic measures and stressed the need for cooperation between employers and employees for the sake of reconstruction. It castigated "pseudo-revolutionary slogans" as pernicious to Allied unity, theorizing that "proletarian class struggle" really meant a "national war" (*Volkskampf*) against the Prussian oppressors of Austria. But as in Germany, the program anticipated the formation of a provisional government.

235

The original plans of the European Advisory Commission called for creation of a tripartite supervisory body in Vienna, while the rest of Austria would be a common British–Soviet responsibility. But after returning from his Moscow consultations, Gusev surprised his Western colleagues by insisting that the Americans should also be given an occupation zone, an invitation Washington initially treated with reluctance.[52] The Soviet ambassador further hinted that "the moment might arise . . . for the Allies to set up an Austrian state in accordance with the declaration of Moscow, without waiting for the German surrender."[53]

The Soviet planning for Austria complemented in an interesting way that for Germany. There was consistency, unnoticed in the subsequent literature, in the encouragement Stalin gave to a movement of the Anglo-American forces from the south to join the Red Army near Vienna; in December, he repeated the suggestion to Harriman.[54] The Russians apparently assumed that the three Allies would enter Austria more or less simultaneously, assume control over their respective occupation zones, and install a provisional government—something of a dry run for the German experiment.

Stalin's suggestion to Harriman, which was never acted upon, conformed with the revised strategic plan the Soviet High Command had adopted in November 1944.[55] The plan envisioned an offensive through Hungary with the objective of reaching Vienna by December 30, a target date which helps to explain why Gusev was pressing so hard in the EAC for clarification of the Austrian zonal arrangement. In the northern sector, the Red Army would have meanwhile advanced as far as Poznań and would be ready to capture the city in the early weeks of 1945. Without a pause, a second stage of the offensive would then begin about January 20 and culminate in an assault on Berlin. The planners expected the second stage to last about thirty days, leading to final victory by the end of February at the latest.

Against the backdrop of the impending summit, the timetable suggested the following scenario: After the liberation of Austria through the combined efforts of all three Allies, the Yalta meeting would coincide with the Soviet assault on Berlin—a campaign likely to result in the collapse of enemy resistance everywhere. The occupation powers would then move into their assigned zones under the overwhelming impact of this decisive Russian military feat. The first among equals, Stalin would be in a unique position to dominate the conference and to have his peers sanction his supremacy in east central Europe, if not more. In particular, the gradual conversion of Germany into a Soviet dependency could proceed under the most auspicious circumstances.

The plan had its pitfalls, however; much as he hoped to outsmart his partners, Stalin mistrusted them all the same. Too spectacular a success (indeed the very sight of the Red Army rolling into the heart of Europe at high speed) risked awakening the capitalists' worst instincts and tempting them to join with the enemy to stem the Bolshevik tide. This was, after all, what growing numbers of even seemingly sober Germans hoped for as Hitler's doom was approaching.[56] To avert the perceived peril, Stalin needed to reassure his allies.

In mid-January, the Soviet leader finally acted to coordinate the respective military moves. During a Moscow visit by Air Marshal Sir Arthur Tedder, Eisenhower's deputy, he agreed to exchange the necessary information.[57] Tedder reached the Soviet capital shortly after a very different set of visitors had arrived incognito, having been summoned to forestall another development potentially alarming to the West. They were representatives of the Yugoslav and Bulgarian Communists, and the main outcome of their conversations with Stalin was indefinite postponement of the planned union of the two countries, which had been ready to be announced.[58]

By this time, the Soviet military timetable had gone awry. The Germans, unmolested by any Anglo-American thrust into Austria, had been able to consolidate their position in Hungary, frustrating the Red Army's planned drive toward Vienna. On the western front, the British and Americans had likewise been stalled and even thrown back in the battle of the Bulge. Stalin quizzed Tedder anxiously, though unsuccessfully, about whether the Nazis were right in boasting that the Western offensive could not be resumed for another two to six months.[59]

If the Nazi estimate were right, the Allied crossing of the great barrier of the Rhine might be delayed until the summer and Berlin might fall to the Red Army while the British and Americans had hardly set foot on German soil. Such a dramatic denouement appeared all the more plausible because the massive transfer of German reserves to the Bulge was likely to have weakened the Germans in the northern sector of the Soviet front (despite their temporary success in the southern one), thus enabling the Russians to proceed toward Berlin not only on schedule but possibly even faster.

The glaring disparity between the Soviet and the Western military fortunes at the beginning of 1945 seemed conducive to the peril that Stalin wanted most to avoid. The threat of a Western–German rapprochement would diminish, however, if he gave his allies timely relief by advancing the second stage of the Russian offensive, whose pace could later be adjusted according to circumstances. So he ordered the campaign to begin on January 12 instead of 20; but although the original plans had specified its duration as a mere thirty days, he hedged his bets and told Tedder that it might take as much as two and a half months[60]—this despite the radically improved strategic outlook.

The first few days of the campaign were a vivid testimony to how decisively the military balance had shifted in favor of the Russians. By early February, the Red Army had advanced 300 miles, reaching the Oder and even establishing several bridgeheads on the western side of the river. A mere 40 miles of open countryside now separated it from Berlin. Panic struck the Nazi chiefs, some of whom expected Soviet armor to reach the city at any time.[61] According to a later assertion by Chuikov, a veteran of the campaign, the capital could have been captured within ten days, and the war thus could have ended in February rather than in May 1945.[62]

In the controversy touched off by Chuikov's sensational claim, most Soviet and Western authorities have disagreed with him. They have dwelt especially on the overextension of the Russian supply lines after the previous rapid advance, a condition which presumably would have made the assault extremely hazardous if not impossible.[63] Yet the operation would have conformed with plans that had been in effect since November and that must have taken this elementary requirement into account. In any case, the order issued on February 4 by Marshal Georgii K. Zhukov, the commander at the Oder front, stated clearly:

It is the mission of the Army Group in the next six days to consolidate achieved successes through active operations, to move up all lagging units, to lay in supplies for two refuelings and two combat munitions units, and to take Berlin with a lightning thrust on February 15–16, 1945.[64]

On the day Zhukov signed the order, the Big Three convened at Yalta.

The Dubious Success

The setting of the Yalta conference, which lasted from February 4 to 11, was not favorable for the West. Since Stalin refused to go anywhere outside his own territory, Roosevelt—a cripple in a wheelchair—had to travel 6,000 miles to meet him. So remote was the Black Sea area that no British and American ships had sailed there since the beginning of the war.[65] As Churchill remarked to Hopkins, "we could not have found a worse place for a meeting if we had spent ten years in looking for it."[66] Stalin did not come to receive Roosevelt and Churchill when they reached the landing strip, still far from the conference site, although he was already in the Crimea.[67] The Western leaders, with their retinues of several hundred officials, were then subjected to a grueling six-hour jeep ride to Yalta, up and down winding mountain roads.[68] There at last was Stalin, amidst the hastily refurbished splendor of the Czar's former summer retreat, his ego undoubtedly gratified by the scene.

But whether these external circumstances, for all their resemblance to Neville Chamberlain's ill-fated pilgrimage to Hitler's "Eagle's Nest" above Berchtesgaden in 1938, materially influenced the course of the conference is another matter. Stalin proved a genial host, with no trace of Hitler's boorishness in his manner. Nor were Churchill and Roosevelt in any mood of appeasement and gloom. Right or wrong, they did not come to avert a crisis; elated by the impending triumph over Nazism, they were self-confident and optimistic about the future. Churchill was tired but mentally alert. Roosevelt, to be sure, was a dying man;[69] yet his illness cannot be conclusively linked with his performance. He was no more or less casual and diffuse a negotiator than he had ever been. As far as the preparation and orderliness of the agenda are concerned, if anything Yalta compared favorably with Teheran.[70]

Appropriately the conferees tackled military matters first. In separate conversations Stalin broached the subject with Churchill and Roosevelt even before the official opening session on February 4, but he gave them contradictory accounts of the situation. He told the Prime Minister that the Oder front had been broken and that the Germans were all but finished; he told the President that there was "very hard fighting going on for the Oder line."[71] Stalin may have been genuinely perplexed about the enemy's residual strength, as military historians have been ever since. But his tone suggests that he vacillated deliberately, trying to ascertain the strategic intentions of his allies. In the talk with Churchill, he again alluded to the desirability of a Western thrust to Vienna from the south.

240

At the first plenary session, the British and Americans mentioned no plans for that particular operation but did reveal their timetable for the western front. There the offensive was to start on February 8 and make possible the crossing of the Rhine at any time after the first of March.[72] This information gave Stalin something to ponder, since the Red Army's directives anticipated the fall of Berlin by that time. As if the perils of this scenario for the war's finale weighed on his mind, he made the unity of the great powers the main conversation topic during the dinner party that followed.

Using his favorite example of Albania as the epitome of insignificance, the Soviet dictator ridiculed the notion that the great powers should ever submit to the judgment of the lesser ones. But if he thought that the affinity of this idea with Roosevelt's concept of "world policemen" would appeal to his audience, he probably was disappointed. Bohlen remarked to Vyshinskii that the American people might have quite a different opinion and challenged him to try changing it. And Churchill offered the metaphor that "the eagle should permit the small birds to sing and care not wherefor they sang."[73] Despite the prevailing friendly atmosphere, the first day did not end on an encouraging note for the Russians.

Further uncertainties cropped up the next day, February 5, during the noon meeting concerned with the coordination of military moves. General Aleksei I. Antonov, the Red Army Chief of Staff, declared that the army's current offensive would continue as long as the weather permitted, a statement tallying with Zhukov's still valid plans "to take Berlin with a lightning thrust on February 15–16." On behalf of the Anglo-American command, General Sir Alan Brooke then confirmed that the Vienna diversion had been definitely ruled out, lest it diminish the force of the main attack from the west. Focusing on a third area where operations might influence the assault on Berlin, the Russians inquired about their allies' intentions in the Baltic. They learned that no land operations were contemplated, just air attacks to hamper enemy movements from Norway to Denmark.[74] The gist of the discussion was that the Western advance would be slow everywhere in comparison with that planned for the Red Army.

After military affairs had been surveyed, Stalin tackled the most urgent item on his agenda: the German question. He did so circuitously by asking for clarification of the common policy on dismemberment.[75] Although not advocating any particular formula himself, he insisted that a phrase mentioning possible dismemberment be inserted into the surrender instrument already approved by the European Advisory Commission. This unexpected initiative, artificially coupling the dormant issue of dismemberment with the already settled issue of surrender terms, puzzled the Western statesmen. Yet a further query—about the policy to be adopted if a group of Germans, having overthrown Hitler, declared a readiness to capitulate—shows what was really on Stalin's mind. The reference to dismemberment, abhorrent to all Germans, would have a chilling effect on any such group that might seek advantage in surrendering to the West alone.[76] The question remained open; at Churchill's suggestion, the three leaders agreed to refer it for further action to their foreign ministers.

Now it was Churchill's turn to introduce the subject closest to his heart: the restoration of France's great-power status as a means to check Russia's growing might.[77] He pleaded vigorously for giving France a share in the occupation of Germany, to help shoulder Britain's overwhelming responsibility for the onerous task. At this point, Roosevelt interjected that United States troops would not stay in Europe longer than two years, a remark often presumed to have filled Stalin with glee.[78] Rather than being overjoyed, the Soviet leader may have been apprehensive. His policies had been aimed at securing, rather than limiting, a temporary Western military presence in central Europe, and the President's remark could herald the unsettling prospect of America's abdicating its obligation to help police the area even before the German problem had been satisfactorily solved.

This prospect put the French role in a different light. Al-

242

though thoroughly contemptuous of France's contribution to victory, Stalin became amenable to Churchill's proposal. He mellowed especially after the Prime Minister, in a friendly allusion to Russia's own aspirations in Poland, had suggested that France's friendship was as essential for Britain as Poland's was for Russia. Besides, Stalin already had his special treaty with France, not to mention the powerful Communist party as a potential watchdog over De Gaulle. So he struck a fair deal by agreeing that France would receive an occupation zone but not a seat in the Allied Control Council; that exclusive club was to be reserved for the truly great.

The Russians also introduced the topic of German reparations. Their plan, outlined by Maiskii, presumed that the reparations would be exacted by the occupation powers collectively, but then the bulk of the yield would be turned over to the Soviet Union.[79] The Russians wanted their share fixed in advance at $10 billion but, anticipating Western objections on the grounds of the frustrating experience with reparations after World War I, they explained that they expected deliveries in kind rather than in cash. To make these desiderata still more palatable, Stalin stressed that he was not yet ready to discuss the related question of forced labor, which was, along with dismemberment, the most alarming question for the Germans and most repulsive for the West. Even so, his partners declined the demands as exorbitant.

Thus the second day of the conference also passed without giving the Russians much to cheer about. The talks had proved more difficult than the previous Western attitude had led Stalin to expect. Under the circumstances, so dramatic a *coup de théâtre* as the planned capture of Berlin might make matters worse rather than better. According to Chuikov's testimony, the Supreme Commander telephoned Zhukov on the next day, February 6, and they had the following conversation:

Stalin: Where are you, what are you doing?
Zhukov: I am at Kolpakchi's headquarters, and all the Army Commanders of the Front are here too. We are planning the Berlin operation.

Stalin: You are wasting your time. We must consolidate on the Oder and then turn all possible forces north, to Pomerania, to join with Rokossovskii and smash the enemy's "Vistula" group.[80]

To his generals' surprise, Stalin ruled that the Berlin operation be postponed indefinitely and forces diverted to the Baltic coast instead.[81] He may have had sound military reasons for pausing before the final attack, but what really matters is that these reasons did not have decisive weight with him until reinforced by political imperatives. Besides, the decision to stop at the Oder entailed no sacrifice. On the contrary, it gave the Red Army extra time to move forward in Hungary, Czechoslovakia, Austria, and toward Denmark—advances less likely to strain the coalition than the attempted seizure of Berlin would have been.

The Russians did not reveal their sensational decision at the conference; however, at the February 6 meeting of the military chiefs Antonov rationalized it indirectly by claiming that the enemy was going to counterattack along the Oder.[82] On the same day, the Soviet government announced its final ratification of the long-pending agreements about the occupation zones and control machinery in Germany, a gesture corroborating the principle of joint responsibility for the country's future.[83] In the matter of Germany's possible dismemberment, Molotov proved accommodating once his Western colleagues agreed to insert a vague statement about it in the instrument of surrender. He maintained that his government was merely interested in studying the problem and that it was not even imperative to establish a special committee, although he agreed with Eden and the new American Secretary of State, Edward R. Stettinius, Jr., to form one later.[84]

Roosevelt was the last of the Big Three to put forth his top-priority item: a compromise proposal on the voting procedures to be used in the United Nations Security Council.[85] Responding to the objections the Russians had raised at Dumbarton Oaks, the elaborate and highly technical document the Americans had prepared was designed to remove the main stumbling block in the way of establishing the world organization. It provided for the great powers' right to veto any motion unless they were themselves parties to a dispute—except for motions involving sanctions, in which case they would merely abstain from voting. In practice, this meant that their own misconduct could still be aired though not acted on against their will.

Stalin pleaded insufficient familiarity with the problems involved. His plea was only an excuse, for he had received the text two months earlier, and his diplomats had raised searching questions about it in Washington since then.[86] In any case, he showed that he well understood the formula's implications for the relations among the great powers. In one of his typical digressions, he expressed concern lest their solidarity be endangered by mere debate about disputes such as those that might arise, say, over Suez or Hong-Kong.[87] A more appropriate example would have been Poland, which must have been in the back of his mind all the time.

Stalin did not introduce the subject of Poland at Yalta, nor did he raise any demands of his own until his Western partners had raised theirs. Roosevelt led the way by stating that he would like Russia to make some concessions but that he would not insist on any. After this clumsy opening, he observed gratuitously that the Poles merely wanted to "save face."[88] It was thus left to Churchill to formulate the problem properly, and he acquitted himself with flair. He stressed that now, after he had already conceded the Curzon line, he must insist on guarantees that would allow Poland to "be mistress in her own house and captain of her soul."[89] This required, first, a new provisional government to replace the unrepresentative Lublin outfit and, second, free elections. After a recess, which Stalin requested to organize his thoughts, the dictator parried in kind. He argued that a truly independent Poland was best served by the maintenance of the Lublin regime and that the whole question of government was in any case an internal Polish matter to be decided without outside intervention. The issues were thus posed as bluntly as they could be, and the conferees sensibly agreed to adjourn.[90]

With the Russians fighting a rearguard action, the two Western leaders attempted to press their advantage. After consulting with Churchill, Roosevelt sent a messenger with a letter to Stalin at the end of the day, February 6. He proposed a whirlwind operation: assorted Polish notables, representing a broad range of political opinion, were to be brought from Poland to Yalta at once and made to agree on the spot about the formation of a new government. The great powers would then recognize that government in return for its pledge to hold elections at the earliest possible date.[91] It would have been a skillful maneuver if adequately executed; however, its authors failed to anticipate Stalin's elaborate obstruction.

When the Big Three convened again the next afternoon, February 7, Stalin claimed that he had only received the missive an hour and a half before, although it had in fact been delivered to his residence the previous night. He continued by asserting that a reply was still being typed up. While the typist was supposedly wrestling with the job (which turned out to be no more than 180 words), the Soviet leader proposed moving ahead with the debate on the voting procedure in the Security Council.[92]

Having thus unobtrusively linked the Polish question with Roosevelt's highest-priority item, Stalin announced that he would accept the American voting formula. There is no reason to assume that he regarded this as an important concession. But he pretended that he did by asking in return for admission of at least two Soviet republics as full-fledged members of the world body, ostensibly a concession compared with the absurd Russian demand for representation of all sixteen of them, which Gromyko had floated at Dumbarton Oaks. Stalin did not feel very strongly about this subject; when his request for the two extra seats had been granted, he showed himself quite willing to forego the advantage by inviting the Americans to claim an equal number of seats, which they never did.[93] The real quid pro quo that he sought concerned Poland, not the United Nations.

In the meantime, Stalin's typist had at last delivered the product, and Molotov read to the assembled statesmen the Soviet counterproposal on Poland.[94] He urged the recognition of both the Curzon and the Oder–Neisse lines. This was the first time the Russians explicitly endorsed the Western Neisse as Poland's future boundary instead of being ambiguous about which of the two streams they meant. They made this endorsement only after careful tactical preparation. In December they had favorably publicized a speech by a Lublin spokesman demanding that boundary. Two days before committing themselves at Yalta, they also let the regime announce the establishment of Polish administration in the territory in question.[95] Even so, the Soviet advocacy of the Western Neisse line caught the British and Americans by surprise.

The Russians further insisted on a mere enlargement, rather than replacement, of the government currently functioning in Poland. The document read by Molotov acknowledged the need for elections, but qualified these by using the fuzzy adjective "general" rather than the more pertinent "free." At the end of his presentation, the Foreign Commissar announced with a straight face that all his efforts to contact the Poles whom Roosevelt and Churchill wanted to invite had unfortunately been in vain and that in any case those men could hardly be brought over to Yalta in time.

The ruse, which the Western representatives meekly left unchallenged, changed the course of the conference. Churchill gave evidence of his confusion when, ignoring the more fundamental questions of the government and the elections, he chose to challenge the Russians on the secondary issue of how much German land the Poles should be allowed to take. He made the memorable remark that "it would be a pity to stuff the Polish goose so full of German food that it got indigestion" but had no effective reply to Stalin's brazen assertion that the Germans had already run away from the area anyway.[96] Although the British and Americans stood firm in rejecting the Western Neisse line, they gave in with regard to the government by settling for the establishment of a tripartite commission that would invite a group of unidentified Poles to a conference in Moscow later, rather than to Yalta immediately.

On the next day, February 8, Churchill tried to regain the initiative by pressing for the elections, which might save Poland's future in the long run.[97] He scored no small success by eliciting Stalin's admission that the vote could be held as early as a month from then. But he inexplicably neglected to pin Stalin down on a firm date. Instead, Churchill offered him a loophole by observing that there was no hurry and that even two months would do. The Soviet leader quickly changed the subject, inquiring with an air of innocence what was holding up the formation of a coalition government in Yugoslavia and what was the situation in Greece.

Stalin's insinuation that his treatment of Poland was not any different from what the British had been doing elsewhere was a fraud. In Yugoslavia it was Tito, rather than Churchill, who had been causing trouble. And whatever the flaws of the Greek regime the British had forcibly propped up, the issue was to uphold a legitimate government rather than to impose an illegitimate one. More to the point, even after the intervention Churchill had been able to address enthusiastic crowds in Athens' main square[98]—a feat Stalin could not dream of achieving in any Polish city. There was a difference in substance, not merely in style, that distinguished a Western democracy from his sort of regime. For the sake of accommodation with him, the Western representatives nevertheless chose to ignore the distinction.

Did the Western leaders conclude, as it might seem in retrospect, that Stalin would do as he pleased in Poland, without regard for their wishes? If they had thought so, they would not have tried so hard to reach an agreement with him. They began making concessions about Poland because they hoped Stalin would find it in his own interest to treat Poland as they desired (although he gave no indication at all that he would). They proceeded on this questionable assumption partly as a result of wishful thinking and partly as a result of pressures by their home constituencies.

The incorrigibly optimistic Roosevelt seems to have anticipated—intuitively rather than rationally—that the Russians would
somehow allow free elections, whereupon the eastern Europeans
would somehow elect pro-Soviet governments, so that in the end
everybody would be happy. Churchill was not given to such
cheap optimism, but he knew that for most of his countrymen a
break with Russia on the eve of common victory was unthinkable.
And since he did not want it either, he told the cabinet after his
return from Yalta that "so far as *Premier Stalin* was concerned, he
was quite sure that he meant well to the world and to Poland."[99]

Stalin too was not ready to risk a break. At the dinner meeting on February 8, he expanded on his innermost feelings in a
toast that had a ring of genuine emotion, which the despot displayed only on the rarest occasions:

In an alliance the allies should not deceive each other. Perhaps that is
naive? Experienced diplomatists may say "Why should I not deceive my
ally?" But I as a naive man think it best not to deceive my ally even if he
is a fool. Possibly our alliance is so firm just because we do not deceive
each other?[100]

If both sides were so eager to avoid a break, then the outcome of
the conference depended very much on diplomatic skill and per-
severance. It was there that the Americans faltered.

Not having bothered to acquaint himself with the intricate
details, Roosevelt accepted at face value Stalin's spurious "historical" claims in the Far East: control of Manchuria and Outer
Mongolia at China's expense, and the annexation of southern Sa-
khalin and the Kurile Islands at Japan's expense. It is true (though
beside the point) that in regard to eastern Europe the West did
not concede anything that the Russians could not take on their
own; in the Far East the situation was quite different. Roosevelt
nevertheless assented to Stalin's demands in return for a Soviet
promise to join the war against Japan after Germany was defeated—an empty accomplishment since the Russians already had
their own strong reasons to join in.[101]

249

On February 9 Stettinius submitted an American proposal incorporating the Soviet principle of only token enlargement of the Lublin regime. This was a major concession, which he tried to lessen by demanding that Western observers be admitted to Poland to assure the impeccability of the subsequent elections. Made without consultation with the British, the move forced Eden to concur reluctantly, merely registering the complaint that "hardly anyone in Great Britain believed that the Lublin Government was representative of Poland."[102] But Eden dissented forcefully when the United States further agreed that the Russian figure of $20 billion worth of reparations, of which half was to be allocated to the Soviet Union, should serve as the basis for future discussion.[103]

Taking advantage of the Anglo-American rift, the Russians made a friendly gesture to the United States by accepting the Stettinius proposal as the basis of discussion. Among the few changes Molotov introduced was that only "non-Fascist and anti-Fascist" parties be allowed to take part in the Polish elections. Rightly mistrustful, Churchill warned that "it would be a great mistake to hurry this question," but Roosevelt thought that everything was now "only a matter of words and details." When the Prime Minister challenged Stalin to clarify what "Fascist" was supposed to mean, he rejoined by referring to the equally vague use of the word in the American-drafted "Declaration of Liberated Europe" that had been submitted to the conference earlier that day.[104] Stalin's reference to this high-sounding manifesto, promising all liberated countries freedom to shape their political destiny, put the Polish controversy into a broader setting.

That the Russians were acutely aware of the broader implications became obvious from Molotov's amendment to the document. He proposed to add the sentence that "strong support . . . be given to those people in these countries who took an active part in the struggle against German occupation." Offered during the debate about the Polish elections, the amendment hardly con-

250

cealed the Soviet intention to rig the vote. Indeed, Molotov went so far as to argue that the whole Declaration "amounted to interference in the affairs of liberated Europe."[105] Recorded only in the unpublished British minutes and lying there unknown ever since, this was perhaps the most illuminating of all the Soviet statements at Yalta.

Molotov withdrew his insert after the Americans, impatient to reach an agreement, had dropped the demand for observers from the draft on Poland. Still troubled about the date of the elections, he suggested the phrase "as soon as practicable" instead of "as soon as possible" but did not succeed. He fared better with another change which he proposed to make in the "Declaration of Liberated Europe" and which his Western colleagues, tired of all this nit-picking, approved without discussion. Instead of pledging to "immediately establish appropriate machinery for the carrying out of the joint responsibilities set forth in this declaration," the signatories were merely obliged to "immediately take measures for the carrying out of mutual consultation."[106] Translated into plain language, this meant that in eastern Europe the peoples' rights of political expression, enunciated by the document, were not to be guaranteed institutionally but left to Soviet discretion.

As the conference drew to an end, much was indeed "a matter of words and details," though not in Roosevelt's sense. The Russians had been trying to adapt the agreement about Poland and the "Declaration of Liberated Europe" in such a way that, according to their own loose interpretation, they would not be technically liable for violations once they began pursuing the arbitrary policies they made no secret of intending to carry out. The effort was only partly successful, and the more restrictive the wording they had to accept, the greater was their urge to secure Roosevelt's forbearance in advance. He was not only the leader of the world's most powerful nation but also a person known for his penchant for a loose interpretation of his own commitments. So, at the penultimate session on February 10, Stalin made a deferen-

251

tial gesture: after Roosevelt announced that he had changed his mind in favor of France's membership in the Allied Control Council for Germany, the Soviet leader followed suit.[107]

Having signed their agreements the following day, the Big Three all radiated happiness. Each believed he had won on the issues he considered primary and had yielded only on the secondary ones. The Americans had sold Stalin their voting formula for the Security Council, thus assuring the creation of the United Nations, and had obtained his firm promise to join the war against Japan. In return, Roosevelt had given in on the Polish question, which he did not think nearly so important.

The British did not underestimate the importance of that question. But they could rationalize that they had not yielded anything they had possessed to begin with while Stalin, by having promised to expand the Lublin government and allow elections, had made real concessions. Furthermore, Churchill, having made a major effort to get France accepted as a great power, had been eminently successful on that score.

Stalin's balance sheet was not so simple. Alone among the Big Three, he could not claim great positive gains, only an important negative one. He had managed to thwart the Western attempts to restrict his freedom of action in Poland, an accomplishment for which the concessions on France and the United Nations had not been a high price to pay. But he had failed to achieve his primary goals concerning Germany, particularly any reparations settlement. Here he could have said, as Churchill did about Poland, that the outcome "was the best I could get,"[108] a rather meager reward for the dexterity Stalin and Molotov had displayed throughout the negotiations.

In a broader sense, Stalin's gain was at once greater and more precarious than it first appears. If his pre-Yalta behavior had suggested uncertainty about how far he could afford to go without antagonizing his allies, then the impression they gave him at the conference was reassuring. In their treatment of Poland especially, they had seemed very much like "weaklings and hypocrites forever ready to yield to pressure and happy to settle for empty promises."[109] But they were not what they seemed to be; and if Stalin believed he was free to do as he liked, he was mistaken. The ambiguity and obfuscation that had pervaded the conference and that he had diligently cultivated made his success indeed a dubious one.

Measured by achievements, Yalta was, despite its later notoriety, the least important of the Allied chiefs' wartime gatherings. No "partition of the world" (as the title of a popular book would have it) was decided there.[110] In all probability, "the map of Europe would look very much the same if there had never been the Yalta conference at all."[111] Yalta was certainly not a glorious occasion for Western statesmanship, but neither was it in any tangible way "Stalin's greatest victory."[112] If it stands out as a landmark, this is because of the precipitous breakdown that soon followed, a shock to all its participants.

Misdeeds, Mistakes, Misperceptions

Within six weeks of Yalta, its substance was weighed and found wanting. In retrospect, this seems an obvious result of the basic conflict of interest that made disintegration of the alliance almost certain once Germany's imminent defeat began to weaken its members' common military exigencies. Yet neither Stalin nor his Western partners had regarded their aims as incompatible. Why did they change their perceptions after the conference had ended on such a confident note? The answer to that question is not at all clear-cut, and the maze of incongruous developments following Yalta makes it particularly perplexing.

On the Russian side, three seemingly unrelated events occurred on February 17. First, the Soviet High Command updated its plan of operations, thus showing that Yalta (unlike Teheran) had military consequences. Second, the Moscow radio made its

253

last appeal for a popular uprising in Germany. And third, the Russians published a comprehensive assessment of the conference by their top commentator, David Zaslavskii.

The Red Army's new directives foresaw a two-pronged offensive on the southern portion of the front: toward the Slovak capital of Bratislava, and south of Vienna.[113] The troops were to start moving on March 10; in fifteen to twenty days they were to advance into Czechoslovakia to the line Pardubice–Brno–Vienna, and in forty to forty-five days as far as Prague. This was not a very fast pace, particularly since no major campaign was scheduled simultaneously in the northern sector, only the diversion along the Baltic coast that Stalin had ordered while the Yalta conference was in session. Like his decision to pause at the Oder, the plan seems to have been designed to synchronize the forward movement with the anticipated Anglo-American advance. On February 20, the wisdom of a defensive strategy in the north was further confirmed by the intelligence estimate the Russians received from General Marshall; it contended that the Germans were preparing for a counterattack in this area, specifically in Pomerania and Upper Silesia.[114]

The ritualistic calls for a people's uprising in Germany were the last substantive item in which Soviet propaganda toward the enemy had deviated from the Western line.[115] By stopping them the Russians reaffirmed their belief in joint treatment of the vanquished, as envisaged by the agreements on Allied governance of Germany that they had ratified on February 6. Significantly, they also scrapped the "Action Program of the Bloc of Militant Democracy"; according to one of its authors, Wilhelm Pieck, it had been "overcome by events."[116] In another gesture of deference to Western sensibilities, the Red Army finally issued orders to curb its soldiers' violence against German civilians.[117]

The first Soviet policy changes in the wake of Yalta thus concerned different aspects of the German question, the issue on which Stalin had received the least satisfaction at the conference. The thrust of the changes was to promote a solution in the spirit of Allied solidarity. But that solidarity had another side as well, described by Zaslavskii in his authoritative evaluation of the summit. Eulogizing it as a triumph of democracy in its "variable forms," he maintained that

England represents democracy in one of its historic types. The United States is another type and the U.S.S.R. yet another. After the elimination of the last traces of fascism and Nazism, the people of liberated Europe will have the possibility of creating democratic institutions according to their own choice. They can take as an example any form of democracy that has been shaped by history.[118]

Rhetoric aside, the discourse expressed a conviction that the conference had licensed the Soviet Union to introduce its particular "form of democracy" in the countries under its control. The practical consequences of that conviction became dramatically evident in another week's time.

On February 24, Communist-sponsored demonstrators rioted in Romania to bring down the government of General Nicolae Rădescu. The Communists called for a new government that they would control and for measures designed to hurt critically their political opponents: radical land reform, punishment of "war criminals," "democratization" of the army. Having lost ground since their abortive attempt to gain the Ministry of the Interior the previous November, they were attempting to reverse the trend.

Soviet complicity in the effort was evident. In January, Romanian party leaders Ana Pauker and Gheorghe Gheorghiu-Dej had traveled to Moscow, and the campaign against Rădescu had gained momentum after they returned to Bucharest.[119] As early as January 20, General Cortlandt Schuyler, the United States military representative there, had apprised Washington of a secret party meeting at which the two emissaries informed their followers of a decision to bring the Communists to power.[120] Finally, the Russians had ordered the bulk of the Romanian troops

255

moved away from the capital to the front, so that the government would find it more difficult to defend itself.[121]

The Soviet intent to intervene thus antedated Yalta. Whether the date of the confrontation was set before or after the conference is less important than the fact that nothing happened at Yalta to dissuade the Russians from going ahead. In particular, Molotov's idea that the "Declaration of Liberated Europe" "amounted to interference in the affairs of liberated Europe," did not receive the rebuff it deserved. Nor, for that matter, had the "percentages agreement" (which had already assigned Romania to the Soviet sphere without so much as a discussion) led the Russians to expect an adverse Western reaction.

The character of the actors determined that the performance would be crude rather than subtle. Once provoked by the Communists, Rădescu responded by charging in a radio address that

those whom the people call "without God and Nation" have planned to set the country on fire and drown it in blood. A handful of individuals led by two venal persons, Ana Pauker and the Hungarian Luca, are attempting to subdue the nation by terror. . . . Under the mask of democracy, a democracy which they have trodden down at every step, these beasts hope to gain power.[122]

The facts were plain enough, but the Premier's language could hardly have been worse, since he was in no position to back tough talk by tough deeds.

On February 27, Vyshinskii descended on Bucharest to teach Romania a lesson. In a style made notorious by Hitler, he bullied a weaker neighbor into submission by an elaborate display of bad manners. Having lectured King Michael on the necessity of appointing the government the Communists wanted, Vyshinskii is said to have slammed the door so hard when he left that the plaster around it cracked badly.[123] Even though Soviet armor appeared in the streets to reinforce Vyshinskii's point, the monarch did not immediately give in—possibly the reason why Stalin did not insist on a cabinet composed exclusively of Communists, as some of his more impatient Bucharest lieutenants would have preferred.[124] The cabinet the King was forced to appoint on March 6 included four other politicians as well. Four days later, Stalin ostentatiously gave it his blessing by finally granting permission to establish Romanian administration in Transylvania.[125]

The new regime was totally subservient to Moscow. If this was a foregone conclusion in view of the nature of the confrontation, the Western reaction was not. Previously, the Western powers had been studiedly indifferent to the Romanian situation, if not openly hostile to non-Communist politicians, who were suspect as potential troublemakers.[126] Now they belatedly protested the Communist takeover, although there was a significant difference between the vigorous American diplomatic action and the half-hearted British one. The Foreign Office rationalized that "we play an admittedly minor role in Roumania and interference there may incite the Russians to interfere elsewhere in our sphere." For his part, Churchill confided to Eden that he was "much concerned lest U[ncle] J[oe] should reproach us for breaking our understanding with him about Roumania at the same time as strife about Poland comes to a head."[127]

In the event, the British were bound to lose in both Romania and Poland. By accident, the tripartite commission (formed at Yalta) to summon Polish notables for consultations about governmental reorganization first met in Moscow the day before the Bucharest riots. Not so accidentally, a deadlock developed rapidly during subsequent meetings, as all the participants discovered the sham of the Yalta accords. Having resolved to keep the power of the Lublin regime intact, the Russians refused to invite for consultations any Poles but their own.[128]

The Russians showed that they had meant their Yalta effort to prevent genuine reorganization of the Lublin regime, regardless of their failure to insert all the necessary loopholes into the formal agreements. And the Western representatives likewise showed that they had meant their insistence on Poland's right to choose its government, although they had not succeeded in spelling out all the necessary safeguards in the agreements. Now the British and Americans were dismayed and the Russians confused; Molotov first agreed to let Western observers into Poland, then reversed himself.[129] Churchill rightly concluded (in a letter he drafted but never sent to Roosevelt) that "if we do not get things right now, it will soon be seen by the world that you and I by putting our signatures to the Crimea settlement have underwritten a fraudulent prospectus."[130] The "Declaration of Liberated Europe" was such a prospectus because of the conflicting interpretations its signatories could read into it if they wished.

Matters might still have turned out differently if unexpected military developments had not intervened. With the enemy resistance in Hungary stronger than anticipated, the Red Army could only inch its way toward Austria, not opening its drive against Vienna until March 16.[131] But the Anglo-American forces took advantage of German failure to blow up the last remaining bridge across the Rhine, at Remagen; they crossed the river on March 7, and began pouring into Germany at high speed. Suddenly the military fortunes were the opposite of what they had been at the time of Yalta. The Russians seemed at a loss. Publicly playing down the remarkable turn of events, they nervously acclaimed "tactical coordination" between their and Western operations—as a postulate rather than a certainty.[132]

Five days after Remagen, on March 12, Harriman told Molotov that Anglo-American representatives had made contact in Berne with the Nazi generals in charge of German forces in Italy and had been examining their offer to surrender. At first hearing the news, the Foreign Commissar did not disapprove but did express a desire that Soviet officers be allowed to participate in the talks.[133] Rumors about enemy efforts to end resistance in the west had been proliferating. As early as mid-February, the Berne correspondent of the London *Daily Dispatch* had reported that General Alfred Kesselring, the German commander in Italy, was ready to withdraw his troops.[134] According to a Nazi intelligence intercept, the Russians at this time alerted Tito to occupy northern Italy swiftly in case the move materialized. [135]

How seriously did Stalin take the possibility of his allies' collusion with the Germans? To anyone suspicious enough to consider such a possibility, the unbelievable Remagen crossing must have seemed *prima facie* evidence of an enemy effort to facilitate an Anglo-American advance and eventually a separate armistice. And indeed, shortly after Yalta Ribbentrop had (with Hitler's approval) secretly instructed all German diplomatic missions to watch for signs of Western willingness to conclude one. He had subsequently sent an aide, Fritz Hesse, to Stockholm to seek actual feelers. [136] On March 15 the Swedish newspaper *Svenska Dagbladet* leaked the news of the mission, on the eve of Molotov's next meeting with Harriman.

Harriman brought a negative reply to the Soviet request to participate in the Berne talks. As instructed, he explained that these were merely preliminary and concerned only the Anglo-American front. [137] Keeping the Russians out of the delicate negotiations was a sensible precaution against scaring the Germans away, but the explanation was clumsy. Though not intended as a snub, it looked like one. It betrayed a deplorable lack of understanding of the Soviet mentality, which was all too evident in Molotov's response. He angrily charged bad faith and arrogantly insisted that the contact be abandoned at once. [138] In view of the Russians' secretiveness about their own previous contacts with the enemy, this was a preposterous demand but otherwise a clever tactical move.

There was nothing improper about the Berne talks; [139] if there had been, the West would hardly have told the Russians about them to begin with. Stalin must have realized that the matter was innocuous, but he might well have worried that the increasingly disturbing signs of German intrigues heralded worse things to come. The recent evanescence of the Yalta spirit, with a suddenness not easily comprehensible, could signal to him that

259

even if the Western powers were not amenable to German overtures now, they might become so as he proceeded with his policies in Poland and elsewhere in eastern Europe. In any case, Stalin's subsequent behavior was indicative of a growing panic.

In again firing volleys at the concept of the "balance of power," the Russians showed their concern about a possible Western–German rapprochement. They claimed that schemes to redress the balance resulted from pressure by "influential groups" in Britain and the United States though not from any design of Churchill's or Roosevelt's.[140] This was, curiously, the same kind of reasoning that many Western officials were inclined to follow in accounting for what they perceived as a puzzling and groundless reversal of the overall Soviet policy. Stettinius, Harriman, and Bohlen speculated that after his return from Yalta Stalin had been criticized in the Politburo for having made too many concessions.[141] Eden and Churchill, too, conjectured that he was under scrutiny in the "Soviet councils" and consequently at pains to prove that he was still pursuing "Soviet interests."[142] The symmetry of the hypotheses advanced on both sides shows how very reluctant the Yalta participants were to admit that they had fooled each other and themselves as well.

As March progressed, the misdeeds, mistakes, and misperceptions multiplied. In Poland, the Russians attempted to negotiate with sixteen remaining leaders of the Home Army, perhaps to ascertain whether at least some of them could be coached to be docile exhibits at the deadlocked Moscow talks. They could not, and on March 27, Soviet agents lured the Poles into a trap, spirited them to Moscow, and jailed them as traitors.[143] This was an outrage by any normal standards, but otherwise only too logical a continuation of previous Soviet conduct.

In contrast, Russian interference in Czechoslovak affairs was less than it seemed. The Communists wrote the program of the new Czechoslovak coalition government, formed in Moscow in the second half of March, and received far more cabinet posts than their numbers justified. That result occurred, however, because their political competitors had not presented a draft of their own and had preferred not to fight during the talks about the government's composition rather than because of any Soviet pressure.[144] In fact, Stalin expressed to Beneš his disapproval of the disproportionate number of ministries the Communists had been able to grab.[145]

If Soviet policies in eastern Europe substantially followed their previous path, for better or for worse, the same was not true in two areas outside Stalin's domain. After the Berne affair, the Russians ended their truce with Britain's client regime in Greece. Raising an outcry about its alleged violations of the "Declaration of Liberated Europe," they held up Romania (of all places) as the country where the document had been implemented in an exemplary fashion.[146] More ominously, on March 19 they announced their intention to terminate their friendship and nonaggression treaty with Turkey.[147]

Though unmistakably more aggressive, the pattern of Soviet policy since Yalta had been erratic and inconsistent rather than premeditated and methodical. Stalin must have anxiously recalled the consequences of his last great miscalculation, concerning Hitler's intentions in 1941. Toward the end of March, Zhukov found him very tired, tense, and visibly depressed.[148] His anguish was hardly alleviated by the thought that all the uncertainties might have been avoided if he had allowed the Red Army to attack Berlin and possibly end the war in February, as originally planned. With a new sense of urgency, he tried to correct what he had neglected.

During March, the Russians began hedging on the principle of joint Allied treatment of Germany, thus preparing for another twist in their tortuous handling of the German question. When the tripartite committee on dismemberment first convened in London on March 7, no substantive discussion took place; when it met again on March 26, Gusev dealt it a *coup de grâce* by announcing that his government did not consider dismemberment obligatory.[149] He disturbed his Western colleagues by his cryptic assertion that the German state would continue to exist despite Hitler's defeat, although he stressed that it had forfeited the right to conduct any foreign relations.[150] What the ambassador was really saying is that Stalin, fearful lest Germany come to terms with the West, wanted to reassure the Germans about the future while preparing the final blow.

To deliver that blow, the Soviet High Command revived its earlier scheme for conquest of Berlin.[151] When Stalin discussed it with Zhukov on March 29, he also mentioned a warning he had supposedly received from a "foreign well-wisher" that the Germans were plotting a separate peace in the west.[152] By coincidence, the next day the BBC reported that, according to a captured enemy officer, no defenses were left between the rapidly advancing Anglo-American forces and the Reich capital. The Russians immediately picked up the item, pointedly asking in *Pravda* "whether these reports are designed to mobilize the spirit of the Germans or whether they pursue some dubious aims."[153]

Further elaborating on those "dubious aims," Antonov charged in a letter to Deane on March 30 that "certain sources" had tried to "divert the attention of the Soviet High Command."[154] He was referring to Marshall's message of February 20, which had claimed that the Germans were going to mount a counterattack in the north whereas in reality they did so in the south, in Hungary. Antonov ignored the fact that a week later Marshall had corrected himself by notifying the Russians before it was too late that revised intelligence estimates indicated a postponement of the northern attack.[155] The Soviet general was insinuating that there had been an American ploy to divert the Red Army from Berlin while hoping to snatch the prize for the West— the very ploy Stalin now planned to use.

By the time Antonov sent his note to Deane, a message from Eisenhower to Stalin, dated March 28, had been received at the American Military Mission in Moscow though not yet forwarded to its final destination. Eisenhower wrote that instead of pressing on toward Berlin, he planned to turn the bulk of his forces south into Bavaria, where he believed the main enemy strength to be concentrated. He further mentioned his intention to join the Russians along the Erfurt–Leipzig–Dresden line and possibly in the Regensburg–Linz area as well.[156]

The message had created a furor in London even before it reached the Russians. The British Chiefs of Staff took exception to Eisenhower's strategy, for they had made plans to capture Berlin with their own forces under Field Marshal Bernard Montgomery, attacking from the Ruhr.[157] On March 31, Churchill protested that the capital might have lost its "military but certainly not its political significance."[158] The British were angered by Eisenhower's failure to consult with them before sending off such an important message. The Supreme Commander, guided strictly by perceived military expediency, had meant no offense, and his independent communication with Stalin, though unprecedented, had been formally within his vast authority. However, Churchill's protest came too late to prevent the dispatch from reaching Stalin.

On March 31, Deane and his British counterpart, Admiral E. R. Archer, had personally delivered the controversial piece into Stalin's hands. Having glanced at it, the Soviet leader immediately remarked that the plan was a good one but that he could not give a definite reply until he had consulted with his generals. As the two chiefs of the Western missions subsequently reported to Washington, Stalin "had apparently been considering Eisenhower's message all through the discussion," at the end of which he again stressed how good the plan was.[159] He reiterated this in his formal reply the next day. Noting that Berlin had "lost its former strategic importance," Stalin observed that Eisenhower's plans conformed with the Russian ones. He added, however, that the Soviet offensive would not start before the second half of May.[160]

Stalin did not mean what he was saying, at least not literally. When he convened his top generals on the same day, April 1, he told them with a sense of urgency that the Western Allies wanted

263

to capture Berlin and that the Red Army must get there first.[161] He evidently thought Eisenhower's unusual message was an elaborate deception and decided to answer it in kind. In his reply he did not actually lie but rather distorted the facts. In his mind, the respective plans did conform with each other in being aimed at Berlin. Stalin further observed that the city had lost its strategic importance; he said nothing about its *political* importance. And when he mentioned the second half of May, he was referring merely to the time, not the place, of an unspecified Soviet offensive. The one against Berlin, which he now ordered, was to start on April 16, and he would notify his allies about it only the day before it began!

Two more Western messages reached the Kremlin on that eventful April Fools' Day of 1945—one from Churchill, the other from Roosevelt. Summing up their criticism of the Russian conduct since Yalta, Stalin's coalition partners issued their most solemn warnings so far. Singling out the Polish question, the Prime Minister wrote that, unless the deadlock were overcome, he would "be bound to confess" a failure of the conference to the "Parliament when they return from the Eastern recess."[162] And the President, deploring the "apparently indifferent attitude of your government," cautioned that the recent developments might "cause the people of the United States to regard the Yalta agreement as having failed."[163] There was symbolic significance in Stalin's receiving these obituaries of Yalta on the day he ordered his troops to take Berlin. There was already an air of the Cold War in this effort to seize control over the remaining unclaimed territory in order to deny it to the adversary.

In the remarkable swing from ostensible harmony to hostile competition, within a mere six weeks, the ambiguous results of the Yalta summit had set the stage. The Western statesmen had contributed their share by rushing agreements for agreements' sake without taking proper care to impress on Stalin how far they really would let him go. Even if we allow for the exalted expectations of their home constituencies, which they had to heed, a

264

more professional diplomacy could have avoided, or lessened, many a pitfall. But it was Stalin who, free from such constraining influences, held the main responsibility for the subsequent breakdown. He knew well that the integrity of the Yalta accord depended on his behavior in eastern Europe.

Since his determination to subdue his new eastern European subjects did not differ before and after the conference, Stalin did not deliberately wreck Yalta. Yet he wrecked it all the same—by first underestimating his partners' opposition and then overestimating it when their response began to show that he and they had misjudged one another. He had shown his ability to retreat before, and he could have chosen to conciliate again, but the peculiar configuration of military developments made him panic.

Under other circumstances, those largely accidental developments need not have mattered. But in conjunction with the other blows that had been shattering the hopes of Yalta, they prompted Stalin to apply what he viewed as precautions against anticipated Western hostility. His perception of a ploy to double-cross him militarily, after he had restrained his own military movements, led him to reverse his long-standing strategy of concerted advance and to aim exclusively for political leverage. Ironically, this momentous reversal elicited in the long run the very hostility he hoped to forestall.

On April 5, Litvinov again spoke frankly to a Western visitor, on this occasion to *New York Times* correspondent Cyrus L. Sulzberger. "A regular Jeremiah, full of gloom," noted Sulzberger, Litvinov mused that "first the Western powers make a mistake and rub us the wrong way. Then we make a mistake and rub you the wrong way."[164] But if Litvinov was now thoroughly pessimistic about the future of the alliance and the whole course of East–West relations, Maiskii tried to minimize the crisis. Cornered by Clark Kerr at about the same time, the former ambassador to London explained it as a transitory manifestation of his compatriots' deep-seated sense of inferiority. More to the point, Kollontai told Clark Kerr that the Russians were bad psychologists, never realizing when others might take offense.[165] So the three Soviet officials most knowledgeable about the Western world were also the most apologetic about their government's policies, indirectly pointing out the real culprit.

If we may draw an analogy with Germany's responsibility for World War I, the Soviet Union "willed" the post-Yalta crisis, much though the West helped to "cause" it.[166] The conflict would not have arisen if Stalin had not all along regarded the suppression of majority will in the neighboring countries as indispensable for the pursuit of what he defined as the Russian national interest. Nor would the situation have deteriorated so precipitously if, once the sham of Yalta had been exposed, Stalin had chosen the path of conciliation rather than confrontation. Even so, the process he had set in motion was not yet irreversible; the impending common victory over Nazism had many dangers but also many opportunities for continued, though strictly limited, collaboration. In determining which trend would prevail, the remaining weeks of the war were crucial.

chapter eight

A Peace Lost?
April—August 1945

The Contest That Never Was

S talin's new resolve to meet his allies' forces as far west as possible had immediate repercussions in Austria and Germany. After the idea that tripartite rule in Austria would serve as a model for German settlement had fallen victim to unforeseen military developments, the Russians kept delaying agreement about the control machinery, the occupation zones, and the administration of Vienna.[1] Now, at the April 4 meeting of the European Advisory Commission, they suddenly demanded a substantial enlargement of their zone, to include the whole of Upper Austria north of the Danube.[2] They reportedly had also assembled in Yugoslavia a Communist-controlled shadow government ready to step in as soon as the Red Army had occupied enough Austrian territory.[3]

Whatever the Soviet plans, they were superseded by an initiative from the Austrians themselves. On April 3, Karl Renner, a veteran Social Democratic politician then in his seventies, stepped forward from retirement to place himself at the Russians' disposal. There was an epic quality in his historic decision, which was prompted, he later said, by his grief at the Red Army's brutality to the inhabitants of his town.[4] Compassionate and intrepid, Renner was also unsentimental and shrewd. He would help the Russians run the country as the head of a provisional government but would insist on popular endorsement of his mandate. Convinced that the victors' unity would not last, he hoped to muster enough Western support to eventually have Austria regain its independence. He was a true son of the eternal Europe that, having almost gone under in its follies and crimes, proved infinitely resourceful in reasserting its vitality against conquerors.

The latest one, Stalin, saw the situation in a different light. Informed of the emergence of Renner (whom Lenin had described as "one of the most despicable lackeys of German imperialism"), he is said to have exclaimed: "The old traitor is still alive? He is just the man we need!"[5] There was a further stain on Renner's record—his public endorsement of the 1938 Nazi *Anschluss*—which, besides his advanced age, seemed to qualify him as a candidate of sufficient pliability. Only the Austrian Communist exiles, who knew better but whom Stalin typically neglected to consult, viewed the choice with misgivings.[6]

The April 27 inauguration of Renner's government in Soviet-occupied Vienna was a Russian bid for supremacy in the whole of Austria, to be exercised through a subservient regime which the Western powers would find hard to reject. Yet, with the Polish and Romanian events fresh in their memories, the British and Americans balked at its recognition. Moscow retaliated by barring them from access to the capital and by stalling the agreements that would have spelled out respective rights and responsibilities in the country.[7] The Red Army meanwhile penetrated deeper, occupying some of the prospective British zone in Styria. Thus, as a result of the turnabout of Soviet policy, Austria emerged as an area of East–West rivalry, together with Germany.

On April 1, the day that Stalin issued his orders to march on Berlin, Ulbricht and his associates had conferred with Dimitrov; five days later, they prepared their new *"Richtlinien."*[8] These mapped out the Communists' tasks in the Russian zone only, rather than in Germany as a whole. Unlike the defunct "Action Program of the Bloc of Militant Democracy," this was a short-term plan of action for the period immediately following the victory. Three task forces of exiles were to be brought into different parts of the Soviet zone on the heels of the Red Army, to act as arms of the occupation administration and particularly to establish a local administration supervised, but not run, by the Communists.[9] These preparations did not mean that the Russians had abandoned the notion of eventually controlling all of Germany and decided to make their own portion into a separate entity, thus disregarding their coalition partners. However, they were taking steps that would facilitate their doing so in case four-power rule failed or, for that matter, never materialized—a possibility which Stalin's recent bid to capture Berlin seemed to make more likely. Gradually but irresistibly the unresolved German problem, although not the cause of the East–West rivalry, was becoming its main catalyst.

The new Communist directives envisaged the publication of a propaganda newspaper, *Deutsche Volkszeitung*, to impress on the German people their co-responsibility for Hitler's crimes. However, before starting the Berlin attack, the Russians explicitly dissociated themselves from any idea of revenge. On April 14, a major *Pravda* article criticized Ehrenburg for having vociferously promoted that idea.[10] Implying that surrender to the Red Army entailed no particular risks, the article rationalized that the preference of German soldiers to lay down arms in the west stemmed not from fear but from a scheme of the Nazi diehards to split the victorious coalition. After Yalta the line toward the Germans had hardened, but now the incipient offensive prompted the Russians to soften it again.

Stalin was not only pushing westward but also trying to hamper his allies' advance eastward. On the eve of the Berlin campaign, he continued his game of deception. He informed Harriman on April 15 that a major Soviet offensive was about to begin, but stated that its target was Dresden rather than Berlin.[11] A week later, after the Red Army had already encircled the capital, Antonov sent a message to Eisenhower in which he claimed additional territory as supposedly belonging to the Russian area of operations. He stated the army's intention to occupy the entire eastern bank of the Elbe, along with the Vltava valley in Bohemia.[12]

On April 22, the news of an imminent enemy surrender in

Denmark prodded the Russians into action in that region as well.[13] Having treated Denmark as a quasi-collaborationist country, Moscow implied that the Danes ought to have to pay for the privilege of admission to the ranks of the liberated. As the price, a Soviet share in the control of the Baltic straits, which Molotov had first demanded from the Nazis in 1940, loomed as a possibility. Soon after the British had indicated at Yalta that they had no immediate military plans in the area, the Soviet navy newspaper *Krasnyi Flot* put forward the thesis that the Baltic was really a Soviet sea; simultaneously, the Russians hinted vaguely that they might liberate both Denmark and Norway.[14] On April 23, the Commissar for the Navy, Admiral Nikolai G. Kuznetsov, approved a plan to capture the Danish island of Bornholm, and soon afterward Soviet reconnaissance parties parachuted into Denmark proper.[15]

As the Berlin operation unfolded, however, Stalin's anxiety lest the Germans and the West join to turn the tables on him counseled caution. At a meeting with his generals on April 17, he called their attention to the claim by a captured enemy soldier that the German army had been instructed to open the gates in the west to stem the tide in the east.[16] And, incredible though it may seem, during the second half of April the Red Army started building *defensive* installations in Austria, including antiaircraft facilities—at a time when an operative German air force no longer existed. Equally astounding, Soviet loudspeakers at the front addressed enemy troops by charging ominously that "the greatest treason of world history is under way. If you don't want to fight on against us on the side of the capitalist powers, come over to us."[17] The reasoning behind such extraordinary moves was plausibly paraphrased in a British Foreign Office estimate that the Russians were

saying to themselves that even if nothing has yet been planned with the German Generals, this does not mean that we [the British and Americans] have given up hope of being able to strike a bargain with them in order to seize as much of Germany as possible without loss of time or men, and thus present the Soviet government with a *fait accompli*. [18]

Did the Western comportment warrant so monstrous a suspicion? By April, the view that "one must get tough with the Russians" was gaining ground; the London Foreign Office noted that nearly all "American, Dominion, and even French diplomats, and most Anglo-American journalists" in Moscow had by then become hardliners. [19] But this applied much more to the Westerners observing the Russians at close range in the Soviet capital than to government officials in Washington and London. The change of mood failed to prompt any change of policy remotely comparable to Stalin's weighty decision to seize as much territory as possible before his perceived Anglo-American competitors did so.

Roosevelt's sudden death on April 12, shocked and distressed Stalin. [20] The familiar and in many ways congenial leader was now replaced by an obscure personality whose Kremlin dossier consisted of hardly more than his 1941 statement that the Nazis and the Bolsheviks should best be left to kill off one another. Before meeting President Truman for the first time on April 23, Molotov confided to the sympathetic ears of ex-Ambassador Davies his government's concern about the uncertainty generated by Roosevelt's death. [21] The Soviet way of combatting that uncertainty, particularly by concluding a formal alliance with the controversial Lublin regime two days before the Foreign Commissar's White House interview, [22] was hardly suited to reassure Roosevelt's successor. Still, the ensuing interview proved an eye-opener for Molotov.

Having been briefed by Harriman and other top officials about the unsatisfactory state of Soviet–American relations, Truman spoke to Stalin's emissary bluntly and to the point—a manner markedly different from Roosevelt's. He asked the aide to convey to the boss in no uncertain terms American displeasure with the Russian policies since Yalta. To Molotov's complaint that he had never been talked to like this in his life, the President

271

supposedly retorted: "Carry out your agreements and you won't get talked to like that."[23] Even if the wording (recorded in Truman's memoirs but not in the official minutes of the interview) may not be authentic, the new tone certainly was. Harriman welcomed the change although he regretted the particular incident, which was likely to give the Russians an impression that there had been a change of policy whereas all that had changed so far was style.[24]

In those tense last weeks of the war, perceptions often mattered more than policies.[25] At the end of April, many Westerners perceived in an article published by French party chief Jacques Duclos, but obviously instigated by Moscow, a Soviet declaration of ideological war. Disguised as a critique of the conciliatory policies of the American Communist party (until then fully sanctioned by Moscow), the gist of the statement was that Communists anywhere must not renounce seizure of power.[26] But the article was not the landmark it might seem; under preparation since November 1944, it did not reflect any change of policy in response to the post-Yalta crisis.[27] According to a suggestion made to me by Duclos himself (for all his lack of candor, an authoritative source), the timing served to indirectly warn the West against any attempted reversal of alliances.[28]

That imaginary danger continued to obsess Moscow despite compelling evidence of Western loyalty to the alliance. On April 25, Churchill passed on to Stalin the information that Himmler had offered to arrange a separate surrender at the western front and had been rebuffed. The Soviet leader responded with "the most cordial message" the Prime Minister ever received from him.[29] Yet when a similar opportunity offered itself to Stalin, he did not reciprocate in kind. On May 1, the day after Hitler's suicide in the ruins of Berlin, upon Goebbels's orders General Hans Krebs tried to negotiate a surrender of the city to the Russians. Although the negotiations ultimately failed, Stalin did not inform his allies—as if there were something to hide.

The hidden thing was a Soviet attempt to gain exclusive control over the government of Hitler's successor, Admiral Karl Doenitz. During the protracted talks between Krebs and Chuikov, who was continuously consulting with the Kremlin by telephone, the Nazi general bargained for Moscow's recognition of the new regime as Germany's legal government.[30] The Russians were amenable, insisting only that the surrender must come first; afterward, they would provide transportation to assemble the scattered members of the Doenitz cabinet under their auspices in Berlin. But Krebs stubbornly demanded recognition first, and therefore the talks broke down. His obstinacy frustrated any possibility of Stalin's launching in Germany a client regime similar to the one he had already launched in Austria. Otherwise, the German experiment might well have turned out more successfully because of pro-Soviet opportunism latent in Doenitz's entourage.[31]

After Krebs's mission had failed, the commander of Berlin surrendered the city unconditionally on May 2. Thus Stalin won the race for the German capital that he imagined himself to be conducting. But on the same day he lost the one for Denmark. Merely hours before the Russians would have reached Lübeck, the British under Montgomery got there first, cutting off the Red Army's access route to Denmark.[32] This outcome only strengthened the Soviet determination to seize at least Bornholm: Two days later, Kuznetsov's secret orders affirmed that the island must be captured "under any circumstances."[33]

Even after Berlin had fallen, substantial enemy forces remained intact in western Czechoslovakia. With German resistance all but finished elsewhere, Eisenhower proposed to turn on them. No sooner did he inform Moscow on May 4 of his intention to advance to the western banks of the Elbe and Vltava rivers— that is, as far as Prague—than Antonov objected.[34] Although in his message prior to the seizure of Berlin the Soviet general had described the eastern bank of the Elbe as the limit of the Red Army's area of operations, he now wanted to extend this to the western ones as well. At the same time, ostensibly to avoid confu-

273

sion of forces, he urged Eisenhower to restrict the American advance in Czechoslovakia to the Budweis–Pilsen–Carlsbad line. Meanwhile the goal of the revised Soviet plans was to capture Prague; the troops were to start moving on May 7 and take the city any time after May 14.[35] The uprising that flared up there on May 5 confounded these plans, setting the stage for a bizarre denouement of the great war.

The uprising broke out independently of the Soviet-directed partisans, who had been active in harrassing the retreating enemy in the Bohemian countryside but otherwise discouraged mass action.[36] Nor had the Czech underground been planning any such action for that particular time.[37] The Communists especially had been badly mauled by recent arrests and executions of their leaders, and the survivors remained out of contact with the Russians.[38] The spontaneous outburst forced the Czech National Council (*Česká národní rada*, CNR), which had been constituted secretly just the day before, to step forward hastily and assume command. Within this makeshift leadership, the CNR's Communist vice-chairman, Josef Smrkovský, soon emerged as the key figure.

The Russians responded to the events in Prague by advancing their timetable from May 7 to May 6.[39] The Americans, too, moved ahead but, in deference to Antonov's wishes, stopped at the Budweis–Pilsen–Carlsbad line. With a keen eye on the politics of the situation, Churchill implored Eisenhower to "advance to Prague if you have the troops and do not meet the Russians earlier."[40] Eisenhower, seeing no military reasons to do so, declined; he shared Marshall's opinion that he would be "loath to hazard American lives for purely political purposes."[41] Compared with these clear and simple, though different, British and American motives, the Soviet ones were complex and murky.

To Stalin, the Prague uprising was suspect. There seemed to be a collusion between its leaders and his archenemies, the Vlasovites. Hoping to earn clemency at the eleventh hour, these Nazi-equipped Russian troops intervened in the fighting on the side of the Czechs on May 6. The radio controlled by the insurgents broadcast Vlasov's appeal, urging the Germans to lay down their arms, and also carried a report about a meeting between him and the CNR chairman.[42] The report was false; the Czechs actually kept their controversial helpers at arm's length.[43] Disillusioned, the luckless Vlasovites left after a day's fighting to seek their last chance by surrendering to the Americans, little knowing that they would be summarily delivered to Stalin anyway.

After Vlasov's withdrawal, the fortunes of the insurgents plummeted. Radio Prague began to plead desperately for help against the advancing Germans. General George S. Patton, commanding the United States Third Army now immobilized fifty miles west of the city, was eager to move. He later reminisced that "we should have gone on to the Moldau [Vltava] River and, if the Russians didn't like it, let them go to hell."[44] For all his flamboyance, however, he would not defy Eisenhower's orders; he could still try to have the Czechs themselves take an initiative that would compel the Supreme Commander to reconsider. Although it is not certain whether this was actually Patton's scheme, a reconnaissance mission was dispatched from his Pilsen headquarters to induce such an initiative. It met with CNR representatives in Prague on May 7.

Two accounts of these crucial talks exist, during which the energetic Smrkovský negotiated on behalf of his less enterprising colleagues.[45] One is his own account, self-serving and written from memory twenty-five years later; the other is a contemporary, but curiously evasive, report by a member of the American team to the Office of Strategic Services. Although all the facts may never be known, the central issue is sufficiently clear: the emissaries made the Czechs believe that the Third Army was ready to move on and liberate Prague within hours, provided a CNR delegation came to Pilsen to formally request this.

The Americans were certainly in a position to meet the request although no promise was ever authorized. But Smrkovský, taking the possibility seriously, successfully resisted the dispatch of any delegation to Patton, to reserve the liberation of the city for the Russians. He was taking a calculated risk, assuming that the insurgents would be able to hold out long enough without American aid. Despite their current plight, this was not an unreasonable assumption, for earlier that day at Reims the German High Command had already concluded an act of surrender, effective at midnight on May 8.

Although Smrkovský was aware of this reassuring development, he did not know that the Russians had repudiated the surrender. Two days before, they had authorized their representative in Eisenhower's Reims headquarters, General Ivan Susloparov, to take part in the surrender negotiations and the general had countersigned the document on behalf of the Soviet government on the morning of May 7.[46] But no sooner did the ink dry than Eisenhower received an urgent message from Antonov describing the surrender as merely preliminary. The Russians insisted that it be followed by a final one, to be signed in their own headquarters at Karlshorst on the outskirts of Berlin.[47]

To Deane, who transmitted the message from Moscow to Reims, this was nothing short of a "bombshell."[48] Moreover, Stalin also tried, albeit unsuccessfully, to dissuade his allies from breaking the news about the Reims surrender to the public.[49] Even when, in conformity with his wishes, the second ceremony got under way at Karlshorst, Zhukov and Vyshinskii raised so many questions about the minutiae of the text and protocol that the final act was not concluded until shortly before midnight on May 8, the time the cease-fire was to become effective.[50]

This last-minute Soviet effort to postpone the official end of the war has never been satisfactorily explained. But the Czech situation provides the clue. While the Russians delayed acknowledging the validity of the German surrender, their armor was roaring from Berlin to Prague. Yet, oddly enough, all this time they did not even attempt to inform the Czechs, much less the Americans, about this ostensibly gallant rescue of an ally in distress. The likely reasons for the conspicuous silence were the unknown quality of the leadership that had so unexpectedly surfaced in Prague, and the uncertainty about whether the Americans might move to liberate Prague after all.

The immediate issues at stake were to prevent the large German forces in Bohemia, not to mention the Vlasovites, from escaping into Western captivity, and to forestall the consolidation in Prague of a suspect leadership that might conceivably interfere with the authority of the Beneš government, already stamped with Soviet approval. The news that the Russians were coming would have induced the enemy to speed up its retreat, thus improving the insurgents' chances of survival. Conversely, if the operation remained secret, the Germans might stay long enough to finish them off, ridding Stalin of a potential embarrassment; hence also the maneuvers with Germany's surrender, calculated to delay the effective cessation of hostilities. Upon closer examination, the motives behind the Soviet drive to Prague were not nearly so gallant as they might seem; indeed, they were ominously reminiscent of those that had sealed the doom of Warsaw in 1944.

The Russian movements, of course, could not be kept secret altogether. Throughout May 8, Czech gendarmerie posts telephoned reports to Prague of the passage of Soviet tanks en route to the capital.[51] Yet the men at the receiving end of the line— members of the insurgents' military staff—neglected to pass this vital information to the CNR.[52] This singular failure of communication may have resulted from incompetence or chaos. But in view of the friction between the military and the political leaders during the uprising, the information may also have been withheld deliberately. Since the military men in fact attempted several times to establish contact with Patton's army on their own, they may have hoped to induce the political leaders to summon American aid at the last moment.[53]

That aid would have been all the more desirable since Smrkovský's gamble to hold out until the Russians could get into town failed on May 8. The morale of the insurgents faltered as the still powerful enemy forces closed in, threatening to overrun Prague with devastating results—a credible enough threat considering the presence of SS desperadoes. On the last day of the war, the Czechs faced an imminent and humiliating defeat.

At this critical moment, the commanding German general, Rudolf Toussaint, offered a compromise that Smrkovský eventually accepted with a heavy heart.[54] Although formally a German surrender, the ensuing agreement was, under the circumstances, a German victory. Not only were all German troops allowed to withdraw unmolested, but they could also keep most of their arms until they reached the American lines—terms very different from the unconditional surrender their superiors had signed the day before at Reims. Both sides implemented the agreement, and hostilities had all but ceased in Prague by the time Germany's official capitulation came into effect at midnight on May 8.

The Russians arrived only hours later. With rare candor, one of their commanders, General Ivan G. Ziberov, later described what he had seen: "When we entered Prague, I had the impression that there was in the city neither an enemy capable of fighting nor any insurgents in their positions."[55] With the enemy gone, the Red Army could only spuriously claim the laurels of a liberator. The Czechs had not liberated themselves either, although they had certainly tried. In that effort, the Vlasovites had helped them more than anyone else, but not enough to make a difference. Only the Americans could have liberated Prague in the true sense of the word, yet they had been dissuaded by both Moscow and the agile Smrkovský. It was an uninspiring ending to the war in the same city where six years earlier the Nazis had triggered its beginning.

On the day the Russians entered Prague, they also captured Bornholm as a result of Western indecision. In response to an urgent Danish plea for an Allied landing on the island, Eisenhower had notified Antonov on May 8 that he intended to meet the request unless this conflicted with Soviet plans. Moscow acted first and replied later; having occupied Bornholm on May 9, the Russians explained that, "as is well known," it was within their zone of operations.[56] But they evacuated it a year later; with the rest of Denmark outside their control, continued occupation of the island became politically counterproductive.

In retrospect, Stalin congratulated himself on the outcome of what he had thought to be a race with his Western competitors but what he subsequently realized had been merely an extension of his power into areas they had voluntarily abstained from entering. Expatiating on Eisenhower's "generosity and chivalry," he later privately admitted that "if it hadn't been for Eisenhower, we wouldn't have succeeded in capturing Berlin."[57] As far as Prague is concerned, in 1946 Marshal Konev spoke in a similar vein at a closed meeting of Soviet officers:

The success of the Prague operation consisted to a large degree in our ability to carry out actions calculated to prevent our allies from getting into Prague. And the situation happened to be such that they could have gotten there. . . . The liberation of Prague was dictated by political and strategic interests. . . . We fulfilled our task and, as you can see, this has produced positive results by strengthening our friendship with the Czechoslovak people and by creating a favorable international situation in postwar Europe.[58]

Both Soviet assessments lend support to Churchill's opinion that it would have been in the West's interest to advance as far east as possible to fill in the vacuum of power while it still existed and thus obtain "bargaining counters . . . [for an] early and speedy show-down and settlement with Russia."[59] If implemented, the Prime Minister's recommendation would not necessarily have resulted in the desired settlement, but it would have put the Western powers in a position to make a better bargain in the showdown. With things as they were, there was to be neither a showdown nor a settlement.

279

The Cramped Détente

The aftermath of the European war was anticlimatic. At first, Stalin even found it hard to believe that Hitler was really finished. To both Western visitors and his own associates, he confided his suspicion that the Nazi chief might still be alive in hiding. He went so far as suppressing a report by Soviet forensic experts certifying that they had positively identified the Führer's corpse in the rubble of Berlin.[60] Perhaps he wanted to keep the report in reserve, to be produced if someone ever tried to pose as Hitler, as so many impostors claiming to be missing czars had done in Russia's past. Or he may have been genuinely worried lest the German leader reappear to create havoc once again, much as Napoleon had done after escaping from Elba.

Ordinary Russians had greater faith in the future than their leader. The day after the victory, thousands of them rallied enthusiastically in front of the American Embassy to celebrate—an act of spontaneity that the Russian capital had not seen for decades and the authorities did not dare to obstruct.[61] Even Stalin could not frivolously disregard the great expectations his subjects cherished after the years of privation and sacrifice. Yet those expectations were potentially dangerous for a regime that needed an enemy to justify its repressive practices. The demise of the Nazi threat heartened the common man; for the dictator and his associates, it left an uncomfortable void.

Unwittingly, the Americans played into Stalin's hands. Having so obligingly helped his drive into central Europe in the last days of the war, they abruptly cut off their lend-lease program immediately afterward—for no better reason than because the end of hostilities had presumably made it redundant.[62] Even ships already at sea with cargo bound for Russia were suddenly recalled to their ports. Although other nations, particularly Britain, were similarly affected, the growing American censure of Soviet conduct in eastern Europe made Moscow appear to be the main

280

target. Thus the Russians had both international and domestic reasons to behave, despite their greatest military triumph, with "marked reserve, if not uncertainty," in Harriman's words.[63]

The situation in the recently occupied territories further contributed to that uncertainty, for the rapid military developments had left the Russians with more than they were prepared to handle. Their scheme to control Austria through the Renner government had been a brilliant, but precarious, improvisation. The Prague operation had likewise been improvised after the unexpected Czech uprising. For Germany, as the chief political advisor of the Soviet military administration, Sergei I. Tiulpanov, later admitted, "the Soviet government possessed no 'occupation blueprint' prepared in advance."[64]

In central Europe, unlike in the traditionally Russophobe countries farther east, Moscow encountered more problems with a friendly Left than with a hostile Right. In Austria, many Communists of old or, perhaps more typically, brand-new vintage slipped into the vacant positions of power with the forbearance of local Soviet commanders. A detachment of Yugoslav-trained Communist partisans even stood guard for Renner at the Vienna Chancellery.[65] In many German cities, the arriving Red Army found spontaneously formed committees eager to promote the creation of a socialist society.[66] In Czechoslovakia, the Prague uprising, in which the Communists had been so influential, had threatened to confound Soviet schemes.

As usual, Moscow dealt unceremoniously with indigenous radicalism. In Austria, the Soviet authorities gradually fired many self-appointed office holders, allowing Renner to replace them with his own personnel.[67] In Germany, Ulbricht and his staff moved swiftly to disband all the leftist committees, ostensibly because of their "inadequate contact with the people."[68] In Czechoslovakia, on the day after its entry into Prague the Red Army rushed in Beneš and his government, to assume power according to the prearranged scenario; the CNR then rapidly faded into obscurity.[69] And Smrkovský, rather than being properly re-

281

warded for helping to keep the Americans out, suffered Soviet disgrace for spoiling the Russian liberation of Prague by his deal with the Germans. (A prominent figure in Czechoslovakia's 1968 reform movement, Smrkovský died a defeated man after Soviet intervention had crushed that movement and reimposed "normalcy.")

With the prospect of a grand bargaining at a forthcoming peace conference, the Russians seemed uncertain about how much of their domain they would be able, or would care, to retain. They gave no signs of being determined to keep a long-term military presence in central Europe, including Hungary. Instead they sought the broadest possible range of collaborators, who were then readily available. They passed over opportunities to install the local Communists in power; later in 1945 and in 1946, they even granted Austria, Hungary, and Czechoslovakia the privilege of free elections. (But in the first two countries the Communists did poorly in the voting, and in the third they began to lose support soon afterward; so those elections were the last free ones allowed in any place under Soviet control.)

The first postwar confrontation between East and West, which took place in mid-May, was not of Russian making. It had been provoked by Yugoslav efforts to grab Venezia Giulia from Italy and Carinthia from Austria, both ventures embarrassing to Moscow. The former risked a clash with the powerful Anglo-American forces in Italy, against which Tito's partisan army had no chance to prevail. The latter threatened to undermine the position of the Renner government, which the Russians had been trying hard to bolster. Stalin therefore curbed the Yugoslav advance into Carinthia, enabling the British to take control of the province. He supported Tito's designs in Venezia Giulia only half-heartedly, lest the confrontation grow into an open clash.[70]

If the blame that the Russians received in the West for the Yugoslavs' behavior was largely undeserved, there was enough in their own behavior elsewhere to justify Western censure. The crisis served as a catalyst of British opposition, as evident especially from the previously unknown record of an important interview between Churchill and Gusev on May 18. Having invited the Soviet ambassador for a luncheon, the Prime Minister gave him an unprecedentedly "brisk talking to." He took the Russian "for a tour of the capitals of Eastern and Central Europe from which Russia's Western Allies were excluded." What is more, he indicated that the demobilization of the Royal Air Force had been suspended, for the British were "resolved to enter upon discussions about the future of Europe with all the strength they had."[71] Churchill staked his hopes on a bargaining session with Stalin at the next summit meeting, which he proposed to convene at the earliest possible date.[72]

The interview helped to keep alive the Russians' suspicions that even after the war the West might join hands with the former enemy to spoil the fruits of their victory. They were particularly anxious about Doenitz, who lingered on as the head of a make-believe government in the north German city of Flensburg. Two days after the Churchill–Gusev meeting, *Pravda* charged that "some Allied circles" wanted to make use of Doenitz's services— which Stalin himself had unsuccessfully tried to engage before.[73] Although three days later the British took the Doenitz group into custody as war criminals, Soviet anxieties persisted.[74]

Again, Litvinov offered a pertinent commentary about the causes of the rising tension. In an off-the-record interview with Snow, which applied to the British as well as the Americans, he asked: "Why did you Americans wait until now to begin opposing us in the Balkans and Eastern Europe? . . . You should have done this three years ago. Now it's too late and your complaints only arouse suspicion here."[75] This was an explanation as independent as it was eminently fair; Russia's striving for power and influence far in excess of its reasonable security requirements was the primary source of conflict, and the Western failure to resist it early enough an important secondary one. Yet the principal contestants still failed to see the realities of the situation as clearly as this dissident did, as their particular moves continued to show.

283

Only a week after Churchill's pep-talk with Gusev, the British went out of their way to gratify Stalin. At Lienz in Austria, they used force and subterfuge to deliver to his henchmen thousands of anti-Soviet refugees—men, women, and children—a testimony to the difficulties in remaining Stalin's ally without becoming infected by him.[76] Despite such confusing appearances, there was a pattern in the Western behavior, as there was in the Soviet behavior. Whereas the Lienz affair and the American lend-lease decision were examples of bureaucratic machines running astray, the actual policies of the two governments were of another order, and also different from each other. The British, despite their aberration, strove to impress Moscow by firmness; the Americans hoped to achieve the same effect by benevolence. Although blurred if viewed in a longer perspective, in mid-1945 the divergence was a conspicuous feature of the international scene.

At his stormy April meeting with Molotov, Truman had acted as if he had hardened the line, but he later heeded Harriman's advice to avoid "any implication of a threat or any indication of political bargaining."[77] At the end of May, the British Embassy in Washington rightly judged that the United States wished "to abide by the Yalta agreements and implement them on Soviet request, whatever the behaviour of the Soviet government."[78] At this time the President dispatched two personal representatives on special missions abroad: Joseph Davies to London to restrain Churchill and Harry Hopkins to Moscow to accommodate Stalin. The choice of the notoriously pro-Soviet Davies could only have been a humiliation, albeit unintended, to Churchill. And Hopkins' Moscow performance did not demonstrate the strength of Western resolve either. It proved a watershed all the same.

On May 26, Hopkins began his Kremlin conversations by trying to get across to Stalin his government's concern about the deterioration of their relations since Yalta, but his indirect approach was hardly suited to impress on the dictator the seriousness of the matter. Hopkins deplored the recent unfavorable turn of American public opinion about Russia but avoided linking the change with any Soviet action. By commending Stalin for having seconded Roosevelt's efforts at a new "structure of world cooperation," he implied instead that the Russian leader could not possibly be blamed.[79] By elimination, the absent British were thus left the villains, and Stalin lost no time in blaming them. He accused them of scheming "to revive the system of *cordon sanitaire*" and of not wishing "to see a Poland friendly to the Soviet Union."[80] Without contesting this palpable untruth, Hopkins replied rather gracelessly that the American policies were different. Although Harriman, who was also present, hastened to add that Anglo-American relations were "very intimate," the impression created was the opposite.[81]

On the next day Hopkins, having failed to specify any American grievances, invited Stalin to state his. Stalin availed himself of the opportunity with gusto and a flair for dramatic effect. He began with an item that could not have bothered him very much but that could be used to bother the Americans—a protest against their ushering the quasi-Fascist Argentina into the United Nations. He further took exception to the Western idea that France be allowed to sit as an equal member on the Allied reparations commission—a proposition he described as "an attempt to humiliate the Russians." Concerning the Yalta agreements on Poland, Stalin assumed a posture of offended innocence. Questioning not only his partners' good will but also their honesty, he ruminated that

despite the fact that they were simple people the Russians should not be regarded as fools, which was a mistake the West frequently made, nor were they blind and could quite well see what was going on before their eyes. It is true that the Russians are patient in the interests of a common cause but their patience has its limits.[82]

After this ominous warning, he charged that the Soviet Union had been treated shabbily, particularly by the abrupt cancellation of the lend-lease program. Ignoring the later restoration

285

of the deliveries, he remonstrated that if their termination had been "designed as pressure on the Russians in order to soften them up then it was a fundamental mistake . . . [for] reprisals in any form would bring about the exact opposite effect." The Soviet leader topped his list with a complaint about a nonevent. He said that he had heard the Western powers were contemplating rejection of the Russian request for the bulk of the captured German navy and merchant marine, and he warned that the consequences of such an act "would be very unpleasant."[83]

Hopkins patiently set the record straight, emphasizing that no offense had been intended. Stalin readily accepted the assurance, thus acknowledging that the presumed grievances had been either groundless or greatly inflated. He had nevertheless won a tactical victory: having cast himself in the role of the aggrieved party, he managed to shift onto the West the onus for the slide toward hostility that had brought the American emissary to Moscow. He subtly imposed on Hopkins the principle that what mattered was not the merit of a case but the manner in which the Russians might choose to interpret it. This shift finally opened the door for an understanding about Poland on Soviet terms.

Hopkins professed ritualistically that "we would accept any government in Poland which was desired by the Polish people and was at the same time friendly to the Soviet government"[84]—as if such a mixture were feasible. More to the point, he volunteered the suggestion that "any present agents of the London government" be eliminated in advance, a step beyond Yalta that Stalin understandably welcomed as "good news."[85] Hopkins spelled out the basic democratic rights that the United States wanted to see safeguarded in Poland but did not object when Stalin reaffirmed his intention to suppress them. Invoking the need to maintain order at the rear of the Red Army, the dictator claimed that those rights "could only be applied in full in peace time, and even then with certain limitations." He particularly insisted that unspecified "Fascist parties" be banned.

In the end, Hopkins acceded to the Soviet formula that the

Lublin government, now residing in Warsaw, be enlarged by a token representation of the London Poles, including especially Mikołajczyk in the largely ornamental post of Deputy Premier. The subsequent unfettered election of a permanent government was left in abeyance. The Polish question was thus settled between Hopkins and Stalin without the British.[86] Although unhappy, the British went along; Churchill had already written off Poland as a lost cause and hoped to exact concessions from the Russians elsewhere. It was rather the Americans who, despite having yielded to Stalin, continued to harbor the illusion that they could compel him to permit free elections although they never had any plan of how to achieve this aim.[87]

No sooner had Hopkins left Moscow for home than Stalin gave eloquent expression to his belief that the West had forfeited any right to concern itself further with Polish affairs. He staged a show trial of fifteen of the sixteen Polish leaders he had entrapped three months before.[88] In doing so, he disregarded Hopkins' explicit warning that such an act would jeopardize the forthcoming Big Three meeting.[89] The lack of Western reaction to this affront implied that the warning need not be taken seriously; the trial and conviction of the captives on trumped-up subversion charges did not impede the work of the tripartite commission entrusted with implementing the Stalin–Hopkins agreement. So confident was Moscow in its ultimate success that it already omitted the word "provisional" from its press references to the Warsaw government. On July 5, after the cosmetic changes in its composition had been made, both Washington and London duly accorded the Warsaw regime full diplomatic recognition.[90]

During his conversations with Hopkins, Stalin had observed that "whether the United States wished it or not, it was a world power and would have to accept world-wide interests."[91] His positive stress on America's global mission, incongruous perhaps in retrospect, again attested to his deep desire to have the strongest world power underwrite the new order he envisaged for eastern Europe. Admittedly, at this late date he hardly needed anyone's fiat to install a regime of his choice in Poland, but he did appreciate that "the solution would carry more weight if it was tripartite."[92] To be sure, the United States had no need to dignify with its consent an arbitrary act that it was unable to prevent; yet in the opinion prevailing in Washington, this was a price worth paying for a possible revival of the Yalta spirit.

The result was a cramped détente more pernicious than an outright confrontation. It rested on Stalin's belief that he could get what he wanted from the Americans without having to worry much about the British. He differentiated ostentatiously the treatment he accorded them. Thus on June 11 he sent an uncommonly gracious note to Truman, thanking him for all the aid the Soviet Union had received from the United States during the war.[93] To Churchill he made no similar gesture; instead, on June 21 he dispatched an insolent message gratuitously aggravating the Venezia Giulia controversy.[94]

Although the British and the Yugoslavs had signed a preliminary accord the day before, Stalin chose to castigate British intransigence.[95] Lashing out especially at Field Marshal Alexander's alleged haughtiness, he endorsed emphatically the Yugoslav territorial claims, which he had treated gingerly a month earlier. On first reading this, Churchill concluded that the time was ripe for "a very great deal of argument conducted between good friends," and drafted a long, spirited reply to that effect. Yet, as so many times before, on second thought he discarded the tough draft and dispatched a brief, conciliatory text instead, although in his memoirs he later wrote as if the original one had been sent.[96] He sensed acutely the waning of Britain's power, which the United States was not yet prepared to replace.

In other areas as well, Moscow began to challenge its weaker adversary, exposing the sham of the détente. In mid-June, a Soviet colonel appeared uninvited at the British headquarters in Oslo, demanding that his government have a voice in all decisions concerning Norway.[97] (This seemed an incipient change of policy after the Russians, having liberated a mere 1,000 square miles of northern Norway in October 1944, had stopped further advance as a sign of their respect for a British area of influence.) No sooner was the request turned down than the Russians announced a desire to share in the international control of Tangier, opposite Britain's Gibraltar.[98] They further gave comfort to Arab efforts to oust British and French troops from Syria and Lebanon.[99] Apart from these probes, the most significant expansion of Stalin's ambitions beyond those already on record concerned Turkey, which was, next to Greece, the bulwark of British influence in the eastern Mediterranean.

Although Russian designs against Turkey were long-standing, their revival at this particular time was hardly accidental. At Yalta, Stalin had announced he would demand a revision of the Montreux convention on the Black Sea straits, a proposition Churchill had promised to back.[100] But this had concerned a revision in consultation with all the signatories of the convention, whereas now the Soviet Union was attempting to impose its will unilaterally by intimidating Turkey. Molotov told the Turkish ambassador on June 7 that a bilateral settlement of the issue was one of the preconditions for renewing the friendship treaty between the two countries, which Moscow had terminated three months before. The others were the establishment of Russian bases in the Dardanelles and Turkey's cession of formerly czarist territories in the Caucasus that the Soviet government had relinquished in 1921. After the Turks had refused to discuss these infringements on their sovereignty, ominous reports of Red Army movements along their frontiers multiplied.[101]

As with Molotov's visit to Berlin in November 1940, Stalin hardly expected all his demands to be met; he more likely viewed them as bargaining points in his anticipated horse-trading with the West.[102] Still, this was a reckless policy. Attributing it to the nefarious influence of Stalin's secret police chief, Lavrenti P. Beria (who as a fellow-Georgian presumably harbored a special animus against the Turks), Khrushchev later singled out the attempt to coerce the Turks as the cardinal Soviet blunder in

1945.[103] In the long run, such provocative behavior in areas where no vital Russian interests were at stake only served to rally other nations against Moscow.

In the short run, however, the three allies were still bent on avoiding confrontation, albeit for different reasons: the United States because it felt strong enough to be accommodating, Britain because it was too weak to risk conflict without American backing, and the Soviet Union because such a situation seemed eminently conducive to advancing its power and influence without effective opposition. Whether the situation could last depended very much on the developments in Germany, that treacherous testing ground of the Allies' willingness and ability to cooperate.

The Stalin–Hopkins talks cleared the way for the inauguration of the Allied Control Council as the victors' supreme executive body in Berlin on June 5.[104] Yet only five days later, the Russians took a step circumventing its authority. On June 10, Zhukov authorized the establishment of political parties in the Soviet zone.[105] This was a sudden decision, which took both the West and the German Communists by surprise; one of their leaders, Ackermann, later recalled how a week before the announcement he had been suddenly pulled out of bed in Leipzig and rushed to Moscow along with several of his comrades for a last-minute briefing.[106]

The move was an incipient Soviet bid for a dominant role in the whole of Germany. As Tiulpanov, the political advisor of the Soviet occupation government, later stressed, the establishment of the parties carried great political weight for the entire country.[107] The four authorized to operate—the Communist, Social Democratic, Christian Democratic, and Liberal—were expected to expand their activities into the other zones as well. By launching a limited number of parties of their own choice, the Russians preempted Western initiative while asserting their intention to take the lead in building Germany's future political system.[108] In doing so, they ruled out neither a temporary four-power regime nor the ultimate preservation of German unity.

At this time, Anglo-American forces still held the extensive portions of the Soviet zone that they had captured in the last days of the war, whereas the Red Army occupied all of Berlin. When the Control Council first met on June 5, Zhukov made its practical operation contingent on mutual withdrawal into the designated zones.[109] Rightly judging the Western presence in the Russian zone as a major trump card for bargaining with Stalin, Churchill ardently wished to delay the withdrawal. But Truman overruled his objections and announced Anglo-American readiness to start moving on June 21.[110]

Stalin did not expect such quick action.[111] Under different pretexts, he pleaded for postponement to July 1.[112] So it was only during the first half of July that the exchange took place, leading to an understanding about Austria as well. The Russians took possession of Thuringia, Saxony-Anhalt, and a part of Mecklenburg, while the Americans, British, and French established themselves in the enclave of West Berlin, which the Red Army had meanwhile all but stripped of industrial equipment—probably the main reason for Stalin's requesting the delay.[113] In Austria, the Russians vacated the portion of Styria that they had occupied and consented to a four-power presence in Vienna. They made good their claim for extension of their zone in Upper Austria but still failed to persuade the West to accept the Renner government.[114]

None of the Austrian arrangements mattered very much; it was, ironically, the ability of the Renner government to eventually free itself from Soviet tutelage and enlist Western support that did matter. But the German real estate deal had fateful consequences. It not only created the Berlin problem but also made possible the country's ultimate partition along the zonal boundaries—something none of the occupation powers bargained for. The sections of Germany originally controlled by the Russians could not possibly have become the nucleus of a viable state later on, especially since those east of the Oder–Neisse line had already been turned over to Poland. But at that time the main significance of the exchange lay elsewhere: the evacuation of the area that Churchill had hoped to use as his main asset to exact concessions from Stalin demonstrated vividly the Anglo-American rift and Britain's impotence.

Speaking at a secret party meeting in May 1945, Stalin's chief Hungarian lieutenant, Mátyás Rákosi, commented on the significance of the rift.[115] He explained to his select audience that the rivalry between the two capitalist powers would facilitate gradual expansion of the Communist orbit, if only precipitate action could be avoided that might draw them together again. He urged moderation in internal affairs, calling for a "great compromise" with his country's middle classes and peasantry. The speech touched on two vital linkages: that between Stalin's perception of weakness in the capitalist world and his desire for promoting Soviet power abroad, and that between his policies in the area already under his sway and the Western opposition to Russia's further expansion. Rákosi's statement conveyed optimism on both counts.

Yet regardless of the deceptive détente, Stalin made his success contingent on exceedingly tenuous premises. One was the inevitability of the West's decline, the other his ability to rule his empire without arousing alarm about his intentions. In the last weeks of the war, he had blundered by overestimating his partners, suspecting a ploy to block his advance. Did he now succumb to the opposite error of underestimating them? The forthcoming summit, set for July 18 at Potsdam, would show.

Potsdam and the Bomb

Having originally proposed the Big Three meeting to force a showdown with Stalin, Churchill was not in the mood for one by the time they met. Haunted by the correct premonition that he would lose in the national elections currently under way, he arrived in Potsdam a mere shadow of his earlier formidable self.[116] Not only was he "tired and below his form. He also suffered from the belief that he knew everything and need not read briefs."[117] Worse still, as Eden noted with exasperation, the Prime Minister was "again under Stalin's spell. He kept repeating 'I like that man.'"[118] And indeed, when the two met tête-à-tête on July 18, there was no showdown. Although they discussed Yugoslavia, Turkey, and other trouble spots, the conversation flowed "without reaching any crucial topic."[119]

Similarly, no argument had marred the first encounter between Stalin and Truman the day before. But the President's crisp self-assurance provided a striking contrast to the British statesman's gloom. With a bluntness all his own, Truman explained to Stalin that since he was "no diplomat, he would not beat around the bush but would operate on a yes or no basis."[120] Elected chairman of the conference, he showed what he meant at the very beginning of the opening session. Blow by blow, he laid out all the troublesome issues he wanted to have settled—from the lack of a common policy on Germany to the breakdown of the Yalta agreements in eastern Europe. Not until afterward did he find time to pause and extend a formal welcome to his two peers.

These initial impressions, indicating to Stalin that Churchill might be less but Truman more difficult to handle than he previously had reason to expect, may have surprised though not necessarily upset the Russian leader. The agenda the Soviet delegation had prepared—yet withheld from the other participants until almost the last moment before the conference opened—dwelt particularly on the recently stated aspirations that Moscow wanted to satisfy largely at Britain's expense.[121] The proposed agenda included not only Tangier, Syria, and Lebanon but also two new items: a request to share in the administration of Italy's former African colonies and a proposal for joint action to remove the Franco regime in Spain. When these topics were first discussed, Churchill was so ill-prepared that his own aides felt embarrassed by his fumbling; Cadogan thought that the Prime Minister "talks the most irrelevant rubbish, and risks giving away our case at every point."[122]

As usual, the items the Russians omitted were as revealing as those they included. The weightiest subjects they proposed concerning Germany were reparations and the disposition of captured enemy ships, indicating that other aspects of the German question were in Stalin's opinion already on their way toward a satisfactory solution. Also the once towering Polish problem had shrunk to demands for Western confirmation of the Oder–Neisse line and the final liquidation of the forlorn government exiled in London. Other items pertaining to the European settlement and listed under the heading "Relationship with the Former Axis Satellite States" in essence proposed that Washington and London give full recognition to the Moscow-made regimes in Bulgaria, Romania, and Hungary. All in all, the subjects the Russians proposed to discuss suggested that they had already received most of what they wanted and were now seeking to get more. As Stalin retorted to Churchill after having been complimented on his recent accomplishments: "Czar Alexander got to Paris."[123]

Admittedly, many substantive issues were covered in the British and American agendas submitted to the Soviet government several days earlier.[124] Thus the treatment of Germany, the procedure for the final peace settlement, and the creation of a Council of Foreign Ministers as the great powers' permanent consultative body, were to be discussed anyway. Even so, the course of the negotiations soon showed that the Russians were more interested in specific gains than in any comprehensive agreements that might tie their hands. The case in point was again Germany, on which the conferees eventually spent most of their time.

At various stages of the talks the Soviet representatives offered seemingly contradictory amendments to the American draft spelling out in detail the principles of treatment of the defeated nation. Molotov, taking exception to the "aspect of centralization" inherent in the document, advanced the formula that only "in so far as it is practicable should the treatment of the German population . . . be the same throughout Germany."[125] However, the Russians were the ones who pressed most adamantly for the creation of "central German agencies"—rudimentary ministries headed by State Secretaries, which would be entrusted first with economic matters and later with other responsibilities as well.[126] Molotov further insisted that those agencies would handle all such matters according to "detailed instructions to be issued by the Control Council," which meant, of course, that if its members disagreed on a particular issue there would be no common policy.[127] In the end, the Allies agreed to treat Germany "as a single economic unit" but subject to "varying local conditions."[128]

At the heart of these confusing Soviet approaches was an effort to reconcile short-term economic aspirations and long-term political ambitions. The Russians were trying to bleed Germany white by wholesale removal of its wealth, yet apparently they hoped to remain credible enough to compete there for political supremacy. Their political bid was implicit in their promotion of the central agencies, as it had been in their independent launching of all-German parties before. They needed an undivided Germany in order to collect the maximum amount of reparations with the help or connivance of the other occupation powers. Yet by pressing this goal they risked a conflict that might well lead to the nation's partition.

It was symptomatic of the shambles of Stalin's German policy that the Russians, much as they tried to succeed in their economic and political pursuits, were also preparing for failure. Accordingly, adequate loopholes were to be built into any agreements they concluded so that they could take an independent course at will, without formally violating their obligations. Perhaps as an additional precaution against any ensuing embarrassment, they insisted that the Allied Control Council be physically located in the American rather than the Soviet sector of Berlin.[129] In addition, the responsibility for any possible breakdown of cooperation was to be shifted onto the West: Stalin made the via-bility of the one-Germany formula dependent on the willingness of the Western powers to deliver from their own zones the exorbitant reparations he coveted. [130]

If the continued unity of Germany rested on such uncertain foundations, so did the whole postwar settlement. Stalin still behaved as if he preferred agreement to discord—but only on his own terms. At Potsdam, he spoke about a world condominium of the great powers representing "the interests of all the United Nations." [131] Yet this was not to be construed to interfere in any way with the advancement of Soviet power. Stalin did not urge the early convocation of a peace conference, which would presumably stabilize the international situation and thus constrain the further growth of that power. Although he wanted the conference convened eventually, he insisted that it be thoroughly prepared by the newly established Council of Foreign Ministers; [132] in the meantime, he would be able to assess the response to his various pending demands and perhaps raise more. Thus the formal conclusion of peace, much like the settlement in Germany, depended ultimately on favorable Western reception of the inflated and growing Soviet desiderata, a prospect which the first days of Potsdam had already made illusory.

Even though Churchill may have risked giving away his case and Truman did not participate in the debate as actively as his initial resolution had seemed to indicate, the Russians made little headway. At the meetings of the foreign ministers, where much of the conference business was transacted, Molotov's peers proved a good match for him. Eden, by now convinced that the "pattern of Russian policy [was becoming] . . . more brazen every day," [133] tried to act tough to counteract his earlier contribution to encouraging that pattern. The new United States Secretary of State, James F. Byrnes, though not so alarmed or burdened, lived up to his reputation as a proficient, and devious, negotiator. Using the Russians' own technique, he exploited the ambiguity of the Yalta understanding that the Soviet claim for $10 billion worth of reparations would serve merely as the basis of discussion. The joint British and American resistance to that claim and to the Soviet demand for recognition of the Western Neisse as Poland's frontier led to an impasse on July 21.[134]

Stalin had been delaying implementation of the agreements about Austria that had been concluded earlier in July; now the time was right to comply, to make his negotiation partners more receptive to his other demands. On July 22, he opened the plenary session by announcing that the Red Army had begun withdrawal to its designated zone in Austria and Western advance units had already entered Vienna.[135] Astute though it was, this timely maneuver brought only meager rewards: Stalin obtained his allies' approval to incorporate the part of East Prussia that he had already incorporated anyway. He also secured an invitation for his Warsaw clients to come to Potsdam and argue in person their case for the Western Neisse. On other matters the deadlock continued. In fact, the outlook for the reparations grew dimmer, as Byrnes hinted that each occupation power might have to collect these from its own zone.[136]

Within four days, Potsdam thus revealed a definite change of atmosphere from Yalta. Admittedly, in dealing with such issues as political freedoms in their respective spheres of influence, the participants still preferred to muddle up their differences in true Yalta fashion. But otherwise, their haggling about the reparations or about the subtleties of the recognition to be accorded Germany's former satellites showed that they retained few illusions about one another. Clearly the urge to reach working agreements had passed, along with the overwhelming military imperative to defeat the common enemy. If anything, the Russians' impending participation in the war against Japan could weaken that imperative, as their contribution was no longer needed. This became particularly true once the United States had successfully tested the atomic bomb, two days before Potsdam began.

What, if any, impact did this epochal event have on the conference? On July 24, Truman broke the news to Stalin with some trepidation, anxious to see how the Soviet ruler would take it after having been kept in the dark by his allies about so crucial a matter. But the man who had raised such tantrums about the innocuous Berne affair four months earlier did not seem to mind at all nor did he seem particularly impressed.[137] Churchill, who watched the scene from a distance, concluded that Stalin simply failed to grasp the weapon's significance—an estimate confirmed by so knowledgeable a Soviet source as Shtemenko.[138] Another reason is that he already knew the "secret." It is all but certain that Klaus Fuchs, the star Soviet spy, had been reporting about the project to Moscow since 1942; when the bomb exploded on the New Mexico test site, Fuchs was right there. Besides, the Russians themselves had been developing a nuclear program since 1943, although not as a matter of high priority.[139] For several reasons, therefore, Molotov could refer to the "revelation" "with something like a smirk on his face" when he met Harriman in Moscow soon after Potsdam.[140]

Actually, even if he had been surprised and shocked, Stalin could hardly have reacted other than as he did. On the defensive at the conference, he could not admit to being impressed without seriously weakening his hand in the negotiations. In this respect the President's casual approach helped him to gloss over the matter. In any case, the topic was not mentioned again at Potsdam in any known conversations with the Russians and, whatever Stalin's feelings, the Soviet negotiating positions remained unaffected.

Far from being intimidated, the Russians explored different avenues to enhance their reparations yield. Seizing on an originally French idea, they proposed joint administration and exploitation of the industrial district of the Ruhr, a plan that would have amounted to a substantive revision of the zonal system.[141] They further raised new claims for reparations from Austria, in the relatively modest sum of $250 million, as well as from Italy.[142] Finally, they tried to force issues by announcing on July 27 the formation in their sector of Berlin of "central German agencies" concerned with economic affairs. Like the political parties six weeks earlier, these were "so formed that they could easily become all-German institutions later on." [143]

On July 25, the conference had been temporarily adjourned so that Churchill and Eden could return to London for the British elections. During the adjournment, Byrnes informally approached Molotov to outline a compromise: apart from the reparations each power would exact from its own zone, industrial equipment was to be delivered to the Soviet Union from the Western-administered part of Germany, but only if foodstuffs and other supplies were sent there from the Russian zone in return. [144] Since it was impossible to even guess what items of value were left in the devastated country, no definite amounts were mentioned in the formal proposal that Byrnes submitted on July 29. He offered Moscow 25 percent of whatever equipment could eventually be found in the Ruhr, provided that the Eastern rather than the Western Neisse became Poland's boundary. [145]

Stalin was not present when this package deal was put forward, having excused himself because of a severe cold. In his absence, Molotov indicated that neither proposal would be acceptable, balking especially at the indefinite reparations total which was to be used to determine the Russian share, and again demanding the Western Neisse. When Stalin was told about Byrnes's offer, however, he found it interesting enough to summon urgently (despite his alleged cold) the Warsaw representatives who had meanwhile arrived in town. Deputy Premier Mikołajczyk, who was likely to leak the contents of the talks to his Western friends, was not invited. [146] As a result, the talks, which took place later on July 29, have been little known; yet the details gradually revealed about them in Polish publications make the episode one of the high points of Potsdam. [147]

Stalin wanted the Poles to part with some of the territory he had promised them, so that he might get in return more reparations for himself. He tried to coax them to give up the Western Neisse and be content with a boundary following the Bober and

Queiss rivers farther east. Aghast, they pleaded for at least the watershed between the two rivers and the Western Neisse. Since both sides apparently held firm, a second meeting became necessary that same evening, during which Stalin's difficult protégés, having recovered from their initial shock, balked at any concessions at all. It was symptomatic of the limits of his dominance that in the end the Soviet ruler promised not to propose any concessions, although it is far from certain that he would have kept his promise if it had come to bargaining with Byrnes. He was spared the test, for the Secretary of State, after Molotov's rebuff and a consultation with Truman, had meanwhile reconsidered the American offer and announced the next day that the United States would accept the Western Neisse after all.[148]

In "improving" his original package, Byrnes also offered the Russians an additional percentage of the Ruhr industrial equipment without any kind of compensation. Moreover, although the Ruhr was part of the British zone, he had proposed his compromise while the British were away, thus promoting an impression that the Anglo-American rift might be widening. Finally, the change of government in London, as a result of the Conservatives' stunning electoral defeat, seemed to justify the conclusion that the British could be written off as a serious factor. If Stalin counted on all these appearances, he was soon proved wrong.

On July 30, the conference resumed with Britain's new Labor leaders. While Prime Minister Clement R. Attlee kept silent most of the time, his Foreign Secretary Ernest Bevin more than made up for his taciturnity; alert and excellently briefed, the seasoned union negotiator was a hardliner by disposition, congenial in many ways to Truman.[149] In any case, the irresistible trend toward closer cooperation between the two Western powers proceeded apace, despite the deceptive appearances to the contrary. It put in question a fundamental premise of Stalin's strategy.

On July 31, Byrnes indicated to Molotov that the revised American package was a take-it-or-leave-it offer, because he and the President intended to leave for home the next day.[150] Hard bargaining ensued as the Russians tried to recoup with minimal losses. Although by then they had scaled down their reparations bill from $10 billion to $4 billion, they were still unable to obtain Western commitment to any definite amount. Nor did they succeed in promoting their plan for internationalization of the Ruhr and in gaining approval for their claims to Austrian and Italian reparations.[151] Stalin therefore raised additional demands, asking particularly for shares in the stock of German firms and for a third of Germany's foreign assets, as well as a third of its gold reserve.[152]

In pressing these demands, the Russians resorted to tactics similar to those Stalin had employed against Hopkins. Toward the end of the conference, they introduced a host of extraneous motions calculated to show their adversaries in the wrong on a variety of issues. They accused the British and Americans of abetting anti-Soviet activites in Germany, of obstructing the repatriation of Soviet citizens from internment camps in Italy, and of neglecting to disarm German troops in Norway. They further challenged Britain to sack the Greek government because of its alleged rule of terror.[153] Having thus charged the West with assorted wrongdoings, they insisted on instant rectification; however, the very preposterousness of the demands indicated that they were designed to induce acceptance of the other Soviet desiderata to compensate for the presumed Western misbehavior.

The tactics that had worked with Hopkins no longer worked at Potsdam, however, and the tone of the verbal exchanges at the final session on August 1 left little doubt that the alliance was over. During a debate about the disposition of Germany's external assets, Stalin prophetically, though unwittingly, proposed a line that anticipated almost exactly the eventual division of Europe. Starting at the Baltic coast, it followed the border between the Western and the Soviet zones of Germany, the Czechoslovak–German frontier, and the zonal boundaries in Austria. The line continued along the northern and eastern limits of

Yugoslavia, as if to presage Tito's later defection from Moscow's fold. With further prophetic insight, Stalin failed to assign Albania to either side. Significantly, of all his additional reparations proposals, this proved the only one acceptable to the conference. It specified that the enemy assets west of the line be sequestered by the West, those east of it by the Soviet Union.[154]

The Russians achieved another minor success before the conference ended. Although the secret final protocol exempted Austria from any obligation to pay reparations, the exemption was deleted from the official public communiqué. The deletion, suggested by Molotov quite casually and approved without closer examination, enabled the Soviet Union to despoil its part of Austria under the disguise of sequestering "German property."[155] Nevertheless, the overall reparations settlement fell far short of Russian wishes. It still mentioned only percentages, and although the total sum available for distribution was to be determined within six months, any practical implementation presupposed the victors' common policy in Germany—something that never existed.[156]

It was ironically France, that object of Stalin's derision, that first proved an obstacle to his German designs. Not having been invited to Potsdam, the French only reluctantly endorsed its decisions while pursuing an independent course. The weakest of the occupation powers, they had the least ambition to seek influence in the other zones but the greatest urge to protect themselves from any outside interference in their own. They resolutely opposed Soviet efforts at joint management of the Ruhr and vetoed any expansion of the "central agencies" the Russians had erected in East Berlin. The occupation power burdened with the worst historic experience with Germany, France alone envisaged its partition as a desirable solution.[157]

Rebuffed in their bid for influence across zonal boundaries, the Russians gradually proceeded to treat their own zone as a separate entity, thus making partition inevitable. Their policy led to suspension of the reparations agreements and paralysis of the Control Council. By 1948 they finally acknowledged the fiasco by

302

ending the removal of capital equipment from their zone and by grudgingly starting its reconstruction instead; this amounted to their fourth major miscalculation in thirty years.[158] Again Germany proved a graveyard of Soviet hopes, and the abortive Berlin blockade of 1948–1949 was yet to come.

The Potsdam negotiators had taken special care to assure that each favor granted to Bulgaria, Romania, and Hungary would also be granted to Italy, and vice versa. The ensuing accords facilitated eventual conclusion of peace treaties with all four countries, as well as with Finland, and their admission to the United Nations—none of which entailed any new Soviet gains. Nor did the Western acquiescence to Polish administration east of the Oder–Neisse line amount to more than the confirmation of an arrangement already in force.[159] It was more consequential that at Potsdam Stalin had failed to advance any of his designs regarding Spain, the Italian colonies, Tangier, or Turkey.

Soviet spokesmen played good sports by publicly praising the results of the conference.[160] But Potsdam was not a success for Moscow; as Khrushchev later admitted, it "was a compromise based on the distribution of power among the Allies at the end of the war."[161] To be sure, the West did not exactly benefit either. Potsdam was no great improvement over Yalta; unlike the Yalta agreements, which had been too vague, the Potsdam ones were specific but on the wrong issues. The conferees missed the last opportunity to make the limits of their respective interests clear to one another, and the advent of the nuclear age changed the perspectives drastically.

Little though the secret explosion of the atom bomb had influenced the Potsdam negotiations, its actual use against Japan shortly after their conclusion revolutionized the whole notion of security. In particular, the dramatic public demonstration of the spectacular new power that the United States alone possessed rendered questionable the value of controlling a land mass—the old-fashioned goal toward which Stalin had expended so much effort and ingenuity during the war.[162] This is not to say that he perceived an immediate threat; the Americans abstained scrupulously from brandishing the weapon to blackmail him, latter-day theories to the contrary notwithstanding.[163] His experience since Yalta also taught him not to panic again. Still, the mere thought that the Americans were in a position to blackmail him if they so desired cast a deep shadow over his wartime gains.[164]

Even though official Soviet comments about the bomb remained restrained and free from reproaches, the tone of satisfaction prevalent after Potsdam had all but disappeared by the end of August.[165] It is not known whether anybody in the ruling oligarchy actually dared to suggest that Stalin may have won the war but lost the peace; it was enough that he had become vulnerable to such a criticism. His serious illness in late summer hardly helped matters.[166] On October 10, *Pravda* announced that the "Generalissimo" was going on vacation and that Molotov would temporarily act as his replacement.[167]

A fortnight later, Stalin gave a glimpse of his state of mind to Harriman, who visited him at the Black Sea resort of Gagra.[168] The dictator's mood was more gloomy than threatening. Without going into specifics, Stalin indicated that now perhaps the time had come for a policy of isolation he had never favored. And although he did not say so, he gave the ambassador the impression that the change was the result of a major reappraisal that had recently taken place in the Kremlin.

The reappraisal can be dated fairly reliably as having occurred in September, when the journal *Bolshevik*, that weathervane of changing Soviet political perceptions, had unexpectedly suspended publication. Meanwhile its editorial board had been throughly shaken up, and when the delayed August issue finally appeared at the end of October, it conspicuously struck a new note of ideological militancy.[169] Whatever else this meant, it is clear that in the altercation Molotov (noted for his aversion to taking chances in foreign policy) had prevailed upon Stalin sufficiently to be appointed his alter ego.

Litvinov, the Cassandra in the Foreign Commissariat, soon found another opportunity to convey his informed opinion about the state of East–West relations. When he met Harriman in November at a Moscow theater performance, Harriman wanted to know what the United States could do to satisfy the Soviet Union. Litvinov replied: "Nothing." When further questioned about what his own government could do to improve matters he gave the same curt answer, adding the enigmatic qualification: "I believe I know what should be done but I am powerless." [170]

If Potsdam had stalled the anemic postwar détente, the advent of the nuclear era finally reversed it. Trying to prove to himself (as well as to his real or potential critics) that he was not resigned to losing the peace after having won the war, Stalin set out to redress the balance by all means at his disposal, including acceleration of Russia's nuclear program. His policy, though it did not preclude occasional concessions and tactical retreats for another two years, was now irrevocable, regardless of anything the West might do short of a nuclear war—an option Stalin rightly discounted. He gradually tightened his grip wherever his power reached, while testing soft spots to expand it farther. In due course, this policy prompted both the imposition of Communist regimes in all countries the Soviet Union had overrun and a confrontation with the West over the issue of where the lines should be drawn.

As the trend toward the ultimate confrontation continued, thriving on an interplay of action and reaction, Soviet theorists wrestled with the question of whether war was inevitable or not. They pondered whether it might result from contradictions among the capitalist powers themselves, that is, from a breakdown in the West which might warrant Russian intervention. Or could an armed conflict ensue instead from the unbridgeable differences between socialism and capitalism, that is, from the growing rivalry between the two superpowers? The conclusion they eventually reached was characteristically ambivalent: There was not a "danger of war" but rather a "threat of a danger of war."[171] Or, in the similarly ambivalent Western terminology, there was now a "Cold War."

In guiding Russia on its road to the Cold War, Stalin was both a victim and an accomplice. He was a victim in the sense that his 1945 military triumph fell short of his hopes—inflated hopes, to be sure, because of his exaggerated and quixotic notion of security. But he was also an accomplice, for he had provoked the adverse Western reaction which, contrary to his expectations, had frustrated those hopes. He might have acted with more restraint if, as Litvinov noted, the Western powers had taken a firm and unequivocal stand early enough. By not doing so, they too had become both accomplices and victims, for their own pious hopes for a stable relationship with Moscow had likewise been frustrated. There was an element of predestination in all this: Stalin could have taken a more enlightened view of what security means—but only if he had not been Stalin. And the Western statesmen could have acted with fewer scruples—but then *they* would have had to be akin to Stalin. Wielding so much greater control over Russian policies than they did over theirs, the dictator may still seem to have been capable of steering away from confrontations more easily. But in the last analysis, his hands were tied by the Soviet system which had bred him and which he felt compelled to perpetuate by his execrable methods; that system was the true cause of the Cold War.

concluding thoughts

What are the lessons of the Cold War? For better or for worse, they are lessons of an irrevocable past; it is remarkable how much those events, hardly more than thirty years old, already have the unmistakable air of another era. In pondering the thoughts and actions of the statesmen of the time, one cannot help noticing how small and simple their world was in comparison with ours. How modest were their tools, how rudimentary their perceptions. Certainly the Americans and Russians have since learned a great deal about one another. It is this sense of a distance traveled that makes irresistible a broad appraisal of the perspectives lost and found.

The longer the perspectives, the more does June 1941 appear as one of the great turning points in history. Not only did Hitler's gratuitous aggression open the door through which the Soviet Union eventually stepped out to become the world's mightiest and perhaps last imperial power; it also provided the dubious justification for Stalin's imperialism. The humiliation of his life, the Nazi treachery imbued Stalin with an extraordinary drive to justify in retrospect the wisdom of the expansionistic policies he had initiated during his abortive association with the German dictator. The experience thus perpetuated rather than discredited the mixture of cynical opportunism and ruthless power politics, disregarding the interests of other nations, that had been the hallmark of the association. Neither Stalin nor his successors have ever repudiated this legacy.

The enduring memory of a narrow escape from catastrophic defeat in 1941 nurtured a cult of military strength in the Soviet Union. The cult has since burgeoned into a militarism so pervasive that critics have sometimes wondered whether it may have acquired a momentum beyond the leaders' ability to control. Having created the biggest war machine the world has ever seen, the Russians have far exceeded any reasonable security requirements. Whether their feeling of security has increased proportionately is doubtful; that such a feeling among other nations has diminished as a consequence is certain.

In bringing the war against Nazi Germany to a victorious end, Stalin created the Soviet empire as a by-product. He had not originally sought a military conquest of the whole area he won. He would have preferred to advance his power and influence there, as elsewhere, by less risky and more subtle means, although he never ruled out resorting to force if the conditions were right; in this respect, his approach differed from that of his successors less than it may seem. But Stalin was unable (contrary to his hopes) to satisfactorily project his power abroad except by force of arms and to maintain it except by putting in charge vassal Communist regimes; as a result, he saddled his country with a cluster of sullen dependencies whose possession proved a mixed blessing in the long run.

Far from providing the ultimate protective shield, the empire enlarged the area whose integrity the Russians had to uphold and also diluted its internal cohesion. In coping with the ensuing challenges, the Soviet leaders since Stalin have greatly refined the art of penetrating other countries without outright conquest and of controlling those previously conquered without excessive resort to force. Despite the refinements, however, the fundamental dilemmas of imperialism they inherited from him are still very much with them, with no resolution in sight. The recurrent Soviet setbacks in uncommitted countries and the smoldering discontent throughout eastern Europe suggest a disconcerting lack of alternatives to force.

In masterminding Russia's ascent during World War II and its aftermath, Stalin proved an accomplished practitioner of the strategy of minimum and maximum aims, a strategy his heirs then continued to pursue with variable success. Apt at both exploiting the existing opportunities and creating new ones, he let his aspirations grow until he realized that he had misjudged the complacency of his Anglo-American partners—as they had misjudged his moderation. So he plunged his country into a confrontation with the West that he had neither desired nor thought inevitable. Not without reason were tributes to his diplomatic proficiency conspicuously missing among the accolades that he afterward stage-managed to impress his subjects by the multiple facets of his presumed genius.

Since Stalin, in pursuing his rising aspirations, took into close account the actual and anticipated Western attitudes, his coalition partners contributed their inseparable share to a development that they soon judged was detrimental to their own vital interests. If the Soviet ruler did not rate nearly so high as a diplomat as his reputation suggested, his American and British opposite numbers surely rated even lower. The great war leaders, Roosevelt and Churchill, failed not so much in their perceptions as in their negligence to prepare themselves and their peoples for the disheartening likelihood of a breakdown of the wartime alliance. The British Prime Minister, whose perceptions were keener, is that much more open to criticism than the American President. In any case, by their reluctance (however understandable) to anticipate worse things to come, the Western statesmen let matters worsen until the hour of reckoning was at hand.

The undistinguished performance of Britain's World War II diplomacy is perhaps the main revelation so far to come out from the recently opened London government archives. Quite apart from the substance of policies, the striking decline of professionalism makes the preceding blunders of appeasement appear

ıry aberrations than as symptoms of the same un-
surmounted crisis of adjustment to the eclipse of power. Nor, to
be sure, did the American diplomacy of those days exactly shine.
Its shortcomings were largely those of innocence and inexperi-
ence, as its subsequent coming of age demonstrated. Since then
the United States foreign policy has, for all its persisting deficiencies, drawn on an expertise beyond any comparison with that
available thirty years ago—surely one of the most encouraging differences between then and now.

It has been a commonplace to observe that nothing could
have prevented the Russians from overruning the countries they
did and installing there regimes of their choice. Indeed, compelling reasons can be cited to explain why the development was inevitable. But this "realistic" argument, which overlooks the difference between Soviet capability and Soviet aims, is a poor guide
to both understanding history and inspiring action. During the
Cold War, it bred the fallacy that Russian expansion could only be
dammed effectively by military means, a reasoning conducive to
the excessive preoccupation with the military attributes of power
that has been characteristic of the American "national security
state."[1] More recently, with the strategic balance ostensibly shifting in favor of the Russians, the same reasoning has often led to
complacency about the spread of Soviet influence. Nowhere has
the ambiguity of the realistic thesis been more evident than in the
continuing controversy about the apparent or real inconsistencies
in the ideas advocated at different times by the leading proponent
of that thesis, George F. Kennan.[2]

Admittedly, the growth of Soviet power and influence need
not always infringe on Western interests. Yet once the proposition is accepted that Moscow possesses the military leverage to
achieve particular political goals, its temptation to actually seek
such goals may become irresistible. In this respect, matters have
not changed substantially since the onset of the Cold War. At the
end of World War II, given Russia's exhaustion and Stalin's sen-
sitivity to the cost of expansion, any Western policy likely to re-

strain him would have had to follow a harder rather than a softer line; it would also have had a better chance to succeed if applied sooner rather than later. Conceivably, even cold-blooded "atomic diplomacy" (the abstention from which failed notably to avert the Cold War) might have achieved the same effect so long as the United States retained its nuclear monopoly. To be sure, these conclusions, however plausible, are merely academic, for no such policies could have materialized in their time.

Nor are these conclusions very helpful now, when the world balance of power is altogether different. In both absolute terms and in relation to the West, the power wielded by Soviet leaders today is dramatically superior to Stalin's. At the same time, in exercising it they have been significantly more restricted. None of them has approximated the dead tyrant in his sheer wickedness. More pertinently, unable to match his authority, his successors have become more susceptible to diverse pressure. Under their guardianship the Soviet regime has, for all its abominations, grown more human and responsive to change.

Yet the transformation, comforting as it is, has not been altogether reassuring. Abroad, Stalin's heirs have sometimes behaved more irresponsibly than he; under greater compulsion to prove themselves by instant success, they have occasionaly been prone to take risks he would have eschewed. For all his aptitude at exploiting opportunities, Stalin would have hardly gone so far as sending missiles to Cuba, ferrying mercenaries to Angola, or peddling arms to unreliable clients around the world. Not every comparison with those who do not quite fit into his shoes casts a bad light on Stalin.

Twenty-five years after Stalin's death, has the Soviet Union at last reached the stage from which it might embark on a bid for global supremacy? Not only does it seem capable of building up its war machine to a point where it could attempt to blackmail others into submission; its actual armament program also suggests the disturbing possibility that at least some of the men in charge might be leaning toward such an insanity. Or, even if they do not

311

lean that way now, the notoriously inefficient Soviet machinery for leadership succession (not to mention the absence of effective institutional safeguards against the abuse of power) offers scant comfort for the future. But, characteristically for the unprecedented open-endedness of the new East–West relationship, this extreme scenario appears no more probable than its very opposite.

More than in Stalin's time, Soviet leaders have had to worry about developments that might abruptly nullify any of their ambitions. Andrei Amalrik's rhetorical question, "Will the Soviet Union Survive until 1984?" may have missed the date but certainly not their profound anxieties about a cataclysmic showdown with China or a sudden disintegration of their multi-ethnic state.[3] With the future so beclouded, Soviet rulers may be well advised to ponder some of the obvious lessons of the Cold War—the cost of underestimating their adversaries, the burden of an empire, the ultimate futility of repression.

To maintain a proper perspective, it is only fair to stress that even the most vexing problems that have faced the West, and the United States especially, tend to pale in comparison with the Soviet predicament; in any case, they lack the same existential urgency. Not even the greatest doomsayers saw fit to suggest in 1976 that a hundred years later the American Republic might no longer be here to celebrate its tricentennial. Even so, its statesmen could do worse than to learn their Cold War lessons right. If their predecessors' failure to impress on Stalin plainly and promptly enough the limits of Western tolerance led to confrontation thirty years ago, the implicit message is hardly less topical in a world packed with instruments of wholesale destruction. And the nuclear balance of terror, however reliable a guardian of peace thus far, is not immune to tampering.

There is a risk of self-righteousness in pressing the argument to its logical conclusion, but there is greater peril in too much modesty. If the evils of the Soviet system were the ultimate cause of the Cold War, the virtues of the Western polity still remain the ultimate hope for averting a conflict that could lead to a holocaust. For only those virtues—moral, political, and economic superiority sustained by both faith in the value of liberty and enough military strength to defend it—can be reliably counted on to give pause to any present and future adversaries that may contemplate gambling on the West's decline. But its vigor also remains the necessary precondition for supplying the Soviet leaders with the incentives needed to promote common interests and mutual survival. And such incentives are no less imperative to help deter an embattled leadership from taking risks out of desperation, to which the tragic Russian experience is so conducive.

Thus there are indeed lessons to be learned from the Cold War, though not the same ones for the East and the West. To say that from the East they require more wisdom, from the West more faith, may seem too simple. Yet the answers to great questions are often that simple. Certainly the price of ignoring the lessons is high and rising. Enlightened statesmanship need not pay it.

abbreviations

BBC	Written Archives Centre, British Broadcasting Corporation, Reading
BGDA	*Beiträge zur Geschichte der deutschen Arbeiterbewegung* (East Berlin periodical)
CNR	Česká národní rada [Czech National Council]
DGFP	*Documents on German Foreign Policy* (Washington: U.S. Government Printing Office, since 1949)
DHCSP	*Dokumenty z historie československé politiky* [Documents on the History of Czechoslovak Politics] (Prague: Academia, 1966)
DPSR	*Documents on Polish-Soviet Relations* (London: Heinemann, 1961–67)
EAC	European Advisory Commission
EAM	Ethnikon Apeleftheretikon Metopon [National Liberation Front]
FDRL	Franklin Delano Roosevelt Library, Hyde Park, New York
FRUS	*Foreign Relations of the United States: Diplomatic Papers* (Washington: U.S. Government Printing Office, since 1922)
FRUS, Potsdam	*Foreign Relations of the United States, The Conference of Berlin (The Potsdam Conference)* (Washington: U.S. Government Printing Office, 1960)
FRUS, Tehran	*Foreign Relations of the United States, The Conferences at Cairo and Tehran 1943* (Washington: U.S. Government Printing Office, 1961)
FRUS, Yalta	*Foreign Relations of the United States, The Conferences at Malta and Yalta 1945* (Washington: U.S. Government Printing Office, 1955)
JCEA	*Journal of Central European Affairs*

315

KRN	Krajowa Rada Narodowa [National Council of the Homeland]
NA	National Archives, Washington, D.C.
Narkomindel	Narodnyi komissariat inostrannykh del [People's Commissariat for Foreign Affairs]
NKVD	Narodnyi komissariat vnutrennikh del [People's Commissariat for Internal Affairs]
OAR	*Odboj a revoluce* (Prague periodical)
OSS	Office of Strategic Services
PRO	Public Record Office, London
RG	Record Group
SCCA	*Correspondence between the Chairman of the Council of Ministers of the U.S.S.R. and the Presidents of the U.S.A. and the Prime Ministers of Great Britain during the Great Patriotic War of 1941–1945: Correspondence with Winston S. Churchill and Clement R. Attlee* (Moscow: Foreign Languages Publishing House, 1957)
SCRT	*Correspondence . . . with Franklin D. Roosevelt and Harry S. Truman* (Moscow: Foreign Languages Publishing House, 1957)
SNR	Slovenská národná rada [Slovak National Council]
SOE	Special Operations Executive
SR	*Slavic Review*
Tass	Telegrafnoe agentstvo Sovetskogo Soiuza [Telegraphic Agency of the Soviet Union]
ZPP	Związek Patriotów Polskich [Union of Polish Patriots]
ZPW	*Z pola walki* (Warsaw periodical)

note on sources

Too numerous and diverse to be itemized separately, the published primary and secondary sources used in this study are listed in the notes to each chapter. A full bibliographical reference appears the first time a source is cited in a chapter, abbreviated ones afterward.

The following collections of unpublished records have been consulted:

National Archives, Washington, D.C., and Suitland, Maryland

RG-59	General Records of the Department of State: Decimal File Lot File (1945)
RG-84	Records of the Foreign Service Posts of the Department of State: United States Embassy Moscow
RG-107	Records of the Office of the Secretary of War
RG-165	Records of the War Department General and Special Staffs: Office of Strategic Services, Research and Analysis Branch Army Intelligence (G-2)
RG-218	Records of the United States Chiefs of Staff: United States Chiefs of Staff Combined Chiefs of Staff
RG-226	Records of the Office of Strategic Services
RG-242	National Archives Collection of Foreign Records Seized (captured German documents on microfilm): T-120 Records of the German Foreign Office T-175 Records of the Reich Leader of the SS and Chief of German Police
RG-319	Records of the Army Staff: Chief of Staff of the Army
RG-331	Records of Allied Operational and Occupation Headquarters, World War II: Supreme Headquarters, Allied Expeditionary Force

RG-334   Records of Interservice Agencies:
          United States Military Mission Moscow

Franklin Delano Roosevelt Library, Hyde Park, New York
Map Room
President's Secretary's File
Hopkins Papers

Harry S. Truman Library, Independence, Missouri
President's Secretary's File

University of Virginia Library, Charlottesville, Virginia
Edward R. Stettinius, Jr., Papers

Columbia University, New York
Oral History Collection:
    Nikita S. Khrushchev Tapes (transcript)
Archive of Russian and East European History and Culture:
    Jaromír Smutný Papers

Public Record Office, London*
CAB 65   War Cabinet Minutes
CAB 66   War Cabinet Memoranda WP and CP Series
CAB 99   War Cabinet Commonwealth and International Conference
FO 181   Embassy and Consular Archives Russia Correspondence
FO 188   Embassy and Consular Archives Sweden Correspondence
FO 371   Foreign Office General Correspondence after 1906 Political
PREM 3   Operational Papers of the Prime Minister's Office

BBC Written Archives Centre, Reading, Berkshire
Daily Digest of World Broadcasts, 1941–45

Bundesarchiv, Koblenz
R 74   Funk-Abhör-Berichte (Sonderdienst Seehaus)

Friedrich Ebert-Stiftung, Bonn–Bad Godesberg
Collection Emigration Sopade

Further incorporated have been information and opinion generously supplied by
the following persons in interviews and correspondence:
Lord Avon (Anthony Eden), British Secretary of State for Foreign Affairs
Sir William Barker, British Minister in Moscow
Werner Best, chief of German civil administration in Denmark
Charles Bohlen, United States Ambassador to Moscow

* Crown copyright of these PRO documents is hereby acknowledged.

Jacques Duclos, member of the Politburo of the French Communist party
Major-General Sir Collin Gubbins, chief of the Special Operations Executive
Sir William Hayter, British Ambassador to Moscow
George F. Kennan, United States Ambassador to Moscow
Wolfgang Leonhard, member of Walter Ulbricht's task force for Germany in
    1945
Ivy Litvinov, wife of Soviet People's Commissar for Foreign Affairs
Otakar Machotka, vice-chairman of the Czech National Council

For the transliteration of Russian names, the simplified Library of Congress system has been used unless transliterated differently in an original source or in common usage.

notes

Introduction

1. Timothy W. Stanley, "Détente: The Continuation of Tension by Other Means," Policy Paper, Security Working Group, Atlantic Council of the United States, 1977.

2. Herbert Feis, quoted in Gar Alperovitz, *Cold War Essays* (New York: Doubleday, 1970), p. 135.

3. William Welch, *American Images of Soviet Foreign Policy* (New Haven: Yale University Press, 1970), p. 299.

4. Khrushchev tapes, transcript, part II, p. 816a, Oral History Collection, Columbia University.

5. Roy Medvedev, *Let History Judge: The Origins and Consequences of Stalinism* (New York: Knopf, 1971).

6. Quite appropriately, the recent revival of "Stalin studies" in the West reflects a keen awareness of the linkage; see especially Robert C. Tucker, ed., *Stalinism: Essays in Historical Interpretation* (New York: Norton, 1977).

7. See Alexander Dallin, "Bias and Blunders in American Studies on the USSR," and John A. Armstrong, "Comments on Professor Dallin's 'Bias and Blunders in American Studies on the USSR,'" *SR* 32 (1973): 564, 580.

Chapter One: Traditions and Antecedents

1. An outstanding recent example is Robert Wesson, *The Russian Dilemma: A Political and Geopolitical View* (New Brunswick, N.J.: Rutgers University Press, 1974).

2. Astolphe de Custine, *La Russie en 1839*, 4 vols. (Paris: D'Amyot, 1843).

3. Karl Marx, in *New York Tribune*, December 30, 1853; Karl Marx and Friedrich Engels, *The Russian Menace to Europe*, ed. Paul W. Blackstock and Bert F. Hoselitz (Glencoe, Ill.: Free Press, 1952), p. 169.

4. Friedrich Engels, "The Foreign Policy of Russian Tsarism," in Marx and Engels, *Russian Menace to Europe*, pp. 25–55, commented on pp. 242–46.

5. See Richard E. Pipes, "Domestic Politics and Foreign Affairs," in *Russian Foreign Policy*, ed. Ivo J. Lederer (New Haven: Yale University Press, 1962), pp. 145–69.

6. Walter Laqueur, *Russia and Germany: A Century of Conflict* (Boston: Little, Brown, 1965), pp. 13–25.

7. Roderic H. Davison, " 'Russian Skill and Turkish Imbecility': The Treaty of Kuchuk Kainardji Reconsidered," *SR* 35 (1976): 463–83.

8. Charles Jelavich, *Tsarist Russia and Balkan Nationalism* (Berkeley: University of California Press, 1958), pp. 1–3.

9. See Michael B. Petrovich, *The Emergence of Russian Panslavism, 1856–1870* (New York: Columbia University Press, 1956), pp. 3–17.

10. David MacKenzie, *The Serbs and Russian Pan-Slavism, 1875–1878* (Ithaca, N.Y.: Cornell University Press, 1967), pp. 1–2.

11. Harold Temperley, "The Treaty of Paris of 1856 and Its Execution," *Journal of Modern History* 4 (1932): 387–414.

12. MacKenzie, *Serbs and Russian Pan-Slavism*, pp. 248–71.

13. Edward Chmielewski, *The Polish Question in the Russian State Duma* (Knoxville: University of Tennessee Press, 1970), pp. 3–21, 170–74.

14. Adam Bromke, *Poland's Politics: Idealism vs. Realism* (Cambridge: Harvard University Press, 1967), pp. 9, 15–16, 22–25.

15. L'udevít Štúr, *Das Slawentum und die Welt der Zukunft*; see Michael B. Petrovich, "L'udevít Štúr and Russian Panslavism," *JCEA* 12 (1952–53): 1–19.

16. Hans Kohn, *Pan-Slavism: Its History and Ideology* (Notre Dame, Ind.: University of Notre Dame Press, 1953), pp. 103–45.

17. Quoted in Otakar Odlozilik, "Russia and Czech National Aspirations," *JCEA* 22 (1962–63), p. 439.

18. William L. Langer, *European Alliances and Alignments, 1871–1890* (New York: Random House, 1966), pp. 417–25.

19. Sergei Sazonov, quoted in A. J. P. Taylor, "The War Aims of the Allies in the First World War," in *Essays Presented to Sir Lewis Namier*, ed. Richard Pares and A. J. P. Taylor (New York: St. Martin's, 1956), p. 481.

20. Quoted in Kohn, *Pan-Slavism*, p. 204.

21. Quoted in Taylor, "War Aims of the Allies," p. 480.

22. Gifford D. Malone, "War Aims Toward Germany," in *Russian Diplomacy and Eastern Europe, 1914–1917* (New York: King's Crown, 1963), pp. 129–31.

23. Merritt Abrash, "War Aims Toward Austria-Hungary: The Czechoslovak Pivot," *ibid.*, pp. 100–14.

24. Andrzej Kamiński, "Czechosłowacja w panslawistycznych planach Wielkorządcy Rosji Admirała Aleksandra W. Kołczaka [Czechoslovakia in the Pan-Slav plans of Admiral Alexander V. Kolchak, the supreme ruler of Russia], *Studia historyczne* 11 (1968): 410–11.

25. Ioannis Sinanoglou, "France Looks Eastward: Perspectives and Policies on Russia, 1914–1918" (Ph.D. diss., Columbia University, 1973), pp. 38–46, 74–75, 91–93.

26. Leon Trotsky, *My Life* (New York: Scribner, 1930), p. 341.

27. Robert H. Johnston, *Tradition versus Revolution: Russia and the Balkans* (New York: Columbia University Press, 1977), appeared after the completion of the present study.

28. Richard Pipes, *The Formation of the Soviet Union* (Cambridge: Harvard University Press, 1964), pp. 34–41.

29. Merle Fainsod, *International Socialism and the World War* (Cambridge: Harvard University Press, 1935), p. 45.

30. Stanley W. Page, *Lenin and World Revolution* (New York: New York University Press, 1959), pp. 3–4, 111–12.

31. James W. Hulse, *The Forming of the Communist International* (Stanford: Stanford University Press, 1964), pp. 79–108.

32. Werner T. Angress, *Stillborn Revolution: The Communist Bid for Power in Germany, 1921–1923* (Princeton: Princeton University Press, 1963), pp. 115, 376–77.

33. Speech by Lenin, April 17, 1919, quoted in David T. Cattell, "The Hungarian Revolution of 1919 and the Reorganization of the Comintern in 1920," *JCEA* 11 (1951–52): 28; Iván Völgyes, "Soviet Russia and Soviet Hungary," in *Hungary in Revolution, 1918*, ed. I. Völgyes (Lincoln: University of Nebraska Press, 1971), pp. 158–69.

34. Alfred D. Low, "The First Austrian Republic and Soviet Hungary," *JCEA* 20 (1960–61): 174–203.

35. Richard Luckett, *The White Generals* (New York: Viking, 1971), p. 165; Paul E. Zinner, *Communist Strategy and Tactics in Czechoslovakia* (London: Pall Mall, 1963), p. 26.

36. Peter A. Toma, "The Slovak Soviet Republic of 1919," *American Slavic and East European Review* 17 (1958): 203–15.

37. Warren Lerner, "Attempting a Revolution from Without: Poland in 1920," in *The Anatomy of Communist Takeovers*, ed. Thomas T. Hammond and Robert Farrell (New Haven: Yale University Press, 1975), pp. 94–106.

38. Władysław Pobóg-Malinowski, *Najnowsza historia polityczna Polski* [The recent political history of Poland], vol. II, part 1 (London: Swiderski, 1956), p. 302.

39. Joseph Rothschild, *The Communist Party of Bulgaria* (New York: Columbia University Press, 1959), pp. 133–51.

40. Norman Davies, *White Eagle, Red Star: The Polish-Soviet War, 1919–20* (London: Macdonald, 1972), pp. 210–19.

41. For example, "Memorandum of Marshal Stalin's Views as Expressed During the Evening of November 28, 1943," *FRUS, Tehran*, p. 513.

42. Quoted in Harald von Riekhoff, *German-Polish Relations, 1918–1933* (Baltimore: Johns Hopkins Press, 1971), p. 87.

43. Hans W. Gatzke, "Russo-German Military Collaboration during the Weimar Republic," *American Historical Review* 63 (1957–58): 565–97.

44. Alexander Dallin, "The Use of International Movements, in *Russian Foreign Policy*, ed. Lederer, p. 323.

45. Henry L. Roberts, *Rumania: Political Problems of an Agrarian State* (New Haven: Yale University Press, 1951), pp. 252–53.

46. Ruth Fischer, *Stalin and German Communism* (Cambridge: Harvard University Press, 1948), pp. 655–56.

47. Ossip Flechtheim, *Die Kommunistische Partei Deutschlands in der Weimarer Republik* (Offenbach a.M.: Bollwerk, 1948), pp. 165–66, 176, 181–82.

48. "Resolution des Exekutivkomitees der Kommunistischen Internationale," April 1, 1933, quoted in Siegfried Bahne, "Die Kommunistische Partei Deutschlands," in *Das Ende der Parteien 1933*, ed. Erich Matthias and Rudolf Morsey (Düsseldorf: Droste, 1960), p. 731.

49. Karlheinz Niclauss, *Die Sowjetunion und Hitlers Machtergreifung* (Bonn: Röhrscheid, 1966), pp. 94–100; cf. the recent controversy touched off by Robert C. Tucker, "The Emergence of Stalin's Foreign Policy," *SR* 36 (1977): 563–89.

50. Quoted in "Soviet Conceptions of Diplomacy," in Vernon V. Aspaturian, *Process and Power in Soviet Foreign Policy* (Boston: Little, Brown, 1971), p. 367.

51. B. M. Leibzon and K. K. Shirinia, *Povorot v politike Kominterna* [The turnabout in the Comintern's policy] (Moscow: Mysl, 1975), pp. 90–106.

52. Niclauss, *Die Sowjetunion und Hitlers Machtergreifung*, pp. 182–99.

53. Robert M. Slusser, "The Role of Foreign Ministry," in *Russian Foreign Policy*, ed. Lederer, pp. 217–30.

54. Francis P. Walters, *A History of the League of Nations*, vol. I (New York: Oxford University Press, 1952), p. 359.

55. Jon D. Glassman, "Soviet Foreign Policy Decision Making," *Columbia Essays in International Affairs: The Dean's Papers, 1967*, vol. III (New York: Columbia University Press, 1968), pp. 380–88.

56. Rudolf L. Tökés, *Béla Kun and the Hungarian Soviet Republic* (New York: Praeger, 1967), pp. 217–18; M. Kamil Dziewanowski, *The Communist Party of Poland* (Cambridge: Harvard University Press, 1976), pp. 149–54.

57. Isaac Deutscher, *Stalin* (New York: Oxford University Press, 1967), pp. 375–77.

58. Robert C. Tucker, *The Soviet Political Mind* (New York: Praeger, 1963), pp. 72–73.

59. Cf. Teddy J. Uldricks, "The Impact of the Great Purges on the People's Commissariat of Foreign Affairs," *SR* 36 (1977): 187–204.

60. Karl Vogelman, "Die Propaganda der österreichischen Emigration in der Sowjetunion für einen selbständigen österreichischen Nationalstaat" (mimeographed Ph.D. diss. University of Vienna, 1973), pp. 20–39.

61. Press statement by Litvinov, March 17, 1938, in *Soviet Documents on Foreign Policy*, ed. Jane Degras, vol. III (London: Oxford University Press, 1953), p. 277.

324

62. Donald N. Lammers, "The May Crisis of 1938: The Soviet Version Considered," *South Atlantic Quarterly* 69 (1970): 480–503; František Lukeš, "Poznámky k československo-sovětským stykům v září 1938" [Comments on Czechoslovak-Soviet contacts in September 1938], *Československý časopis historický* 16 (1968): 703–29.

63. Memorandum by Bohlen on Churchill-Stalin conversation on November 29, 1943, *FRUS, Tehran*, p. 837.

64. Bohdan B. Budurowycz, *Polish-Soviet Relations, 1932–1939* (New York: Columbia University Press, 1963), pp. 127–44.

65. Quoted in Jan Křen and Václav Kural, "Ke stykům mezi československým odbojem a SSSR v letech 1939–1941," [Contacts between the Czechoslovak resistance and the USSR in 1939–1941], *Historie a vojenství*, 1967, p. 440.

66. For a recent interpretation of the ambiguities of the British act, see Simon Newman, *March 1939: The British Guarantee to Poland* (New York: Oxford University Press, 1976).

67. Seeds to Halifax, April 18, 1939, *Documents on British Foreign Policy, 1919–1939*, 3d. ser., vol. V (London: His Majesty's Stationery Office, 1952), pp. 228–29; note by Weizsäcker on conversation with Merekalov, April 17, 1939, *DGFP*, D, vol. VI, pp. 267–68.

68. Donald C. Watt, "The Initiation of the Negotiations Leading to the Nazi-Soviet Pact: A Historical Problem," in *Essays in Honour of E. H. Carr*, ed. C. Abramsky (Hamden: Archon, 1974), pp. 152–70.

69. Walter Duranty, *Stalin & Co.: The Politburo—the Men Who Run Russia* (London: Secker and Warburg, 1949), p. 93.

70. For the different opinions, see: Gustav Hilger and Alfred G. Meyer, *The Incompatible Allies* (New York: Macmillan, 1953), p. 290; W. Averell Harriman and Elie Abel, *Special Envoy to Churchill and Stalin* (New York: Random House, 1975), p. 94; Paul Schmidt, *Statist auf diplomatischer Bühne* (Frankfurt a.M.: Athäneum, 1949), p. 516; and especially Charles E. Bohlen, *Witness to History* (New York: Norton, 1973), pp. 379–81.

71. Louis Fischer, *The Life and Death of Stalin* (London: Cape, 1953), p. 162.

72. *Khrushchev Remembers* (Boston: Little, Brown, 1970), pp. 127–28.

73. "German-Soviet Boundary and Friendship Treaty," September 28, 1939, *DGFP*, D, vol. VIII, p. 166.

74. Wiktor Sukiennicki, "The Establishment of the Soviet Regime in Eastern Poland in 1939," *JCEA* 23 (1963–64): 191–218.

75. Gottwald to Communist Party Central Committee, November 19, 1939, Gustav Bareš and Oldřich Janeček, eds., "Depeše mezi Prahou a Moskvou" [The dispatches between Prague and Moscow], *Příspěvky k dějinám KSČ* 7 (1967): 402.

76. *Bolshevik*, 1939, no. 22, pp. 84–86.

77. Philip J. Jaffe, *The Rise and Fall of American Communism* (New York: Horizon, 1975), pp. 38–49.

78. Note on Ribbentrop-Stalin-Molotov conversations, August 23–24, 1939, *DGFP*, D, vol. VII, p. 227.

79. Khrushchev tapes, transcript, part I, p. 802, Oral History Collection, Columbia University; David Kirby, "The Baltic States, 1940–50," in *Communist Power in Europe 1944–1949*, ed. Martin McCauley (New York: Barnes and Noble, 1977), pp. 25–26.

80. James E. McSherry, *Stalin, Hitler, and Europe*, vol. II (Cleveland: World, 1970), pp. 50–66.

81. Khrushchev tapes, transcript, part II, p. 805, Oral History Collection, Columbia University.

82. Wolfgang W. Birkenfeld, "Stalin als Wirtschaftspartner Hitlers," *Vierteljahrschrift für Sozial- und Wirtschaftsgeschichte* 53 (1966): 492–99.

83. Margarete Buber, *Under Two Dictators* (London: Gollancz, 1949), pp. 151–66; František Janáček, "Linie a ideologie KSČ, 1939–1941" [The policy line and ideology of the Communist party of Czechoslovakia, 1939–1941], *OAR* 4, no. 4 (1966): 31–52; Victor Gollancz, *Where Are You Going?* (London: Gollancz, 1940).

84. Gilbert Mathieu, "The French and Belgian Communist Parties in Relation to Soviet Objectives towards Western Europe in 1940 and 1944" (Ph.D. diss., University of Wisconsin, 1971), pp. 38–82.

85. Janusz K. Zawodny, *Death in the Forest* (Notre Dame, Ind.: University of Notre Dame Press, 1962), pp. 127–28.

86. *Khrushchev Remembers*, p. 134.

87. C. A. Macartney, *October Fifteenth: A History of Modern Hungary, 1929–1945*, vol. I (Edinburgh: Edinburgh University Press, 1956), pp. 404–5.

88. Elisabeth Barker, *British Policy in South-East Europe in the Second World War* (London: Macmillan, 1976), p. 25.

89. Robert Cecil, *Hitler's Decision to Invade Russia in 1941* (New York: McKay, 1976), pp. 68–84.

90. Andreas Hillgruber, *Hitler, König Carol und Marschall Antonescu* (Wiesbaden: Steiner, 1965), pp. 89–107.

91. Marshall L. Miller, *Bulgaria during the Second World War* (Stanford: Stanford University Press, 1975), pp. 33–35.

92. H. Peter Krosby, *Finland, Germany and the Soviet Union, 1940–1941: The Petsamo Dispute* (Madison: University of Wisconsin Press, 1968), pp. 55–61.

93. Ferdinand Beer et al., *Dějinná křižovatka* [The historic crossroads] (Prague: Nakladatelství politické literatury, 1964), pp. 72–86.

94. Kurt Krupinski, *Die Komintern seit Kriegsausbruch* (Berlin: Stollberg, 1941), pp. 89–105.

95. Otto Molden, *Der Ruf des Gewissens: Der österreichische Freiheitskampf, 1939–1945* (Vienna: Herold, 1958), p. 166; Josef Novotný, "Činnost KSČ v letech 1938–1941" [The activities of the Communist party of Czechoslovakia in 1938–1941], *OAR* 4, no. 4 (1966): 113–14.

96. Record of Molotov-Ribbentrop conversation, held on November 13, dated November 18, 1940, *DGFP*, D, vol. XI, pp. 562–70, and draft agreements on pp. 508–10.

97. Record of Molotov-Hitler conversation, held on November 13, dated November 15, 1940, *ibid.*, pp. 550–62.

98. Schulenburg to German Foreign Office, November 26, 1940, *ibid.*, pp. 714–15.

99. See Philipp W. Fabry, *Der Hitler-Stalin Pakt, 1939–1941: Ein Beitrag zur Methode sowjetischer Aussenpolitik* (Darmstadt: Fundus, 1962), pp. 365–67.

100. Macartney, *October Fifteenth*, vol. I, pp. 370, 468.

101. Křen and Kural, "Ke stykům mezi československým odbojem a SSSR," p. 732; interview with Maiskii, "Svědek doby" [A witness of the times], *Kulturní tvorba* (Prague), July 1, 1965.

102. František Moravec, *Master of Spies* (Garden City, N.Y.: Doubleday, 1975), pp. 188–89; Emil Strankmüller, "Československé ofenzivní zpravodajství od března 1939" [Czechoslovak intelligence since March 1939], *OAR* 8, no. 1 (1970): 210–19.

103. Treaty of April 5, 1941, in *Yugoslavia and the Soviet Union, 1939–1973*, ed. Stephen Clissold (London: Oxford University Press, 1975), pp. 122–23.

104. Maury Lisann, "Stalin the Appeaser," *Survey* 76 (1970): 57–60.

105. Luka Fertilio, "Izlet bez iluzija . . ." [A trip without illusions], *Hrvatska revija* (Buenos Aires) 10 (1960): 625.

106. Schulenburg to German Foreign Office, April 13, 1941, *DGFP*, D, vol. XII, p. 537.

107. Barton Whaley, *Codeword Barbarossa* (Cambridge: M.I.T. Press, 1973), pp. 222–43.

108. John Erickson, *The Road to Stalingrad* (New York: Harper, 1975), pp. 87–98.

109. Harrison E. Salisbury, *The Nine Hundred Days* (New York: Harper, 1969), pp. 67–81; Stefan T. Possony, "Hitlers Unternehmen 'Barbarossa' und die Rolle des sowjetischen Geheimdienstchefs Berija," *Beiträge zur Konfliktforschung* 5, no. 3 (1975): 99–114.

110. *Khrushchev Remembers*, p. 167.

111. "Memorandum of Marshal Stalin's Views as Expressed During the Evening of November 28, 1943," by Bohlen, *FRUS, Tehran*, p. 513.

112. Svetlana Alliluyeva, *Only One Year* (New York: Harper, 1969), p. 392.

Chapter Two: The Minimum Aims

1. Ivan M. Maiskii, "Dni ispytanii" [The days of trial], *Novyi Mir* 40, no. 12 (1964): 163; Nikita S. Khrushchev, "The Crimes of the Stalin Era," *New Leader*, 1956, suppl., p. 40.

2. N. N. Voronov, "At Supreme Headquarters," in *Stalin and His Generals*, ed. Seweryn Bialer (New York: Pegasus, 1970), p. 210.

3. Speech by Stalin, July 3, 1941, in *Soviet Foreign Policy during the Patriotic War*, ed. Andrew Rothstein, vol. I (London: Hutchinson, 1944), pp. 21–24; Maiskii, "Dni ispytanii," p. 165.

4. Translation of address by Litvinov, July 8, 1941, Box 217, Russia, Hopkins Papers, FDRL.

5. Stalin's secret order no. 0019, July 16, 1941, quoted in Alexander Dallin, *German Rule in Russia, 1941–1945* (London: Macmillan, 1957), p. 64.

6. Speech by Stalin, May 24, 1945, J. V. Stalin, *War Speeches, Orders of the Day, and Answers to Foreign Press Correspondents During the Great Patriotic War* (London: Hutchinson, 1946), p. 139.

7. W. Averell Harriman and Elie Abel, *Special Envoy to Churchill and Stalin* (New York: Random House, 1975), p. 275.

8. John Erickson, *The Road to Stalingrad* (New York: Harper and Row, 1975), pp. 142, 176, 227.

9. "Our Policy in Soviet-Nazi War Stated," *New York Times*, June 24, 1941.

10. Speech by Churchill, June 22, 1941, and entry by Colville, Winston S. Churchill, *The Grand Alliance* (Boston: Houghton Mifflin, 1950), pp. 370–73.

11. Raymond H. Dawson, *The Decision to Aid Russia, 1941* (Chapel Hill: University of North Carolina Press, 1959), pp. 110–25.

12. F. I. Golikov, "Sovetskaia voennaia missiia v Anglii i SShA v 1941 godu" [The Soviet military mission in England and the U.S.A. in 1941], *Novaia i noveishaia istoriia*, 1969, no. 3, pp. 100–11; *ibid.*, no. 4, pp. 102–10.

13. Cited in Elisabeth Barker, *British Policy in South-East Europe in the Second World War* (London: Macmillan, 1975), pp. 127–28.

14. Llewellyn Woodward, *British Foreign Policy in the Second World War*, vol. II (London: Her Majesty's Stationery Office, 1971), pp. 11–14.

15. Records of Sikorski-Maiskii conversations, July 5 and 11, and Eden to Zaleski, July 17 and 18, 1941, *DPSR*, vol. I, pp. 117–19, 128–32, 138–39; see Michał Sokolnicki, *Dziennik ankarski, 1939–1943* [The Ankara diary] (London: Gryf, 1965), pp. 292–93.

16. "Agreement between the Governments of Poland and the Union of Soviet Socialist Republics," July 30, 1941, in *War and Peace Aims of the United Nations*, ed. Louise W. Holborn, vol. I (Boston: World Peace Foundation, 1943), p. 354.

17. "Znachenie sovetsko-polskogo soglasheniia" [The significance of the Soviet-Polish agreement], *Pravda*, August 4, 1941.

18. Theodore A. Wilson, *The First Summit: Roosevelt and Churchill at Placentia Bay 1941* (Boston: Houghton Mifflin, 1969), pp. 173–202.

19. Woodward, *British Foreign Policy in the Second World War*, vol. II, p. 209.

20. "Address of the Ambassador of the Soviet Union (Maisky) to the Inter-Allied Meeting, London, September 24, 1941," in *Documents on American Foreign Relations*, ed. Leland M. Goodrich, vol. IV, *1941–42* (Boston: World Peace Foundation, 1942), pp. 214–16.

21. Stalin to Churchill, July 18, 1941, *SCCA*, pp. 12–13.

22. Bialer, ed., *Stalin and His Generals*, pp. 61–62; see Robert E. Sherwood, *Roosevelt and Hopkins* (New York: Harper, 1950), p. 333.

23. Minutes of Eden–Stalin conversation, December 16, 1941, and Annex I, II, WP (42) 8, CAB 66/20, PRO.

24. *Ibid*. The mention of the extension of Poland to the Oder is omitted in Eden's January 5, 1942, summary of the conversation, the substantive parts of which are printed in Churchill, *The Grand Alliance*, pp. 628–29; nor is this point mentioned in Woodward's official history, *British Foreign Policy in the Second World War*, vol. II, pp. 220–36.

25. James E. Chaney to George C. Marshall, March 21, 1942, 019 Russia, 1942–43, Records of the Army Staff, RG-319, NA.

26. A. J. P. Taylor, "The War Aims of the Allies in the First World War," in *Essays Presented to Sir Lewis Namier*, ed. Richard Pares and A. J. P. Taylor (New York: St. Martin's, 1956), p. 480.

27. Report by Eden on conversation with Maiskii, May 5, 1942, Memorandum no. 190, CAB 66/24, PRO.

28. Draft by Molotov, quoted in Memorandum no. 220, May 25, 1942, CAB 66/24, PRO.

29. Berle to J. Edgar Hoover, July 10, 1941, *FRUS*, 1941, vol. I, pp. 789–90; Sumner Welles, "Two Roosevelt Decisions: One Debit, One Credit," *Foreign Affairs* 29 (1950–51): 189.

30. Memorandum on conversation between Welles and Halifax, March 30, 1942, *FRUS*, 1942, vol. III, pp. 537–38; Jan Ciechanowski, *Defeat in Victory* (New York: Doubleday, 1947), p. 107.

31. Churchill to Roosevelt, March 7, 1942, in *Roosevelt and Churchill: Their Secret Wartime Correspondence*, ed. Francis L. Loewenheim et al. (New York: Saturday Review Press–Dutton, 1975), p. 186.

32. Entry for February 24, 1942, *The Diaries of Sir Alexander Cadogan* (London: Cassell, 1971), p. 437; Memorandum by Eden, February 8, 1942, W. P. (42) 69, CAB 66/21, PRO.

33. Memorandum by Eden, April 10, 1942, W. P. (42) 156, CAB 66/23, PRO; Woodward, *British Foreign Policy in the Second World War*, vol. II, pp. 244–45.

34. "British-Soviet Negotiations Looking Forward to the Conclusion of a Treaty of Political Character with Particular Reference to Soviet Suggestions that Certain Territories Taken Over by the Soviet Union during the Period September 1, 1939–June 22, 1941, Be Recognized as Soviet Territory," February 4, 1942, *FRUS*, 1942, vol. III, pp. 505–12.

35. See Robert Garson, "The Atlantic Alliance, Eastern Europe and the Origins of the Cold War: From Pearl Harbor to Yalta," in *Contrast and Connection: Bicentennial Essays in Anglo-American History*, ed. H. C. Allen and Roger Thompson (London: Bell, 1976), pp. 296–320.

36. Memorandum of a conversation by the Acting Secretary of State, March 12, 1942, *FRUS*, 1942, vol. III pp. 532–33; Thompson to Secretary of State, March 26, 1942, *ibid.*, pp. 535–36.

37. *The Memoirs of Cordell Hull* (New York: Macmillan, 1948), vol. II, p. 1172; see Harriman and Abel, *Special Envoy to Churchill and Stalin,* pp. 135–36.

38. Minutes of Eden-Molotov conversations, Memorandum No. 220, CAB 66/24; 66th conclusions, War Cabinet meeting, May 25, 1942, W.M. (42), CAB 65/30, PRO.

39. Roosevelt to Stalin, April 12, 1942, *SCRT,* p. 23.

40. Memorandum on Roosevelt-Molotov conference, May 30, 1942, *FRUS,* 1942, vol. III, p. 577; see also Mark A. Stoler, *The Politics of the Second Front: American Military Planning and Diplomacy in Coalition Warfare, 1942–1943* (Westport, Conn.: Greenwood Press, 1977), pp. 43–51.

41. White House press release, June 11, 1942, *FRUS,* 1942, vol. III, p. 594; Harriman and Abel, *Special Envoy to Churchill and Stalin,* pp. 137–39.

42. Woodward, *British Foreign Policy in the Second World War,* vol. II, p. 259.

43. From the Soviet and the Western vantage points, respectively, the Russian side of the enduring controversy is recorded exhaustively in I. N. Zemskov, "Diplomaticheskaia istoriia otkrytiia vtorogo fronta v Evrope (1941–1944 gg.)" [The diplomatic history of the launching of the Second Front in Europe], *Mezhdunarodnaia zhizn,* 1970, nos. 3, 5, 11; *ibid.,* 1974, nos. 4, 6, 9, 12; *ibid.,* 1975, nos. 2, 3; and in James R. Hawkes, "Stalin's Diplomatic Offensive: The Politics of the Second Front, 1941–1943" (Ph.D. diss., University of Illinois, 1966).

44. Milovan Djilas, *Conversations with Stalin* (New York: Harcourt, 1962), p. 73.

45. Harriman and Abel, *Special Envoy to Churchill and Stalin,* p. 399; see Robert H. McNeal, "Roosevelt through Stalin's Spectacles," *International Journal* 18 (1962–63): 194–206.

46. Memoranda by Samuel H. Cross and Harry Hopkins on Roosevelt–Molotov conversation, May 29, 1942, *FRUS,* 1942, vol. III, pp. 568–69, 572–74; see Willard Range, *Franklin D. Roosevelt's World Order* (Athens, Ga.: University of Georgia Press, 1959), pp. 172–83.

47. Winston S. Churchill, *The Hinge of Fate* (Boston: Houghton Mifflin, 1950), pp. 493, 501.

48. For evidence that purely military reasons accounted for the delay, see Maurice Matloff and Edwin M. Snell, *Strategic Planning for Coalition Warfare, 1941–1942* (Washington, D.C.: Department of the Army, 1953), especially pp. 217–32, 322–27.

49. Harriman and Abel, *Special Envoy to Churchill and Stalin,* p. 89; see Robert H. Jones, *The Roads to Russia* (Norman: University of Oklahoma Press, 1969), pp. 61, 86–87, 109–10, 129, 240–50.

50. Alfred Bilmanis, *A History of Latvia* (Princeton: Princeton University Press, 1951), pp. 403–4; V. Stanley Vardys, "The Partisan Movement in Postwar Lithuania," *SR* 22 (1963): 502.

51. Stalin to Roosevelt, August 4, 1941, *SCRT,* p. 11.

2. Minimum Aims

52. Peter Gosztony, *Hitlers Fremde Heere: Das Schicksal der nichtdeutschen Armeen im Ostfeldzug* (Düsseldorf: Econ, 1976), pp. 54–64, 110–14.

53. Memorandum by Orme Sargent, May 31, 1944, W.P. (44) 289, CAB 66/50, PRO.

54. Marshall L. Miller, *Bulgaria during the Second World War* (Stanford: Stanford University Press, 1975), p. 62; Gosztony, *Hitlers Fremde Heere*, p. 110.

55. According to Mario D. Fenyo, *Hitler, Horthy and Hungary: German-Hungarian Relations, 1941–1944* (New Haven: Yale University Press, 1972), pp. 2–3, and Kristóffy's widow, in *Studies for a New Central Europe* 3, no. 2 (1972): 70, Molotov offered to back a Hungarian bid for the part of Transylvania still in Romanian hands; however, Elek Karsai, *Stalo sa v Budine v Sándorovskom paláci* [It happened at the Sándor Palace in Buda] (Bratislava: Vydavateľstvo politickej literatúry, 1966), p. 512, cites Kristóffy's June 23 report that Molotov took no position on the subject.

56. N. F. Dreisziger, "New Twist to an Old Riddle: The Bombing of Kassa (Košice), June 26, 1941," *Journal of Modern History* 44 (1972): 232–42.

57. Order of the Day, February 23, 1942, in *Soviet Foreign Policy during the Patriotic War*, ed. Rothstein, vol. I, p. 36.

58. Report by Stalin, November 6, 1942, *ibid.*, p. 29; Erwin Zucker-Schilling, *Er diente seiner Klasse* (Vienna: Globus, 1971), p. 62.

59. Ruth von Mayenburg, *Blaues Blut und rote Fahnen* (Vienna: Molden, 1969), p. 292.

60. Alfred J. Rieber, *Stalin and the French Communist Party, 1941–1947* (New York: Columbia University Press, 1962), pp. 42–51; Mary Dau, "The Soviet Union and the Liberation of Denmark," *Survey* 76 (1970): 64–72.

61. Note by Beneš on conversation with Maiskii, August 28, 1941, quoted in Eduard Táborský, "Beneš and Stalin—Moscow 1943 and 1945," *JCEA* 13 (1953–54): 165.

62. Leopold Grünwald, "Der 'Sudetendeutsche Freiheitssender' der Kommunistischen Partei der Tschechoslowakei (1941 bis 1945)," in *Beiderseits der Grenze*, ed. Horst Köpstein (Berlin: Deutscher Militärverlag, 1965), pp. 38–50.

63. Narkomindel to Maiskii, July 3, 1941, *Dokumenty i materiały do historii stosunków polsko-radzieckich* [Documents and materials on the history of Polish-Soviet relations], vol. VII (Warsaw: Książka i Wiedza, 1973), p. 221.

64. Note by Eden on conversation with Maiskii, July 4, 1941, *DPSR*, vol. I, p. 116.

65. Peter Gosztony, "Über die Entstehung der Nationalkomitees und der nationalen Militärformationen der osteuropäischen Nationen in der Sowjetunion während des Zweiten Weltkrieges," *Militärgeschichtliche Mittleilungen* 12 (1973): 38–40; Oldřich Janeček, "Boj o hegemonii v československém vojsku v SSSR (1942–1945) [The struggle for hegemony in the Czechoslovak army in the USSR], *Příspěvky k dějinám KSČ* 4 (1964): 201–7.

66. Memorandum by Sikorski on conversation with Stalin, January 12, 1942, *DPSR*, vol. I, p. 264–65.

67. Notes on Sikorski-Churchill conversation, January 31, 1942, *ibid.*, p. 274. Sikorski

remains the only source of Stalin's statement; General Władysław Anders' account of the Sikorski-Stalin talks does not mention the Oder frontier.

68. Note on Sikorski-Stalin conversation, December 4, 1941, *DPSR*, vol. I, pp. 244–45.

69. Wladyslaw W. Kulski, "The Lost Opportunity for Russian-Polish Friendship," *Foreign Affairs* 25 (1946–47): 676.

70. See Eden to O'Malley, October 6, 1943, in *The Great Powers and the Polish Question, 1941–45*, ed. Antony Polonsky (London: London School of Economics and Political Science, 1976), pp. 155–57.

71. "Polish-Czechoslovak Agreement, November 11, 1940," in Leften S. Stavrianos, *Balkan Federation* (Hamden, Conn.: Archon, 1964), pp. 307–8.

72. Churchill, *The Hinge of Fate*, pp. 802–3; Churchill to Eden, October 21, 1942, *ibid.*, p. 562.

73. Dušan Plenča, *Medjunarodni odnosi Jugoslavije u toku Drugog svjetskog rata* [The international relations of Yugoslavia during World War II] (Belgrade: Institut društvenih nauka, 1962), p. 32.

74. Note by Smutný on conversation with Beneš, July 12, and on Beneš's conversation with Maiskii, July 9, 1942, *DHCSP*, vol. I, p. 241.

75. Minutes of Eden-Stalin meeting, December 16, 1941, Memorandum W.P. (42) 8, January 5, 1942, CAB 66/20, PRO.

76. "Polish-Czechoslovak Agreement, January 23, 1942," and "Greek-Yugoslav Pact, January 15, 1942," in Stavrianos, *Balkan Federation*, pp. 309–13.

77. "Survey of Reactions of Allied Government Circles to M. Stalin's Reported Post-War Intentions and Their Forward-Looking Views," March 2, 1942, Box 15, President's Secretary's File, FDRL.

78. Note on Morawski-Bogomolov conversation, March 2, 1942, *DPSR*, I, p. 285.

79. Józef Kowalski, "Rozgłośnia im. Tadeusza Kościuszki (Fragment wspomnienia)" [The Tadeusz Kościuszko broadcasting station: A fragment of a memoir], *ZPW* 4, no. 4 (1961): 345.

80. Memorandum by Eden, April 10, 1942, W.P. (42) 156, CAB 66/23, PRO.

81. Memorandum by Roosevelt, March 7, 1942, *FRUS*, 1942, vol. III, p. 113.

82. Plenča, *Medjunarodni odnosi Jugoslavije*, p. 113; Constantin Fotitch, *The War We Lost* (New York: Viking, 1948), p. 173.

84. Tito to Comintern, August 11, 1942, in *Yugoslavia and the Soviet Union, 1939–1973*, ed. Stephen Clissold (London: Oxford University Press, 1975), pp. 139–40.

85. "Statement on Attitude toward Albania," December 18, 1942, *War and Peace Aims of the United Nations*, ed. Holborn, vol. I, pp. 376–77.

86. Note by Smutný on Beneš-Molotov conversations, June 9, 1942, *DHCSP*, I, p. 273.

87. Atherton to Welles, March 23, 1942, *FRUS*, 1942, vol. III, p. 121.

88. See notes by Smutný on conversations with Beneš, July 12, 1941, and August 27,

1943, *DHCSP*, vol. I, pp. 241 and 362, and Stephen Borsody, *The Triumph of Tyranny* (New York: Macmillan, 1960), pp. 231–42.

89. Quoted in Oldřich Janeček, "Na cestě k národní frontě" [The road to the National Front], *OAR* 7, no. 4 (1969): 196.

90. Reinhardt to Secretary of State, May 5, 1942, *FRUS*, 1942, vol. III, p. 433.

91. Piotr S. Wandycz, "Recent Traditions of the Quest for Unity," in *The People's Democracies after Prague*, ed. Jerzy Lukaszewski (Bruges, Belgium: De Tempel, 1970), p. 59.

92. Raczyński to Jan Masaryk, March 20, 1943, in Stefania Stanisławska, "Korespondencja w sprawie konfederacji polsko-czechosłowackiej w latach 1940–1943" [Correspondence on the Polish-Czechoslovak confederation in 1940–1943], *Studia z najnowszych dziejów powszechnych* 4 (1963): 303; Jaroslav Valenta, "Pol'sko a uzavretie československo-sovietskej spojeneckej zmluvy roku 1943" [Poland and the conclusion of the Czechoslovak-Soviet alliance in 1943], *Slovanské štúdie, História* 9 (1967): 43–44.

93. Stalin to Churchill, July 23, 1942, *SCCA*, p. 56.

94. "Estimate of the Situation and Possibilities of Action," October 16–November 10, 1942, Poland 1942–43, President's Secretary's File, FDRL; Marian Kukiel, "Strategiczne koncepcje generała Sikorskiego w Drugiej wojnie światowej" [General Sikorski's strategic concepts during World War II], *Belona* (London) 37, no. 3 (1955): 16–24.

95. Mark A. Stoler, "The 'Second Front' and American Fear of Soviet Expansion, 1941–1943," *Military Affairs* 39, no. 3 (1975): 136–41.

96. Note by Smutný on conversation with Beneš, July 21, 1942, *DHCSP*, vol. I, p. 278; Biddle to Secretary of State, January 20, 1943, 840.50/1256, RG-59, NA.

97. Veselin Khadzhinikolov, *Georgi Dimitrov i s'vetskata obshchestvennost, 1934–1945* [Georgi Dimitrov and Soviet public life] (Sofia: B'lgarskata Akademiia na Naukite, 1972), p. 318.

98. Message by Comintern, June 22, 1941, in *Yugoslavia and the Soviet Union*, ed. Clissold, p. 128.

99. Speech by Molotov, June 22, 1941, in *Soviet Foreign Policy during the Patriotic War*, ed. Rothstein, vol. I, pp. 75–76.

100. "Iz dokumentov kompartii Germanii" [From documents of the Communist Party of Germany], *Kommunisticheskii Internatsional* 23, nos. 6–7 (1941): 123.

101. "Entwurf eines Aufrufes an die deutschen Soldaten," June 26, 1941, Walter Ulbricht, *Zur Geschichte der deutschen Arbeiterbewegung: Aus Reden und Aufsätzen*, vol. II, Suppl. 2 (Berlin: Dietz, 1968), p. 221.

102. Woodward, *British Foreign Policy in the Second World War*, vol. II, p. 14.

103. "Appell an das deutsche Volk, unterzeichnet von 158 deutschen Soldaten," *Sie kämpften für Deutschland* (Berlin: Ministerium für Nationale Verteidigung, 1959), pp. 114–21; Willy Wolff, "Zur Beratung der 158 kriegsgefangenen deutschen Soldaten im Oktober 1941 in der Sowjetunion," *Zeitschrift für Militärgeschichte* 2 (1963): 42–52.

104. "Obrashchenie TsK KPG k nemetskomu narodu i nemetskoi armii" [An Appeal by the Central Committee of the KPD to the German people and the German army], *Pravda*, October 16, 1941; K. L. Sselesnjow, "Mit Walter Ulbricht im sowjetischen Kriegsgefangenenlager (Oktober 1941)," *BGDA* 11 (1969): 816.

105. Alexander Fischer, *Sowjetische Deutschlandpolitik im Zweiten Weltkrieg* (Stuttgart: Deutsche Verlags-Anstalt, 1975), pp. 18, 166.

106. "Vorschläge für die Tätigkeit der Auslandssender beim Moskauer Rundfunk," June 25, 1941, in Ulbricht, *Zur Geschichte der deutschen Arbeiterbewegung*, vol. II, 2, pp. 218–20.

107. Ernst Fischer, *An Opposing Man* (London: Lane, 1974), p. 366.

108. Peter Gosztony, "Die ungarische antifaschistische Bewegung in der Sowjetunion während des Zweiten Weltkrieges," *Militärgeschichtliche Mitteilungen* 9 (1972): 91.

109. E. Fisher, "Ot narodnogo fronta k obshchenatsionalnomu frontu" [From the popular front of the national front], *Kommunisticheskii Internatsional*, 24, nos. 8–9 (1942): 26–30.

110. "Lupta poporului român pentru libertate şi independenţa naţionalã" [The struggle of the Romanian people for freedom and national independence], September 6, 1941, *Documente din Istoria Partidului Comunist din România* [Documents on the history of the Communist party of Romania] (Bucharest: Editura Partidului Muncitoresc Român, 1953), pp. 340–51.

111. Stephen Peters, "Ingredients of the Communist Takeover in Albania," in *The Anatomy of Communist Takeovers*, ed. Thomas T. Hammond and Robert Farrell (New Haven: Yale University Press, 1975), p. 275.

112. Marian Malinowski, "Grupa Inicjatywna PPR" [The task force of the Polish Workers' Party], *ZPW* 8, no. 4 (1965): 57–85.

113. Jerzy Pawłowicz, "Uwagi na temat kształtowania się strategii PPR i międzynarodowego ruchu robotniczego w okresie II wojny światowej" [The formation of the strategy of the Polish Workers' Party and of the International Workers' Movement during World War II], *ZPW* 7, no. 1 (1964): 33; Janeček, "Na cestě k národní frontě," pp. 176–84.

114. Comintern to Tito, March 5, 1942, in *Yugoslavia and the Soviet Union*, ed. Clissold, pp. 145–46.

115. Comintern to Tito, November 1942, *ibid.*, p. 150.

116. "Über die politische Linie und die nächsten Aufgaben der Kommunistischen Partei der Tschechoslowakei," January 5, 1943, in *Slovenské národné povstanie: Dokumenty* [The Slovak national uprising: Documents], ed. Vilém Prečan (Bratislava: Vydavateľstvo politickej literatúry, 1965), p. 42.

117. Ernst Fischer, *An Opposing Man*, p. 282.

118. Erickson, *The Road to Stalingrad*, pp. 240–41.

119. Veljko Vlahović, "Internacionalizam Komunističke Partije Jugoslavije na delu" [The internationalism of the Communist Party of Yugoslavia in practice], *Socijalizam* 2, no. 2 (1959): 53.

120. Moša Pijade, *La fable de l'aide soviétique à l'insurrection nationale yougoslave* (Paris: Le Livre Yougoslave, 1950), pp. 17–65.

121. Nissan Oren, *Bulgarian Communism* (New York: Columbia University Press, 1971), pp. 175–77.

122. Jiří Doležal, *Jediná cesta* [The only way] (Prague: Naše vojsko, 1966), pp. 132–33; C. A. Macartney, *October Fifteenth*, vol. II (Edinburgh: University of Edinburgh Press, 1956), p. 35.

123. Bickham Sweet-Escott, *Baker Street Irregular* (London: Methuen, 1965), pp. 117–18.

124. Speech by Stalin, November 7, 1941, in *Soviet Foreign Policy during the Patriotic War*, ed. Rothstein, vol. I, p. 34.

125. Georgi K. Zhukov, "First Victory," in *Stalin and His Generals*, ed. Bialer, pp. 330–35; Erickson, *The Road to Stalingrad*, pp. 286–87, 292.

126. Order of the Day, February 23, 1942, in *Soviet Foreign Policy during the Patriotic War*, ed. Rothstein, vol. I, p. 37.

127. Churchill, *The Hinge of Fate*, p. 335.

128. V. P. Morozov, "Nekotorye voprosy organizatsii strategicheskogo rukovodstva v Velikoi Otechestvennoi voine" [Problems of the organization of strategic leadership in the Great Patriotic War], *Istoriia SSSR*, 1975, no. 3, p. 23.

129. "Borba narodov Evropy protiv okkupantov" [The struggle of Europe's peoples against their occupiers], *Kommunisticheskii Internatsional* 24, nos. 10–11 (1942): 69.

130. Speech by Václav Kopecký, May 18, 1942, no. 1036, *Daily Digest of World Broadcasts*, BBC; Janeček, "Na cestě k národní frontě," pp. 189, 194.

131. Speech by Jean-Richard Bloch, May 19, 1942, no. 1037, *Daily Digest of World Broadcasts*, BBC; Rieber, *Stalin and the French Communist Party*, pp. 23–29.

132. Wolfgang Schumann and Karl Drechsler, eds., *Deutschland im Zweiten Weltkrieg*, vol. II (Berlin: Akademie, 1975), p. 216; Hermann Mitteräcker, *Kampf und Opfer für Österreich* (Vienna: Stern, 1963), pp. 98–99; radio news items, May 19, 1942, no. 1037, *Daily Digest of World Broadcasts*, BBC.

133. Clissold, ed., *Yugoslavia and the Soviet Union*, pp. 16–18.

134. Comintern to Tito, April and September 1942, *ibid.*, pp. 143 and 140.

135. Government-in-exile to Mihajlović, November 30, 1942, and Comintern to Tito, February 11, 1943, *ibid.*, pp. 140 and 144.

136. Comintern to Tito, February 13, 1943, *ibid.*, p. 156.

137. A. I. Pushkash, "Iz istorii borby progressivnykh sil Vengrii protiv Khortistskogo rezhima" [From the history of the struggle of Hungary's progressive forces against the Horthy regime], *Voprosy istorii*, 1957, no. 4, p. 88.

138. Oren, *Bulgarian Communism*, pp. 180–87.

139. Vojtech Mastny, *The Czechs under Nazi Rule* (New York: Columbia University Press, 1971), p. 221.

140. Heinz Höhne, *Codeword DIREKTOR: The Story of the Red Orchestra* (New York: Coward, McCann, and Geoghegan, 1972), pp. 157–65; the standard East German book is Karl Heinz Biernat and Luise Kraushaar, *Die Schulze-Boysen/Harnack-Organisation im antifaschistischen Kampf* (Berlin: Dietz, 1970).

141. *Die Kommunisten im Kampf für die Unabhängigkeit Österreichs* (Vienna: Stern, 1958), pp. 139–40.

142. David J. Dallin, *Soviet Espionage* (New Haven: Yale University Press, 1955), pp. 264–68; Leopold Trepper, *The Great Game* (New York: McGraw-Hill, 1977), pp. 179–85.

143. "Hinweise zur propagandistischen Auswertung der Erfahrungen aus den Diskussionen mit Kriegsgefangenen," September 12, 1942, in Ulbricht, *Zur Geschichte der deutschen Arbeiterbewegung*, vol. II, suppl. 1, pp. 159–62; OSS report A-4953, May 6, 1943, 33855 C, OSS, RG-226, NA.

144. "Programm der Vaterländischen Front," July 17, 1942, in *Bulgariens Volk im Widerstand*, ed. Peter Georgieff and Basil Spiru (Berlin: Rütten und Loening, 1962), pp. 95–99.

145. Oren, *Bulgarian Communism*, p. 232.

146. "Aufruf zur Bildung der Freiheitsfront," October 22–23, 1942, in *Die Kommunisten im Kampf für die Unabhängigkeit Österreichs*, pp. 146–51; Karl Vogelmann, "Die Propaganda der österreichischen Emigration in der Sowjetunion für einen selbständigen österreichischen Nationalstaat" (mimeographed Ph.D. diss., University of Vienna, 1973), pp. 115–19.

147. "Marsiglia 1943: Discussione tra PCI e 'Giustizia e libertà,'" *Rinascità* 22, no. 12 (March 20, 1965): 21.

148. "Friedensmanifest," December 6, 1942, *Zur Geschichte der deutschen antifaschistischen Widerstandsbewegung* (Berlin: Verlag des Ministeriums für Nationale Verteidigung, 1957), pp. 174–80.

149. *Beratung der nationalen Friedensbewegung in Deutschland* (Moscow: Verlag für fremdsprachige Literatur, 1943), pp. 12–39.

150. Anton Ackermann, "Das Nationalkomitee 'Freies Deutschland'—miterlebt und mitgestaltet," in *Im Kampf bewährt*, ed. Heinz Vosske (Berlin: Dietz, 1969), p. 323; see Klaus Mammach, "Georgi Dimitroffs Hilfe für die KPD im antifaschistischen Kampf," *BGDA* 14 (1972): 581.

151. "Bit zakhvatchikov vo vsekh okkupirovannykh stranakh" [Fight the aggressors in all the occupied countries], *Kommunisticheskii Internatsional* 24, no. 7 (1942): 2–6.

152. František Janáček, "Na okraj historické komparace" [Comments on historical comparison], in *Národní fronta a komunisté* [The national front and the Communists] (Prague: Naše vojsko, 1968), p. 334.

153. Bohuslav B. Kymlicka, "The Origins and Establishment of National Committees in Czechoslovakia, 1943–1945," (certificate essay, Program on East Central Europe, Columbia University, 1961), pp. 2–3.

154. Wolfgang Leonhard, *Child of the Revolution* (Chicago: Regnery, 1958), pp. 176–87.

155. Horst Duhnke, *Die KPD von 1933 bis 1945* (Cologne: Kiefenheuer and Witsch, 1972), pp. 368–75; Vogelmann, "Die Propaganda der österreichischen Emigration in der Sowjetunion," pp. 282–91.

Chapter Three: Hazy Perspectives

1. Portions of this section have appeared in my article, "Stalin and the Prospects of a Separate Peace in World War II," *American Historical Review* 77 (1972): 1365–88, and are reprinted here with permission of the editor.

2. E. A. Boltin, "Die Wesenszüge der sowjetischen Strategie in der Endphase des Grossen Vaterländischen Krieges," in *Befreiung und Neubeginn,* ed. Bernhard Weissel (Berlin: Akademie, 1968), p. 65.

3. E. Razin, "Lenin o sushchnosti voiny" [Lenin on the nature of war], *Bolshevik* 1943, no. 1, p. 47.

4. Speech by Stalin, November 6, 1942, in *Soviet Foreign Policy during the Patriotic War,* ed. Andrew Rothstein, vol. I (London: Hutchinson, 1944), p. 49.

5. Peter Kleist, *The European Tragedy* (London: Gibbs and Phillips, 1965), pp. 139–41.

6. S. W. Roskill, *The War at Sea, 1939–45,* vol. II (London: His Majesty's Stationery Office, 1950), pp. 400–401; Llewellyn Woodward, *British Foreign Policy in the Second World War,* vol. II (London: Her Majesty's Stationery Office, 1971), p. 566.

7. William H. Standley and Arthur A. Ageton, *Admiral Ambassador to Russia* (Chicago: Regnery, 1955), pp. 341–42.

8. Order of the Day, February 23, 1943, in *Soviet Foreign Policy during the Patriotic War,* ed. Rothstein, vol. I, pp. 53–57; cf. memorandum by Bohlen, February 23, and Standley to Secretary of State, February 24, 1943, *FRUS,* 1943, vol. III, pp. 506–9.

9. Churchill to Stalin, March 11, 1943, and Stalin to Churchill, March 15, 1943, *SCCA,* pp. 99–102, 106.

10. Alan Clark, *Barbarossa: The Russian-German Conflict, 1941–1945* (New York: Morrow, 1965), pp. 269–71; cf. John A. Lukacs, *The Great Powers and Eastern Europe* (New York: American Book, 1953), pp. 502–3.

11. Survey of topics discussed in the program of the Deutscher Volkssender, dissemination report A-12777, October 9, 1943, 45621 C, OSS, RG-226, NA.

12. Quoted in Woodward, *British Foreign Policy during the Second World War,* vol. II, p. 555.

13. Narkomindel to Polish Embassy, January 16, 1943, *DPSR,* vol. I, pp. 473–74; see William J. Couch, "General Sikorski, Poland, and the Soviet Union" (Ph.D. diss., University of Chicago, 1970), pp. 281–94.

14. Aleksandr E. Korneichuk, "Vossoedenie ukrainskogo naroda v nedrakh svoego gos-

sudarstva" [Reunion of the Ukrainian people in the bosom of its state], *Pravda*, February 20, 1943.

15. Statement by Tass, March 3, 1943, in *Soviet Foreign Policy during the Patriotic War*, ed. Rothstein, vol. I, pp. 264–65; Fryderyk Zbiniewicz, "Rola komunistów polskich w organizowaniu i działalności Związku Patriotów Polskich oraz polskich sił zbrojnych w ZSRR" [The role of the Polish Communists in the organization and activities of the Union of Polish Patriots and the Polish armed forces in the USSR], *ZPW* 4, no. 4 (1961): 93–94.

16. Wilfred von Oven, *Finale Furioso: Mit Goebbels bis zum Ende* (Tübingen: Graebert, 1974), entries for September 1 and November 25, 1943, pp. 120–21, 192–93.

17. For that reason any items on Katyn are missing from the otherwise comprehensive compilation edited by Krystyna Szczepańska and Bożena Zielińska, *Bibliografia Wojny Wyzwoleńczej Narodu Polskiego, 1939–1945* [Bibliography of the liberation war of the Polish people] (Warsaw: Wydawnictwo Ministerstwa Obrony Narodowej, 1973).

18. Soviet radio bulletin, April 15, 1943, in *Zbrodnia Katyńska w świetle dokumentów* [The Katyn crime in the light of documents] (London: Gryf, 1962), p. 86.

19. "Polskie sotrudniki Gitlera" [The Polish collaborators of Hitler], *Pravda*, April 19, 1943.

20. Churchill to Stalin, April 24, 1943, *SCCA*, pp. 121–22; Roosevelt to Stalin, April 26, 1943, *SCRT*, p. 61; Molotov to Romer, April 25, 1943, *DPSR*, vol. I, pp. 533–34.

21. OSS report A-5094, May 11, 1943, USSR 3700, RG-165, NA; cf. "The Problem of a Separate Peace between Germany and Russia," enclosed with Biddle to Secretary of State, June 26, 1943, 740.00119 EW/1530, RG-59, NA.

22. OSS report A-9469, August 9, 1943, USSR 6900, RG-165, NA; see also Polish Intelligence report no. 1297, early May 1943, *ibid.*, and Michał Sokolnicki, *Dziennik ankarski* (London: Gryf, 1965), entry for May 8, 1943, p. 513.

23. These terms are not mentioned specifically in relation to the April incident but recur in intelligence reports from late 1942 to the fall of 1943, such as London SI report, November 3, 1942, USSR 3850, or OSS report A-1820, February 5, 1943, USSR 6900, RG-165, NA; see also Kleist, *European Tragedy*, p. 140.

24. Order of the Day, May 1, 1943, in *Soviet Foreign Policy during the Patriotic War*, ed. Rothstein, vol. I, p. 58.

25. Lynn E. Davis, *The Cold War Begins: Soviet-American Conflict over Eastern Europe* (Princeton: Princeton University Press, 1974), p. 46; "U.K. Documents Hold Russia Guilty of the Katyn Massacre," *International Herald Tribune*, July 6, 1972.

26. Alexander Werth, *Russia at War* (New York: Dutton, 1964), p. 669.

27. "Godovshchina sovetsko-angliiskogo soiuznogo dogovora" [The anniversary of the Soviet-English alliance agreement], *Pravda*, May 26, 1943; "Koalitsiia rozhdenaia voinoi i prizvannaia obespechit pobedonosnyi mir" [A coalition born of war and destined to secure a victorious peace], *Voina i rabochii klass*, June 15, 1943, pp. 3–9.

28. For example, A. Erusalimskii, " 'Mirnye' manevry germanskogo imperializma" [The "peace" maneuvers of German imperialism], *Krasnaia Zvezda*, May 15, 1943.

29. Roosevelt to Stalin, May 5, and Stalin to Roosevelt, May 26, 1943, *SCRT*, pp. 63–64, 66.

30. Werth, *Russia at War*, pp. 674–76; Georgi K. Zhukov, *Marshal Zhukov's Greatest Battles* (New York: Harper, 1969), p. 221.

31. "Razgrom germano-italianskikh voisk v Tunise" [The defeat of the German–Italian armies in Tunisia], *Pravda*, May 12, 1943.

32. Roosevelt to Stalin, received June 4, and Stalin to Roosevelt, June 11, 1943, *SCRT*, pp. 67–71; Ivan Maisky, *Memoirs of a Soviet Ambassador* (New York: Scribner, 1968), pp. 364–65.

33. "Dva goda Otechestvennoi voiny Sovetskogo soiuza" [Two years of the Patriotic War of the Soviet Union], *Pravda*, June 22, 1943.

34. N. Malinin [pseud.], "O tseliakh voiny" [Concerning the war aims], *Voina i rabochii klass*, July 1, 1943, p. 11.

35. *New York Times*, June 17, 1943, p. 3.

36. Statement by Tass, June 18, 1943, in *Soviet Foreign Policy during the Patriotic War*, ed. Rothstein, vol. I, p. 269; *New York Times*, June 18, 1943, p. 4.

37. OSS report A-9647, August 9, 1943, and Herschel Johnson (Stockholm) to Secretary of State, June 17, 1943, USSR 6900, RG-165, NA; Wiskeman to Warner, August 11 and 23, 1943, N 4591/66/38 and N 4898/66/38, FO 371/36956, PRO; Kleist, *European Tragedy*, pp. 144–50.

38. Paul Schwarz and Guy Richards, "A Secret Russian Mission That Almost Changed History," *Liberty*, July 5, 1947, p. 26; *Izvestia*, July 29, 1947.

39. There is no evidence, however, to support the contention by noted British military historian Sir Basil H. Liddell Hart that Molotov and Ribbentrop negotiated behind the German lines near Kirovograd in June 1943; Basil H. Liddell Hart, *History of the Second World War* (New York: Putnam, 1970), p. 488.

40. For the best analysis of the victory's significance, see Joseph E. Thach, Jr., "The Battle of Kursk" (Ph.D. diss., Georgetown University, 1971), esp. pp. 1–4, 444–62.

41. "Manifest des Nationalkomitees 'Freies Deutschland' an die Wehrmacht und an das deutsche Volk," July 12–13, 1943, in *Sie kämpften für Deutschland* (Berlin: Ministerium für Nationale Verteidigung, 1959), pp. 146–51.

42. Karl O. Paetel, *Versuchung oder Chance?* (Göttingen: Musterschmidt, 1965), p. 249; *Sie kämpften für Deutschland*, p. 167; Walther von Seydlitz, *Stalingrad—Konflikt und Konsequenz: Erinnerungen* (Oldenburg: Stalling, 1977), pp. 285–92.

43. For contrasting examples, cf. Heinz Schumann and Heinz Kühnrich, "Der Kampf der deutschen Antifaschisten für ein freies, friedliebendes und demokratisches Deutschland

und seine Übereinstimmung mit den Zielen der Sowjetunion im zweiten Weltkrieg," *BGDA* 2, suppl. (1960): 69–96, and Peter Strassner, *Verräter: Das Nationalkomitee "Freies Deutschland"—Keimzelle der sogennanten DDR* (Munich: Schild, 1960).

44. Kurt Pätzold and Manfred Weissbecker, "Kritische Bemerkungen zum Bericht 'Die deutsche Widerstandsbewegung und die Alliierten zur Zeit des zweiten Weltkrieges' von Walter Bartel," *Zeitschrift für Geschichtswissenschaft*, 10 (1962): 331–32.

45. Quoted in Heinrich von Einsiedel, *I Joined the Russians* (New Haven: Yale University Press, 1953), p. 161.

46. Note by Likus, August 9, 1943, frames 130779-80, roll 162, microcopy T-120, RG-242, NA; Walter Schellenberg, *The Labyrinth* (New York: Harper, 1956), p. 370; Kleist, *European Tragedy*, pp. 154–56.

47. Entry for September 23, 1943, *The Goebbels Diaries* (Garden City, N.Y.: Doubleday, 1948), p. 477.

48. Entry for August 15, 1943, *The Von Hassell Diaries* (Garden City: Doubleday, 1947), p. 315.

49. Kaltenbrunner to Bormann, August 28, 1944, in Ernst Kaltenbrunner, *Spiegelbild einer Verschwörung* (Stuttgart: Seewald, 1961), pp. 308–9; entry for December 5, 1943, *Von Hassell Diaries*, p. 327.

50. This according to Hans Bernd Gisevius, *To the Bitter End* (Boston: Houghton Mifflin, 1947), p. 486; Stauffenberg's eastern orientation is denied in the standard biography, Joachim Kramarz, *Stauffenberg* (New York: Macmillan, 1967), pp. 178–79.

51. Shandor Rado [Sándor Radó], *Pod psevdonimom Dora* [Under the code name of Dora] (Moscow: Voenizdat, 1973), pp. 184–85.

52. Bruno Löwel, "Die Gründung des NKFD im Lichte der Entwicklung der Strategie und Taktik der KPD," *BGDA* 5 (1963): 618–19.

53. Paul Carell [Paul K. Schmidt], *Scorched Earth: Hitler's War on Russia*, vol. II (London: Harrap, 1970), pp. 97–114.

54. Seydlitz, *Stalingrad—Konflikt und Konsequenz*, pp. 277–80; Bodo Scheurig, *Free Germany* (Middletown, Conn.: Wesleyan University Press, 1970), pp. 54–72; Alfred Sywottek, *Deutsche Volksdemokratie: Studien zur politischen Konzeption der KPD* (Düsseldorf: Bertelsmann, 1971), pp. 129–30.

55. Wolfgang Leonhard, *Child of the Revolution* (Chicago: Regnery, 1958), pp. 256–58.

56. Kleist, *European Tragedy*, pp. 164–71; the feeler is confirmed in a retrospective report by the Nazi Security Service, "Vermerk betreffend Sowjet-Kontakt," August 4, 1944, frames 124-25, roll 579, microcopy T-175, RG-242, NA.

57. Broadcast by Martin Legmann, "German Army's Task Now to Ask for Armistice," September 1, 1943, *Daily Digest of World Broadcasts*, II, 4 B, BBC.

58. Toshikazu Kase, *Journey to the Missouri* (New Haven: Yale University Press, 1950), pp. 162–63; for other Japanese mediation attempts, see Bernd Martin, *Deutschland und Japan im Zweiten Weltkrieg* (Göttingen: Musterschmidt, 1969), pp. 110–21, 172–88.

59. Stalin to Roosevelt, September 8, 1943, *SCRT*, pp. 90–91.

60. Gromyko to Hull, September 14, 1943, *FRUS*, 1943, vol. III, pp. 696–97; Foreign Office to British Embassy Moscow, September 18, 1943, FO 181/975/5, PRO.

61. Herschel Johnson (Stockholm) to Secretary of State, September 29, 1943, *FRUS*, 1943, vol. III, pp. 698–99.

62. "Interview between Mr. Gordon Young and Mme Kollontay," N 5967/499/38, FO 371/36992, PRO; the date of the interview was September 22.

63. Robert E. Sherwood, *Roosevelt and Hopkins* (New York: Harper, 1948), p. 734.

64. Navy Intelligence report, October 15, 1943, Germany 6900, RG-165, NA; British Embassy Bern to Foreign Office, October 1, 1943, C 11735/55/18, FO 371/34438, PRO; Albert C. Wedemeyer, *Wedemeyer Reports!* (New York: Holt, 1958), p. 92; memorandum by Harvey H. Smith, September 20, 1943, Germany 6900, RG-165, NA.

65. See sources cited in footnotes 24, 36, 60, and 61 above, and statement by Tass, July 17, 1943, in *Soviet Foreign Policy during the Patriotic War*, ed. Rothstein, vol. I, p. 269–70.

66. Minute by Bentinck, October 15, 1943, on letter by More to Strang, September 23, 1943, FO 371/37031, PRO.

67. Maurice Matloff, *Strategic Planning for Coalition Warfare, 1943–1944* (Washington, D.C.: Department of the Army, 1959), pp. 286–87; cf. *The War Diary of Breckinridge Long* (Lincoln: University of Nebraska Press, 1966), pp. 320–21.

68. Harry Hopkins, "We Can Win in 1945," *American Magazine* 136, no. 4 (October 1943): 100.

69. "Russia's Position," August 2, 1943, *FRUS, Conferences at Washington and Quebec*, p. 625.

70. Schumann and Kühnrich, "Der Kampf der deutschen Antifaschisten für ein freies, friedliebendes und demokratisches Deutschland und seine Übereinstimmung mit den Zielen der Sowjetunion im zweiten Weltkrieg."

71. An outstanding example was the Czechoslovak-Polish-Yugoslav symposium held in October 1966 in Belgrade; the papers presented there were later published under the title *Národní fronta a komunisté* [The National Front and the Communists] (Prague: Naše vojsko, 1968), with parallel editions in Polish and Serbo-Croatian.

72. See especially Gabriel Kolko, *The Politics of War* (New York: Random House, 1968), pp. 3–9; also Angus Calder, *The People's War* (New York: Pantheon, 1969), p. 18.

73. For details, see Alfred Rieber, *Stalin and the French Communist Party* (New York: Columbia University Press, 1962), pp. 59–60, 84–85, and Joan Barth Urban, "Moscow and the Italian Communist Party: 1926–1945" (Ph.D. diss., Harvard University, 1967), pp. 289–303.

74. Susanne S. Lotarski, "The Communist Takeover in Poland," in *The Anatomy of Communist Takeovers*, ed. Thomas T. Hammond and Robert Farrell (New Haven: Yale University Press, 1975), p. 347.

75. Nowotko to Dimitrov, September 11, 1942, "Perepiska Generalnogo Sekretaria IK KI G. M. Dimitrova s rukovodstvom Polskoi Rabochei Partii (1942–43)" [Correspondence between secretary general of the executive committee of the Communist International G. M. Dimitrov and the leadership of the Polish Workers' Party], *Novaia i noveishaia istoriia*, 1964, no. 5, p. 116.

76. Nicholas Bethell, *Gomułka: His Poland and His Communism* (London: Longmans, 1969), pp. 52–53.

77. Nissan Oren, *Bulgarian Communism* (New York: Columbia University Press, 1971), pp. 167–68.

78. The estimate for Romania by Matei Socor, former party regional secretary for Moldavia; for Hungary, see Peter Gosztony, "Die ungarische antifaschistische Bewegung in der Sowjetunion während des Zweiten Weltkrieges," *Militärgeschichtliche Mitteilungen* 9 (1972): 91.

79. C. A. Macartney, *October Fifteenth*, vol. II (Edinburgh: University of Edinburgh Press, 1956), pp. 78–79.

80. Vojtech Mastny, *The Czechs under Nazi Rule* (New York: Columbia University Press, 1971), pp. 172–73.

81. Jozef Jablonický, *Z ilegality do povstania* [From the underground to the uprising] (Bratislava: Epocha, 1969), p. 195.

82. Comintern to Tito, March 5, 1942, in *Yugoslavia and the Soviet Union* (New York: Oxford University Press, 1975), p. 146.

83. F. W. Deakin, "Great Britain and European Resistance," in *European Resistance Movements*, vol. II (Oxford: Pergamon, 1964), p. 110.

84. Walter R. Roberts, *Tito, Mihailović, and the Allies* (New Brunswick, N.J.: Rutgers University Press, 1973), pp. 106–12; Dan Morgan, "Yugoslav Officials Annoyed At WWII Resistance Book," *Washington Post*, August 19, 1973; Milovan Djilas, *Wartime* (New York: Harcourt, 1977), pp. 229–45.

85. Milorad M. Drachkovitch, "The Comintern and the Insurrectional Activity of the Communist Party of Yugoslavia in 1941–1942," in *The Comintern: Historical Highlights*, ed. Milorad M. Drachkovitch and Branko Lazitch (New York: Praeger, 1966), pp. 205–6.

86. Paul Schoup, "The Yugoslav Revolution: The First of a New Type," in *The Anatomy of Communist Takeovers*, ed. Hammond and Farrell, pp. 258–59.

87. Stephen E. Palmer, Jr., and Robert R. King, *Yugoslav Communism and the Macedonian Question* (Hamden, Conn.: Archon, 1971), pp. 95–106; Svetozar Vukmanović-Tempo, *Revolucija koja teče: Memoari* [The revolution continues: Memoirs] (Belgrade: Komunist, 1971), vol. I, pp. 349–55.

88. Włodzimierz Dąbrowski, "Wspomnienia działacza PPR" [Recollections of a party activist], *ZPW* 4, no. 4 (1961): 262–63.

89. Marian Malinowski, "Kształtowanie się założeń programowych polskiego ruchu robotniczego w latach 1939–1942" [The program formation of the Polish workers' movement in 1939–1942], *ibid.*, p. 43.

3. Hazy Perspectives

90. Bethell, *Gomułka*, pp. 53–54; see Andrzej Korbonski, "The Polish Communist Party 1938–1942," *SR* 26 (1967): 441–44.

91. Jan Pivoluska, "K niektorým otázkám zahraničnej orientácie slovenského odboja do roku 1943" [Problems of foreign policy orientation in the Slovak resistance until 1943], *Slovanské štúdie, História* 9 (1967): 75–80; Ferdinand Beer et al., *Dějinná křižovatka* (Prague: Nakladatelství politické literatury, 1964), pp. 108–19.

92. *Odboj a revoluce, 1938–1945* [Resistance and revolution] (Prague: Naše vojsko, 1965), p. 207; Stanislav Kotršál, "O činnosti III. ilegálního vedeni KSČ" [The Activities of the third underground leadership of the Communist party of Czechoslovakia], *OAR* 5, no. 4 (1967): 17–32.

93. Horst Duhnke, *Die KPD von 1933 bis 1945* (Cologne: Kiepenheuer und Witsch, 1972), pp. 485–504.

94. Gerhard Rossmann, "Der Weg zur Gründung des Nationalkomitees 'Freies Deutschland' in Leipzig," *Zeitschrift für Geschichtswissenschaft* 13 (1965): 1040–41; George Kennan and Hermann Weber, "Aus dem Kadermaterial der illegalen KPD, 1943," *Vierteljahrshefte für Zeitgeschichte* 20 (1972): 422–46.

95. Otto Winzer, *Zwölf Jahre Kampf gegen Faschismus und Krieg* (Düsseldorf: Das Neue Wort, 1955), p. 191.

96. Arvid Lundgren, "Internationalen sjöngs i nazi-Tyskland" [The Internationale was sung in Nazi Germany], *Ny Tid* (Stockholm), June 6, 1947; Karl Mewis, *Im Auftrag der Partei* (Berlin: Dietz, 1971), pp. 302–5.

97. Vinzent Porombka, "Als Fallschirmspringer im illegalen Einsatz," in *Im Kampf bewährt*, ed. Heinz Vosske (Berlin: Dietz, 1969), pp. 105–41.

98. "Hitlers Krieg ist verloren!" in Gertrud Glondajewski and Heinz Schumann, *Die Neubauer-Poser-Gruppe* (Berlin: Dietz, 1957), pp. 105–7.

99. Erich Köhn, "Der Weg zur Gründung des Nationalkomitees 'Freies Deutschland' in Leipzig," *Zeitschrift für Geschichtswissenschaft* 13 (1965): 27–31.

100. Werner Plesse, "Zum antifaschistischen Widerstandskampf in Mitteldeutschland," *ibid.*, 2 (1954): 836–37; Duhnke, *Die KPD von 1933 bis 1945*, pp. 615–19.

101. Kotršál, "O činnosti III. ilegálního vedení KSČ," p. 33; Beer et al., *Dějinná křižovatka*, pp. 169–75.

102. Kotršál, "O činnosti III. ilegálního vedení KSČ," pp. 34–38.

103. *Ibid.*, and in Vetiška's less than candid memoirs appropriately entitled *Skok do tmy* [The jump into darkness] (Prague: Nakladatelství politické literatury, 1966), pp. 68–69, 116–47.

104. Oldřich Sládek, *Kryci heslo: Svoboda* [Codeword freedom] (České Budějovice: Nakladatelství České Budějovice, 1967), pp. 147, 167; Josef Klečka, "O zradě" [On treason], *OAR* 5, no. 4 (1967): 47–52.

105. Vilém Kahan, "O některých nedostatcích v konspiratívní činnosti [Some shortcomings in the conspiratorial activities], *OAR* 5, no. 4 (1967): 97–98.

106. M. R. D. Foot, *SOE in France* (London: Her Majesty's Stationery Office, 1966), pp. 124–25, 473.

107. Macartney, *October Fifteenth*, vol. I, pp. 99, 156.

108. "List otwarty KC PPR do Delegatury Rządu Emigracyjnego" [An open letter by the central committee of the Polish Workers' Party to the Delegation of the government-in-exile], January 15, 1943, in *Stosunki polsko-radzieckie w latach 1917–1945* [Polish-Soviet relations in 1917–1945], ed. Tadeusz Cieślak and Euzebiusz Basiński (Warsaw: Książka i Wiedza, 1967), pp. 332–39.

109. Tadeusz Żeńczykowski, "Rozmowy Delegatura Rządu-PPR w 1943 roku w świetle faktów" [The 1943 conversations between the government Delegation and the Polish Workers' party in the light of the facts], *Zeszyty historyczne* 27 (1974): 104–29.

110. *Ibid.*, p. 119; Jan Nowak, "Sprawa generała Berlinga" [The affair of General Berling], *ibid.*, 37 (1976): 54–57.

111. "O co walczymy" [What we are fighting for], March 1, 1943, in *Kształtowanie się podstaw programowych Polskiej Partii Robotniczej w latach 1942–1945* [The program formation of the Polish Workers' party in 1942–1945] (Warsaw: Książka i Wiedza, 1958), pp. 93–96; Dimitrov to Finder, April 2, 1943, "Perepiska Generalnogo Sekretaria IK KI G.M. Dimitrova s rukovodstvom Polskoi Rabochei Partii," p. 122.

112. Comintern to Tito, May 1943, in *Yugoslavia and the Soviet Union*, ed. Clissold, p. 157.

113. For example, Kermit E. McKenzie, *Comintern and World Revolution* (New York: Columbia University Press, 1964), p. 190, or Franz Borkenau, *European Communism* (New York: Harper, 1953), p. 282.

114. Adam Ulam, *Expansion and Coexistence* (New York: Praeger, 1968), p. 346.

115. Leonhard, *Child of the Revolution*, p. 218; Enrique Castro Delgado, *Mi fe se perdió en Moscú* (Mexico City: Horizontes, 1951), pp. 222–23.

116. Macartney, *October Fifteenth*, vol. II, p. 158.

117. Pero Morača, "Odnosi izmedju Komunističke partije Jugoslavije i Kominterne od 1941. do 1943. godine" [The relations between the Communist party of Yugoslavia and the Comintern from 1941 to 1943], *Jugoslovenski Istorijski Casopis*, 1969, no. 1–2, p. 128.

118. "Statement of the Praesidium of the E.C.C.I. on the Dissolution of the Communist International," May 21, 1943, in *The Communist International, 1919–1943*, ed. Jane Degras, vol. III (London: Oxford University Press, 1965), pp. 477–79.

119. Jesús Hernández, *La grande trahison* (Paris: Fasquelle, 1953), p. 249.

120. See Annie Kriegel, "La dissolution du 'Komintern,' " *Revue d'histoire de la deuxième guerre mondiale* 68 (1967): 33–43, and Robert H. McNeal, *International Relations among Communists* (Englewood Cliffs, N.J.: Prentice-Hall, 1967), pp. 11–12.

121. An earlier version of this section appeared as my article, "Spheres of Influence and

Soviet War Aims in 1943," in *Eastern Europe in the 1970s*, ed. Sylva Sinanian, Istvan Deak, and Peter C. Ludz (New York: Praeger, 1972), pp. 87–107.

122. Memorandum by Cross on Roosevelt-Molotov conversation, June 1, 1942, *FRUS*, 1942, vol. III, p. 580.

123. Eden to Clark Kerr on conversation with Maiskii, March 10, 1943, N 1605/315/38, FO 371/36991, PRO.

124. In its original version, the Curzon line left Lvov on the Soviet side; Witold Sworakowski, "An Error Regarding Eastern Galicia in Curzon's Note to the Soviet Government of 11 July, 1920," *JCEA* 4 (1944–45): 1–26; cf. Norman Davies, *White Eagle, Red Star* (London: Macdonald, 1972), pp. 169–71.

125. Woodward, *British Foreign Policy in the Second World War*, vol. III (London: Her Majesty's Stationery Office, 1971), p. 133.

126. John L. Gaddis, *The United States and the Origins of the Cold War* (New York: Columbia University Press, 1972), p. 33.

127. Ralph B. Levering, *American Opinion and the Russian Alliance* (Chapel Hill: University of North Carolina Press, 1976), pp. 97–145, 159–68.

128. Edward H. Carr, *Conditions of Peace* (London: Macmillan, 1942), p. 206.

129. "Britain, Russia and Europe: Conditions of Continental Security," *Times* (London), March 10, 1943.

130. David J. Dallin, *Russia and Postwar Europe* (New Haven: Yale University Press, 1943), p. 188.

131. *New York Times*, March 21, 1943, p. E3.

132. "A Four Years' Plan," March 21, 1943, in Winston Churchill, *Onwards to Victory* (Boston: Little, Brown, 1944), p. 51.

133. Andrzej Marek [Alfred Lampe], "Miejsce Polski w Europie" [Poland's place in Europe], *Wolna Polska* (Moscow), April 16, 1943, reprinted in *Stosunki polsko-radzieckie w latach 1917–1945*, ed. Cieślak and Basiński, pp. 339–45.

134. F. A. Voigt, "The Need for an Invincible Poland," *Time and Tide* 22 (1941): 1119; Włodzimierz T. Kowalski, *Walka dyplomatyczna o miejsce Polski w Europie* [The diplomatic struggle for Poland's place in Europe] (Warsaw: Książka i Wiedza, 1966), pp. 336–37.

135. Edward Raczyński, *In Allied London* (London: Weidenfeld and Nicolson, 1962), pp. 140–41.

136. Eden to Dormer, January 22, 1943, in *The Great Powers and the Polish Question*, ed. Antony Polonsky (London: London School of Economics and Political Science, 1976), pp. 115–16; see Viktoria Vierheller, *Polen und die Deutschland-Frage, 1939–1949* (Cologne: Wissenschaft und Politik, 1970), pp. 27–29.

137. Marian Orzechowski, *Odra-Nysa Łużycka-Bałtyk w polskiej myśli politycznej okresu Drugiej wojny światowej* [The Oder, Western Neisse and Baltic in Polish political

thought during World War II] (Wrocław: Zakład Narodowy imienia Ossolińskich, 1969), pp. 65, 71–72.

138. Bogomolov to Narkomindel, March 20, and Narkomindel to Bogomolov, April 21 and 23, 1943, *Sovetsko-chekhoslovatskie otnosheniia vo vremia Velikoi Otechestvennoi Voiny* [Soviet–Czechoslovak relations during the Great Patriotic War] (Moscow: Gospolitizdat, 1960), pp. 65, 71–72.

139. Piotr S. Wandycz, *Czechoslovak-Polish Confederation and the Great Powers* (Bloomington: Indiana University Press, 1956), pp. 92–93.

140. Note by Smutný on Beneš–Bogomolov conversation, April 24, 1943, *DHCSP*, vol. I, p. 327.

141. Speech at the University of Chicago, May 24, 1943, in *President Beneš on War and Peace: Statements by Dr. Edvard Beneš, President of the Czechoslovak Republic during His Visit to the United States and Canada in May and June 1943* (New York: Czechoslovak Information Service, 1943), p. 91; other references on pp. 30, 32–33, 51–58, 126–27.

142. *New York Herald Tribune*, May 29, 1943.

143. *FRUS*, 1943, vol. III, p. 529; *Memoirs of Dr. Eduard Beneš* (Boston: Houghton Mifflin, 1955), pp. 180–87; cf. Eden to Nichols, June 16, 1943, in *Great Powers and the Polish Question*, ed. Polonsky, p. 133.

144. Roosevelt to Stalin, May 5, 1943, *SCRT*, pp. 63–64.

145. Standley to Secretary of State, May 25, 1943, *FRUS*, 1943, vol. III, pp. 653–55.

146. Note by Butler on conversation with Maiskii, June 1, 1943, FO 181/976/8, PRO.

147. "Vystuplenie Benesha" [An address by Beneš], *Pravda* and *Izvestia*, May 22, 1943; Ripka to Beneš on conversation with Bogomolov, June 6, 1943, *Sovetsko-chekhoslovatskie otnosheniia*, p. 85.

148. B. L., "Rudolf Slansky," *Ost-Probleme* 3 (1951): 1530; L. Lesny, "Der Slansky-Process," *Osteuropa* 3 (1953): 2.

149. Note by Smutný on Beneš–Eden conversation, June 17, 1943, *DHCSP*, vol. I, p. 335; minute by J. M. Roberts, October 5, 1943, C 11407/525/12, FO 371/34340, PRO.

150. Note by Smutný on conversation with Beneš, November 1, 1943, *DHCSP*, vol. I, p. 407; Ladislav K. Feierabend, *Beneš mezi Washingtonem a Moskvou* [Beneš between Washington and Moscow] (Washington, D.C.: privately printed, 1966), pp. 84–88.

151. Report by Eden at War Cabinet meeting, July 5, 1943, Minutes no. 93(43), CAB 65, PRO; Bogomolov to Narkomindel, June 19, 1943, *Sovetsko-chekhoslovatskie otnosheniia*, pp. 86–88.

152. Aide-mémoire by Sobolev, July 26, 1943, and Foreign Office memorandum, August 5, 1943, N 4691/66/38, and memorandum by Sobolev, August 30, 1943, N 5015/66/38, FO 371/36956, PRO.

153. Fierlinger to Beneš on conversation with Korneichuk, July 14, 1943, *Sovetsko-chekhoslovatskie otnosheniia*, p. 99.

154. Note by J. M. Roberts on conversation with Jan Masaryk, August 27, 1943, C 11107/525/12, FO 371/34340, PRO.

155. Jaromír Smutný, "Vývoj vztahů československo-sovětských" [The development of Czechoslovak–Soviet relations], vol. I, pages not numbered, unpublished manuscript on microfilm, Smutný Papers, Archive of Russian and East European History and Culture, Columbia University.

156. Molotov to Clark Kerr, June 7, 1943, C 7263/155/18, FO 371/34449, PRO.

157. Note in the same folder; see also Viktor L. Israelian, Antigitlerovskaia koalitsiia [The anti-Hitler coalition] (Moscow: Mezhdunarodnye otnosheniia, 1964), p. 268.

158. Macartney, October Fifteenth, vol. II, pp. 176–77.

159. Gosztony, "Die ungarische antifaschistische Bewegung in der Sowjetunion," pp. 98–101; Nikolai I. Lebedev, Rumyniia v gody Vtoroi Mirovoi Voiny [Romania during World War II] (Moscow: Mezhdunarodnye otnosheniia, 1961), pp. 158–59.

160. "Chto skryvaetsia za proektom Vostochnoevropeiskoi federatsii ili konfederatsii?" [What is concealed behind the project of the eastern European federation or confederation?], Voina i rabochii klass, July 15, 1943, pp. 23–27; cf. "Soviet Attitude to Federations in Eastern Europe," August 10, 1943, 4906/315/38, FO 371/36992, PRO.

161. "Suggested Principles Which Would Govern the Conclusion of Hostilities with the European Members of the Axis," July 14, 1943, FRUS, 1943, vol. I, p. 708–10.

162. Roosevelt and Churchill to Stalin, August 19, 1943, SCRT, pp. 79–82.

163. Stalin to Roosevelt and Churchill, August 22, 1943, SCRT, p. 84; For subsequent American-Soviet exchanges concerning the commission, see file 711—Advisory Council, U.S. Embassy Moscow, RG-84, NA.

164. Stalin to Roosevelt and Churchill, September 12, 1943, FRUS, 1943, vol. I, p. 786; the passage does not appear in the Soviet edition of the message, SCRT, pp. 93–94; see also Molotov to Clark Kerr, October 14, 1943, Sovetsko-frantsuzskie otnosheniia vo vremia Velikoi Otechestvennoi Voiny [Soviet-French relations during the Great Patriotic War] (Moscow: Gospolitizdat, 1959), p. 217.

165. A. B., "O Voenno-Politicheskoi Komissii soiuznykh stran" [The Military-Political Commission of the Allied nations], Voina i rabochii klass, October 1, 1943, pp. 4–5; cf. Bruce Kuklick, "The Genesis of the European Advisory Commission," Journal of Contemporary History 4, no. 4 (1969): 189–201.

166. Eden to Clark Kerr on conversation with Maiskii, August 31, 1943, N 4977/66/38, FO 371/36956, PRO.

167. Arthur M. Schlesinger, Jr., "Origins of the Cold War," Foreign Affairs 46 (1967–68): p. 29, italics added.

168. Robert I. Gannon, The Cardinal Spellman Story (Garden City, N.Y.: Doubleday, 1962), pp. 222–24.

169. See Gaddis, The United States and the Origins of the Cold War, pp. 133–34.

170. "Post-War Settlement," Memorandum no. 292, by Eden, July 1, 1943, CAB 66/38, PRO.

171. Michael Howard, *The Mediterranean Strategy in the Second World War* (London: Weidenfeld and Nicolson, 1968), pp. 50–53, 63, 70; see F. W. D. Deakin, "The Myth of an Allied Landing in the Balkans during the Second World War (with Particular Regard to Yugoslavia)," in *British Policy towards Wartime Resistance in Yugoslavia and Greece,* ed. Phyllis Auty and Richard Clogg (New York: Barnes and Noble, 1975), pp. 93–116.

172. See. A. J. P. Taylor, "The Statesman," and Basil H. Liddell Hart, "The Military Strategist," in A. J. P. Taylor et al., *Churchill Revised* (New York: Dial, 1969), pp. 57 and 221–22.

173. "Post-War Settlement," Memorandum no. 292, by Eden.

174. Memorandum no. 447, by Churchill, October 11, 1943, CAB 66/41, PRO.

175. Memorandum no. 438, by Eden, October 5, 1943, CAB 66/41, PRO.

Chapter Four: The Crucial Conferences

1. The first two sections of this chapter have appeared in a slightly different version as an article, "Soviet War Aims at the Moscow and Teheran Conferences of 1943," *Journal of Modern History* 47 (1975): 481–504, and are reprinted here with the permission of the University of Chicago Press.

2. Harriman to Secretary of State, November 9, 1943, *FRUS,* 1943, vol. III, p. 596.

3. Translated as "Teaching of Economics in the Soviet Union," *American Economic Review* 34 (1944): 501–30; see Raya Dunayevskaia, "A New Revision of Marxian Economics," *ibid.,* pp. 531–37.

4. Evgenii Varga, "Vozmeshchenie ushcherba gitlerovskoi Germaniei i ee soobshchnikami" [Reparation of the damages by Hitlerite Germany and her accomplices], *Voina i rabochii klass,* October 15, 1943, pp. 4–10.

5. "The Consideration of Measures to Shorten the Duration of the War against Hitlerite Germany and Her Allies in Europe," October 19, 1943, *FRUS,* 1943, vol. I, pp. 771–72; Sobolev to Eden, September 29, 1943, annex C to Memorandum no. 434, CAB 66/41, PRO.

6. Eden to Clark Kerr, September 18, 1943, *FRUS,* 1943, vol. I, pp. 525–26; "Note on the Secretary of State's Meeting with the Allied Foreign Ministers," October 7, 1943, C 11823/11823/62, FO 371/34409, PRO.

7. "Draft Agenda for Tripartite Conference," September 14, 1943, *FRUS,* 1943, vol. I, pp. 521–22.

8. Clark Kerr to Foreign Office, November 5, 1943, N 6575/3666/38, FO 371/37031, PRO; see Hamilton to Secretary of State, September 30, 1943, *FRUS,* 1943, vol. I, pp. 535–36.

9. Clark Kerr to Foreign Office, November 5, 1943, N 6575/3666/38, FO 371/37031, PRO.

10. The literature about the Moscow and Teheran conferences is extensive but mostly repetitive. Among original accounts, William H. McNeill, *America, Britain and Russia: Their Co-operation and Conflict, 1941–1946* (London: Oxford University Press, 1953), pp. 328–37, 348–68, has withstood the test of time remarkably well; the discussion in Herbert Feis, *Churchill—Roosevelt—Stalin: The War They Waged and the Peace They Sought* (Princeton: Princeton University Press, 1967), pp. 191–279, is thoughtful and informative though characteristically inconclusive; Robert Beitzell, *The Uneasy Alliance* (New York: Knopf, 1972), pp. 153–365, based on published sources only, is often perceptive in detail but lacking a clear line of argument; the best analysis is in John W. Wheeler-Bennett and Anthony Nicholls, *The Semblance of Peace* (New York: Macmillan, 1972), pp. 103–21, 143–67.

11. Mallet (Stockholm) to Foreign Office on conversation with Razin, October 27, 1943, FO 188/419, PRO.

12. Record of meeting, October 20, 1943, *FRUS*, 1943, vol. I, pp. 583–86; statements by Generals Ismay and Deane, October 20, 1943, *ibid.*, pp. 774–81.

13. Stalin to Churchill, September 3, 1941, *SCCA*, p. 21, italics added.

14. *The Memoirs of General Lord Ismay* (New York: Viking, 1960), pp. 326–27.

15. Deane to Marshall, October 29, 1943, subject file Italy, U.S. Military Mission Moscow, RG-334, NA.

16. Maurice Matloff, *Strategic Planning for Coalition Warfare, 1943–1944* (Washington, D.C.: Department of the Army, 1959), pp. 302–4; see Robert W. Coakley and Richard M. Leighton, *Global Logistics and Strategy, 1943–1945* (Washington, D.C.: Office of the Chief of Military History, 1968), p. 275.

17. Tito to Moscow, early October, 1943, in *Yugoslavia and the Soviet Union*, ed. Stephen Clissold (New York: Oxford University Press, 1975), p. 151; Dušan Plenča, *Medjunarodni odnosi Jugoslavije u toku Drugog svjetskog rata* (Belgrade: Institut društvenih nauka, 1962), pp. 210–12.

18. Summary of proceedings, session of October 23, 1943, *FRUS*, 1943, vol. I, pp. 617–18; Minutes of Hopkins-Eden-Molotov meeting, November 30, 1943, *FRUS, Tehran,* p. 575.

19. "Information from the Soviet Delegation Concerning the Situation in Bulgaria," *FRUS*, 1943, vol. I, pp. 712–14.

20. "British Note to the Soviet Chargé Concerning Question of Agreement between Major and Minor Allies on Post-War Questions," *ibid.*, pp. 725–26.

21. Memorandum by Eden, September 28, 1943, W.P. (43) 423, CAB 66/41, PRO; 135th Conclusions, Minute 4, October 5, 1943, W.M. (43), CAB 65/40, PRO.

22. Llewellyn Woodward, *British Foreign Policy in the Second World War*, vol. II (London: Her Majesty's Stationery Office, 1971), pp. 642–44.

23. W. Averell Harriman and Elie Abel, *Special Envoy to Churchill and Stalin* (New York: Random House, 1975), p. 245.

24. Summary of proceedings, session of October 24, 1943, *FRUS*, 1943, vol. I, p. 625.

25. Record of Molotov-Beneš conversation, December 14, 1943, in Vojtech Mastny, ed., "The Beneš-Stalin-Molotov Conversations in December 1943: New Documents," *Jahrbücher für Geschichte Osteuropas* 20 (1972): 387.

26. Summary of proceedings, session of October 24, 1943, *FRUS*, 1943, vol. I, pp. 626–27; see British record of proceedings, pp. 41–42, N 6921/3666/38, FO 371/37031, PRO.

27. Philip Mosely, *The Kremlin and World Politics* (New York: Random House, 1960), p. 19.

28. Eden to Foreign Office, October 24, 1943, C 12467/525/12, FO 371/34340, PRO.

29. Cadogan to Churchill, October 25, 1943, C 12505/525/12, FO 371/34340, PRO.

30. Eden to Churchill, October 24, 1943, N 6263/3666/38, FO 371/37030, PRO; in his memoirs, Eden has confirmed that his main objective at the conference was creation of a "machinery for consultation between Allies on European questions," Anthony Eden, *The Reckoning* (Boston: Houghton Mifflin, 1965), pp. 410–11.

31. Churchill to British Embassies in Washington and Moscow, October 16, 1943, enclosures, C 11655/525/12, FO 371/34340, PRO.

32. "Statement of the Soviet Delegation on Point 8 of the Agenda," *FRUS*, 1943, vol. I, pp. 726–27.

33. "Draft of Declaration on Joint Responsibility for Europe," *ibid.*, pp. 736–37.

34. Summary of proceedings, session of October 25, 1943, *ibid.*, p. 634.

35. Summary of proceedings, session of October 26, 1943, *ibid.*, pp. 637–39; "The Future of Poland and Danubian and Balkan Countries, Including the Question of Federations," *ibid.*, pp. 762–63.

36. Summary of proceedings, session of October, 21, 1943, *ibid.*, pp. 596–97, 600.

37. *Ibid.*, pp. 599 and 641.

38. Summary of proceedings, sessions of October 22, 23, 27, and 29, 1943, *ibid.*, pp. 604–13, 620–21, 650–53, 662–64; "European Advisory Commission," *ibid.*, pp. 756–57; "Advisory Council for Italy," *ibid.*, pp. 758–59.

39. "Proposal of the Soviet Union in Regard to Italy," *ibid.*, pp. 714–15; "Declaration Regarding Italy," *ibid.*, pp. 759–60; the Soviet Union endorsed a British-sponsored declaration which reserved to Anglo-American commanders in liberated France the exclusive right to exercise power and supervise its subsequent transfer to French authorities enjoying their confidence, "Civil Affairs for France," *ibid.*, pp. 760–61.

40. See Hull to Winant, December 23, 1943, *ibid.*, p. 812; William Strang, *Home and Abroad* (London: Deutsch, 1956), p. 202.

41. "U.S. Proposal with Regard to the Treatment of Germany," *FRUS*, 1943, vol. I, pp. 720–23.

42. Summary of proceedings, session of October 25, 1943, *ibid.*, pp. 631–32.

43. Memorandum by Hull on conversation with Stalin, October 30, 1943, *ibid.*, p. 687.

350

44. Harriman to Acting Secretary of State, October 31, 1943, *ibid.*, p. 690; Strang, *Home and Abroad*, p. 200.

45. "Amended Draft on Austria," *FRUS*, 1943, vol. I, p. 724; Mosely, *Kremlin and World Politics*, pp. 276–77.

46. "Declaration on Austria," *FRUS*, 1943, vol. I, p. 761; on the British origins of the declaration, see Elisabeth Barker, *Austria, 1918–1972* (Coral Gables: University of Miami Press, 1973), pp. 137–47.

47. Summary of proceedings, session of October 30, 1943, *FRUS*, 1943, vol. I, p. 679.

48. *Ibid.*, p. 680.

49. Speech of November 18, 1943, quoted in *The Memoirs of Cordell Hull* (New York: Macmillan, 1948), vol. II, pp. 1314–15; see Robert A. Divine, *Second Chance* (New York: Atheneum, 1967), pp. 154–55.

50. *Washington Post*, November 12, 1943, p. 8.

51. *New York Herald Tribune*, November 7, 1943.

52. Notes on Eden-Mikołajczyk conversations, November 12, and December 22, 1943, *DPSR*, vol. II, pp. 77 and 120.

53. In a letter to me on July 17, 1970, Eden wrote that "there is really nothing which I can now add to what I wrote then."

54. Eden, *The Recknoning*, p. 565.

55. "K itogam Moskovskoi konferentsii" [On the results of the Moscow conference], *Voina i rabochii klass*, November 1, 1943, pp. 1–4.

56. Deane to Marshall on conversation with Molotov, November 6, 1943, subject file Italy, U.S. Military Mission Moscow, RG-334, NA.

57. Deane to Marshall on conversation with Voroshilov, November 11, 1943, subject file Italy, U.S. Military Mission Moscow, RG-334, NA: cf. John R. Deane, *The Strange Alliance* (New York: Viking, 1947), p. 32.

58. Litvinov at press conference on November 10, 1943, summarized in Harriman to Secretary of State, November 10, 1943, *FRUS*, 1943, vol. I, pp. 700–702.

59. "K voprosu o federatsiiakh 'malykh' gossudarstv v Evrope" [The question of the federations of "small" states in Europe], *Izvestia*, November 18, 1943.

60. On Soviet influence in wartime Iran, see George Lenczowski, *Russia and the West in Iran, 1918–1948* (Ithaca, N.Y.: Cornell University Press, 1949), pp. 193–234.

61. The evidence concerning the alleged Nazi plot is of the most spurious kind, leaving ample room for the possibility that Stalin deliberately exaggerated the danger: Laslo Havas, *Hitler's Plot to Kill the Big Three* (New York: Cowles, 1969); Viktor Egorov, *Zagovor protiv Evriki* [The plot against EUREKA] (Moscow: Sovetskaia Rossiia, 1968).

62. Roosevelt's "Log of the Trip," *FRUS, Tehran*, pp. 463–64; Harriman and Abel, *Special Envoy to Churchill and Stalin*, pp. 262–64.

63. In contrast, Chief of Imperial General Staff Hastings Ismay wondered whether "microphones had already been installed in anticipation," in *Memoirs of General Lord Ismay*, p. 337.

64. Valentin Berezhkov, *Tegeran 1943: Na konferentsii Bolshoi troiki i v kuluarakh* [Teheran 1943: At the conference of the Big Three and in the lobbies] (Moscow: Novosti, 1971), p. 27.

65. Elliott Roosevelt, *As He Saw It* (New York: Duell, Sloan and Pearce, 1946), p. 175.

66. *FRUS, Tehran*, p. 482; in a letter to me on March 16, 1973, Bohlen reaffirmed that he "was with Mr. Roosevelt as his interpreter and Pavlov was with Stalin."

67. Note on Stalin-Roosevelt conversation, November 28, 1943, *Tegeran—Ialta—Potsdam: Sbornik dokumentov* [Teheran—Yalta—Potsdam: A collection of documents] (Moscow: Mezhdunarodnye otnosheniia, 1970), pp. 33–36; Bohlen minutes, Roosevelt-Stalin meeting, November 28, 1943, *FRUS, Tehran*, pp. 483–86.

68. Bohlen and Combined Chiefs of Staff minutes, plenary meeting of November 28, 1943, *ibid.*, pp. 487–508; British minutes, CAB 99/25, PRO; Soviet minutes, *Tegeran—Ialta—Potsdam*, pp. 37–47.

69. Statement by Eden at Cabinet meeting, December 13, 1943, W.M. (43), 169th Conclusions, Minute 2, CAB 65/40, PRO; The code names in the quote refer to the plans for the cross-Channel attack, invasion of southern France, and landing on the Andaman Islands, respectively.

70. Entry for November 29, 1943, *The Diaries of Sir Alexander Cadogan* (London: Cassell, 1971), p. 580.

71. Stalin was the most insistent during a private conversation with Churchill on November 30 when the Prime Minister made his last eloquent plea for the Mediterranean campaign; British minutes of the conversation in Memorandum W.P. (44) 9, January 7, 1944, CAB 66/45, PRO; see Soviet minutes, *Tegeran—Ialta—Potsdam*, pp. 76–81.

72. Feis, *Churchill—Roosevelt—Stalin*, p. 258; cf. *FRUS, Tehran*, pp. 500–501.

73. Bohlen and Combined Chiefs of Staff minutes, plenary meeting of November 30, 1943, *FRUS, Tehran*, pp. 576–81; Soviet minutes, *Tegeran—Ialta—Potsdam*, pp. 82–85.

74. Bohlen minutes, luncheon meeting, November 30, 1943, *FRUS, Tehran*, pp. 566–67; British minutes, no. 3, Memorandum W.P. (44) 8, January 7, 1944, CAB 66/45, PRO; see also Edward Weisband, *Turkish Foreign Policy, 1943-1945* (Princeton: Princeton University Press, 1973), p. 198.

75. "Decision on the Federative Organization of Yugoslavia," November 29, 1943, in *War and Peace Aims of the United Nations*, ed. Louise W. Holborn, vol. II (Boston: World Peace Foundation, 1948), pp. 1107–8.

76. Tito to Moscow, December 1, 1943, in *Yugoslavia and the Soviet Union*, ed. Clissold, p. 152; Vladimir Dedijer, *Tito* (New York: Simon and Schuster, 1953), p. 209.

77. Walter R. Roberts, *Tito, Mihailović and the Allies* (New Brunswick, N.J.: Rutgers University Press, 1973), pp. 175–79.

78. Mosely, *Kremlin and World Politics*, p. 200.

79. *Memoirs of Dr. Eduard Beneš* (Boston: Houghton Mifflin, 1955), pp. 252–53, 287; note on Eden-Mikołajczyk conversation, December 22, 1943, *DPSR*, vol. II, p. 117.

80. Notes on suggested Stettin–Vienna bombing line, December 1944, C 17528/134/12, FO 371/38927, PRO; General Sir Colin Gubbins, the wartime chief of the SOE, confirmed in a letter to me on July 16, 1969, that no strategic line ever existed.

81. Sergei M. Shtemenko, *The Soviet General Staff at War* (Moscow: Progress, 1970), p. 198.

82. Record of the Molotov-Beneš conversation, December 16, 1943, and memorandum on Stalin–Beneš conversation, December 18, 1943, in Mastny, "The Beneš-Stalin-Molotov Conversations," pp. 397, 399.

83. Molotov to Harriman, November 12, 1943, *FRUS*, 1943, vol. I, pp. 502–3; Molotov to Clark Kerr, November 12, 1943, FO 181/975/5, PRO.

84. Bohlen minutes, dinner meeting, November 28, 1943, and Bohlen's "Memorandum of Marshal Stalin's Views as Expressed during the Evening of November 28, 1943," *FRUS, Tehran*, pp. 510–11, 513; British minutes of Churchill–Stalin conversation, November 28, 1943, no. 1 in Memorandum W.P. (44) 8, January 7, 1944, CAB 66/45, PRO; record of this meeting is omitted in the Soviet publication of the Teheran minutes.

85. Bohlen minutes, meeting of December 1, 1943, *FRUS, Tehran*, pp. 600–603; British minutes, no. 8 in Memorandum W.P. (44) 8, January 7, 1944, CAB 66/45, PRO; Soviet minutes, *Tegeran—Ialta—Potsdam*, pp. 93–95.

86. Bohlen minutes, dinner meeting, November 29, 1943, *FRUS, Tehran*, pp. 553–54; the published Soviet minutes omit the incident.

87. Bohlen minutes, dinner meeting, November 28, 1943, *FRUS, Tehran*, p. 509.

88. Bohlen minutes, Roosevelt-Stalin meeting, November 28, 1943, *ibid.*, pp. 484–85; Bohlen minutes, Roosevelt-Stalin meeting, November 29, 1943, *ibid.*, p. 532; Ware minutes, Hopkins-Eden-Molotov luncheon meeting, November 30, 1943, *ibid.*, pp. 568–71; Stalin's more unflattering remarks about the French do not appear in the published Russian minutes.

89. "Memorandum of Marshal Stalin's Views," November 28, 1943, *FRUS, Tehran*, p. 514.

90. K. V., "Sudba Avstrii" [The Fate of Austria], *Voina i rabochii klass*, November 15, 1943, pp. 14–17.

91. Bohlen minutes, meeting of December 1, 1943, *FRUS, Tehran*, p. 602; Ruth von Mayenburg, *Blaues Blut und rote Fahnen* (Vienna: Molden, 1969), p. 331.

92. British minutes of Churchill–Stalin conversation, November 28, 1943, no. 1 in Memorandum W.P. (44) 8, January 7, 1944, CAB 66/45, PRO; Bohlen minutes, meeting of December 1, 1943, *FRUS, Tehran*, pp. 603–4; Soviet minutes, *Tegeran—Ialta—Potsdam*, p. 96.

93. Speech of November 6, 1941, in *Soviet Foreign Policy during the Patriotic War*, ed. Andrew Rothstein, vol. I (London: Hutchinson, 1944), p. 32; Notes on Sikorski-Churchill conversation on January 31, 1942, on Sikorski-Stalin conversations in December 1941, *DPSR*, vol. I, p. 274.

94. Bohlen minutes, dinner meeting, November 29, 1943, *FRUS, Tehran*, p. 555.

95. Finder to Dimitrov, April 17, 1943, "Perepiska Generalnogo Sekretaria IK KI G. M. Dimitrova s rukovodstvom Polskoi Rabochei Partii" [Correspondence between secretary general of the executive committee of the Communist International G. M. Dimitrov and the leadership of the Polish Workers' party], *Novaia i noveishaia istoriia*, 1964, no. 5, p. 123.

96. Minutes of Churchill-Stalin conversation, November 28, 1943, no. 1, Memorandum W.P. (44) 8, January 7, 1944, CAB 66/45, PRO; cf. Bohlen minutes, dinner meeting, November 28, 1943, *FRUS, Tehran*, p. 512.

97. Bohlen minutes, Roosevelt-Stalin meeting, December 1, 1943, *ibid.*, p. 594; for other references to the conversation, see footnote on that page; cf. Bohlen, *Witness to History*, pp. 151–52.

98. Minutes of meeting, December 1, 1943, nos. 6 and 8, Memorandum W.P. (44), 8, January 7, 1944, CAB 66/45, PRO; both the Bohlen minutes of the same meeting in *FRUS, Tehran*, pp. 597–600, 603–4, and the Soviet ones in *Tegeran—Ialta—Potsdam*, pp. 92–93, 95, omit many details mentioned in the British minutes.

99. Memorandum W.P. (43) 528, November 22, 1943, CAB 66/43, PRO.

100. "Memorandum of Conversation with President Roosevelt," October 5, 1943, *FRUS, 1943*, vol. I, p. 542.

101. See Winston S. Churchill, *Hinge of Fate* (Boston: Houghton Mifflin, 1950), p. 477, and Elliott Roosevelt, *As He Saw It*, pp. 174–76.

102. Churchill to Eden, January 16, 1944, PREM 3/399/6, PRO.

103. B. Shatov, "O Lige natsii" [On the League of Nations], *Voina i rabochii klass*, December 15, 1943, p. 10; cf. Harriman to Secretary of State, December 14, 1943, *FRUS, 1943*, vol. III, pp. 608–609.

104. Record of Molotov–Beneš conversation, December 16, 1943, in Mastny, "The Beneš-Stalin-Molotov Conversations," p. 398.

105. Statement by Ambassador Vladimir Novikov to Greek Vice Premier Georgios Roussos, quoted in Heinz Richter, *Griechenland zwischen Revolution und Konterrevolution* (Frankfurt a.M.: Europäische Verlagsanstalt, 1973), p. 459.

106. Memorandum by Bohlen, December 15, 1943, *FRUS, Tehran*, p. 846.

107. Bogomolov to Narkomindel, August 24, 1943, *Sovetsko-chekhoslovatskie otnosheniia vo vremia Velikoi Otechestvennoi Voiny* [Soviet-Czechoslovak relations during the Great Patriotic War] (Moscow: Gospolitizdat, 1960), pp. 103–5.

108. Note by Smutný on conversation with Beneš, September 28, 1943, *DHCSP*, vol. I, p. 379.

109. Narkomindel to Bogomolov, October 2, 1943, *Sovetsko-chekhoslovatskie otnosheniia*, pp. 108–9.

110. Raymond J. Sontag, *A Broken World, 1919–1939* (New York: Harper and Row, 1971), pp. 365–66.

111. Note by Smutný on Eden-Masaryk conversation, October 8, 1943, *DHCSP*, vol. I, p. 388.

112. Essay by Smutný, October 4, and note by Smutný, August 22, 1943, *ibid.*, pp. 384, 362.

113. Note by Smutný on Eden-Masaryk conversation, October 8, 1943, *ibid.*, p. 388.

114. Note by Smutný, October 4, 1943, *ibid.*, pp. 383–87.

115. Beneš to Fierlinger, October 13, 1943, Fierlinger to Beneš, October 19 and 21, 1943, *ibid.*, pp. 396–97, 401–404.

116. For the final text of the treaty, see *War and Peace Aims of the United Nations*, ed. Holborn, vol. II, pp. 761–63.

117. Cadogan to Churchill, October 25, 1943, C 12505/525/12, FO 371/34340, PRO.

118. Report on Mikołajczyk–Beneš conversation, November 13, 1943, *DPSR*, vol. II, pp. 78–80; Nichols to Frank K. Roberts, November 17, 1943, C 13831/525/12, FO 371/34341, PRO.

119. Nichols to Roberts, November 4, 1943, and minute by Eden, C 13087/525/12, FO 371/34340, PRO.

120. Ladislav K. Feierabend, *Beneš mezi Washingtonem a Moskvou* [Beneš between Washington and Moscow] (Washington, D.C.: privately printed, 1966), p. 76; Jaromír Smutný, "Vývoj vztahů československo-sovětských" [The development of Czechoslovak-Soviet relations], vol. I, pages not numbered, Smutný Papers, Archive of Russian and East European History and Culture, Columbia University.

121. Smutný, "Vývoj vztahů československo-sovětských"; memorandum on conversation between Beneš and H. Fish Armstrong, November 21, 1944, 740.00119 EAC/11-2544, RG-59, NA.

122. For example, F. A. Voigt, "Constants in Russian Foreign Policy," *The Nineteenth Century and After* 134 (1943): 246.

123. Record of Beneš–Molotov conversation, December 14, 1943, in Mastny, "The Beneš-Stalin-Molotov Conversations," p. 380.

124. Record of Beneš-Molotov conversation, December 16, 1943, *ibid.*, p. 390.

125. Record of Beneš-Molotov conversation, December 14, 1943, *ibid.*, p. 384.

126. *Ibid.*, pp. 381–82.

127. Record of Beneš–Molotov conversation, December 16, 1943, and summary by Smutný, *ibid.*, pp. 391–93, 402.

128. Record of Beneš-Stalin conversation, December 12, 1943, *ibid.*, pp. 376–80.

129. Records of Beneš-Stalin and Beneš-Molotov conversations, December 12 and 14, 1943, *ibid.*, pp. 378, 379, 382, 385–87.

130. Notes on conversations on December 15, 16, and 18, 1943, *Cesta ke Květnu* [The road to May], vol. I, pt. 1 (Prague: Academia, 1965), pp. 47–57; the quotation is on p. 47.

131. Nichols to Roberts, November 17, 1943, C 13831/525/12, FO 371/34341, PRO.

132. Record of Beneš-Molotov conversation, December 16, 1943, in Mastny, "The Beneš-Stalin-Molotov Conversations," pp. 388–90; "Přehledná zpráva o průběhu jednání o pomoc spojenců pro ozbrojený odpor na Slovensku" [A survey of the negotiations on the Allies' aid for an armed uprising in Slovakia], December 12, 1944, in *Slovenské národné povstanie* [The Slovak National Uprising], ed. Vilém Prečan (Bratislava: Vydavateľstvo politickej literatúry, 1965), pp. 868–69; a copy of the memorandum about expulsion of the Sudeten Germans is in folder C 1350/1347/12, FO 371/38945, PRO.

133. "Návrh podkladu pro jednání s britskými politickými činiteli" [Draft guidelines for the negotiations with British political representatives], August 17, 1943, in *Slovenské národné povstanie*, ed. Prečan, pp. 85–86; "Požadavky na SSSR" [Demands on the USSR], *ibid.*, pp. 117–19.

134. Frederick Morgan, *Overture to Overlord* (London: Hodder and Stoughton, 1950), pp. 126–28.

135. Entry for December 1, 1943, war diary of the Operations Department of the Staff for the Formation of the Armed Forces, in *Slovenské národné povstanie*, ed. Prečan, p. 115.

136. Ladislav K. Feierabend, *Soumrak československé demokracie* [The twilight of Czechoslovak democracy] (Washington, D.C.: privately printed, 1967), p. 13.

137. "Protocol on the Exchange of Opinion between . . . Beneš . . . Molotov . . . and . . . Stalin," in Mastny, ed., "The Beneš-Stalin-Molotov Conversations," pp. 399–402.

138. Johann W. Brügel, *Tschechen und Deutsche, 1939–1946* (Munich: Nymphenburger Verlagshandlung, 1974), pp. 188–89.

139. Radio address on December 21, 1943, Edvard Beneš, *Šest let exilu a druhé světové války* [Six years of exile and the Second World War] (Prague: Orbis, 1947), p. 227.

140. Harriman to Secretary of State, December 18, 1943, *FRUS*, 1943, vol. III, pp. 728–30; *The Complete War Memoirs of Charles de Gaulle* (New York: Simon and Schuster, 1964), pp. 534–35; Winston S. Churchill, *Closing the Ring* (Boston: Houghton Mifflin, 1951), p. 452; note by Mikołajczyk on conversation with Beneš, January 10, 1944, *DPSR*, vol. II, pp. 129–32.

141. Report to the State Council, February 3, 1944, Beneš, *Šest let exilu a druhé světové války*, pp. 369–77.

142. Quoted in Edvard Táborský, "Beneš and Stalin—Moscow 1943 and 1945," *JCEA* 13 (1953–54): 162.

143. On the Soviet concept of treaties, see Jan F. Triska and Robert M. Slusser, *The Theory, Law, and Policy of Soviet Treaties* (Stanford: Stanford University Press, 1962), pp. 29–31, 397–406.

144. D. Monin, "Chekhoslovakiia pod gitlerovskim gnetom" [Czechoslovakia under Hit-lerite oppression], *Voina i rabochii klass*, January 1, 1944, pp. 4–10.

145. František Janáček et al., "KSČ a politika národní fronty, 1938–1945" [The Commu-nist party of Czechoslovakia and the National Front policy], in *Národní fronta a komunisté* [The National Front and the Communists], (Prague: Naše vojsko, 1968), pp. 80–83.

146. Bohuslav B. Kymlicka, "The Origins and Establishment of National Committees in Czechoslovakia" (certificate essay, Program on East Central Europe, Columbia University, 1961), pp. 5–11.

147. "Declaration by the Government of the U.S.S.R. on the Question of the Polish-Soviet Frontier," January 11, 1944, *DPSR*, vol. II, pp. 132–34.

148. Włodzimierz T. Kowalski, "Walka ZSRR o uznanie ludowego państwa polskiego" [The struggle of the USSR for recognition of the Polish people's state], *Z dziejów stosun-ków polsko-radzieckich* 2 (1956): 57–58.

149. Speech by Molotov, February 1, 1944, *Izvestia*, February 2, 1944.

150. Mario Toscano, "Resumption of Diplomatic Relations between Italy and the Soviet Union during World War II," in his *Designs in Diplomacy* (Baltimore: Johns Hopkins Press, 1970), pp. 294–95.

151. Memorandum by Gromyko, March 19, 1944, *FRUS, 1944*, vol. III, pp. 1062–65; cf. Norman Kogan, *Italy and the Allies* (Cambridge: Harvard University Press, 1956), pp. 63–64.

Chapter Five: From Teheran to Lublin

1. Maurice Matloff and Edwin S. Snell, *Strategic Planning for Coalition Warfare, 1941–1942* (Washington, D.C.: Department of the Army, 1953), p. 380; for the origins of the formula, see Anne Armstrong, *Unconditional Surrender* (New Brunswick, N.J.: Rutgers University Press, 1961), pp. 12–40, and Raymond G. O'Connor, *Diplomacy for Victory* (New York: Norton, 1971), pp. 31–56.

2. "Declaration of Four Nations on General Security," November 1, 1943, *FRUS, 1943*, vol. I, pp. 755–56.

3. Eden to Foreign Office, November 29, 1943, quoted in Churchill to Roosevelt, January 2, 1944, *FRUS, Tehran*, p. 863.

4. "Unconditional Surrender," Memorandum W.P. (44) 125 by Eden, February 19, 1944, C 3029/236/62, FO 371/39024, PRO.

5. Harriman to Hull, January 6, 1944, and Hull to Roosevelt, January 14, 1944, *FRUS, 1944*, vol. I, pp. 581 and 493; on the Soviet concept of unconditional surrender, see John L. Chase, "Unconditional Surrender Reconsidered," *Political Science Quarterly* 70 (1955): 268–72, and Reimer Hansen, *Das Ende des Dritten Reiches: Die deutsche Kapitulation 1945* (Stuttgart: Klett, 1966), pp. 23–26.

6. Roosevelt to Hull, January 17, 1944, *FRUS*, 1944, vol. I, pp. 493–94; see Wallace Carroll, *Persuade or Perish* (Boston: Houghton Mifflin, 1948), pp. 309–10, and Charles E. Bohlen, *Witness to History* (New York: Norton, 1973), p. 157.

7. Memorandum W.P. (44) 33 by Churchill, January 15, 1944, CAB 66/45, PRO.

8. Walther von Seydlitz, *Stalingrad—Konflikt und Konsequenz: Erinnerungen* (Oldenburg: Stalling, 1977), pp. 328–30; Gerhard Leschkowitz, "Zu einigen Fragen des Nationalkomitees 'Freies Deutschland,'" *Zeitschrift für Geschichtswissenschaft* 10, suppl. (1962): 195–96; Arnold Sywottek, *Deutsche Volksdemokratie* (Düsseldorf: Bertelsmann, 1971), pp. 134–36.

9. Horst Laschitza, *Kämpferische Demokratie gegen Faschismus* (Berlin: Deutscher Militärverlag, 1969), pp. 90–97.

10. *Ibid.*, p. 125.

11. "Terms of Surrender for Germany," "Military Occupation of Germany," January 15, 1944, *FRUS*, 1944, vol. I, pp. 112–54; a French occupation zone was not yet considered; see Tony Sharp, *The Wartime Alliance and the Zonal Division of Germany* (New York: Oxford University Press, 1975), pp. 34–35.

12. Foreign Office to British Embassy Moscow, February 10, 1944, U 960/3/70, FO 371/40580, PRO; Winant to Secretary of State, February 3, 9, and 24, 1944, 740.00119 EAC/69, 81, 96, RG-59, NA.

13. "Slukhi iz Kaira" [Rumors from Cairo], *Pravda*, January 17, 1944.

14. Lord Killearn (Cairo) to Foreign Office, January 20, 1944, N 448/442/38, FO 371/43359, PRO.

15. Entry for January 17, 1944, *The Diaries of Sir Alexander Cadogan* (London: Cassell, 1971), p. 597; Churchill to Stalin, January 24, 1944, *SCCA*, pp. 188–90.

16. Gilles Perrault, *The Red Orchestra* (New York: Simon and Schuster, 1969), pp. 324–26, 491; Heinz Höhne, *Codeword DIREKTOR* (New York: Coward, McCann, and Geoghegan, 1972), pp. 220–32.

17. Gusev to Eden, February 3, 1944, N 839/442/38, FO 371/43360, PRO; Gromyko to Hull, February 3, *FRUS*, 1944, I, pp. 498–99; letter by Best to me, May 5, 1974.

18. B. Shatrov, " 'Mirnye' manevry germanskogo imperializma" [The "peace" maneuvers of German imperialism], *Voina i rabochii klass*, February 15, 1944, pp. 8–12.

19. "1918 and 1944: No Historical Analogy," commentary by Major Herbert Stösslein, January 11, 1944, II, 4 B, *Daily Digest of World Broadcasts*, BBC.

20. Balfour to Molotov, December 26, 1943, FO 181/975/5, PRO.

21. Churchill to Eden, January 16, 1944, PREM 3/399/6, PRO.

22. Memorandum by the Representative of the Soviet Union to the European Advisory Commission, "Terms of Surrender for Germany," February 18, 1944, *FRUS*, 1944, vol. I, pp. 173–79.

23. Minutes of EAC meeting, March 3, 1944, U 1869/3/70, FO 371/40580, PRO.

24. Minutes of EAC meeting, March 17, 1944, U 2297/3/70, FO 371/40580, PRO.

25. See Philip E. Mosely, *The Kremlin and World Politics* (New York: Random House, 1960), pp. 133–38, 168–71.

26. *FRUS*, 1944, vol. I, p. 178.

27. Minutes of EAC meeting, March 3, 1944, U 1869/3/70, FO 371/40580, PRO.

28. According to the Russian secretary of the EAC, the Soviet delegation was ready to make concessions on almost any point but the prisoners of war; note by C.W.T. [Charles W. Thayer] on conversation with Prigornyi, April 26, 1944, Box 9603, Stettinius Papers, University of Virginia.

29. *FRUS*, 1944, vol. I, p. 178.

30. *Ibid.*, p. 174.

31. Winant to Secretary of State, March 10, 1944, *FRUS*, 1944, vol. I, pp. 197–99; William Strang, *Home and Abroad* (London: Deutsch, 1956), p. 207.

32. See Hans-Günter Kowalski, "Die 'European Advisory Commission' als Instrument alliierter Deutschlandplanung 1943–1945," *Vierteljahrshefte für Zeitgeschichte* 19 (1971): 268–72, 281.

33. George Slocombe, "Stalin's Peace Terms," *Sunday Express*, March 12, 1944; Tass statement, March 15, 1944, in *Soviet Foreign Policy during the Patriotic War*, ed. Andrew Rothstein, vol. II (London: Hutchinson, 1945), p. 203.

34. "25 Artikel zur Beendigung des Krieges," March 5, 1944, in *Verrat hinter Stacheldraht?* ed. Bodo Scheurig (Munich: Deutscher Taschenbuchverlag, 1965), pp. 174–85; BBC monitoring transcript, folder 199, Emigration Sopade, Ebert-Stiftung.

35. Notes by Pieck on statements by Ulbricht, April 17 and 24, 1944, in Walter Ulbricht, *Zur Geschichte der deutschen Arbeiterbewegung*, vol. II, pt. 1 (Berlin: Dietz, 1955), pp. 176–79; Sywottek, *Deutsche Volksdemokratie*, pp. 142–44; Laschitza, *Kämpferische Demokratie gegen Faschismus*, pp. 115–17.

36. Soviet memorandum for United States government, March 31, 1944, quoting Soviet reply to Clark Kerr, March 29, 1944, *FRUS*, 1944, vol. I, pp. 587–88.

37. John H. Wuorinen (ed.), [Arvi Korhonen], *Finland and World War II* (New York: Ronald, 1948), p. 161; Thede Palm, *The Finnish-Soviet Armistice Negotiations of 1944* (Stockholm: Almqvist and Wicksell, 1971), pp. 32–33, Llewellyn Woodward, *British Foreign Policy in the Second World War*, vol. III (London: Her Majesty's Stationery Office, 1971), p. 134.

38. G. A. Gripenberg, *Finland and the Great Powers* (Lincoln: University of Nebraska Press, 1965), pp. 281–317; for Finnish minutes of the March 27–29 negotiations in Moscow, see Palm, *Finnish-Soviet Armistice Negotiations*, pp. 65–96.

39. Record of Beneš-Molotov conversation, December 16, and memorandum on Beneš-Stalin conversation, December 18, 1943, in Vojtech Mastny, ed., "The Beneš-Stalin-Molotov Conversations in December 1943," *Jahrbücher für Geschichte Osteuropas* 20 (1972): 392, 399.

40. Peter Gosztony, "Die ungarische antifaschistische Bewegung in der Sowjetunion," *Militärgeschichtliche Mitteilungen* 9 (1972) 100–105.

41. Mario D. Fenyo, *Hitler, Horthy, and Hungary* (New Haven: Yale University Press, 1972), pp. 146–47; C. A. Macartney, *October Fifteenth*, vol. II (Edinburgh: University of Edinburgh Press, 1956), p. 215.

42. Alexandre Cretzianu, *The Lost Opportunity* (London: Cape, 1957), p. 128.

43. Platon Chirnoâga, *Istoria politică şi militâra a râzboiului Românei contra Rusiei Sovietice* [A political and military history of Romania's war against Soviet Russia] (Madrid: n.p., 1965), p. 146–47.

44. Frederic C. Nano, "The First Soviet Double Cross: A Chapter in the Secret History of World War II," *JCEA* 12 (1952–53): 240–45; Elisabeth Barker, *British Policy in South-East Europe in the Second World War* (London: Macmillan, 1976), p. 229.

45. Statement by Molotov, April 2, 1944, in *Soviet Foreign Policy during the Patriotic War*, ed. Rothstein, vol. II, pp. 65–66.

46. Order by Colonel Kuznetsov to NKVD units of the Second Ukrainian Army Group, April 13, 1944, in *Pogranichnye voiska v gody Velikoi Otechestvennoi Voiny* [The border troops during the Great Patriotic War] (Moscow: Nauka, 1968), p. 516.

47. Sergei M. Shtemenko, *Generalnyi shtab v gody voiny* [The general staff during the war], vol. II (Moscow: Voenizdat, 1973), pp. 43–44.

48. Alexander Cretzianu, "The Rumanian Armistice Negotiations: Cairo, 1944," *JCEA* 11 (1951–52): 251–55.

49. Nano, "First Soviet Double Cross," pp. 246–53.

50. Klement Gottwald, "Istoricheskii den dlia narodov Chekhoslovakii" [A historic day for the peoples of Czechoslovakia], *Pravda*, April 10, 1944.

51. Basil H. Liddell Hart, *The German Generals Talk* (New York: Morrow, 1948), pp. 215–16.

52. Shtemenko, *Generalnyi shtab v gody voiny*, vol. II, p. 43.

53. M. Galaktionov, "Vtorzhenie v Evropu—sokrushitelnyi udar po Germanii ili zatizhnaia borba za istorshchenie" [The invasion of Europe: A crushing blow to Germany or a protracted war of attrition], *Voina i rabochii klass*, March 15, 1944, pp. 4–6; see Frederick C. Barghoorn, *The Soviet Image of the United States* (New York: Harcourt, 1950), p. 65.

54. Marshall to Roosevelt, March 31, 1944, Records of the Chief of Staff of the Army, RG-319, NA.

55. John R. Deane, *The Strange Alliance* (New York: Viking, 1947), pp. 149–50.

56. Survey of messages between Generals Deane and Burrows and General Antonov, May 23, 1944, CCS 381 USSR (2-27-44) * Sec. 1, RG-218, NA.

57. Sergei M. Shtemenko, *The Soviet General Staff at War* (Moscow: Progress, 1970), p. 230.

58. Fryderyk Zbiniewicz, *Armia Polska w ZSRR* [The Polish army in the USSR] (Warsaw: Wydawnictwo Ministerstwa Obrony Narodowej, 1963), p. 305; Antonín Benčík *et al.*, *Partyzánské hnuti v Československu za druhé světové války* [The partisan movement in Czechoslovakia during World War II] (Prague: Naše vojsko, 1961), pp. 159–62; Gosztony, "Die ungarische antifaschistische Bewegung in der Sowjetunion," pp. 105–6.

59. Roger W. Pethybridge, *A History of Postwar Russia* (New York: New American Library, 1970), p. 28, mentions "the desertion of thousands of Red Army men in Rumania in the summer of 1944" without indicating a source.

60. G. Brovarskii, "Obiazannosti i prava chlenov partii" [The obligations and rights of party members], *Pravda*, May 15, 1944; M. Kalinin, "Mogushchestvo sovetskogo gosudarstva" [The might of the Soviet state], *Bolshevik*, 1944, nos. 7–8, pp. 20–37; "O marksistsko-leninskom vospitanii kadrov sovetskoi intelligentsii" [The Marxist-Leninist education of the cadres of the Soviet intelligentsia], *ibid.*, no. 9, pp. 1–7.

61. Winant to Secretary of State, May 9, 1944, *FRUS*, 1944, vol. I, pp. 55–56.

62. Boris Shtein, "Ob Atlanticheskoi Khartii" [The Atlantic Charter], *Voina i rabochii klass*, May 1, 1944, pp. 18–21.

63. Order of the Day, May 1, 1944, in *Soviet Foreign Policy during the Patriotic War*, ed. Rothstein, vol. II, pp. 22–24.

64. Nichols to Roberts, April 5, 1944, C 4585/1347/12, FO 371/38945, PRO; Gromyko to Hull, April 15, 1944, *FRUS*, 1944, vol. III, pp. 518–19; for the text of the agreement, see *War and Peace Aims of the United Nations*, ed. Louise W. Holborn, vol. II (Boston: World Peace Foundation, 1948), pp. 767–69.

65. Decision by the Central Committee of the Communist Party of the Ukraine, June 17, 1944, in *Slovenské národné povstanie* [The Slovak National Uprising], ed. Vilém Prečan (Bratislava: Vydavateľstvo politickej literatúry, 1965), p. 211; Zbiniewicz, *Armia Polska w ZSRR*, p. 306; Gosztony, "Die ungarische antifaschistische Bewegung in der Sowjetunion," p. 106.

66. Hamilton to Secretary of State, May 28, 1945, 891—Reviews of Trend of Soviet Press—1944, U.S. Embassy Moscow, RG-84, NA; Burrows to British Chiefs of Staff, May 19, 1944, N 3220/3220/38, FO 371/43417, PRO.

67. Aide-mémoire for British Embassy, May 24, 1944, 800—Germany, U.S. Embassy Moscow, RG-84, NA; "Overtures by German Generals and Civilian Opposition For a Separate Armistice," May 16, 1944, *FRUS*, 1944, vol. I, p. 510.

68. "K dvuletiiu anglo-sovetskogo soiuznogo dogovora i sovetsko-amerikanskogo soglasheniia" [The second anniversaries of the British–Soviet alliance treaty and of the Soviet–American agreement], *Voina i rabochii klass*, June 1, 1944, pp. 1–3.

69. Vasilii I. Chuikov, *The Fall of Berlin* (New York: Holt, 1967), pp. 17–18, 24.

70. Stalin to Churchill, June 6, 1944, *SCAA*, p. 224; Stalin to Roosevelt, June 7, 1944, *SCRT*, p. 145.

71. Ilya G. Ehrenburg, "Bitva Frantsii" [France's battle], *Pravda*, June 11, 1944.

72. Nikita S. Khrushchev, *World without Arms, World without Wars* (Moscow: Foreign Languages Publishing House, 1959), p. 165; see Matthew P. Gallagher, *The Soviet History of World War II: Myths, Memories, and Realities* (New York: Praeger, 1963), p. 29.

73. "Deliveries of armaments, strategical raw materials, industrial equipment and food-stuffs to the Soviet Union by the United States of America, Great Britain and Canada," *Pravda*, June 11, 1944, in *Soviet Foreign Policy during the Patriotic War*, ed. Rothstein, vol. II, pp. 86–88.

74. "Reply by J. V. Stalin to a question put by a *Pravda* correspondent," June 13, 1944, *ibid.*, p. 25.

75. Harriman to Roosevelt, June 28, 1944, Box 11, Map Room, FDRL; see Deane, *The Strange Alliance*, p. 153.

76. Winant to Secretary of State, June 10, 22, and July 1, 1944, *FRUS*, 1944, vol. I, pp. 233, 235–39, 450.

77. Stalin to Churchill, June 6, 1944, *SCCA*, p. 224.

78. Earl F. Ziemke, *Stalingrad to Berlin: The German Defeat in the East* (Washington: Office of the Chief of Military History, 1968), p. 296; Sergei M. Shtemenko, "Na severnom flange sovetsko-germanskogo fronta letom i oseniu 1944 goda" [At the northern section of the Soviet–German front in the summer and fall of 1944], *Voennoistoricheskii zhurnal* 14, no. 6 (1972): 63–66.

79. Palm, *Finnish-Soviet Armistice Negotiations*, pp. 55–56, 97–160.

80. Harriman to Roosevelt, June 11, 1944, President–Harriman, January 1–June 30, 1944, Box 11, Map Room, FDRL.

81. Herschel Johnson (Stockholm) to Secretary of State, June 26, 1944, *FRUS*, 1944, vol. I, pp. 523–25; Henrik Lindgren, "Adam von Trotts Reisen nach Schweden, 1942–1944," *Vierteljahrshefte für Zeitgeschichte* 18 (1970): 274–91.

82. Patrick Seale and Maureen McConville, *Philby: The Long Road to Moscow* (London: Hamish Hamilton, 1973), p. 178.

83. Report by Security Service, "Vermerk betreffend Sowjet-Kontakt," August 4, 1944, frames 124–25, roll 579, microcopy T-175, RG-242, NA; Kleist's activities were noted in OSS reports A-32337 and A-32759-a, July 8 and 13, 1944, RG-226, NA.

84. Bernd Martin, *Deutschland und Japan im Zweiten Weltkrieg* (Göttingen: Musterschmidt, 1969), p. 194.

85. Paraphrase of telegram by British Foreign Office, July 23, 1944, *FRUS*, 1944, vol. I, pp. 538–39; Clark Kerr to Vyshinskii, August 21, and Vyshinskii to Clark Kerr, September 4, 1944, C 12685-86/180/18, FO 371/39088, PRO.

86. "Appell des Nationalkomitees 'Freies Deutschland' und Volk und Wehrmacht," July 22, 1944, BBC monitoring transcript, folder 201, Emigration Sopade, Ebert-Stiftung.

87. N. Bodrov, "Sobytiia v Germanii" [The events in Germany], *Pravda*, July 22, 1944; *idem*, "Borba v Germanii prodolzhaetsia" [The struggle in Germany continues], *ibid.*, July 24, 1944.

88. "Report on the Rumors of July 22," July 22, 1944, 800—Soviet Union—General, U.S. Embassy Moscow, RG-84, NA.

89. "Mezhdunarodnoe obozrenie" [International survey], *Pravda*, July 23 and 30, 1944.

90. Walther von Seydlitz, "Was ist am 20. Juli geschehen—was muss weiter geschehen?" August 10, 1944, folder 201, Emigration Sopade, Ebert-Stiftung; "Funk-Abhör-Berichte," July–November 1944, Sonderdienst Seehaus, R 74, Bundesarchiv Koblenz.

91. Harriman to Secretary of State, September 11, 1944, 891—Reviews of Trend of Soviet Press—1944, U.S. Embassy Moscow, RG-84, NA; see Barghoorn, *Soviet Image of the United States*, pp. 66–67; Alexander Werth, *Russia at War* (New York: Dutton, 1964), p. 944.

92. Deane, *The Strange Alliance*, pp. 153–54.

93. Bodo Scheurig, *Free Germany* (Middletown, Conn.: Wesleyan University Press, 1970), pp. 183–201.

94. "To the People and the Wehrmacht," December 8, 1944, *ibid.*, pp. 252–55.

95. Alexander Fischer, *Sowjetische Deutschlandpolitik im Zweiten Weltkrieg* (Stuttgart: Deutsche Verlags-Anstalt, 1975), p. 204.

96. M. Iovchuk, "O moralno-politicheskom porazhenii gitlerovskoi Germanii v khode voiny" [The moral and political defeat of Hitlerite Germany during the war], *Bolshevik*, 1944, no. 22, pp. 8–18.

97. Kaltenbrunner to Himmler, October 9, 1944, and Kleist to Schellenberg, October 10, 1944, frames 131–32, 138–46, roll 579, microcopy T-175, RG-242, NA; Donovan to Roosevelt, October 12, 1944, OSS October 1944, Box 169, President's Secretary's File, FDRL.

98. Alexander Dallin, "Vlasov and Separate Peace: A Note," *JCEA* 16 (1956–57): 394–96.

99. "Russia—Seven Years Later," September 1944, George F. Kennan, *Memoirs, 1925–1950* (Boston: Little, Brown, 1967), p. 520.

100. On Soviet relations with the Polish government-in-exile and the British mediation, see Llewellyn Woodward, *British Foreign Policy in the Second World War*, vol. II (London: Her Majesty's Stationery Office, 1971), pp. 627–57, and vol. III (London: Her Majesty's Stationery Office, 1971), pp. 154–202.

101. For the best study of Stalin's wartime relations with the Polish Communists, see Itō Takayuki, "The Genesis of the Cold War: Confrontation over Poland, 1941–44," in *The Origins of the Cold War in Asia*, ed. Nagai Yonosuke and Iriye Akira (Tokyo and New York: University of Tokyo Press and Columbia University Press, 1977), pp. 147–202.

102. *Dokumenty i materiały do historii stosunków polsko-radzieckich* [Documents and materials on the history of Polish-Soviet relations], vol. VII (Warsaw: Książka i Wiedza, 1973), p. 406, n. 2; Fryderyk Zbiniewicz, "Rola komunistów polskich w organizowaniu i działalności Związku Patriotów Polskich" [The role of the Polish Communists in the organization and activities of the Union of Polish Patriots], *ZPW* 4, no. 4 (1961): 93–94.

103. Berling in *Zielony Sztandar* (Warsaw), October 12, 1972, cited in Tadeusz Żeńczy-

kowski, "Rozmowy Delegatura Rządu-PPR" [The conversations between the government Delegation and the Polish Workers' party], *Zeszyty historyczne* 27 (1974): 119; Berling to NKVD, April 8, 1943, in *Dokumenty i materiały do historii stosunków polsko-radzieckich*, vol. VII, pp. 395–96.

104. Berling to Gomułka, November 20, 1956, in Jan Nowak, "Sprawa generała Berlinga" [The affair of General Berling], *Zeszyty historyczne* 37 (1976): 42.

105. Zbiniewicz, *Armia Polska w ZSRR*, pp. 46–47.

106. "Zagadnienie" [The problem], September 12, 1943, in "Z archiwów polskich komunistów" [From the archives of the Polish Communists], *Zeszyty historyczne* 26 (1973): 194–202 (on p. 202, the document is erroneously dated 1945): cf. Antoni Przygoński, "Z rozważań Alfreda Lampe o nowej Polsce" [Alfred Lampe's thoughts on a new Poland], *ZPW* 7, no. 2 (1964): 98–115.

107. Jerzy Pawłowicz, "Polityka PPR w sprawie utworzenia demokratycznej reprezentacji narodu (marzec–grudzień 1943 r.)" [The policy of the Polish Workers' party on the establishment of a democratic people's representation, March–December 1943], *ZPW* 4, no. 4 (1961): 50–53.

108. Zbiniewicz, *Armia Polska w ZSRR*, pp. 149–60.

109. See Jerzy Pawłowicz, "Uwagi na temat kształtowania się strategii PPR" [The formation of the strategy of the Polish Workers' party], *ZPW* 7, no. 1 (1964): 36–39.

110. Zbiniewicz, *Armia Polska w ZSRR*, pp. 161–69, 178.

111. *Ibid.*, pp. 169–71; draft program of the Polish National Committee, November–December 1943, in *Kształtowanie się podstaw programowych PPR* [The program formation of the Polish Workers' party] (Warsaw: Książka i Wiedza, 1958), pp. 474–87.

112. Maria Wilusz, ed., "Protokoły Prezydium Zarządu Głównego Związku Patriotów Polskich w ZSRR (czerwiec 1943–lipiec 1944 r.)" [Minutes of the supreme leadership of the Union of Polish Patriots in the USSR (June 1943–July 1944)], *Archiwum ruchu robotniczego*, vol. II (Warsaw: Książka i Wiedza, 1975), pp. 73–74; W. Namiotkiewicz and B. Rostropowicz, eds., *Ludzie, fakty, refleksje* [People, facts, and reflections] (Warsaw: Wydawnictwo Ministerstwa Obrony Narodowej, 1961), pp. 116–20.

113. Record of Beneš–Stalin conversation, December 12, 1943, in Mastny, "The Beneš–Stalin–Molotov Conversations in December 1943," p. 379.

114. Clark Kerr to Foreign Office, February 20, 1944, N 896/42/38, FO 371/43312, PRO.

115. Władysław Gomułka, "Polemika z 'Archiwum Ruchu Robotniczego,' " [Polemics with the "Archives of the Workers' Movement"], *Zeszyty historyczne* 39 (1977): pp. 5–9; "Manifest demokratycznych organizacji społeczno-politycznych i wojskowych w Polsce" [A manifesto by democratic social, political and military organizations in Poland], December 15, 1943, in *Stosunki polsko-radzieckie w latach 1917–1945* [Polish-Soviet relations in 1917–1945], ed. Tadeusz Cieślak and Euzebiusz Basiński (Warsaw: Książka i Wiedza, 1967), pp. 368–73.

116. "Deklaracja programowa Krajowej Rady Narodowej [The platform of the KRN],

"Dekret Krajowej Rady Narodowej o utworzeniu Armii Ludowej" [Decree by the KRN on the establishment of the People's Army], January 1, 1944, *ibid.*, pp. 374–78.

117. Gomułka, "Polemika z 'Archiwum Ruchu Robotniczego,' " p. 5.

118. *Ibid.*, pp. 18–19.

119. *Ibid.*, pp. 8–10, 14–16; Irena Skarlińska, ed., "Protokoł pierwszego posiedzenia Krajowej Rady Narodowej" [Minutes of the first session of the National Council of the Homeland], *Archiwum ruchu robotniczego*, vol. II (Warsaw: Książka i Wiedza, 1975), pp. 8–62; cf. an eyewitness account of the KRN's inaugural session, Stanisława Sowińska, *Lata walki* [The years of struggle] (Warsaw: Książka i Wiedza, 1962), pp. 231–36.

120. M. Kamil Dziewanowski, *The Communist Party of Poland* (Cambridge: Harvard University Press, 1959), p. 386.

121. "Układ sił politycznych" [The configuration of the political forces], Gomułka to Central Bureau of the Polish Communists in the USSR, January 12, 1944, in *Kształtowanie się podstaw programowych PPR*, pp. 205–20.

122. Jerzy Pawłowicz, *Strategia frontu narodowego PPR* [The National Front strategy of the Polish Workers' party] (Warsaw: Książka i Wiedza, 1965), p. 191; Władysław Góra, *Powstanie władzy ludowej w Polsce* [The emergence of the people's power in Poland] (Warsaw: Książka i Wiedza, 1972), pp. 83, 90–92, the best study of the subject.

123. Central Committee of the Polish Workers' party to Dimitrov, March 7, 1944, "Z archiwów polskich komunistów," pp. 186–90.

124. Zbiniewicz, *Armia Polska w ZSRR*, pp. 172–76.

125. "Declaration by the Government of the U.S.S.R. on the Question of the Polish-Soviet Frontier," January 11, 1944, *DPSR*, vol. II, pp. 132–34; see Włodzimierz T. Kowalski, "Walka ZSRR o uznanie ludowego państwa polskiego" [The USSR's struggle for the recognition of the Polish people's state], *Z dziejów stosunków polsko-radzieckich* 2 (1956): 57–58.

126. Jan M. Ciechanowski, *The Warsaw Rising of 1944* (Cambridge: Cambridge University Press, 1974), pp. 191–94; memorandum by Raczyński for British government, April 7, 1944, PREM 3/355/15, PRO.

127. Jerzy Pawłowicz, *Z dziejów konspiracyjnej KRN* [From the history of the underground KRN] (Warsaw: Książka i Wiedza, 1961), pp. 170–71; Stanisława Sowińska, *Rozszumiały się wierzby . . .* [The willows wept] (Warsaw: Iskry, 1961), pp. 173–82.

128. Peter H. Irons, " 'The Test Is Poland': Polish Americans and the Origins of the Cold War," *Polish American Studies* 30, no. 2 (1973): 30–31.

129. *Pravda*, April 29, 1944.

130. Memorandum by DeWitt C. Poole for Roosevelt on conversation with Orlemański, May 27, 1944, Box 13, President's Secretary's File, FDRL.

131. Memorandum by Lange for Roosevelt, May 17, 1944, *DPSR*, vol. II, pp. 235–40; cf. Clark Kerr to Eden, May 19, 1944, in *The Great Powers and the Polish Question*, ed. An-

tony Polonsky (London: London School of Economics and Political Science, 1976), pp. 197–99.

132. Pawłowicz, *Strategia frontu narodowego*, pp. 169–70. Włodzimierz T. Kowalski, *ZSRR a granica na Odrze i Nysie Łużyckiej* [The USSR and the Oder-Neisse line] (Warsaw: Wydawnictwo Ministerstwa Obrony Narodowej, 1965), p. 138; Bolesław Drobner, *Bezustanna walka*, vol. III: *Wspomnienia, 1936–1944* [The unending struggle: memoirs, 1936–1944] Warsaw: Państwowy Instytut Wydawniczy, 1967), pp. 197–98.

133. Report by Grabski on conversations with Lebedev, in Stanisław Kirkor, "Rozmowy polsko-sovieckie w 1944 roku" [The Polish-Soviet conversations in 1944], *Zeszyty historyczne* 22 (1972): 41–64; *idem*, "Urywek wspomnień: O rozmowach z ambasadorem Lebiediewem w Londynie w maju i czerwcu 1944 r." [A fragment of memoirs: Conversations with Ambassador Lebedev in London in May and June 1944], *ibid.* 18 (1970): 99–108.

134. "Priem tov. I. V. Stalinym upolnomochennykh Natsionalnogo Soveta Polshi" [The reception of plenipotentiaries of the National Council of Poland by comrade J. V. Stalin], *Vneshniaia politika Sovetskogo Soiuza v period Otechestvennoi Voiny* [Foreign policy of the Soviet Union during the Patriotic War], vol. II (Moscow: Ogiz, 1946), p. 137.

135. Eden to Clark Kerr on conversation with Gusev, May 26, 1944, PREM 3/355/15, PRO.

136. Note by Harriman on conversation with Stalin, June 10, 1944, 711—Poland, U.S. Embassy Moscow, RG-84, NA.

137. Record of meeting between Harriman and KRN delegation, June 11, 1944, 711—Poland, U.S. Embassy Moscow, RG-84, NA.

138. Władysław Gomułka, *Przemówienia, 1962* [Speeches, 1962] (Warsaw: Książka i Wiedza, 1963), p. 26; Wsiewołod Wołczew, "Stosunek ruchu oporu na Lubelszczyźnie do ZSRR i radzieckich sił zbrojnych w ostatnim okresie okupacji" [The relationship of the resistance in the Lublin area to the USSR and Soviet armed forces during the last period of the occupation], *Z dziejów stosunków polsko-radzieckich* 6 (1970): 162.

139. Harriman to Secretary of State, June 12, 1944, Russia 1944, Box 68, President's Secretary's File, FDRL.

140. Note by Harriman on conversation with Molotov, June 13, 1944, 711—Poland, U.S. Embassy Moscow, RG-84, NA.

141. Pawłowicz, *Strategia frontu narodowego*, p. 170; the author erroneously identifies the chief Russian negotiator in London as Gusev rather than Lebedev.

142. Record of Romer–O'Malley conversation, June 26, 1944, PREM 3/355/12, PRO; Schoenfeld to Secretary of State, July 9, 1944, *FRUS*, 1944, vol. III, pp. 1295–96.

143. "Rezolucja Zarządu Głównego Związku Patriotów Polskich w ZSRR" [Resolution of the supreme leadership of the Union of Polish Patriots in the USSR], June 23, 1944, in "Protokoły Prezydium Zarządu Głównego," ed. Wilusz, pp. 130–31. Fryderyk Zbiniewicz, "U źródeł powstania PKWN i Wojska Polskiego" [The origins of the Polish Committee of National Liberation and the Polish Army], *ZPW* 7, no. 4 (1964): 50.

144. Stalin to Roosevelt, June 24, 1944, *SCRT*, p. 148.

145. Clark Kerr to Foreign Office, July 1, 1944, cited in Harriman to Secretary of State, July 4 and 5, 1944, 711—Poland, U.S. Embassy Moscow, RG-84, NA; cf. Góra, *Powstanie władzy ludowej w Polsce*, p. 142.

146. Władysław Bieńkowski, "Nasze stanowisko" [Our standpoint], *Trybuna Wolności*, July 1, 1944, reprinted in *Kształtowanie się podstaw programowych PPR*, pp. 255–56.

147. Gomułka, "Polemika z 'Archiwum Ruchu Robotniczego,' " pp. 29–30; Ludomir Smosarski, ed., "Dyskusje w PPR w sprawie zjednoczenia sił demokratycznych (notatki protokołarne z posiedzień KC PPR maj–czerwiec 1944 r.)" [The debates in the Polish Workers' party on the unification of democratic forces: Notes from the central committee sessions in May–June 1944], *Archiwum ruchu robotniczego*, vol. II (Warsaw: Książka i Wiedza, 1975), pp. 154–63.

148. Gomułka, "Polemika z 'Archiwum Ruchu Robotniczego,' " pp. 21–28; Nicholas Bethell, *Gomułka* (New York: Holt, 1969), pp. 144–62.

149. Ciechanowski, *The Warsaw Rising*, pp. 206–8.

150. Włodzimierz T. Kowalski, *Polityka zagraniczna RP, 1944–1947* [The foreign policy of the Polish Republic, 1944–1947] (Warsaw: Książka i Wiedza, 1971), p. 360; information from the Osóbka-Morawski and Berling memoirs has been divulged by several Polish historians who were allowed to peruse the manuscripts.

151. *Ibid.*, pp. 2–3; Edward Puacz, "Sprawa granic Polski w układach między P.K.W.N. i ZSSR" [The question of Poland's frontiers in the agreements between the Polish Committee of National Liberation and the USSR], *Zeszyty historyczne* 15 (1969): 202–7; Drobner, *Bezustanna walka*, vol. III, p. 200.

152. Memorandum by Lange for Roosevelt, May 17, 1944, *DPSR*, vol. II, p. 237.

153. Edward Osóbka-Morawski, "Wspomnienie z Poczdamu" [A recollection from Potsdam], *Polityka* (Warsaw), July 24, 1965; Kowalski, *ZSRR a granica na Odrze i Nysie Łużyckiej*, pp. 142–46.

154. Osóbka-Morawski and Wasilewska to Stalin, July 15, 1944, in "Protokoły Prezydium Zarządu Głównego," ed. Wilusz, pp. 149–50; Włodzimierz T. Kowalski, "Międzynarodowe tło powstania Polskiego Komitetu Wyzwolenia Narodowego" [The international background of the establishment of the Polish Committee of National Liberation], *ZPW* 7, no. 3 (1964): 31–55.

155. Central Bureau of the Polish Communists in the USSR to Central Committee of the Polish Workers' party, July 18, 1944, "Z archiwów polskich komunistów," pp. 191–94.

156. "Manifest Polskiego Komitetu Wyzwolenia Narodowego" [Manifesto by the Polish Committee of National Liberation], July 22, 1944, in *Stosunki polsko-radzieckie*, ed. Cieślak and Basiński, pp. 284–90.

157. Marian Orzechowski, *Odra-Nysa Łużycka-Bałtyk w polskiej myśli politycznej okresu Drugiej wojny światowej* [The Oder, Western Neisse and Baltic in Polish political thought during World War II] (Wrocław: Zakład Narodowy imienia Ossolińskich, 1969), p. 155.

158. Agreement between the Polish Committee of National Liberation and the Soviet government, July 27, 1944, in *Stosunki polsko-radzieckie*, ed. Cieślak and Basiński, pp. 399–400; the date of the agreement is printed incorrectly as June 27.

159. Włodzimierz T. Kowalski, "Problem granicy polsko-niemieckiej przed konferencją w Jałcie" [The Problem of the Polish–German Frontier before the Yalta Conference], *Sprawy międzynarodowe* 15, no. 5 (1962): 55–56.

160. Record of Mikołajczyk–Stalin conversation, August 3, 1944, *DPSR*, vol. II, p. 316.

161. Record of Churchill-Stalin conversations, October 16, 1944, PREM 3/434/4, PRO.

162. Zygmunt Sobieski, "Reminiscences from Lwow, 1939–1946," *JCEA* 6 (1946–47): 368.

163. *Khrushchev Remembers: The Last Testament* (Boston: Little, Brown, 1974), pp. 155, 159, 163.

164. Cited from manuscript of Osóbka-Morawski's memoirs in Puacz, "Sprawa granic Polski," p. 205.

165. Churchill to King George VI, October 15, 1944, PREM 3/434/8, PRO.

Chapter Six: The Birth of an Empire

1. Jan M. Ciechanowski, *The Warsaw Rising of 1944* (Cambridge: Cambridge University Press, 1974), pp. 217, 268–71; cf. Aleksander Skarzyński, *Polityczne przyczyny powstania warszawskiego* [The political causes of the Warsaw Uprising] (Warsaw: Państwowe Wydawnictwo Naukowe, 1964), pp. 143–200.

2. Ciechanowski, *The Warsaw Rising*, pp. 218–42.

3. Note on Mikołajczyk-Stalin conversation, August 9, 1944, *DPSR*, vol. II, p. 336; Hanns von Krannhals, *Der Warschauer Aufstand 1944* (Frankfurt a.M.: Bernard und Graefe, 1962), pp. 81–86. Jerzy Kirchmayer, *Powstanie warszawskie* [The Warsaw Uprising] (Warsaw: Książka i Wiedza, 1959), pp. 56–63.

4. I. A. Makarenko, "K Varshave!" [On to Warsaw!], *Pravda*, August 2, 1944.

5. Broadcasts of July 29 and August 1, 1944, nos. 1839 and 1842, *Daily Digest of World Broadcasts*, BBC.

6. Zbigniew S. Siemaszko, "Powstanie Warszawskie—kontakty z ZSSR i PKWN" [The Warsaw Uprising: Contacts with the USSR and the Polish Committee of National Liberation], *Zeszyty historyczne* 16 (1969): 9–10.

7. Alexander Werth, *Russia at War* (New York: Dutton, 1964), p. 876.

8. Note on Mikołajczyk-Stalin conversation, August 3, 1944, *DPSR*, vol. II, p. 315.

9. Note on Mikołajczyk-Stalin conversation, August 9, 1944, *ibid.*, p. 337.

6. Birth of an Empire

10. Włodzimierz Wołoszyn, *Na warszawskim kierunku operacyjnym* [Conducting the Warsaw operation] (Warsaw: Wydawnictwo Ministerstwa Obrony Narodowej, 1964), p. 78.

11. Report by Sovinformburo, *Pravda*, August 16, 1944.

12. Statement by Tass, August 13, 1944, in *Soviet Foreign Policy during the Patriotic War*, ed. Andrew Rothstein, vol. II (London: Hutchinson, 1945), p. 204.

13. Stalin to Churchill, August 16 and 22, 1944, *SCCA*, pp. 254–55.

14. "Summary of Discussions with Russian Government on Aid to Warsaw," PREM 3/352/11, PRO.

15. Tadeusz Walichnowski, "Znaczenie sojuszu polsko-radzieckiego w okresie walki o władzę ludową w Polsce" [The significance of the Polish-Soviet alliance during the struggle for the people's power in Poland], *Z dziejów stosunków polsko-radzieckich* 8 (1971): 105.

16. Tadeusz Bór-Komorowski, *The Secret Army* (London: Gollancz, 1950), p. 294.

17. Józef Sęk Małecki, *Armia Ludowa w powstaniu warszawskim* [The People's Army in the Warsaw Uprising] (Warsaw: Iskry, 1962), p. 130.

18. Andrzej Korbonski, "The Warsaw Uprising Revisited," *Survey* 76 (1970): 95; also oral information from Jan M. Ciechanowski, October 1974.

19. Churchill to Stalin, August 12 and 20, 1944, *SCCA*, pp. 252, 254.

20. Churchill to Bracken, August 23, and Bracken to Churchill, August 24, 1944, PREM 3/352/12, PRO.

21. Jozef Jablonický, *Z ilegality do povstania* [From the underground to the uprising] (Bratislava: Epocha, 1969), though mainly on the background of the uprising, is superior to Wolfgang Venohr, *Aufstand für die Tschechoslowakei: Der slowakische Freiheitskampf von 1944* (Hamburg: Wegner, 1969).

22. Golian to Ingr, June 15, 1944, in *Slovenské národné povstanie* [The Slovak National Uprising], ed. Vilém Prečan (Bratislava: Vydavateľstvo politickej literatúry, 1965), pp. 210–11.

23. "Christmas Agreement" of 1943 on the creation of the SNR, *ibid.*, pp. 125–26; see Píka and Drtina to Beneš, August 29, 1944, *ibid.*, p. 351, and memoir by one of the SNR's non-Communist founders, Ján Lettrich, "K 25. výročiu Vianočnej dohody" [The 25th anniversary of the Christmas agreement], *Naše snahy* (Toronto) 5, no. 1 (1969): 3–6.

24. Ladislav K. Feierabend, *Soumrak československé demokracie* [The twilight of Czechoslovak democracy] (Washington, D.C.: n.p., 1967), pp. 91–92; Jozef Jablonický, "Slovenská otázka v období národnej a demokratickej revolúcie" [The Slovak question in the period of the national and democratic revolution] in *Slováci a ich národný vývin* [The Slovaks and their national development] (Bratislava: Slovenská akadémia vied, 1966), pp. 269–90.

25. Ingr to Píka, July 10, 1944, in *Slovenské národné povstanie*, ed. Prečan, pp. 227–28; Ferdinand Beer et al., *Dějinná křižovatka* [The historic crossroads] (Prague: Nakladatelství politické literatury, 1964), pp. 266–67.

6. Birth of an Empire

26. Jablonický, Z ilegality do povstania, pp. 318–38; Beer et al., Dějinná křižovatka, pp. 232–33.

27. Memorandum by Čatloš, July 1944, in Slovenské národné povstanie, ed. Prečan, pp. 262–63.

28. Jablonický, Z ilegality do povstania, pp. 341–52.

29. Peter Gosztony, Hitlers Fremde Heere (Düsseldorf: Econ, 1976), p. 449.

30. "O některých úkolech národně-osvobozeneckého hnutí na Slovensku" [Some tasks of the national liberation movement in Slovakia], August 23, 1944, in Slovenské národné povstanie, ed. Prečan, pp. 310–12; cf. Jablonický, Z ilegality do povstania, p. 356.

31. Directive by General Timofei Strokach, August 24, 1944, quoted in Antonín Benčík et al., Partyzánské hnutí v Československu za druhé světové války [The partisan movement in Czechoslovakia during World War II] (Prague: Naše vojsko, 1961), pp. 188–89; cf. Khrushchev to Stalin, August 15, 1944, in Slovenské národné povstanie, ed. Prečan, pp. 294–95.

32. Andrei A. Grechko, Cherez Karpaty [Across the Carpathians] (Moscow: Voenizdat, 1970), pp. 54–55; Sergei M. Shtemenko, Generalnyi shtab v gody voiny [The general staff during the war], vol. II (Moscow: Voenizdat, 1973), p. 229.

33. Zdeněk Fierlinger, Ve službách ČSR [In the service of Czechoslovakia], vol. II (Prague: Svoboda, 1951), pp. 339–41; note by Vyshinskii on conversation with Fierlinger and Píka, August 31, 1944, in Slovenské národné povstanie, ed. Prečan, p. 380.

34. Gottwald to Molotov, September 2, 1944, ibid., pp. 403–4.

35. Jablonický, Z ilegality do povstania, pp. 493–507.

36. Foreign Office to British Embassy Moscow, September 9, 1944, C 12077/1342/12, FO 371/38942, PRO.

37. Llewellyn Woodward, British Foreign Policy in the Second World War, vol. III (London: Her Majesty's Stationery Office, 1971), pp. 215–16; Churchill to Roosevelt, September 4, 1944, and draft of message by Churchill to Stalin, quoted in draft of message by Churchill to Roosevelt, September 3, 1944, PREM 3/352/12, PRO.

38. Edward Puacz, "Powstanie Warszawskie w protokołach P.K.W.N." [The Warsaw Uprising in the minutes of the Polish Committee of National Liberation], Zeszyty historyczne 10 (1966): 178–79; Władysław Gomułka, "Polemika z 'Archiwum Ruchu Robotniczego' " [Polemics with the "Archives of the Workers' Movement"], ibid. 39 (1977): 12.

39. Eden to Churchill, September 10, 1944, PREM 3/352/12, PRO; Velikaia Otechestvennaia Voina Sovetskogo Soiuza, 1941–1945: Kratkaia istoriia [The Great Patriotic War of the Soviet Union, 1941–1945: A Short History] (Moscow: Voenizdat, 1965), p. 383.

40. Bór-Komorowski, The Secret Army, p. 343.

41. Clark Kerr to Foreign Office, September 24, 1944, PREM 3/353/11, PRO; Krannhals, Der Warschauer Aufstand, pp. 153–62; Wołoszyn, Na warszawskim kierunku operacyjnym, pp. 215–303; the appealing but implausible story that Berling, following the call of

his conscience, acted in defiance of Stalin's orders presumes a latitude no officer of his rank enjoyed under Soviet command; cf. Jan Nowak, "Sprawa generała Berlinga" [The affair of General Berling], *Zeszyty historyczne* 37 (1976): 58–60, and polemics by Zbigniew S. Siemaszko, *ibid.* 38 (1976): 224–27.

42. Bór-Komorowski, *The Secret Army*, p. 342.

43. Siemaszko, "Powstanie Warszawskie—kontakty z ZSSR i PKWN," p. 57.

44. "To the Polish Nation," October 3, 1944, *DPSR*, vol. II, p. 398.

45. On this subject, Peter A. Toma's article, "Soviet Strategy in the Slovak Uprising of 1944," *JCEA* 19 (1959); 290–98, has been superseded by subsequent evidence.

46. Grechko, *Cherez Karpaty*, pp. 160, 179; Gustáv Husák, *Svedectvo o Slovenskom národnom povstani* [A testimony on the Slovak National Uprising] (Bratislava: Vydavateľstvo politickej literatúry, 1964), pp. 272–76.

47. *Velikaia Otechestvennaia Voina Sovetskogo Soiuza: Kratkaia istoriia*, pp. 403–4.

48. "Přehledná zpráva o průběhu jednání o pomoc spojenců pro ozbrojený odpor na Slovensku" [A survey of the negotiations on the Allies' aid for an armed uprising in Slovakia, December 12, 1944, in *Slovenské národné povstanie*, ed. Prečan, p. 873; *Cesta ke Květnu* [The road to May], vol. I, pt. 1 (Prague: Academia, 1965), pp. 253, 274; Grechko, *Cherez Karpaty*, p. 30.

49. Address by Šverma, October 3, 1944, in *Slovenské národné povstanie*, ed. Prečan, pp. 631–34; Beer et al., *Dějinná křižovatka*, pp. 388–94; Feierabend, *Soumrak československé demokracie*, p. 94.

50. Order by Konev, October 7, 1944, in *Slovenské národné povstanie*, ed. Prečan, p. 939.

51. For details, see *Cesta ke Květnu*, vol. I, pt. 1, pp. 193–94, 215–17, 235–36, 239, 245–48, 252–53.

52. "Assistance to the Slovak Army and Partisans," September 7 and 12, 1944, Czechoslovakia, 9-7-44, Records of the Combined Chiefs of Staff, 381, RG-218, NA.

53. "Přehledná zpráva o průběhu jednání o pomoc spojenců," December 12, 1944, in *Slovenské národné povstanie*, ed. Prečan, pp. 872–83; Donovan to Roosevelt, September 23 and October 20, 1944, OSS: September, October, 1944, President's Secretary's File, FDRL.

54. Wesley F. Craven and James L. Cate, eds., *The Army Air Forces in World War II*, vol. III (Chicago: University of Chicago Press, 1951), p. 317; according to Frank P. King, "British Policy and the Warsaw Rising," *Journal of European Studies* 4 (1974): 1–18, the British gave Warsaw maximum support, probably more than justified by strictly military considerations.

55. Minutes by J. M. Roberts, Warner, and Eden, August 31, 1944, C 11772/1343/12, FO 371/38941, PRO.

56. "Lide český!" [To the Czech People!], September 16, 1944, in *Slovenské národné povstanie*, ed. Prečan, pp. 510–11; see also p. 590.

371

57. Píka to Ingr, and Fierlinger to Ripka, September 14, 1944, *ibid.*, pp. 221, 491; Benčík *et al.*, *Partyzánské hnutí v Československu*, pp. 325–31.

58. For the SOE activities in 1944, see folder FO 371/38927, PRO.

59. Hollis to Roberts, October 7, 1944, C 13611/134/12, FO 371/38927, PRO.

60. Brooke to Ingr, November 13, 1944, Czechoslovakia, 9-7-44, Records of the Combined Chiefs of Staff, 318, RG-218, NA.

61. Karel Veselý-Štainer, *Cestou národního odboje* [On the road of national resistance] (Prague: Sfinx, 1947), pp. 146–55.

62. Message by the "Clay" group, November 11, 1944, C 16522/1343/12, FO 371/38944, PRO.

63. Extract from minutes of Foreign Office–SOE meeting, November 14, 1944, C 16039/1343/12, FO 371/38944, PRO; Veselý-Štainer, *Cestou národního odboje*, pp. 167–82.

64. *Osvobozhdenie iugo-vostochnoi i tsentralnoi Evropy voiskami 2-go i 3-go Ukrainskikh Frontov* [The liberation of southeastern and central Europe by the troops of the 2nd and 3rd Ukrainian army groups] (Moscow: Nauka, 1970), pp. 58–59.

65. Entry for August 21, 1944, Lord Charles Moran, *Winston Churchill: The Struggle for Survival* (Boston: Houghton Mifflin, 1966), p. 173.

66. Woodward, *British Foreign Policy in the Second World War*, vol. III, p. 116; folder FO 371/43636, PRO.

67. Stephen Fischer-Galati, *The New Rumania* (Cambridge: M.I.T. Press, 1967), pp. 18–22.

68. Vasile Liveanu, "Le problème du pouvoir dans l'insurrection nationale armée antifasciste et antiimpérialiste en Roumanie," *Revue des études sud-est européennes* 12 (1974): 477–78.

69. Dumitru Dămăceanu, "Pregătirea militară a însurecției armate sub conducerea Partidului Comunist din Romînia" [The military preparation for the armed insurrection under the leadership of the Communist party of Romania], *Scînteia*, August 9, 1964.

70. Liveanu, "Le problème du pouvoir dans l'insurrection nationale," pp. 479–80.

71. The best-informed Western account of the coup is Arthur G. Lee, *Crown against Sickle* (London: Hutchinson, 1950), pp. 59–79; for a description by a participant, former adjutant to the king, see Emilian Ionescu, "Momente din timpul doborîrii dictaturii militare-fasciste" [Recollections from the time of the overthrow of the military-fascist dictatorship], *Analele* 11, no. 6 (1965): 30–37.

72. Ghita Ionescu, *Communism in Rumania* (London: Oxford University Press, 1964), pp. 84–85.

73. Squires (Istanbul) to Secretary of State, May 19, 1944, 800—Communism, U.S. Embassy Moscow, RG-84, NA.

74. Werth, *Russia at War*, pp. 902–4.

75. Henry L. Roberts, *Rumania* (New Haven: Yale University Press 1951), pp. 243, 259–60; Seymour Freidin, "Romanian Red Denies Fraud in Electoral Lists," *New York Herald Tribune*, November 15, 1946, p. 13.

76. Nissan Oren, *Bulgarian Communism* (New York: Columbia University Press, 1971), pp. 205–20.

77. Summary of Soviet notes to Bulgaria, U.S. Embassy Moscow to Department of State, May 27, 1944, *FRUS*, 1944, vol. III, pp. 330–33.

78. Records of conversations among Harriman, Clark Kerr, and Vyshinskii, February 18, 1944, and between Harriman and Molotov, March 19, 1944, 711—Bulgaria, U.S. Embassy Moscow, RG-84, NA.

79. A. Liarov, "Bolgaria—voennyi soiuznik gitlerovskoi Germanii" [Bulgaria: A military ally of Hitlerite Germany], *Voina i rabochii klass*, May 15, 1944, pp. 10–13; see memorandum by Orme Sargent, May 31, 1944, W.P. (44) 289, CAB 66/50, PRO.

80. Oren, *Bulgarian Communism*, pp. 237–39; Marshall L. Miller, *Bulgaria during the Second World War* (Stanford: Stanford University Press, 1975), pp. 176–77.

81. Memorandum by William Strang, August 27, 1944, W.P. (44) 475, CAB 66/54, PRO.

82. Record of conversation among Harriman, Clark Kerr, and Molotov, August 26, 1944, 711—Bulgaria, U.S. Embassy Moscow, RG-84, NA.

83. Oren, *Bulgarian Communism*, p. 252.

84. Winant to Secretary of State, August 29, 1944, *FRUS*, 1944, III, pp. 377–78.

85. Speech of August 2, 1944, in *Winston Churchill: His Collected Speeches, 1897–1963*, ed. Robert R. Rhodes, vol. VII(London: Chelsea House, 1974), p. 6983.

86. Woodward, *British Foreign Policy in the Second World War*, vol. III, p. 139.

87. N. Bodrov, "Falshivye manevry bolgarskogo pravitelstva" [The devious maneuvers of the Bulgarian government], *Pravda*, August 31, 1944.

88. Miller, *Bulgaria during the Second World War*, p. 209; Oren, *Bulgarian Communism*, p. 251.

89. Sergei D. Biriuzov, *Sovetskii soldat na Balkanakh* [The Soviet soldier in the Balkans] (Moscow: Voenizdat, 1963), p. 172.

90. *Osvobozhdenie iugo-vostochnoi i tsentralnoi Evropy*, pp. 216, 219; Shtemenko, *Generalnyi shtab v gody voiny*, vol. II, p. 165.

91. Record of conversation among Harriman, Clark Kerr, and Molotov, September 5, 1944, 711—Bulgaria, U.S. Embassy Moscow, RG-84, NA.

92. Oren, *Bulgarian Communism*, pp. 253–54; Miller, *Bulgaria During the Second World War*, pp. 209–10, 214–15.

93. Miller, *Bulgaria during the Second World War*, pp. 215–16.

94. Oren, *Bulgarian Communism*, pp. 254–58.

95. Peter Gosztony, "Der 9. September 1944: Eine Studie zur Frage der Neutralität und

Wehrbereitschaft am Beispiel der September-Ereignisse 1944 in Bulgarien," in *Neutrale Kleinstaaten im Zweiten Weltkrieg* (Münsingen: Tages-Nachrichten, 1973), pp. 85–108.

96. Evangelos Kofos, *Nationalism and Communism in Macedonia* (Salonica: Institute for Balkan Studies, 1964), pp. 138–40; Svetozar Vukmanović-Tempo, *Revolucija koja teče* [The revolution continues], vol. I (Belgrade: Komunist, 1971), p. 413–26; Piotr S. Wandycz, "Recent Traditions of the Quest for Unity," in *The People's Democracies after Prague*, ed. Jerzy Lukaszewski (Bruges, Belgium: De Tempel, 1970), pp. 71–75.

97. Vladimir Dedijer, *Tito* (New York: Simon and Schuster, 1953), pp. 232–35, 267–68; Nissan Oren, *Revolution Administered: Agrarianism and Communism in Bulgaria* (Baltimore: Johns Hopkins Press, 1973), pp. 85–86.

98. Stephen Peters, "Ingredients of the Communist Takeover in Albania," in *The Anatomy of Communist Takeovers*, ed. Thomas T. Hammond and Robert Farrell (New Haven: Yale University Press, 1975), pp. 287–90; Vladimir Dedijer, *The Battle Stalin Lost* (New York: Viking, 1971), p. 194.

99. Leften S. Stavrianos, *The Balkans since 1453* (New York: Rinehart, 1958), pp. 792–95; D. George Kousoulas, *Revolution and Defeat: The Story of the Greek Communist Party* (London: Oxford University Press, 1965), pp. 192–93.

100. Stephen G. Xydis, *Greece and the Great Powers, 1944–1947* (Salonica: Institute for Balkan Studies, 1963), p. 564.

101. *Ibid.*, p. 38; C. M. Woodhouse, *The Struggle for Greece, 1941–1949* (London: Hart-Davis, MacGibbon, 1976), pp. 92–96; John O. Iatrides, *Revolt in Athens* (Princeton: Princeton University Press, 1972), pp. 74–76.

102. Stephen G. Xydis, "The Secret Anglo-Soviet Agreement on the Balkans of October 9, 1944," *JCEA* 15 (1955–56): 266–67.

103. Oren, *Revolution Administered*, p. 89; Woodhouse, *The Struggle for Greece*, pp. 90–91, 93.

104. Shtemenko, *Generalnyi shtab v gody voiny*, vol. II, p. 250.

105. C. A. Macartney, *October Fifteenth*, vol. II (Edinburgh: University of Edinburgh Press, 1956), pp. 349–50; Gustav Hennyey, "Ungarns Weg aus dem Zweiten Weltkrieg," *Wehrwissenschaftliche Rundschau* 12 (1962): 716.

106. Bela Vago, "Romania," in *Communist Power in Europe, 1944–1949*, ed. Martin McCauley (New York: Barnes and Noble, 1977), p. 115.

107. C. A. Macartney, "Ungarns Weg aus dem Zweiten Weltkrieg," *Vierteljahrshefte für Zeitgeschichte* 14 (1966): 79–105; A. Rozsnyói, "October Fifteenth, 1944," *Acta Historica* 8 (1961): 57–105; Nicholas Horthy, *Memoirs* (New York: Speller, 1957), pp. 228–29.

108. M. Korom, "Az ideiglenes Nemzetgyülés és a kormány létrehozásanak elökészitése" [The preparation for the establishment of the provisional National Assembly and government], *Párttörténeti Közlemények* 20, no. 4 (1974): 116; I am indebted to William O. McCagg, of Michigan State University, for calling my attention to this remarkable document; see also Macartney, *October Fifteenth*, vol. II, p. 354.

109. William O. McCagg, Jr., "Communism and Hungary, 1944–46 (Ph.D. diss., Columbia University, 1965), pp. 100–102.

110. Churchill to Smuts, October 8, 1944, PREM 3/434/8, PRO.

111. Winston S. Churchill, *Triumph and Tragedy* (Boston: Houghton Mifflin, 1953), pp. 227–28.

112. See John A. Lukacs, "The Night Stalin and Churchill Divided Europe," *New York Times Magazine,* October 5, 1969, pp. 36–50.

113. Record of Churchill-Stalin meeting, October 9, 1944, PREM 3/434/2, PRO.

114. V. Trukhanovsky, *British Foreign Policy during World War II* (Moscow: Progress, 1970), pp. 406–8.

115. PREM 3/66/7, PRO; There is no reason to accept the hypothesis by Charles E. Bohlen, in *Witness to History* (New York: Norton, 1973), p. 163, that the tick applied to Romania only.

116. Draft record of Churchill-Stalin meeting, October 9, 1944, FO 181/990/2, PRO.

117. Record of Eden-Molotov meeting, October 10, 1944, PREM 3/434/2; Eden to Sargent, October 11, 1944, C 14105/10/21, FO 371/39255, PRO.

118. Record of Eden-Molotov meeting, October 11, 1944, PREM 3/434/2, PRO.

119. Churchill, *Triumph and Tragedy,* pp. 231–35.

120. W. Averell Harriman and Elie Abel, *Special Envoy to Churchill and Stalin* (New York: Random House, 1975), p. 358.

121. Records of Eden-Molotov meetings, October 10 and 11, 1944, PREM 3/434/2, PRO.

122. Eden to Sargent, October 11, 1944, C 14105/10/21; Eden-Molotov correspondence, October 13–15, 1944, PREM 3/434/4, PRO; Woodhouse, *Struggle for Greece,* p. 99.

123. Antonov to Faraghó, October 14, 1944, and minutes of first military meeting, October 14, 1944, PREM 3/434/3, PRO.

124. Milovan Djilas, *Conversations with Stalin* (New York: Harcourt, 1962), p. 114.

125. Comment by Wilson on memorandum by Clark Kerr, September 23, 1944, N 5598/183/38, FO 371/43336, PRO; cf. John Slessor, *The Central Blue* (New York: Praeger, 1957), p. 612.

126. Harriette L. Chandler, "The Transition to Cold Warrior: The Evolution of W. Averell Harriman's Assessment of the U.S.S.R.'s Polish Policy," *East European Quarterly* 10 (1976): 229–45.

127. Harriman to Hopkins, September 10, 1944, *FRUS,* 1944, vol. IV, p. 989.

128. Harriman to Secretary of State, September 20, 1944, *ibid.,* p. 993.'

129. Memorandum W. P. (44) 436, by Eden, August 9, 1944, CAB 66/436, PRO.

130. W. Averell Harriman, "Our Wartime Relations with the Soviet Union and the Agreements Reached at Yalta," *Department of State Bulletin* 25 (1951): 379.

131. George F. Kennan, "Excerpts from a Draft Letter Written at Some Time during the First Months of 1945," *SR* 27 (1968): 481–84.

132. H. Gordon Skilling, "Group Conflict in Soviet Politics," in *Interest Groups in Soviet Politics*, ed. H. G. Skilling and Franklyn Griffiths (Princeton: Princeton University Press, 1971), pp. 399–404.

133. The question is thoroughly analyzed in William O. McCagg, Jr., *Stalin Embattled, 1943–1948* (Detroit: Wayne State University Press, 1978).

134. Djilas, *Conversations with Stalin*, pp. 77–78; Svetlana Alliluyeva, *Twenty Letters to a Friend* (New York: Harper, 1967), p. 11.

135. Shtemenko, *Generalnyi shtab v gody voiny*, vol. II, p. 250; *The Memoirs of Marshal Zhukov* (New York: Delacorte, 1971), p. 267.

136. Djilas, *Conversations with Stalin*, pp. 62, 70–71; Dedijer, *Tito*, pp. 232–33; *Khrushchev Remembers* (Boston: Little, Brown, 1970), p. 58.

137. Cf. record of Stalin–De Gaulle conversation, December 2, 1944, *Sovetsko-frantsuzskie otnosheniia vo vremia Velikoi Otechestvennoi Voiny* [Soviet-French relations during the Great Patriotic War] (Moscow: Gospolitizdat, 1959), p. 345.

138. Vernon V. Aspaturian, "The Union Republics and Soviet Nationalities as Instruments of Soviet Territorial Expansion," in *Process and Power in Soviet Foreign Policy*, ed. Aspaturian (Boston: Little, Brown, 1971), pp. 453–54, 465, 474.

139. *Idem, The Union Republics in Soviet Diplomacy* (Geneva: Droz, 1960), pp. 70–71; the retrospective theory that the constitution was changed to enable the Soviet Union to later claim multiple representation in the United Nations deserves little credence because of the still rudimentary state of the world organization project at that time; see Konstantyn Sawczuk, *The Ukraine in the United Nations Organization* (New York: Columbia University Press, 1975), pp. 8–10.

140. Robert Slusser, ed., *Soviet Economic Policy in Postwar Germany: A Collection of Papers by Former Soviet Officials* (New York: Research Program on the U.S.S.R., 1953), p. 41.

141. Harriman to Secretary of State, January 4, 1945, *FRUS*, 1945, vol. V, pp. 942–43; Harriman and Abel, *Special Envoy to Churchill and Stalin*, pp. 384–87.

142. For the best statement of the opposing view, see Thomas G. Paterson, *Soviet-American Confrontation: Postwar Reconstruction and the Origins of the Cold War* (Baltimore: Johns Hopkins University Press, 1973), pp. 33–56.

143. Memorandum by Spaak for Foreign Office, enclosed with Memorandum W.P. (44) 181, March 24, 1944, CAB 66/48, PRO.

144. "Security in Western Europe and the North Atlantic," July 20, 1944, U 6691/748/70, "Comments by the Chiefs of Staff on Policy towards Western Europe," July 27, 1944, U 6793/748/70, FO 371/40741 A, and U 8097/748/70, FO 371/40741 B, PRO.

145. Gromyko to Narkomindel, February 25, 1944, *Sovetsko-frantsuzskie otnosheniia*, p. 241.

146. Cf. Heinrich Bodensieck, *Provozierte Teilung Europas? Die britisch-nord-amerikanische Regionalismus-Diskussion und die Vorgeschichte des Kalten Krieges* (Opladen: Leske, 1970), esp. pp. 76–77.

147. Krystyna Kersten, "Niektóre problemy kształtowania się władzy ludowej w okresie dzaiałania Polskiego Komitetu Wyzwolenia Narodowego" [Some problems concerning the development of the people's power under the Polish Committee of National Liberation], *Kwartalnik historyczny* 71 (1964): 344–45; Beer et al., *Dějinná křižovatka*, p. 462.

148. Henry L. Roberts, *Rumania*, p. 262.

149. Oren, *Revolution Administered*, pp. 88–89.

150. Bohlen minutes of Roosevelt-Stalin conversation, November 29, 1943, *FRUS, Tehran*, pp. 529–33.

151. See Vojtech Mastny, "The Cassandra in the Foreign Commissariat: Maxim Litvinov and the Cold War," *Foreign Affairs* 54 (1975–76); 366–76; parts of the article are excerpted here by permission, from *Foreign Affairs*, January 1976, Copyright 1975 by Council on Foreign Relations, Inc.

152. Memorandum on conversation by Welles, May 7, 1943, *FRUS*, 1943, vol. III, pp. 522–24.

153. English translation, "Regarding International Security Organization," Enclosure no. 1 to despatch no. 719, July 25, 1944, U.S. Embassy Moscow, RG-84, NA.

154. Harriman to Secretary of State, August 23, 1944, 711.9—Armistice, U.S. Embassy Moscow, RG-84, NA.

155. "Memorandum on an International Security Organization, by the Soviet Union," August 12, 1944, *FRUS*, 1944, vol. I, pp. 706–11.

156. Record of interview with Litvinov, by Edgar Snow, October 6, 1944, Russia 1945, President's Secretary's File, FDRL.

157. Harriman to Secretary of State, August 23, 1944, 711.9—Armistice, U.S. Embassy Moscow, RG-84, NA.

158. Record of interview with Litvinov, by Snow, October 6, 1944.

159. Cf. Alexander Dallin, *The Soviet Union and the United Nations* (New York: Praeger, 1962), pp. 22–23; Tom Campbell, *Masquerade Peace* (Tallahassee: Florida State University Press, 1972), pp. 36–37.

160. "Note on conversation between M. Mikołajczyk and Marshal Stalin," *DPSR*, vol. II, pp. 338–39; Edward J. Rozek, *Allied Wartime Diplomacy: A Pattern in Poland* (New York: Wiley, 1958), p. 247.

161. Valentin Berezhkov, *Gody diplomaticheskoi sluzhby* [The years of diplomatic service] (Moscow: Mezhdunarodnye otnosheniia, 1972), pp. 290–91.

162. Harriman to Secretary of State, September 19, 1943, *FRUS*, 1944, vol. I, p. 827.

163. Harriman and Abel, *Special Envoy to Churchill and Stalin*, pp. 242–43.

164. Record of interview with Litvinov, by Snow, October 6, 1944; the subsequent quotations are from the same interview unless indicated otherwise.

165. Snow to Roosevelt, December 28, 1944, and Roosevelt to Snow, January 2, 1945, Russia 1945, President's Secretary's File, FDRL.

Chapter Seven: The Hopes and Blows of Yalta

1. Stalin to Roosevelt, October 19, 1944, SCRT, p. 165.

2. Stalin-Malinovskii conversation, October 28, 1944, Osvobozhdenie iugo-vostochnoi i tsentralnoi Evropy [The liberation of southeastern and central Europe] (Moscow: Nauka, 1970), pp. 321–22.

3. Roosevelt to Stalin, received November 19, and Stalin to Roosevelt, November 23, 1944, SCRT, pp. 168–70.

4. "Izbranie prezidenta Ruzvelta obespecheno" [President Roosevelt's election assured], Izvestia, November 5, 1944; Frederick C. Barghoorn, The Soviet Image of the United States (New York: Harcourt, 1950), p. 89.

5. Sergei M. Shtemenko, "Kak planirovalas posledniaia kampania po razgromu gitlerovskoi Germanii" [How the last campaign for the defeat of Hitlerite Germany was planned], Voennoistoricheskii zhurnal 7, no. 5 (1965): 56–64: Gallman to Secretary of State, November 6, 1944, FRUS, 1944, vol. I, p. 384; Horst Laschitza, Kämpferische Demokratie gegen Faschismus (Berlin: Deutscher Militärverlag, 1969), pp. 189–93.

6. C. A. Macartney, October Fifteenth, vol. II (Edinburgh: University of Edinburgh Press, 1956), pp. 457–58.

7. M. Korom, "Az ideiglenes Nemzetgyülés és a kormány létrehozásanak elökészitése" [The preparation for the establishment of the provisional National Assembly and Government], Párttörténeti Közlemények 20, no. 4 (1974): 115–23, 126.

8. Louise W. Holborn, ed., War and Peace Aims of the United Nations, vol. II (Boston: World Peace Foundation, 1943), pp. 112–19.

9. Zdeněk Fierlinger, Ve službách ČSR [In the service of Czechoslovakia], vol. II (Prague: Svoboda, 1951), pp. 431–58.

10. Němec to Fierlinger, November 11, 1944, in František Němec and Vladimír Moudrý, The Soviet Seizure of Subcarpathian Ruthenia (Toronto: Anderson, 1955), pp. 102–5; Johann W. Brügel, "Der Fall Karpathorussland," Europa-Archiv 8 (1953): 6023.

11. Iurii V. Ilnytskyi, Narysy istorii Zakarpatskoi Partiinoi Orhanizatsii [Outlines of the history of the Trans-Carpathian District party organization] (Uzhgorod: Karpaty, 1968), p. 265.

12. John A. Armstrong, Ukrainian Nationalism (New York: Columbia University Press, 1963), pp. 294–95.

13. Jan Křen and Václav Kural, "Ke stykům mezi československým odbojem a SSSR" [Contacts between the Czechoslovak resistance and the USSR], *Historie a vojenství*, 1967, p. 446; Jaromír Smutný, "Vývoj vztahů československo-sovětských" [The development of Czechoslovak-Soviet relations], vol. I, no page numbers, Smutný Papers, Archive of Russian and East European History and Culture, Columbia University.

14. Fierlinger to Němec, January 26, 1945, in Němec and Moudrý, *Soviet Seizure of Subcarpathian Ruthenia*, pp. 355–57.

15. Notes by Gottwald on postwar policy, April 1944, *Cesta ke Květnu* [The road to May], vol. I, pt. 1 (Prague: Academia, 1965), p. 107.

16. "Zaiavlenie glavy chekhoslovatskoi pravitelstvennoi delegatsii dlia osvobozhdennoi territorii Chekhoslovakii" [Statement by the head of the Czechoslovak government delegation for the liberated territory of Czechoslovakia], *Pravda*, October 26, 1944.

17. Němec and Moudrý, *Soviet Seizure of Subcarpathian Ruthenia*, p. 92; see John A. Armstrong, *The Soviet Bureaucratic Elite: A Case Study of the Ukrainian Apparatus* (New York: Praeger, 1959), pp. 108–10.

18. I. F. Evseev, *Narodnye komitety Zakarpatskoi Ukrainy—organy gosudarstvennoi vlasti (1944–1945)* [The national committees of the Transcarpathian Ukraine as organs of governmental power (1944–1945)] (Moscow: Gosudarstvennoe izdatelstvo iuridicheskoi literatury, 1954), pp. 63, 52.

19. Květa Kořalková, "Československo a polská prozatímní vláda r. 1944–1945" [Czechoslovakia and the Polish provisional government in 1944–1945], *Slovanský přehled*, 1966, p. 195; see Włodzimierz T. Kowalski, *Polityka zagraniczna RP* [The foreign policy of the Polish republic] (Warsaw: Książka i Wiedza, 1971), pp. 15–16.

20. Harriman to Secretary of State, January 10, 1945, *FRUS, Yalta*, p. 452.

21. Stalin to Beneš, January 23, and Beneš to Stalin, January 31, 1945, *Cesta ke Květnu*, vol. 1, pt. 1, pp. 476–77, 481–82.

22. Cf. A. W. De Porte, *De Gaulle's Foreign Policy, 1944–1948* (Cambridge: Harvard University Press, 1968), pp. 74–83.

23. Winant to Roosevelt, December 31, 1944, President-Winant 1944, Box 11, Map Room, FDRL; Llewellyn Woodward, *British Foreign Policy in the Second World War*, vol. III (London: Her Majesty's Stationery Office, 1971), pp. 91–95; Stalin to Churchill, December 3, 1944, *SCCA*, pp. 280–81.

24. Records of conversations on December 6, 1944, *Sovetsko-frantsuzskie otnosheniia vo vremia Velikoi Otechestvennoi Voiny* [Soviet-French relations during the Great Patriotic War] (Moscow: Gospolitizdat, 1959), pp. 356–62; Charles de Gaulle, *The Complete War Memoirs of Charles de Gaulle* (New York: Simon and Schuster, 1964), pp. 736–57; W. Averell Harriman and Elie Abel, *Special Envoy to Churchill and Stalin* (New York: Random House, 1975), pp. 375–78.

25. Aveling (Brussels) to Foreign Office, October 28, 1944, C 15045/11585/4, FO 371/38897, PRO; Duff Cooper to Foreign Office, November 25, 1944, Z 7933/5766/17, FO

371/42084; minute by Harrison on Knatchbull-Hugessen to Harvey, November 18, 1944, C 16118/11585/4, FO 371/38898, PRO.

26. Gilbert Mathieu, "The French and Belgian Communist Parties in Relation to Soviet Objectives towards Western Europe in 1940 and 1944" (Ph.D. diss., University of Wisconsin, 1971), pp. 135, 156–57.

27. David Anderson, "Belgium Quieter After 4-Day Crisis," *New York Times*, November 30, 1944. For the best account, see Geoffrey Warner, "Allies, Government, and Resistance: The Belgian Political Crisis of November 1944"; I am indebted to Professor Warner, of the University of Hull, for letting me use the manuscript before its scheduled 1978 publication in the *Transactions of the Royal Historical Society*.

28. John O. Iatrides, *Revolt in Athens* (Princeton: Princeton University Press, 1972), pp. 221, 276–80. See Richard Clogg, "The Greek Government-in-exile: some British perspectives," paper presented at the Conference on Governments in Exile in London during the Second World War, Imperial War Museum, London, October 26, 1977.

29. N. Malinin, "K voprosu o sozdanii mezhdunarodnoi organizatsii bezopasnosti" [The question of the establishment of an international security organization], *Voina i rabochii klass*, December 15, 1944, pp. 10–13.

30. Nils M. Udgaard, *Great Power Politics and Norwegian Foreign Policy* (Oslo: Universitetsforlaget, 1973), pp. 67–68.

31. Harriman to Roosevelt, December 15, 1944, and memorandum by Pasvolsky on conversation with Gromyko, January 13, 1945, *FRUS, Yalta*, pp. 378–79, and 75.

32. Incidents summarized in FO 371/48045, and Balfour to Warner, November 10, 1944, N 7494/6965/38, FO 371/43448, PRO.

33. Kennan to Bohlen, cited in Charles E. Bohlen, *Witness to History* (New York: Norton, 1973), p. 175.

34. Speech by Stalin, November 6, 1944, in *Soviet Foreign Policy during the Patriotic War*, ed. Andrew Rothstein, vol. II (London: Hutchinson, 1945), p. 31.

35. "Aktionsprogramm des Blockes der Kämpferischen Demokratie," in Horst Laschitza, "Zwei Dokumente der KPD aus den Jahren 1944 und 1945 für das neue, demokratische Deutschland," *BGDA* 7 (1965): 261–63; see Alexander Fischer, *Sowjetische Deutschlandpolitik im Zweiten Weltkrieg* (Stuttgart: Deutsche Verlags-Anstalt, 1975), pp. 103–8.

36. Laschitza, *Kämpferische Demokratie gegen Faschismus*, pp. 193–209, esp. 199; "Die gegenwärtige Lage und die Aufgaben des Nationalkomitees 'Freies Deutschland,'" January 16–17, 1945, in Walter Ulbricht, *Zur Geschichte der deutschen Arbeiterbewegung*, vol. II, suppl. 1 (Berlin: Dietz, 1968), p. 202; see Fischer, *Sowjetische Deutschlandpolitik*, pp. 108–19.

37. Laschitza, *Kämpferische Demokratie gegen Faschismus*, p. 200.

38. See Tony Sharp, *The Wartime Alliance and the Zonal Division of Germany* (New York: Oxford University Press, 1975), pp. 14–20.

39. Gallman to Secretary of State, November 6, 11, and 12, 1944, *FRUS*, 1944, vol. I, pp. 384–85, 391–92, 403–404; for the texts of the agreements, see *FRUS, Yalta*, pp. 121–27.

40. Laschitza, *Kämpferische Demokratie gegen Faschismus*, p. 199.

41. "Unsere Aufgaben," November 12, 1944, and "Die gegenwärtige Lage," January 16–17, 1945, in Ulbricht, *Zur Geschichte der deutschen Arbeiterbewegung*, vol. II, suppl. 1, pp. 183–85, 199–203.

42. Churchill to Roosevelt, October 22, 1944, in *Roosevelt and Churchill: Their Secret Correspondence*, ed. Francis L. Loewenheim et al. (New York: Dutton, 1975), p. 591.

43. Record of Churchill-Stalin meeting, October 17, 1944, PREM 3/434/2, PRO.

44. Memorandum by Harriman on conversation with Maiskii, January 20, 1945, *FRUS, Yalta*, pp. 176–78.

45. "Die gegenwärtige Lage," January 16–17, 1945, in Ulbricht, *Zur Geschichte der deutschen Arbeiterbewegung*, vol. II, suppl. 1, p. 202; see Arnold Sywottek, *Deutsche Volksdemokratie* (Düsseldorf: Bertelsmann, 1971), p. 155.

46. Bruce Kuklick, *American Policy and the Division of Germany: The Clash with Russia over Reparations* (Ithaca, N.Y.: Cornell University Press, 1972), pp. 47–73.

47. Churchill to Roosevelt, October 22, 1944, in *Roosevelt and Churchill*, ed. Loewenheim et al., p. 591; Laschitza, *Kämpferische Demokratie gegen Faschismus*, p. 199.

48. Harriman to Secretary of State, January 10, 1945, *FRUS, Yalta*, p. 453.

49. In "Aktionsprogramm des Blockes der Kämpferischen Demokratie," in Laschitza, "Zwei Dokumente der KPD," p. 262.

50. S. N. Borshchev, *Ot Nevy do Elby* [From the Neva to the Elbe] (Leningrad: Lenizdat, 1970), p. 282; German excerpt from POW interrogations, January 26, 1945, frame 909, microfilm 582, microcopy T-78, RG-242, NA; for a critical Soviet account of the atrocities, see Peter Gosztony, "Die Tagebuchaufzeichnungen eines russischen Artillerieoffiziers in Deutschland im Frühjahr 1945," *Wehrwissenschaftliche Rundschau* 19 (1969): 512–24.

51. *Die Kommunisten im Kampf für die Unabhängigkeit Österreichs* (Vienna: Stern, 1955), pp. 152–63; Karl Vogelmann, "Die Propaganda der österreichischen Emigration für einen selbständigen österreichischen Nationalstaat" (Ph.D. diss., University of Vienna, 1973), pp. 141–50.

52. Winant to Secretary of State, November 24 and 27, 1944, *FRUS*, 1944, vol. I, pp. 470–72.

53. Proceedings of EAC session, November 6, 1944, 65 A 987, Box 1291, Lot 52 M 64, RG-59, NA.

54. Message by Deane, December 24, 1944, cited in Joint Staff Mission (Washington) to Air Ministry (London), December 26, 1944, PREM 3/398/3, PRO.

55. Shtemenko, "Kak planirovalas posledniaia kampania," pp. 58, 61.

56. Cf. Arthur L. Smith, Jr., "Churchill et l'armée allemande (1945): Quelques spéculations sur les origines de la guerre froide," *Revue d'histoire de la deuxième guerre mondiale* 24, no. 93 (1974): 65–78.

57. Alfred D. Chandler, Jr., ed., *The Papers of Dwight David Eisenhower* (Baltimore: Johns Hopkins Press, 1970), vol. IV, pp. 2458–59.

58. Vladimir Dedijer, *The Battle Stalin Lost* (New York: Viking, 1971), pp. 187–89.

59. Arthur Tedder, *With Prejudice: The War Memoirs* (London: Cassell, 1966), p. 647.

60. John R. Deane, *The Strange Alliance* (New York: Viking, 1947), p. 156.

61. Entry for January 31, 1945, Wilfred von Oven, *Finale Furioso* (Tübingen: Graebert, 1974), p. 564.

62. Vasilii I. Chuikov, "Konets tretego reikha" [The end of the Third Reich], *Oktiabr*, 1964, no. 4, pp. 128–32; cf. Erich Kuby, *The Russians and Berlin 1945* (New York: Hill and Wang, 1968), pp. 21–27.

63. Georgi K. Zhukov, *Marshal Zhukov's Greatest Battles* (New York: Harper, 1969), pp. 274–81; Nikolai A. Antipenko, *Na glavnom napravlenii* [In the main direction] (Moscow: Nauka, 1967), pp. 209–20; Reuben Ainsztein, "The Russian Road to Berlin 1944–45," *International Affairs* (London) 46 (1970): 91–101.

64. Chuikov quoted in *Stalin and His Generals*, ed. Seweryn Bialer (New York: Pegasus, 1969), p. 503.

65. "Log of the Trip," entry for February 3, 1945, *FRUS, Yalta*, p. 550.

66. Winston S. Churchill, *Triumph and Tragedy* (Boston: Houghton Mifflin, 1953), p. 342.

67. The official Soviet explanation, that Stalin had not yet arrived in the Crimea, is denied by Yalta participant Admiral Nikolai G. Kuznetsov, "Pobednaia vesna 1945 goda" [The victorious spring of 1945], *Novaia i noveishaia istoriia*, 1970, no. 1, p. 156.

68. William D. Leahy, *I Was There* (New York: McGraw-Hill, 1950), p. 296; Edward R. Stettinius, Jr., *Roosevelt and the Russians* (Garden City, N.Y.: Doubleday, 1949), p. 81.

69. Jim Bishop, *FDR's Last Year* (New York: Morrow, 1974), esp. pp. 294–95.

70. There is no official record of the proceedings. The unpublished British minutes (preserved in PREM 3/51/4, 5, 6, and 9, PRO) differ from the American ones (printed in *FRUS, Yalta*) in only a few, sometimes enlightening, details. The Soviet record published in *Tegeran—Ialta—Potsdam* [Teheran—Yalta—Potsdam] (Moscow: Mezhdunarodnye otnosheniia, 1970), though less detailed than the Western minutes, does not differ from them substantially, except for politically motivated deletions of embarrassing passages, such as those concerning the Soviet advocacy of Germany's dismemberment; see Johann W. Brügel, "Teheran, Jalta und Potsdam aus sowjetischer Sicht," *Europa-Archiv* 21 (1966): 803–10. The best analytical study of the conference is Diane S. Clemens, *Yalta* (New York: Oxford University Press, 1970), its painful pro-Stalin slant notwithstanding.

71. "Record of an Informal Conversation between the Prime Minister, Marshal Stalin, and

Others," February 4, 1945, PREM 3/51/9, PRO; Bohlen minutes of Roosevelt-Stalin meeting, February 4, 1945, *FRUS, Yalta*, pp. 570–71.

72. Bohlen minutes of first plenary meeting, February 4, 1945, *ibid.*, p. 576.

73. Bohlen minutes of tripartite dinner meeting, February 4, 1945, *ibid.*, pp. 589–90.

74. Combined Chiefs of Staff minutes of first tripartite military meeting, February 5, 1945, *ibid.*, pp. 597, 600–601.

75. Bohlen minutes of second plenary meeting, February 5, 1945, *ibid.*, pp. 611–16.

76. Bohlen later speculated that Stalin wanted "to get the others fully committed to the [dismemberment] idea, so their views would be useful in Soviet propaganda in Germany after the war," in *Witness to History*, p. 183; cf. Horst Duhnke, *Stalinismus in Deutschland* (Cologne: Verlag für Politik und Wirtschaft, 1955), p. 32.

77. Bohlen minutes of second plenary meeting, February 5, 1945, *FRUS, Yalta*, pp. 616–19.

78. For example, André Fontaine, *History of the Cold War*, vol. I (New York: Random House, 1968), p. 230, or Thomas W. Wolfe, *Soviet Power and Europe, 1945–1970* (Baltimore: Johns Hopkins Press, 1970), pp. 14–15.

79. Bohlen minutes of second plenary meeting, February 5, 1945, *FRUS, Yalta*, pp. 619–23.

80. Reproduced from memory by Chuikov, who witnessed the conversation, in his book *The Fall of Berlin* (New York: Holt, 1967), p. 120; Zhukov has contested the date, which Chuikov originally gave as February 4, but not the substance of the incident; Clemens, *Yalta*, p. 91.

81. The offensive into Pomerania was ordered on February 8; E. A. Boltin and S. J. Rostschin, "Konnte die Sowjetarmee Berlin im Februar 1945 einnehmen?" *Zeitschrift für Militärgeschichte* 5 (1966): 721.

82. Combined Chiefs of Staff minutes of second tripartite military meeting, February 6, 1945, *FRUS, Yalta*, p. 648.

83. *Ibid.*, p. 118.

84. Page minutes of meetings of foreign ministers, February 6 and 7, 1945, *ibid.*, pp. 656–57, 700–701.

85. Bohlen minutes of third plenary meeting, February 6, 1945, *ibid.*, pp. 661–67.

86. Stalin to Roosevelt, December 19, 1944, *SCRT*, pp. 178–79; Harriman to Secretary of State, December 19, 1944, and memorandum by Pasvolsky on conversation with Gromyko, January 11, 1945, *FRUS, Yalta*, pp. 60–61, and 68–73.

87. Bohlen minutes of third plenary meeting, February 6, 1945, *ibid.*, pp. 664–67.

88. Matthews minutes of third plenary meeting, February 6, 1945, *ibid.*, p. 677; see Hugh B. Hammett, "America's Non-Policy in Eastern Europe and the Origins of the Cold War," *Survey* 89 (1973): 156–57.

89. Bohlen minutes of third plenary meeting, February 6, 1945, *FRUS, Yalta*, p. 668.

90. *Ibid.*, pp. 669–71.

91. Roosevelt to Stalin, February 6, 1945, *ibid.*, pp. 727–28; Churchill, *Triumph and Tragedy*, p. 372.

92. Bohlen minutes of fourth plenary meeting, February 7, 1945, *FRUS, Yalta*, pp. 711–15.

93. Stalin to Roosevelt, February 11, 1945, *ibid.*, pp. 967–68.

94. Bohlen minutes of fourth plenary meeting, February 7, 1945, *ibid.*, p. 716.

95. Stefan Endrikhovskii, "Vossoedenie polskikh zemel v Polskom gossudarstve" [Stefan Jędrzychowski, The unification of the Polish lands in the Polish state], *Pravda*, December 18, 1944; *New York Times*, February 6, 1945.

96. Bohlen minutes of fourth plenary meeting, February 7, 1945, *FRUS, Yalta*, p. 717.

97. Bohlen minutes of fifth plenary meeting, February 8, 1945, *ibid.*, pp. 779–81.

98. Churchill, *Triumph and Tragedy*, p. 396; see Iatrides, *Revolt in Athens*, p. 230.

99. War Cabinet minutes, February 19, 1945, *The Great Powers and the Polish Question*, ed. Antony Polonsky (London: London School of Economics and Political Science, 1976), p. 251.

100. Churchill, *Triumph and Tragedy*, pp. 362–63.

101. Bohlen minutes of Roosevelt-Stalin meeting, February 8, 1945, *FRUS, Yalta*, pp. 768–70.

102. Page minutes of the meeting of foreign ministers, February 9, 1945, *ibid.*, pp. 803–5.

103. *Ibid.*, pp. 807–9.

104. Bohlen minutes of sixth plenary meeting, February 9, 1945, *ibid.*, pp. 842–43, 846–48; "Declaration of Liberated Europe," *ibid.*, pp. 862–63.

105. British minutes of meeting of foreign ministers, February 9, 1945, CAB 99/31, PRO.

106. Page minutes of meeting of foreign ministers, February 10, 1945, *FRUS, Yalta*, pp. 872–73.

107. Bohlen minutes of seventh plenary meeting, February 10, 1945, *ibid.*, pp. 899–900.

108. Churchill, *Triumph and Tragedy*, p. 385.

109. Fontaine, *History of the Cold War*, vol. I, p. 256.

110. Arthur Conte, *Yalta ou le partage du monde* (Paris: Laffont, 1964).

111. Testimony by Bohlen before the Senate Committee on Foreign Relations, *Hearings on the Nomination of Charles E. Bohlen*, U.S. Senate, 83d Cong., 1st sess., 1953, p. 34.

112. Chester Wilmot, *The Struggle for Europe* (New York: Harper, 1952), p. 628.

384

113. Shtemenko, "Kak planirovalas posledniaia kampania," p. 497; *Osvobozhdenie iugo-vostochnoi i tsentralnoi Evropy*, p. 68; A. I. Eremenko, "Pobednaia vesna" [The victorious spring], in *9 maia 1945 goda* [May 9, 1945], ed. A. M. Samsonov (Moscow: Nauka, 1970), pp. 244, 252–53.

114. Marshall to Deane for Antonov, February 20, 1945, subject file Europe, U.S. Military Mission Moscow, RG-334, NA.

115. Sywottek, *Deutsche Volksdemokratie*, pp. 163–64.

116. Laschitza, *Kämpferische Demokratie gegen Faschismus*, pp. 136–38.

117. Donovan to Roosevelt, March 9, 1945, OSS March 1945, 1st to 15th, Box 171, President's Secretary's File, FDRL; cf. editorial "Nashe mshchenie" [Our revenge], *Krasnaia zvezda*, February 9, 1945.

118. David Zaslavskii, "The Rout of Germany," domestic radio commentary, February 17, 1945, no. 2042, *Daily Digest of World Broadcasts*, BBC.

119. Henry L. Roberts, *Rumania* (New Haven: Yale University Press, 1951), pp. 262–63.

120. Schuyler to Department of War, January 20, 1945, subject file Romania, U.S. Military Mission Moscow, RG-334, NA.

121. Henry L. Roberts, *Rumania*, p. 263.

122. Radio address by Rădescu, February 24, 1945, no. 2049, pt. I, *Daily Digest of World Broadcasts*, BBC.

123. James F. Byrnes, *Speaking Frankly* (New York: Harper, 1947), pp. 50–51.

124. Stephen Fischer-Galati, *The New Rumania* (Cambridge: M.I.T. Press, 1967), pp. 28–29.

125. Groza and Tătărescu to Stalin, and Stalin to Groza and Tătărescu, *Pravda*, March 10, 1945.

126. Bela Vago, "Romania," in *Communist Power in Europe, 1944–1949*, ed. Martin McCauley (New York: Barnes and Noble, 1977), p. 116.

127. Quoted *ibid.*, p. 120; Secretary of State to Harriman, March 12, Harriman to Molotov, March 14, and British Embassy Washington to Department of State, "Aide-Mémoire," March 19, 1945, *FRUS*, 1945, vol. V, pp. 510–13, 518.

128. Harriman to Secretary of State, February, 24, 1945, *FRUS*, 1945, vol. V, pp. 123–25.

129. Harriman to Secretary of State, March 1, 6, and 23, 1945, *ibid.*, pp. 134, 142–44, 178.

130. Draft of letter by Churchill to Roosevelt, March 8, 1945, PREM 3/374/9, PRO.

131. *Osvobozhdenie iugo-vostochnoi i tsentralnoi Evropy*, pp. 428–59.

132. Broadcasts on March 8 and 9, 1945, nos. 2061 and 2063, *Daily Digest of World*

Broadcasts, BBC; Paul Winterton, "The Aims of the U.S.S.R. in Europe," *International Affairs* (London) 22 (1946): 16.

133. Grew to Harriman, March 11, and Harriman to Grew, March 12, 1945, *FRUS*, 1945, vol. III, pp. 723–25.

134. Donovan to Roosevelt, February 26, 1945, OSS, February 1945, Box 171, President's Secretary's File, FDRL.

135. Silvio Bertoldi, *I Tedeschi in Italia* (Milan: Rizzoli, 1964), pp. 186–87.

136. Reimer Hansen, "Ribbentrops Friedensfühler im Frühjahr 1945," *Geschichte in Wissenschaft und Unterricht* 18 (1967): 716–30.

137. Stettinius to Harriman, March 15, 1945, *FRUS*, 1945, vol. III, 730–31.

138. Harriman to Stettinius, March 16, 1945, *ibid.*, pp. 731–32.

139. For the evidence, see the American record of the talks in Donovan to Roosevelt, March 8, 9, 10, 12, 13, 21, 29, and April 1, and 4, 1945, OSS March–April 1945, Box 171, President's Secretary's File, FDRL.

140. A. Sokolov, "Senator Vandenberg i ego skhema" [Senator Vandenberg and his scheme], *Voina i rabochii klass*, March 1, 1945, pp. 19–23; A. Georgiev, "O knige Uoltera Lippmana 'Voennye tseli SShA' " [On Walter Lippmann's book *U.S. War Aims*], *Pravda*, March 16, 1945.

141. Stettinius, *Roosevelt and the Russians*, pp. 310–11. Harriman and Abel, *Special Envoy to Churchill and Stalin*, pp. 444–45; Bohlen, *Witness to History*, p. 217.

142. Anthony Eden, *The Reckoning* (Boston: Houghton Mifflin, 1965), p. 604.

143. Zbigniew Stypulkowski, *Invitation to Moscow* (London: Thames and Hudson, 1951), pp. 211–32.

144. *Cesta ke Květnu*, vol. I, pt. 1, pp. 380–92, 445.

145. Harriman to Secretary of State on conversation with Beneš, March 31, 1945, *FRUS*, 1945, vol. IV, p. 432; see Klieforth to Secretary of State, June 4, 1945, 860 F.00/6-445, RG-59, NA.

146. Stephen G. Xydis, *Greece and the Great Powers* (Salonica: Institute for Balkan Studies, 1963), pp. 89–90.

147. Edward Weisband, *Turkish Foreign Policy* (Princeton: Princeton University Press, 1973), p. 305.

148. *The Memoirs of Marshal Zhukov* (New York: Delacorte, 1971), p. 582.

149. Philip E. Mosely, *The Kremlin and World Politics* (New York: Random House, 1960), pp. 142–45; Gusev to Eden, quoted in Winant to Secretary of State, March 29, 1945, *FRUS*, 1945, vol. III, pp. 205–6.

150. Minutes of EAC meeting, March 23, 1945, 65 A 987, Box 1291, Lot 52 M 64, RG-59, NA.

151. Shtemenko, "Kak planirovalas posledniaia kampania," p. 69.

152. *Memoirs of Marshal Zhukov*, p. 588.

153. M. Galaktionov, "Nastuplenie soiuznikov na zapade" [The Allies' offensive in the west], *Pravda*, April 2, 1945.

154. Antonov to Deane, March 30, 1945, *SCCA*, p. 319.

155. Marshall to Deane for Antonov, February 27, 1945, WAR-44444, Military Mission Moscow, RG-334, NA.

156. Eisenhower to Deane and Archer for Stalin, March 28, 1945, in *Papers of Dwight David Eisenhower*, ed. Chandler, vol. IV, p. 2551; Stephen E. Ambrose, *Eisenower and Berlin, 1945: The Decision to Halt at the Elbe* (New York: Norton, 1967).

157. Hollis to Churchill, March 29, 1945, PREM 3/141/5, PRO.

158. Churchill to Eisenhower, March 31, 1945, PREM 3/341/5, PRO.

159. Archer and Deane to Department of War, April 1, 1945, PREM 3/341/5, PRO.

160. Stalin to Eisenhower, April 1, 1945, in *Papers of Dwight David Eisenhower*, ed. Chandler, vol. IV, p. 2584.

161. Cornelius Ryan, *The Last Battle* (New York: Simon and Schuster, 1966), pp. 243–51; Ivan S. Konev, *Year of Victory* (Moscow: Progress, 1969), p. 79.

162. Churchill to Stalin, March 31, 1945, *SCCA*, pp. 309–10.

163. Roosevelt to Stalin, received April 1, 1945, *SCRT*, pp. 201–4.

164. Cyrus L. Sulzberger, "Litvinov a Lonely Jeremiah Who Foresaw the 'Cold War,' " *New York Times*, January 3, 1952, p. 9.

165. Clark Kerr to Foreign Office, April 6, 1945, N 3745/165/18, FO 371/47881, PRO.

166. Cf. Imanuel Geiss, "The Outbreak of the First World War and German War Aims," *Journal of Contemporary History* 1, no. 3 (1966): 90–91.

Chapter Eight: A Peace Lost?

1. Kirk to Secretary of State, March 17, 1945, *FRUS*, 1945, vol. III, pp. 26–27.

2. Winant to Secretary of State, April 4, 1945, *ibid.*, p. 41.

3. Harold Callender, "Soviet Domination in Reich Foreseen," *New York Times*, February 2, 1945; Adolf Schärf, *Österreichs Erneuerung* (Vienna: Wiener Volksbuchhandlung, 1955), p. 29.

4. Karl Renner, *Denkschrift über die Geschichte der Unabhängigkeitserklärung Österreichs und Bericht über drei Monate Aufbauarbeit* (Zurich: Europa, 1946), pp. 9–21.

5. David J. Dallin, "Stalin, Renner und Tito: Österreich zwischen drohender Sowjetisierung und den jugoslawischen Gebietsansprüchen im Frühjahr 1945," *Europa-Archiv* 13 (1958): 11030; according to Shtemenko's implausible assertion, even before Renner's

initiative Stalin had ordered a search for him to solicit his services; Sergei M. Shtemenko, *Generalnyi shtab v gody voiny* [The general staff during the war], vol. II (Moscow: Voenizdat, 1973), p. 356.

6. Erwin Zucker-Schilling, *Er diente seiner Klasse* (Vienna: Globus, 1971), p. 71.

7. Kennan to Secretary of State, April 29 and May 1, 1945, *FRUS*, 1945, vol. III, pp. 100–101, 108.

8. Carola Stern, *Ulbricht: A Political Biography* (New York: Praeger, 1965), p. 92; "Richtlinien über die Arbeit der deutschen Antifaschisten in dem von der Roten Armee besetzten deutschen Gebiet," in Horst Laschitza, "Zwei Dokumente der KPD aus den Jahren 1944 und 1945," *BGDA* 7 (1965): 263–68.

9. Heinz Vosske, "Über die Initiativgruppe des Zentralkomitees der KPD in Mecklenburg-Vorpommern," *BGDA* 6 (1964): 424–37.

10. G. Aleksandrov, "Tovarishch Erenburg uproshchaet" [Comrade Ehrenburg oversimplifies], *Pravda*, April 14, 1945; see Ilya Ehrenburg, *The War: 1941–1945* (New York: New American Library, 1964), p. 177.

11. U.S. Military Mission Moscow to Eisenhower, April 16, 1945, PREM 3/396/14, PRO.

12. John Ehrman, *Grand Strategy*, vol. VI (London: Her Majesty's Stationery Office, 1956), p. 157; Forrest C. Pogue, "The Decision to Halt at the Elbe (1945)," in *Command Decisions*, ed. Kent R. Greenfield (New York: Harcourt, 1959), p. 384.

13. Archer and Olsen to Antonov, April 22, 1945, subject file Germany, U.S. Military Mission Moscow, RG-334, NA.

14. Mary Dau, "The Soviet Union and the Liberation of Denmark," *Survey* 76 (1970): 76–77.

15. A. Basov, "Desant na ostrov Bornkholm" [The landing on Bornholm Island], *Voennoistoricheskii zhurnal* 8, no. 5 (1966): 29; minutes of War Cabinet meeting no. 58 (45), May 4, 1945, CAB 65/50, PRO.

16. Sergei Shtemenko, "Na poslednikh rubezhakh v Evrope" [Along the last frontiers of Europe], *Voennoistoricheskii zhurnal* 13, no. 4 (1971): 66.

17. Lothar Rendulic, *Gekämpft, gesiegt, geschlagen* (Wels and Munich: Welsermühl, 1957), p. 376.

18. Memorandum by Orme Sargent, April 2, 1945, N 4281/165/18, FO 371/47881, PRO.

19. Frank K. Roberts to C. F. A. Warner, April 25, 1945, N 4919/165/18, FO 371/47881, PRO; minutes of conference between Combined Chiefs of Staff and Deane, April 20, 1945, CCS 092 USSR (3-27-45), Sec. 1, Records of Combined Chiefs of Staff, RG-218, NA.

20. Memorandum by Harriman on conversation with Stalin, April 13, 1945, *FRUS*, 1945, vol. V, pp. 826–27; W. Averell Harriman and Elie Abel, *Special Envoy to Churchill and Stalin* (New York: Random House, 1975), pp. 440–42.

21. Martin J. Sherwin, *A World Destroyed* (New York: Knopf, 1975), p. 171.

22. Tadeusz Cieślak and Euzebiusz Basiński, eds., *Stosunki polsko-radzieckie w latach*

1917–1945 [Polish-Soviet relations in 1917–1945] (Warsaw: Książka i Wiedza, 1967), pp. 438–40.

23. Harry S. Truman, *Memoirs: Year of Decisions* (Garden City, N.Y.: Doubleday, 1955), p. 82; cf. Bohlen minutes of Truman-Molotov conversation, April 23, 1945, Foreign Affairs, Box 187, President's Secretary's File, Harry S. Truman Library.

24. Harriman and Abel, *Special Envoy to Churchill and Stalin*, p. 454.

25. See Stanley Hoffmann, "Revisionism Revisited," in *Reflections on the Cold War*, ed. Lynn H. Miller and Ronald W. Pruessen (Philadelphia: Temple University Press, 1974), pp. 3–26.

26. English translation, "On the Dissolution of the Communist Party of the United States," *Daily Worker* (New York), May 24, 1945.

27. See Philip J. Jaffe, *The Rise and Fall of American Communism* (New York: Horizon, 1975), pp. 77–78.

28. Duclos to me, March 27, 1975.

29. Churchill to Stalin and Stalin to Churchill, April 25, 1945, *SCCA*, pp. 333–35.

30. Record of Krebs-Chuikov negotiations, Vsevolod Vishnevskii, "The Surrender of Berlin, 1945," *International Affairs* (Moscow) 7, no. 3 (1961): 96–104; Vasili I. Chuikov, *The Fall of Berlin* (New York: Holt, 1967), pp. 213–30.

31. Marlis G. Steinert, *Twenty-Three Days: The Final Collapse of Nazi Germany* (New York: Walker, 1969), pp. 255, 258–60.

32. *The Memoirs of Field-Marshal the Viscount Montgomery of Alamein* (Cleveland: World, 1958), pp. 297–98.

33. Basov, "Desant na ostrov Bornkholm," p. 30.

34. Eisenhower to U.S. Military Mission Moscow, May 4 and 6, and U.S. Military Mission Moscow to Eisenhower, May 5, 1945, "Correspondence between SHAEF and Soviet High Command Concerning Decisions to Halt Allied Forces in Czechoslovakia," *Department of State Bulletin*, May 22, 1949, pp. 666–67.

35. *Istoriia Velikoi Otechestvennoi Voiny Sovetskogo Soiuza* [A history of the Great Patriotic War of the Soviet Union], vol. V (Moscow: Voenizdat, 1963), pp. 319–20.

36. Instructions to Soviet partisans in Bohemia by General Andreev, May 1, 1945, cited in Jiří Doležal, *Jediná cesta* [The only way] (Prague: Naše vojsko, 1966), p. 226.

37. Minutes of CNR meeting, May 7, 1945, in Ivan Šťovíček, "Zápis o zasedání ČNR ve dnech 4.–9. května 1945" [The record of the meetings of the CNR on May 4–9, 1945], *Historie a vojenství*, 1967, no. 4, p. 1007.

38. Jiří Doležal, "Komunisté a povstání" [The Communists and the uprising], *Život strany* (Prague) 8 (1965): pp. 480–82.

39. Shtemenko, "Na poslednikh rubezhakh v Evrope," pp. 86–87; for the best study of the Prague uprising, see Stanislav Zámečník, "Květnové povstání českého lidu" [The May uprising of the Czech people], *Historie a vojenství*, 1965, no. 1, suppl., pp. 47–100.

40. Churchill to Eisenhower, May 7, 1945, in Winston S. Churchill, *Triumph and Tragedy* (Boston: Houghton Mifflin, 1953), p. 507.

41. Alfred D. Chandler, Jr., ed., *The Papers of Dwight David Eisenhower*, vol. IV (Baltimore: Johns Hopkins Press, 1970), p. 2662; Acting Secretary of State Joseph C. Grew favored Churchill's position; Grew to Caffery, May 7, 1945, *FRUS*, 1945, vol. IV, pp. 448–49.

42. Šťovíček, "Zápis o zasedání ČNR," pp. 995, 999; broadcast by Radio Prague, May 7, 1945, no. 2121, part I, *Daily Digest of World Broadcasts*, BBC.

43. Albert Pražák, *Náš odboj proti Němcum* [Our resistance to the Germans] (Prague: Zemská rada osvětová, 1946), pp. 22–23; Josef Smrkovský, "Za pravdou o pražském povstání" [For the truth about the Prague uprising], *Zemědělské noviny* (Prague), May 5–6, 1945; Otakar Machotka, "Česká národní rada za revoluce" [The Czech National Council during the revolution], in *Pražské povstání 1945* [The Prague uprising of 1945] (Washington: Rada svobodného Československa, 1965), pp. 39–41.

44. George S. Patton, *War As I Knew It* (Boston: Houghton Mifflin, 1947), p. 327.

45. Josef Smrkovský, "Proč neosvobodili Prahu Američané?" [Why was Prague not liberated by the Americans?], *Student* (Prague) 3, no. 25 (1967); OSS dissemination report, A-57389, June 28, 1945, L 57494, RG-165; cf. Machotka, "Česká národní rada za revoluce," p. 42.

46. Eisenhower to Combined Chiefs of Staff and British Chiefs of Staff, May 5, 1945, in *The Papers of Dwight David Eisenhower*, ed. Chandler, vol. IV, pp. 2687–88; Shtemenko, *Generalnyi shtab v gody voiny*, vol. II, 432–33.

47. Antonov to Deane and Archer, May 7, 1945, subject file Germany, U.S. Military Mission Moscow, RG-334, NA.

48. John R. Deane, *The Strange Alliance* (New York: Viking, 1947), p. 169.

49. Stalin to Churchill, May 7, 1945, *SCCA*, p. 351; William D. Leahy, *I Was There* (New York: McGraw-Hill, 1950), pp. 357–63.

50. Arthur Tedder, *With Prejudice* (London: Cassell, 1966), p. 685.

51. *Osvobození Československa Rudou armádou* [The liberation of Czechoslovakia by the Red Army] (Prague: Naše vojsko, 1965), vol. II, p. 373.

52. Vladimír Ježek, *Voláme všechny: Československý revoluční vysílač na vlně 414,5 metru ve dnech 5.-9.května 1945* [Calling everybody: The Czechoslovak revolutionary radio station on the wavelength of 414.5 meters on May 5–9, 1945] (Prague: Nakladatelství politické literatury, 1966), pp. 64–66.

53. Šťovíček, "Zápis o zasedání ČNR," pp. 1011, 1015; OSS dissemination report, A-57020, June 12, 1945, L 57022, RG-165, NA; Václav Král, *Osvobozeni Československa* [The liberation of Czechoslovakia] (Prague: Academia, 1975), pp. 328, 336–41.

54. Karel Bartošek, *Pražské povstáni 1945* [The Prague uprising of 1945] (Prague: Naše vojsko, 1965), pp. 221–30.

55. Ivan G. Ziberov, "Jak byla osvobozena Praha v květnu 1945" [How Prague was liberated in May 1945], *Historie a vojenství*, 1965, no. 2, p. 152.

56. Eisenhower to U.S. Military Mission Moscow, May 8, and Antonov to Deane and Archer, May 10, 1945, subject file Germany, U.S. Military Mission Moscow, RG-334, NA.

57. *Khrushchev Remembers* (Boston: Little, Brown, 1970), pp. 220–21.

58. Quoted in *Osvobození Československa Rudou armádou*, vol. II, pp. 389–90.

59. Churchill to Eden, May 4, 1945, in Churchill, *Triumph and Tragedy*, p. 503.

60. Robert E. Sherwood, *Roosevelt and Hopkins* (New York: Harper, 1948), pp. 892, 912; James F. Byrnes, *Speaking Frankly* (New York: Harper, 1947), p. 68; Lev Bezymenski, *The Death of Adolf Hitler: Unknown Documents from Soviet Archives* (New York: Harcourt, 1968), p. 66.

61. George F. Kennan, *Memoirs, 1925–1950* (Boston: Little, Brown, 1967), pp. 240–42.

62. George C. Herring, Jr., *Aid to Russia* (New York: Columbia University Press, 1973), pp. 203–6.

63. Harriman to Secretary of State, July 11, 1945, *FRUS*, 1945, vol. V, p. 865.

64. Sergej I. Tjulpanow, "Die Rolle der Sowjetischen Militäradministration im demokratischen Deutschland," in *50 Jahre Triumph des Marxismus-Leninismus* (Berlin: Dietz, 1967), p. 34.

65. Adolf Schärf, *April 1945 in Wien* (Vienna: Wiener Volksbuchhandlung, 1948), pp. 33–34, 51–53, 60–62.

66. Manuel Gottlieb, *The German Peace Settlement and the Berlin Crisis* (New York: Paine-Whitman, 1960), pp. 4–12.

67. For the best account of conditions in Soviet-occupied Austria, see Douglas W. Houston, "Karl Renner and Austria in 1945," *Austrian History Yearbook* I (1965): 122–49.

68. Ulbricht to Dimitrov, May 9, 1945, in Walter Ulbricht, *Zur Geschichte der deutschen Arbeiterbewegung*, vol. II (Berlin: Dietz, 1966), p. 419; Cf. Erich W. Gniffke, *Jahre mit Ulbricht* (Cologne: Wissenschaft und Politik, 1966), pp. 35–36.

69. Otakar Machotka, "Česká národní rada po revoluci" [The Czech National Council after the revolution], in *Pražské povstání 1945*, pp. 111–22.

70. Bogdan C. Novak, *Trieste, 1941–1954: The Ethnic, Political, and Ideological Struggle* (Chicago: University of Chicago Press, 1970), pp. 161–68, 198–99; David J. Dallin, "Stalin, Renner und Tito," pp. 11030–34.

71. Note by Clark Kerr on Churchill-Gusev conversation, May 18, 1945, PREM 3/396/12, PRO.

72. Churchill to Stalin, May 26, 29, June 1, 1945, *SCCA*, pp. 360–62.

73. "Mezhdunarodnoe obozrenie" [International survey], *Pravda*, May 20, 1945.

74. Reimer Hansen, *Das Ende des Dritten Reiches* (Stuttgart: Klett, 1966), pp. 194–95.

391

75. Edgar Snow, *Journey to the Beginning* (London: Gollancz, 1959), p. 357.

76. On this awkward subject, Mark R. Elliott, "The Reparation Issue in Soviet-American Relations, 1944–1947," (Ph.D. diss., University of Kentucky, 1974), p. 1, and Nicholas Bethell, *The Last Secret* (New York: Basic Books, 1974), pp. 97–98, are superior to Julius Epstein, *Operation Keelhaul* (Old Greenwich, Conn.: Devin-Adair, 1974), pp. 76–82.

77. Notes on Stettinius-Harriman meeting, May 9, 1945, *FRUS*, vol. V, p. 998; cf. Harriman and Abel, *Special Envoy to Churchill and Stalin*, pp. 459–60, 463.

78. British Embassy Washington to Foreign Office, May 29, 1945, FO 181/1005/7, PRO.

79. Memorandum by Bohlen on Hopkins-Stalin conversation, May 26, 1945, *FRUS, Potsdam*, vol. I, pp. 26–27.

80. *Ibid.*, p. 28.

81. *Ibid.*, p. 30.

82. Memorandum by Bohlen on Hopkins-Stalin conversation, May 27, 1945, *ibid.*, p. 32.

83. *Ibid.*, p. 33.

84. *Ibid.*, p. 38.

85. "Memorandum of the Fourth Hopkins-Stalin Conversation," May 30, 1945, *FRUS*, 1945, vol. V, pp. 304–5.

86. Cf. J. R. Thackrah, "Aspects of American and British Policy towards Poland from the Yalta to the Potsdam Conferences, 1945," *Polish Review*, 21, no. 4 (1976): 30.

87. Lynn E. Davis, *Cold War Begins* (Princeton: Princeton University Press, 1974), pp. 236–39.

88. The sixteenth was too ill to appear in court; see Zbigniew Stypulkowski, *Invitation to Moscow* (London: Thames and Hudson, 1951), pp. 313–33; Harriman to Secretary of State, June 18, 1945, *FRUS*, 1945, vol. V, pp. 348–50.

89. Memorandum by Hopkins on conversation with Stalin, June 1, 1945, *FRUS, Potsdam*, vol. I, pp. 58–59.

90. Harriman to Secretary of State, June 29, 1945, *ibid.*, p. 729; "Statement by the President," July 5, 1945, *ibid.*, p. 735.

91. Memorandum by Bohlen on Hopkins-Stalin conversation, May 27, 1945, *ibid.*, p. 39.

92. Memorandum by Bohlen on Hopkins-Stalin conversation, May 30, 1945, *ibid.*, p. 55.

93. Stalin to Truman, June 11, 1945, *SCRT*, p. 244.

94. Stalin to Churchill, June 21, 1945, *SCCA*, pp. 368–69.

95. Llewellyn Woodward, *British Foreign Policy in the Second World War*, vol. III (London: Her Majesty's Stationery Office, 1971), p. 380.

96. Churchill to Stalin, June 24, 1945, *SCCA*, p. 370; Churchill, *Triumph and Tragedy*, pp. 560–61.

97. Eisenhower to U.S. Military Mission Moscow, in Gammel and Deane to Antonov, June 16, 1945, subject file Germany, U.S. Military Mission Moscow, RG-334, NA.

98. Grew to Winant, July 2, 1945, *FRUS, Potsdam*, vol. I, pp. 989–90.

99. Novikov to Grew, June 1, 1945, *FRUS*, 1945, vol. VIII, pp. 1128–29.

100. Matthews minutes of seventh plenary meeting, February 10, 1945, *FRUS, Yalta*, pp. 909–10.

101. Stephen G. Xydis, "The 1945 Crisis over the Turkish Straits," *Balkan Studies* 1 (1960): 70–77.

102. Cf. Fletcher S. Crowe III, "The Soviet Union and the Turkish Straits, 1933–1945," (Ph.D. diss., Florida State University, 1973), pp. i-xxxviii.

103. *Khrushchev Remembers: The Last Testament* (Boston: Little, Brown, 1974), pp. 295–96.

104. "Declaration Regarding the Defeat of Germany and the Assumption of Supreme Authority," June 5, 1945, in *Documents on Germany under Occupation, 1945–1954*, ed. Beate Ruhm von Oppen (London: Oxford University Press, 1955), pp. 29–35.

105. "Establishment of Anti-Fascist Parties and Free Trade Unions in the Soviet Zone," June 10, 1945, *ibid.*, pp. 37–38.

106. Anton Ackermann, "Der neue Weg zur Einheit," in *Vereint sind wir alles: Erinnerungen an die Gründung der SED* (Berlin: Dietz, 1966), p. 81; cf. Wolfgang Leonhard, " 'Es muss demokratisch aussehen . . .': Vor 20 Jahren begann die 'Gruppe Ulbricht' ihre Arbeit—Legende und Wirklichkeit," *Die Zeit*, May 14, 1965.

107. Sergej I. Tjulpanow, "Die Rolle der SMAD bei der Demokratisierung Deutschlands," *Zeitschrift für Geschichtswissenschaft* 15 (1967): 248; cf. Ernst Lemmer, *Manches war doch anders* (Frankfurt a.M.: Scheffler, 1968), p. 243.

108. Cf. Henry Krisch, *German Politics under Soviet Occupation* (New York: Columbia University Press, 1974), pp. 51–52; and Ekkehart Krippendorf, *Die Liberal-Demokratische Partei Deutschlands in der sowjetischen Besatzungszone 1945/1948* (Düsseldorf: Droste, 1962), pp. 22–23.

109. Eisenhower to Joint Chiefs of Staff, June 6, 1945, *FRUS*, 1945, vol. III, p. 328.

110. Truman to Stalin, received June 15, 1945, *SCRT*, p. 245; Churchill, *Triumph and Tragedy*, pp. 604–5.

111. *Khrushchev Remembers*, p. 221; cf. Robert Murphy, *Diplomat among Warriors* (Garden City, N.Y.: Doubleday, 1964), p. 273.

112. Stalin to Truman, June 16, 1945, *SCRT*, p. 247.

113. "Factory Equipment Removals from the American Zone of Berlin," July 27, 1945, *FRUS, Potsdam*, vol. II, pp. 889–92.

114. Winant to Secretary of State, June 20, 1945, 740.00119 EAC/6-2045, RG-59, NA; Agreement on Control Machinery in Austria, July 4, 1945, *FRUS, Potsdam*, vol. I, pp.

351–55; Philip E. Mosely, *The Kremlin and World Politics* (New York: Random House, 1960), pp. 20–21.

115. Gyula Schöpflin, "A magyar kommunista párt útja, 1945–1950" [The road of the Hungarian Communist party], *Latohatár* (Munich) 6 (1955): 241–42.

116. Entry for July 22, 1945, in Lord Charles Moran, *Winston Churchill: The Struggle for Survival* (Boston: Houghton Mifflin, 1966), p. 300.

117. In the opinion of the former Secretary to the British delegation, Sir William Hayter, quoted in Charles L. Mee, Jr., *Meeting at Potsdam* (New York: Evans, 1975), p. 136; this is the most penetrating study of the conference, even though Mee's thesis that the Big Three deliberately fostered conflict among themselves does not stand up to the evidence.

118. Anthony Eden, *The Reckoning* (Boston: Houghton Mifflin, 1965), p. 632.

119. Record of Churchill-Stalin conversation, July 18, 1945, PREM 3/430/6, PRO; Churchill, *Triumph and Tragedy*, p. 634.

120. Memorandum by Bohlen on Truman-Stalin meeting on July 17, 1945, dated March 28, 1960, *FRUS, Potsdam*, vol. II, p. 1584. The American, British, and Soviet minutes of the Potsdam meetings do not differ substantially from one another but the Soviet ones, in *Tegeran—Ialta—Potsdam* [Teheran–Yalta–Potsdam] (Moscow: Mezhdunarodnye otnosheniia, 1970), give a more detailed account of Stalin's statements.

121. Memorandum for Mr. Dunn, by Bohlen, July 17, 1945, *FRUS, Potsdam*, vol. II, pp. 46–47.

122. Entry for July 18, 1945, *The Diaries of Sir Alexander Cadogan* (London: Cassell, 1971), p. 765.

123. W. Averell Harriman, *America and Russia in a Changing World* (Garden City, N.Y.: Doubleday, 1971), p. 44.

124. Aide-mémoire, July 3, 1945, *FRUS, Potsdam*, vol. I, pp. 206–208; Secretary of State to Winant, July 5, 1945, *ibid.*, pp. 226–27; cf. Harriman to Secretary of State, July 8, and memorandum by Page on Harriman-Molotov conversation, July 11, 1945, *ibid.*, pp. 233 and 236.

125. Thompson minutes of the first meeting and State Department minutes of the tenth meeting of foreign ministers, July 18 and 30, 1945, *ibid.*, vol. II, pp. 72 and 492.

126. Thilo Vogelsang, "Die Bemühungen um eine deutsche Zentralverwaltung, 1945/46," *Vierteljahrshefte für Zeitgeschichte* 18 (1970): 510–28.

127. Thompson minutes of the first and fifth meetings of foreign ministers, July 18 and 22, 1945, *FRUS, Potsdam*, vol. II, pp. 75 and 233; "Political Principles for Germany," July 30, 1945, *ibid.*, p. 824.

128. "Protocol of the Proceedings of the Berlin Conference," August 1, 1945, *ibid.*, p. 1484.

129. Lucius D. Clay, *Decision in Germany* (Garden City, N.Y.: Doubleday, 1950), p. 33.

130. On the reparations question at Potsdam, Manuel Gottlieb, *The German Peace Settle-*

ment and the Berlin Crisis (New York: Paine-Whitman, 1960), pp. 38–42, grasps the real issues better than Bruce Kuklick, *American Policy and the Division of Germany* (Ithaca, N.Y.: Cornell University Press, 1972), pp. 141–66.

131. Minutes of second plenary session, July 18, 1945, *Tegeran—Ialta—Potsdam*, p. 217.

132. Minutes of first plenary session, July 17, 1945, *ibid.*, pp. 211–14.

133. Eden, *The Reckoning*, p. 634.

134. "On the question of Western Frontier of Poland," July 20, 1945, *FRUS, Potsdam*, vol. II, p. 1138; Department of State minutes of fifth plenary meeting, July 21, 1945, *ibid.*, pp. 203–15.

135. Minutes of sixth plenary session, July 22, 1945, *Tegeran—Ialta—Potsdam*, p. 275.

136. "Plan of reparations from Germany" and "On Advance Deliveries from Germany," July 23, 1945, *FRUS, Potsdam*, vol. II, pp. 863–85; Bohlen minutes of Byrnes-Molotov meeting, *ibid.*, p. 275.

137. Truman, *Memoirs: Year of Decisions*, p. 416.

138. Churchill, *Triumph and Tragedy*, p. 670; Sergei M. Shtemenko, *The Soviet General Staff at War* (Moscow: Progress, 1970), pp. 347–48.

139. Arnold Kramish, *Atomic Energy in the Soviet Union* (Stanford: Stanford University Press, 1959), pp. 53–54, 97–107; Leslie R. Groves, *Now It Can Be Told* (New York: Harper, 1962), p. 167.

140. Harriman and Abel, *Special Envoy to Churchill and Stalin*, p. 491.

141. "Notes on Soviet Suggestions That the Ruhr Be Internationalized," July 20, 1945, *FRUS, Potsdam*, vol. II, pp. 183–84; "On Ruhr Industrial District," July 30, 1945, *ibid.*, pp. 1000–1001; cf. Boris Meissner, "Der Kreml und das Ruhrgebiet," *Osteuropa* 1 (1951): 81–88.

142. "Regarding Reparations from Austria" and "Regarding Reparations from Italy," July 24, 1945, *FRUS, Potsdam*, vol. II, pp. 666 and 1092–93.

143. Tjulpanow, "Die Rolle der Sowjetischen Militäradministration im demokratischen Deutschland," p. 59.

144. Bohlen minutes of Byrnes-Molotov meeting, July 27, 1945, *FRUS, Potsdam*, vol. II, pp. 449–52.

145. Bohlen minutes of Truman-Molotov meeting, July 29, 1945, *ibid.*, pp. 471–76; proposal by the United States delegation, July 29, 1945, *ibid.*, p. 1150.

146. Diary entry by Mikołajczyk, July 29, 1945, *ibid.*, p. 1539.

147. Włodzimierz T. Kowalski, *Walka dyplomatyczna o miejsce Polski w Europie* [The diplomatic struggle for Poland's place in Europe] (Warsaw: Książka i Wiedza, 1966), p. 628; *idem, Polityka zagraniczna RP* [The foreign policy of the Polish republic] (Warsaw: Książka i Wiedza, 1971), p. 58.

148. "Western Frontier of Poland," July 30, 1945, *FRUS, Potsdam*, vol. II, pp. 1150–51; Bohlen minutes of Byrnes-Molotov meeting, July 30, 1945, *ibid.*, p. 480.

149. Cf. "Truman-Attlee meeting," July 28, 1945, *ibid.*, p. 459.

150. Byrnes, *Speaking Frankly*, p. 85; *Idem, All in One Lifetime* (New York: Harper, 1958), p. 302.

151. "Proposal on Reparations from Germany," July 29, 1945, *FRUS, Potsdam*, vol. II, pp. 913–14; Department of State minutes of tenth meeting of foreign ministers, July 30, 1945, *ibid.*, pp. 484–92, 496–97.

152. "Reparations from Germany," July 31, 1945, *ibid.*, pp. 1593–94; minutes of eleventh plenary session, July 31, 1945, *Tegeran—Ialta—Potsdam*, pp. 339–40.

153. *Tegeran—Ialta—Potsdam*, p. 354; Department of State minutes of eleventh meeting of foreign ministers, August 1, 1945, *FRUS, Potsdam*, vol. II, pp. 549–50; Soviet aide-mémoires, July 23, 25, 30, 1945, *ibid.*, pp. 1163, 1036–37, 684, 1165–66, 1592.

154. Thompson minutes of twelfth plenary meeting, August 1, 1945, *FRUS, Potsdam*, vol. II, pp. 566–67; "Protocol of the Proceedings of the Berlin Conference," August 1, 1945, *ibid.*, pp. 1486–87.

155. *Ibid.*, p. 1490; Department of State minutes of thirteenth plenary meeting, August 1, 1945, *ibid.*, pp. 591–92.

156. "Protocol of the Proceedings of the Berlin Conference," August 1, 1945, *ibid.*, pp. 1485–87.

157. Notes by Bidault, cited in Caffery to Secretary of State, August 7, 1945, *ibid.*, pp. 1551–55; Ernst Deuerlein, "Frankreichs Obstruktion deutscher Zentralverwaltungen 1945," *Deutschland-Archiv* 4 (1971): 466–91.

158. J. P. Nettl, *The Eastern Zone and Soviet Policy in Germany, 1945–50* (London: Oxford University Press, 1951), pp. 206, 299, 304–5.

159. "Protocol of the Proceedings of the Berlin Conference," August 1, 1945, *FRUS, Potsdam*, vol. II, pp. 491–92.

160. "Istoricheskie resheniia Berlinskoi Konferentsii trekh derzhav" [The historic decisions of the Berlin conference of the three powers], *Bolshevik*, 1945, no. 15, pp. 1–11; cf. Jens Hacker, *Sowjetunion und DDR zum Potsdamer Abkommen* (Cologne: Wissenschaft und Politik, 1969).

161. *Khrushchev Remembers*, p. 224.

162. Cf. Harriman to Secretary of State, November 29, 1945, 713—Atomic Energy, U.S. Embassy Moscow, RG-84, NA.

163. The thesis, stated the most forcefully in Gar Alperovitz, *The Atomic Diplomacy* (New York: Simon and Schuster, 1965), has been refuted in Robert J. Maddox, *The New Left and the Origins of the Cold War* (Princeton: Princeton University Press, 1973), pp. 63–78, and in Thomas T. Hammond, "Did the United States Use Atomic Diplomacy against Russia in 1945?" in *From the Cold War to Détente*, ed. Peter J. Potichnyj and Jane P. Shapiro (New York: Praeger, 1976), pp. 26–56.

164. Cf. Barton J. Bernstein, "Roosevelt, Truman, and the Atomic Bomb, 1941–1945: A Reinterpretation," *Political Science Quarterly* 90 (1975): 63–64; Kramish, *Atomic Energy in the Soviet Union*, pp. 81–89.

165. Summary of lecture by A. S. Erusalimskii, "The Berlin Conference of the Three Great Powers," August 23, 1945, N 11605/165/38, FO 371/47883, PRO; Clark Kerr to Bevin, September 6, 1945, N 12165/165/38, FO 371/47883, PRO.

166. Svetlana Alliluyeva, *Twenty Letters to a Friend* (New York: Harper, 1967), p. 188.

167. *Pravda*, October 10, 1945.

168. Harriman and Abel, *Special Envoy to Churchill and Stalin*, pp. 511–15.

169. B. Thomas Trout, "Soviet Policy-Making in the Cold War: Domestic and Foreign Policy Relationships, 1946–1947," (Ph.D. diss., Indiana University, 1972), pp. 69–70.

170. Harriman to Secretary of State, November 22, 1945, *FRUS*, 1945, vol. V, p. 921.

171. Trout, "Soviet Policy-Making in the Cold War," pp. 76–84.

Concluding Thoughts

1. Daniel Yergin, *Shattered Peace: The Origins of the Cold War and the National Security State* (Boston: Houghton Mifflin, 1977), pp. 12–13.

2. Charles Gati, ed., *Caging the Bear* (Indianapolis: Bobbs-Merrill, 1974), pp. 9–53; cf. C. Ben Wright, "Mr. 'X' and Containment," and "George F. Kennan Replies," *SR* 35 (1976): 1–36; John L. Gaddis, "Containment: A Reassessment," *Foreign Affairs* 55 (1976–77): 873–87; Eduard Mark, "The Question of Containment: A Reply to John Lewis Gaddis," *ibid.* 56 (1977–78): 430–41; and comments by George F. Kennan and Eduard Mark, *ibid.*, 643–47.

3. Andrei Amalrik, *Will the Soviet Union Survive until 1984?* (New York: Harper, 1970).

index

405